MOMIGLIANO AND ANTIQUARIANISM: FOUNDATIONS OF THE MODERN CULTURAL SCIENCES

Arnaldo Momigliano, 1983. Photo courtesy of Riccardo Di Donato.

MOMIGLIANO AND ANTIQUARIANISM

FOUNDATIONS OF THE MODERN CULTURAL SCIENCES

Edited by Peter N. Miller

Published by the University of Toronto Press in association with
the UCLA Center for Seventeenth- and Eighteenth-Century Studies and
the William Andrews Clark Memorial Library

© The Regents of the University of California 2007
Toronto Buffalo London
Printed in Canada

ISBN 978-8020-9207-6

Printed on acid-free paper

Library and Archives Canada Cataloguing in Publication

Momigliano and antiquarianism : foundations of the modern cultural
sciences / edited by Peter N. Miller.

(UCLA Center/Clark series)
Includes bibliographical references and index.
ISBN 978-0-8020-9207-6

1. Momigliano, Arnaldo – Criticism and interpretation.   2. History,
Ancient – Historiography.   I. Miller, Peter N., 1964–   II. Series:
UCLA Clark Memorial Library series

D53.A2M64 2006   930   C2006-905435-5
2007

This book has been published with the help of a grant from the UCLA Center
for Seventeenth- and Eighteenth-Century Studies.

University of Toronto Press acknowledges the financial support for its
publishing activities of the Government of Canada through the Book
Publishing Industry Development Program (BPIDP).

University of Toronto Press acknowledges the financial assistance
to its publishing program of the Canada Council for the Arts and
Ontario Arts Council.

In honour of Wallace MacCaffrey

Where could one find a feeling for the seriousness of research called to explore the fathomless depths of knowledge? How seldom is there any forbearance towards bold efforts that were unsuccessful, or patience for slow developments!

Goethe, *Geschichte der Farbenlehre*

Contents

Acknowledgments

This book originated as a conference at the William Andrews Clark Library in Los Angeles. It is a pleasure to able to thank the director, Peter Reill, and the fine staff who made that event such a pleasant experience. That it does not remain only a pleasant memory is due to the University of Toronto Press, to its two anonymous readers, and to Ron Schoeffel, who shepherded the book from start to finish. Theresa Griffin offered careful copy-editing when it was most needed, and Anne Laughlin flawlessly supervised the end-game. I thank Professors Glenn Most, Michael P. Steinberg, Anthony Grafton, Riccardo Di Donato, Deborah L. Krohn, and Naomi C. Miller for their helpful comments at various points in the making of the book. I especially thank Di Donato in his capacity as executor of the Momigliano estate for his generosity in providing us with these great photographs of Momigliano. Most of all, I have to thank the contributors to this volume: for their freely given labour, for its extraordinarily high quality, and for their unfailing patience and punctuality.

Finally, my work on this book, as on all my other projects, has been ably assisted by librarians at the Bard Graduate Center: Greta Ernest, Heather Topcik, Erin Elliott, Rebecca Friedman, and Cheryl Costello.

I am very happy to be able to dedicate this book to Wallace MacCaffrey. It was in his classes at Harvard two decades ago that I took my first steps towards becoming a historian. A book about one great scholar and teacher seems to me the best way to say thank you to another one.

Contributors

Peter Burke, a Fellow of Emmanuel College, was Professor of Cultural History at the University of Cambridge until his retirement in 2004. His books range from *The Renaissance Sense of the Past* (1969) to *Languages and Communities in Early Modern Europe* (2004).

Michael C. Carhart is assistant professor of history at Old Dominion University. He is the author of *Human Nature, Human Culture: Enlightenment Social Science* (Harvard University Press, 2007).

Riccardo Di Donato is Professor of Greek Language and Literature, and Chair of the Department of Classical Philology at the University of Pisa. He collaborated with Momigliano in the latter's Pisan seminars (1970–86) and is Curator of the Archivio Arnaldo Momigliano (Pisa).

Marc Fumaroli is honorary professor at the Collège de France, and member of the Académie Française and of the Académie des Inscriptions et Belles Lettres. The author of many books about the European tradition of classical learning, he is currently preparing a study of the Count of Caylus and the French origins of the eighteenth-century 'retour à l'antique.'

Anthony Grafton teaches European history at Princeton University.

Ingo Herklotz is Professor in the History of Art at the University of Marburg (Germany), and previously held teaching positions at the Universities of Rome, Konstanz, and Basel. He has been a visiting professor at the Bibliotheca Hertziana in Rome, the Getty Research Institute at Los Angeles, and the Institut National d'Histoire de l'Art at Paris.

Moshe Idel is Professor in the Department of Jewish Thought and Philosophy, Hebrew University, Jerusalem. His scholarship focuses on the history of Kabbalah and Jewish mysticism. He is the author of, most recently, *Enchanted Chains: Techniques and Rituals in Jewish Mysticism* (2005) and *Kabbalah and Eros* (2005).

Suzanne Marchand teaches European intellectual history at Louisiana State University in Baton Rouge. She is the author of *Down from Olympus: Archaeology and Philhellenism in Germany, 1750–1970*, as well as several other essays on the history of the humanities in Germany and Austria.

Peter N. Miller is Professor and Chair of Academic Programs at the Bard Graduate Center in New York City.

Wilfried Nippel holds the Chair of Ancient History at the Humboldt University in Berlin. He has published extensively on Athenian democracy, the Roman Republic, the history of political thought, and the history of classical studies. He is one of the editors of the German edition of Momigliano's essays.

Guy G. Stroumsa is Martin Buber Professor of Comparative Religion at The Hebrew University of Jerusalem. His recent works include *La fin du sacrifice: mutations religieuses de l'antiquité tardive* (Paris, 2005) and *Le rire du Christ, essais sur le Christianisme antique* (Paris, 2006).

Contributors

Peter Burke, a Fellow of Emmanuel College, was Professor of Cultural History at the University of Cambridge until his retirement in 2004. His books range from *The Renaissance Sense of the Past* (1969) to *Languages and Communities in Early Modern Europe* (2004).

Michael C. Carhart is assistant professor of history at Old Dominion University. He is the author of *Human Nature, Human Culture: Enlightenment Social Science* (Harvard University Press, 2007).

Riccardo Di Donato is Professor of Greek Language and Literature, and Chair of the Department of Classical Philology at the University of Pisa. He collaborated with Momigliano in the latter's Pisan seminars (1970–86) and is Curator of the Archivio Arnaldo Momigliano (Pisa).

Marc Fumaroli is honorary professor at the Collège de France, and member of the Académie Française and of the Académie des Inscriptions et Belles Lettres. The author of many books about the European tradition of classical learning, he is currently preparing a study of the Count of Caylus and the French origins of the eighteenth-century 'retour à l'antique.'

Anthony Grafton teaches European history at Princeton University.

Ingo Herklotz is Professor in the History of Art at the University of Marburg (Germany), and previously held teaching positions at the Universities of Rome, Konstanz, and Basel. He has been a visiting professor at the Bibliotheca Hertziana in Rome, the Getty Research Institute at Los Angeles, and the Institut National d'Histoire de l'Art at Paris.

Moshe Idel is Professor in the Department of Jewish Thought and Philosophy, Hebrew University, Jerusalem. His scholarship focuses on the history of Kabbalah and Jewish mysticism. He is the author of, most recently, *Enchanted Chains: Techniques and Rituals in Jewish Mysticism* (2005) and *Kabbalah and Eros* (2005).

Suzanne Marchand teaches European intellectual history at Louisiana State University in Baton Rouge. She is the author of *Down from Olympus: Archaeology and Philhellenism in Germany, 1750–1970*, as well as several other essays on the history of the humanities in Germany and Austria.

Peter N. Miller is Professor and Chair of Academic Programs at the Bard Graduate Center in New York City.

Wilfried Nippel holds the Chair of Ancient History at the Humboldt University in Berlin. He has published extensively on Athenian democracy, the Roman Republic, the history of political thought, and the history of classical studies. He is one of the editors of the German edition of Momigliano's essays.

Guy G. Stroumsa is Martin Buber Professor of Comparative Religion at The Hebrew University of Jerusalem. His recent works include *La fin du sacrifice: mutations religieuses de l'antiquité tardive* (Paris, 2005) and *Le rire du Christ, essais sur le Christianisme antique* (Paris, 2006).

MOMIGLIANO AND ANTIQUARIANISM: FOUNDATIONS OF THE MODERN CULTURAL SCIENCES

Introduction: Momigliano, Antiquarianism, and the Cultural Sciences

PETER N. MILLER

Arnaldo Momigliano was one of the great historians of the twentieth century. His contribution to the study of the ancient world has been enormous. His command of Roman, Greek, and Jewish history was legendary. But he was also a historian who cared deeply about the history of historical study. And from 1950 onwards, in a career that began in the early 1930s, he devoted the lion's share of his intellectual energies to exploring the history of historiography. These essays, beginning with 'Ancient History and the Antiquarian' (1950), brought Momigliano to the wider attention of modern historians, but also to historians of art, archaeology, and the social sciences.

At the centre of this story, or, rather more precisely, the thread that runs through this story, is history's debt to antiquarianism. Momigliano explored the role and resonances of antiquarianism in ancient Greece and Rome, and its position vis-à-vis what counted then as 'history,' but devoted the bulk of his attention to the seventeenth and eighteenth centuries. There, he discerned the crucial encounter between the methods that antiquaries had developed for studying subjects abandoned by 'historians,' namely, old, non-political matters that required research into sources, and the rhetorically gifted writers of history who needed to prove that their stories were true. And although antiquarianism and antiquaries continued on into the nineteenth and twentieth centuries, Momigliano kept coming back to this late seventeenth- and early-eighteenth-century moment.

Nevertheless, Momigliano knew much about things he chose not to write about. His reader, in turn, learns to pay close attention to the asides casually tossed off in footnotes, in book reviews, and on the periphery of essays devoted to other subjects. And on these margins, Momigliano was willing to hazard the suggestion that if one would pursue not the afterlife of antiquarianism *within* history – which was his own interest – but rather its survival *outside* it, in other disciplines, one would find connections to anthropology, art history, archaeology, sociology, and history of religion. This nexus, between antiquarianism and what were called 'the cultural sciences' (*Kulturwissenschaften*) during Momigliano's germanophone youth, and which he once or twice let slip as 'cultural history' – probably in appreciation of Burckhardt's achievement – allows us to hang on to Momigliano's own scaffolding the sketch of a history of antiquarianism from the fifteenth century to the twentieth.

Today, the historical study of culture is at the centre of historical scholarship. But this is an extremely recent phenomenon. A hundred years ago, cultural history would have been seen as a decidedly marginal approach, sidelined as amateurish by political and economic historians alike. A hundred years before that, at the beginning of its life, cultural history was perceived to be a form of counter-philosophy, or at best a form of philosophical history, viewing human development through the lens of 'culture' rather than abstract reason. In all cases, what the history of culture promised was some insight into the nature of human civilization – that idea, or spirit, or thing (depending upon the author's intellectual persuasion) – that could then explain the varied manifestations of human creativity across the widest possible range, from politics to private life, and from philosophy to the plastic.[1]

What changed, in the twentieth century, and especially in its second half, to raise the prominence of cultural history was the increasing number of sophisticated tools the scholar had at his or her disposal for plumbing the depths of the past. Where the lone genius of a Burckhardt was able to discover in art, ritual, autobiography, society, and religion the 'meaning' of the Italian Renaissance, scholars now have at their disposal the elaborate methodologies, and secondary literatures, of art history, archaeology, anthropology, economic history, sociology, and history of religion, as well as quantitative approaches once barely conceivable.

In Germany, the short twentieth century that ended in 1933 witnessed the first attempts to combine these perspectives and approaches. With the cover provided by the achievements of Max Weber and Gustav Schmoller, the more adventurous historians – by and large still necessarily 'political historians' – adopted 'sociology' as their comparative framework. Otto Hintze's career suggests how this change moved into the mainstream.[2] Momigliano's friend and exact contemporary Carlo Antoni charted this progress from *Historismus* to Sociology in a series of essays published in *Studi germanici* in the 1930s, and in collective form in 1940.[3] Whether Momigliano followed Antoni's line of argument or arrived at it independently cannot be determined. The famous Institut für Sozialforschung (Institute for Social Research) in Frankfurt would be an example of sociology as a polydisciplinary integrator in a Marxist mode.

The Kulturwissenschaftliche Bibliothek Warburg (Warburg Library for the Cultural Sciences), established by Aby Warburg in Hamburg around 1905, put the emphasis on culture, not politics. It offers probably the best, or most successful, example of the attempt to pursue topics in the history of culture using the range of tools developed by the various new disciplines, but with no respect for those disciplines' own borders. In its elliptical reading room, historians of religion worked alongside art historians, anthropologists alongside philosophers.

Momigliano, who was closely associated with the Warburg Institute in London, to which the Kulturwissenschaftliche Bibliothek was hastily and fortunately translated in May 1933, was fascinated by the development of these research agendas. And in the second half of his career he was excited by the possibilities they offered for understanding the ancient world. Indeed, he was much more interested in these 'cultural sciences' than in cultural history per se. And though he was a bit saddened, I think, that the engine of methodological development had shifted outside Ancient History – that what had been the most methodologically innovative region of history became a 'borrower' after so long being a 'donor' – he was open-minded enough to welcome innovation wherever it came from. And indeed, in recent years there has been a cross-pollination of the practice of history by the cultural sciences, producing some of the profession's most notable works, for example those of Carlo Ginzburg, Natalie Zemon Davis, and Caroline Walker Bynum.

The survival of the antiquarian in modern cultural history, however, is to be tracked not only through its genetic relationship with the cultural sciences but also in the persistence of method. This, too, can be traced back to Momigliano's achievement. First of all, as he pointed out, even as historians in the eighteenth and nineteenth centuries adopted the tools of the antiquary, they consigned the acquisition of these tools to the preparatory courses in university. Institutionally speaking, then, the 'auxiliary sciences' or *Hilfswissenschaften* were the direct and generally despised methodological legacy of the antiquarian. But with the breakdown in the old hierarchy of history – politics on top, then maybe economics, and everything else down at the bottom – in the twentieth century, the despised preliminary tools emerged as bearers of astonishing power, in works such as Michael McCormick's revision of early medieval history and Michel Pastoureau's studies of heraldry. Second, the importance Momigliano attached to method in the history of history's development, and especially to the antiquaries' contribution, inspired younger scholars to dig into those twisted roots of history in early modern scholarly practice. The work of Anthony Grafton and Alain Schnapp, for example, and that of their students, emerges from this genealogy.

The history of the cultural sciences as it has and has not been sketched out by Momigliano is the subject of our book. This involves us, first, in a close examination of Momigliano's account of early modern antiquarianism and, second, in an examination of his map of its connections to art history, anthropology, archaeology, sociology, and history of religion. These investigations will make plain that our theme cannot simply be lifted from Momigliano's pages, and that though the direction of the story he hints at, of antiquarianism's transformation into these varied approaches to the historical study of culture, is correct, his own way of presenting it is lapidary, and often reflects very different intellectual aims. I am not suggesting that Momigliano's work needs to be read against the grain if it is to serve as the template for such a history. But we will need to expand where Momigliano's own interests led him to contract, and to put our emphases where Momigliano chose not to put his – again for perfectly viable reasons of his own.

Our project, then, is twofold. It begins with philological reconstruction of what Momigliano did say – Is Momigliano's account of early modern antiquarianism sufficient? – and then moves to add to what he did not, or what he merely hinted at. Only at the end of this process, hopefully, will more of our main theme be apparent. And, at that point, we will be able to say of Momigliano that, in addition to being a great historian of the ancient world, and a great historian of the methods that have been developed to study the ancient world, he also laid bare one of the most central intellectual developments of modern times, the birth of the cultural sciences.

Arnaldo Dante Momigliano was born in 1908 in the small Piedmontese town of Caraglio, near Cumeo, into an upper-middle-class observant Jewish family. He was schooled at home until going off to the University of Turin in 1925. Four years later he headed to Rome, following his teacher Gaetano De Sanctis. By 1932 he had gained a position in Greek history at the University of Rome – in fact replacing his teacher, who had refused to take the oath of allegiance to the Fascist regime. The very early Momigliano produced three monographs in four busy years: *Prime linee di storia della tradizione maccabaia* (1931), *L'opera dell'imperatore Claudio* (1932), and *Filippo il Macedone* (1934). Finally, in 1936 he was the winner of a contest for the Chair of Roman History – an astonishingly rapid ascent to the pinnacle of Italian academic life.

This was all to end in 1938. Stripped of his chair by the Racial Laws, Momigliano decided to leave Italy. By the end of March 1939, he was in Paris. He continued on to England. His first notebook from this period is dated Oxford, 22 May. Oxford was where he spent the war years. He remained there, in the company of figures such as Beryl Smalley, Iris Murdoch, Franz Steiner, and Elias Canetti. Much of his intellectual life soon was being lived at the Warburg Institute, in London, especially after his appointment to a chair in ancient history at University College in 1951, just up the road from the W.I. (there was a brief period of commuting from Oxford to Bristol in 1947–51). London was to be Momigliano's main base of operations for the next two and a half decades. In 1964 he began directing a seminar at the Scuola Normale Superiore in Pisa, which continued through 1987. In 1975, upon his retirement from London, he was appointed Alexander H. White Visiting Professor in the Committee on Social Thought at the University of Chicago, a position that led him to Hyde Park for a term every year. The peripatetic life, with its three poles of London, Chicago, and Pisa but with many radiating tangents, was his until his death in September 1987.

Momigliano began life as a scholar by writing books. But after his exile to English, as Anthony Grafton observes in his contribution here, Momigliano took up the lecture and the essay. And though writing in his third or fourth language, he became a great stylist. Much of the power of his arguments derived from their conciseness and turn of phrase. Comparison of the essays and books of the Italian era with the nine (ultimately there will be ten) volumes of essays and reviews that began to appear in 1955 as *Contributi alla storia degli studi classici* offers evidence of this changed style. The books he did publish from this second life all had their beginnings in the lecture series: *The Origin of Greek Biography* (1971), *Alien Wisdom* (1975), and, posthumously, *The Classical Foundations of Modern Historiography* (1990).

In the years since his death in 1987, and largely through the efforts of Riccardo Di Donato, large chunks of Momigliano's unpublished oeuvre have come to light and been catalogued. Di Donato's contribution to this volume follows in a series of articles that use the archive to fill in the bare bones of an intellectual biography.[4] In the massive outpouring of memoirs and appreciation that followed his death, various aspects of Momigliano's work, and the contexts in which he worked, have been clarified.[5] But Momigliano has not yet made that transition from a remembered figure to a fully historical one. Our volume, with its focus on one rather small point in the vast heavens of Momigliano, is an attempt to move him in that direction.

A final prefatory note: Momigliano was a great biographer. He often relied on the frame provided by a life to expose complex conceptual issues. This was not just a matter of art; it was an example of the wisdom or just plain common sense demanded of the historian, especially of the historian of historiography. For as long as Momigliano worked on historiography, he knew himself to be working on historians. And as he showed time and again, the personal history that was lived shaped the ancient history that was written. We have here adopted something of this method. For while the history of antiquarianism, or of the foundations of the cultural sciences, could have been constructed differently, it is true both to Momigliano's contribution to these questions and to his contribution to how we understand the making of history, to put his life at the centre of our question.

I. The Ancient Historian and the Antiquarian

The Article

'Ancient History and the Antiquarian' is probably Momigliano's most famous essay. It has certainly been his most influential. And for many people it is, simply, *the* history of antiquarianism. It was first read as a paper at the Warburg Institute in January 1949 and then published in the *Journal of the Warburg and Courtauld Institutes* in December 1950.[6] It was reprinted in Momigliano's first *Contributo alla storia degli studi classici* in 1955 and again in *Studies in Historiography* in 1966. Rarely has one relatively short piece come so thoroughly to be identified with an entire field of learning.

It is also an extremely complex piece of intellectual architecture. It begins with an 'Introduction' followed by three sections – 'The Origins of Antiquarian Research,' 'The Controversy of the 17th and 18th Centuries on the Value of Historical Evidence' (divided into three parts), and 'The Conflicts between Antiquarians and Historians in the 18th and 19th Centuries' (divided into two parts) – and ends with two appendices.

Momigliano begins by contrasting a 'new humanism' with 'the traditional one.' After a brilliant, and typically dichotomous, presentation of the social foundation of the eighteenth-century classicizing revolution that takes in the Grand Tour, Herculaneum, and the Greek, Celtic, and Gothic Revivals, he concludes by dismissing it all. 'This is the conventional view of the Age of the Antiquaries,' which he described as incomplete yet not needing to be challenged. 'But' – and this is where the argument is joined – 'the Age of the Antiquaries meant not only a revolution in taste; it meant a revolution in historical method' setting standards 'of historical method which we can hardly call obsolete today.'[7]

The central issue, as presented immediately following by Momigliano, was the distinction between 'original' and 'derivative authorities' (primary and secondary sources), which 'became the common patrimony of historical research only in the late seventeenth century,' though 'of course' it had also been found earlier. 'In the formation of the new historical method' – this distinction – 'the so-called antiquaries played a conspicuous part and posed essential problems.'

Momigliano then concluded the 'Introduction' by laying out the axes of the essay. First, to describe 'the origins of antiquarian research.' Second, to understand 'why the antiquaries played such a part in the reform of historical method in the *eighteenth* century [my emphasis].' Third, to explain why the old distinction between antiquarian and historical studies ceased to make any sense in the nineteenth century. A section of the essay is devoted to each.

'The Origins of Antiquarian Research' begins with an apology for Momigliano's being unable to refer the reader to 'a History of Antiquarian Studies. But none exists.'[8] After some brief terminological comments – he endorsed the received view that historians wrote diachronically and antiquaries synchronically, that historians selected facts relevant to making an argument whereas antiquaries collected material whether pertinent to a problem's solution or not – he turned to ancient Greece. This perspective offered a further distinction: between treatises focused on the history of the very recent political past, and those that explored the customs and institutions, especially religious and political, of the distant past.

The Romans absorbed this division between history and antiquities, and added a distinction of their own. Varro is credited with the term *antiquitates* and its shape: 'a systematic survey of Roman life according to the evidence provided by language, literature, and custom.' His fourfold division into public, private, sacred, and military antiquities was lost in the Middle Ages – this thousand years was dismissed in a sentence – but was revived again with Flavio Biondo in the fifteenth century. (Momigliano gracefully noted that 'the stages of the rediscovery of the Varronian idea from Petrarch to Biondo cannot detain us.')[9]

'Antiquarius' as 'a lover, collector and student of ancient traditions and remains – though not a historian – is one of the most typical concepts of fifteenth- and sixteenth-century humanism,' Momigliano writes. The antiquaries of the sixteenth century who are explicitly mentioned – Rosinus, Sigonio, Orsini, Augustín, Lipsius – improved on Varro by combining literary with material evidence and by extending the Roman paradigm to Greek and eventually to northern and oriental lands. They did not describe themselves as historians and did not try to use their evidence to rewrite the accounts of ancient history left by ancient historians. These, according to Momigliano, were read 'to provide materials for moral and political reflections' and for literary style.[10]

Similarly, according to Momigliano, those concerned with how to do history – the authors of the *artes historicae* that sprang up in the sixteenth century – did not concern themselves with antiquaries and antiquities. The former they viewed as 'imperfect historians' who saved materials 'too fragmentary to be the subject of proper history.'[11]

All this applied to the study of the ancient, classical world. But when attention began to be turned to the histories of France, Germany, and England – the northern, new world born out of the collapse of Rome – all rules were suspended. The same people who were antiquaries in their relationship to ancient Rome were historians when writing what we would now call 'medieval' history. Momigliano gave as examples Sigonio in Italy and Leland in England.

But 'the situation changed in the second part of the seventeenth century.' That was when the sanctity – and separateness – of ancient history was lost, and the methods and evidence of the antiquaries were used to evaluate and reassess the literary sources of the past, in other words, to correct the ancient historians. But, Momigliano asserted, 'the new importance attributed to non-literary evidence is understandable only against the background of the great reform of historical method which took place in the second part of the seventeenth century.'[12] This assertion leads into the most striking aspect of the article: the explanatory role of the 'Pyrrhonian' controversy of the seventeenth and eighteenth centuries.

Over the next fifteen pages (in an article of 35 pages) Momigliano provided background to the controversy over the implications of Pyrrhonian scepticism in the second half of the seventeenth century, and asserted that the 'emphasis on non-literary evidence' was an attempt to rebut, or refute, the possibility of that kind of overwhelming scepticism undermining historical truth. To the ancient sceptic Pyrrho was attributed, mostly through the writings of Sextus Empiricus, which were widely diffused from the second half of the sixteenth century, the view that the very possibility of certain knowledge did not exist. Moralists (like Montaigne) grappled with this sceptical revival immediately; it took historians a whole century to realize that their work, too, was imperilled. The discredit of the historians was answered, with a kind of glee, by the antiquaries. Jacques Spon (1679), 'with the ardour of an apostle of a new method,' Ezechiel Spanheim (1671), and Francesco Bianchini (1697) are cited as proclaiming the superiority of the archaeological, or material, record over the literary. Momigiliano notes that many antiquaries were also natural philosophers or doctors, and says, simply, that 'they brought something of the scientific method of direct observation into historical research.'[13]

Though the Pyrrhonians protested that material evidence could also be fabricated, they failed to persuade, according to Momigliano. So much so, that when the Historical Institute was founded at Göttingen in 1766 it was devoted to those 'auxiliary' sciences, which, as C.G. Heyne explained in the inaugural speech, 'make historical arguments true' ('historicis argumentis fidem faciunt'). Momigliano notes that there had been others, before, who preferred material to literary evidence – the examples given are Ciriaco d'Ancona and Antonio Agustín – but that these figures 'do not alter the fact that non-literary evidence became especially authoritative in the late seventeenth and early eighteenth centuries.'[14] With the successes of paleography (Mabillon), iconography (Montfaucon), epigraphy (Maffei) and numismatics (Spanheim), the eighteenth-century antiquary was able to stand tall – taller, even, perhaps – alongside his age-old rival, the historian.[15] Momigliano offers eighteenth-century Etruscology as 'an example of the extensive use of non-literary evidence.'

The rise of philosophical history spelled the end of the antiquaries' short-lived supremacy. When Montesquieu, Voltaire, and then the Scots began to ask questions about how present civilization – in its broadest meaning – developed, they turned to the realm of *content* that hitherto had been abandoned by political historians to the antiquaries. Institutions, religion, manners: the conditions of the present were traced right back to these ancient structures. But in the meantime, led by Gibbon, historians interested in writing narratives of political affairs had been sensitized to the need for good evidence and so began to reach for the *tools* developed by the antiquaries.[16]

Momigliano explains away the survival of antiquaries into the nineteenth century, despite their inability to tell a story, by stressing the suitability of the collecting and classifying mentality for the study of institutions. He then turns from the antiquaries to the philologists who shaped Classics in nineteenth-century Germany, F.A. Wolf, F. Ast, E. Platner, F. Ritschl, and A. Boeckh. When G.G. Gervinus (1837) and J.G. Droysen (1868) ignored antiquities (*Altertumswissenschaft*) in their textbooks on *Historik*, the battle, Momigliano opined, was over, even if people would still write *Kunst-*, *Kultur-*, *Kriegs-*, *Privat-*, and *Staatsaltertümer* for some time to come. Despite stressing German sources, Momigliano asserted that the same general trend could be found true for French historiography as well.[17]

The 'idea of *antiquitates*,' he concluded, 'is now dead because the corresponding idea of political history founded upon literary evidence is dead. The historians have recognized that the traditional subject of antiquarian research can be tranformed into chapters of the history of civilization with all the necessary apparatus of erudition.'[18] With the reform of history in the twentieth century, antiquarianism had, literally, lost its raison d'être.

And then, as if an afterthought – or a eulogy – Momigliano ended with words praising the antiquary not only for his contribution to historical method – 'his preference for the original documents, his ingenuity in discovering forgeries, his skill in collecting and classifying the evidence' – which was the substance of the entire article – but 'above all' for 'his unbounded love of learning,' which had hitherto been entirely ignored.

The Article in Its Time and Place

'Ancient History and the Antiquarian' had an immediate and enormous impact. For many scholars, for many years, it has served as that history of antiquarianism the absence of which Momigliano had lamented. But it is an essay that is full of riddles.

The first challenge faced by the interpreter is to locate the essay in space and time. Without any obvious antecedents in Momigliano's already vast oeuvre and without obvious links to what he had been working on in the preceeding years, the essay appears to have burst full-grown from its author's head. Even the coincidental fact of its being the only article published by Momigliano in 1950 seems to bespeak its unique status.

The second challenge is to disentangle the essay's history from its interpretation. Where and how did Momigliano's own, very particular, intellectual interests lead him to emphasize some points and to minimize, or obscure, others? Once it becomes clear that 'Ancient History and the Antiquarian' cannot be relied upon as a history of antiquarianism, it follows that the crucial question is, what might such a history look like? The first challenge is dealt with in this section, the second in the one that follows.

To begin with, is the essay as isolated from Momigliano's work as appears from the published material? And is there anything in the Archive that helps explain its appearance in 1950?

Momigliano's two great, key essays of the Italian years are 'The Historical Genesis and Current Function of the Concept of Hellenism' (1935) and 'The Modern Historiography of the Roman Empire' (1936). In them, with a maturity extraordinary in a historian under thirty, Momigliano tackled the history of historiography. This was intended as a problem-solving approach, returning as if *ad fontes* to the beginning of what had become long-playing and rather long-winded historical debates whose key principles had become blurred or distorted with the passage of time. The firm foundation of origins – Momigliano did not fear for the murkiness of eternal regress – provided him with a perspective from which the fashions of a secondary literature could be seen as just that, and then put aside.

The invention of Hellenism is credited to Herder, Humboldt, Wolf, Boeckh, Hegel, and, above all, Droysen; that of the modern historiography of the Empire to the seventeenth-century Jansenist scholar Sebastian Le Nain de Tillemont. Droysen seems to have represented for Momigliano an opportunity already lost. Between the two editions of his biography of Alexander the Great, Droysen turned away from Hellenism studied from the point of view of cultural history (the union of Greece with the Orient that culminated in Christianity) to an explanation of it based on political history (Philip of Macedon as Bismarck).

And yet even so, Droysen continued to emphasize that the later Hellenistic world was united by common language, social structure, institutions of public law, religious and political ideals, and economic characteristics – 'enough to make one think about a relatively unified civilization.'[19] In other words, Droysen remained working with a definition that was expressed in the terms of cultural history, even if these were now 'pointed' towards a political story. But Droysen's discarded cultural historical project still bore some fruit, Momigliano wrote, since it inspired later historians like Franz Cumont – Momigliano seems not yet to know of the work of Franz Boll and his acolyte Aby Warburg – to study the syncretistic cults of the Empire.[20]

Even in this essay, which shows Momigliano most in the grasp of Romantic neo-humanism, he demonstrates a critical awareness of its origins. He recognized in C.G. Heyne, the teacher of Humboldt at Göttingen and of Herder through his books, a valuable and living connection to an explicitly antiquarian tradition that was empirical. He repeated Heyne's judgment that Winckelmann had broken with this approach at the expense of his 'historische Richtigkeit.'[21]

Where the German study of Hellenism failed, according to Momigliano – and Droysen's inability to complete his history is paradigmatic – was in its inability to take the measure of the Roman Empire. And this, in turn, was traced back, as Momigliano showed in the next essay, to the turn in the historiography that separated the history of the Empire from the history of the Church. This began, according to Momigliano, at the very beginning of modern historical study in the seventeenth century with the Jansenist Le Nain de Tillemont. As an Augustinian, Tillemont did not believe that sacred history needed any support from merely profane facts; but as a scholar on the leading edge of methodological practice, he would write a history only with the greatest care for the evidence employed.

Nor is this attention to Tillemont's method isolated. Momigliano surveys much of the landscape to which he would return more than a decade later. He refers to Tillemont's sophistication compared to predecessors such as the sixteenth-century Roman historian Carlo Sigonio, as well as to the important contribution made by the French 'polyhistors' and legal historians of the *mos Gallicus*, Bodin, Baudouin, and Hotman. In a footnote, Momigliano allowed that the case of Baudouin 'points the way to a clear deepening between the earlier emphasis on the development of juridical thought and this one here [Tillemont's],' and declares, 'It is my intention to follow it.'[22] Gibbon, too, makes an appearance (along with other themes and people Momigliano would come back to over the years, including the German hermeneutical tradition, ecclesiastical history, Vico, Montesquieu, the French nineteenth-century tradition, and Mommsen). Gibbon is presented as the forerunner of the historiographical reform movement that would include Robertson and Hume and that was inspired by the 'old pre-enlightenment erudition' he had assimilated.[23] But the crucial importance of Gibbon in 1936 is defined in terms of this presentation of the end of antiquity – not in terms of methodology, of the combination of erudition and philosophy.

A year later, in 1937, when Momigliano again turned to Gibbon, he explained the force of the *Decline and Fall* in terms of its 'unique mixture' of 'enlightenment rationalism and reconstructive fantasy, that was a prelude to romantic historiography.'[24]

This focus on Tillemont would later provide Momigliano with an entrée to the anti-Pyrrhonist literature of the seventeenth century. The list of eighteenth-century sources on pre-Roman Italy that is printed as an appendix to 'Ancient History and the Antiquarian' reflects research done for this project. But in the 1930s Momigliano's polestar is nineteenth-century German historiography.

Tillemont and Bossuet – the other figure mentioned at the beginning of the account – seem to have been important to Momigliano for personal reasons, too. Their faith in the narrative of sacred history had given them the confidence, or freedom, to do without it, to tell the story of the world as if there were no divine inspiration. Momigliano may have been attracted by their faith, as he was many years later by that of Jacob Bernays, about whom he wrote so eloquently that 'having received a faith, he did not have to look to history for one.'[25] He could have said the same of these Jansenists. Speaking in the first person, he acknowledged sharing their sense of the problem. 'The question was whether one would have to presuppose for the facts of profane history the same punctual and continuous intervention of God that was the character of sacred history. The answer, *also for me* [my emphasis], lies at the centre of [Bossuet's] *Discours*': that God works in human history through human means.[26] For Momigliano, as he told us later, the gift of Spinoza before his bar mitzvah had provided him with answers enough. But had it? We will return to this question.

The great break in Momigliano's life, whose implications were still shaping his work decades later, was his decision to leave Italy after he had been dispossessed of his job. He could have decided to hang on in Turin, teaching Jewish children likewise dispossessed of educational opportunities – as he did in the months between November 1938 and March 1939 – and await the future. Instead, he departed for Paris and thence England. Momigliano's attempt to stave off the application of the Racial Laws in his particular case because of his father's long-time affiliation with the Fascist party, and his equally self-interested later attempt to win more speedily his freedom from British detention on account of his long-time anti-fascism have been made much of recently; they seem rather the desperate attempt of the victim of a shipwreck to find firm footing amid a gathering storm.[27]

Momigliano had come to England with a project 'Peace and Liberty in the Ancient World,' on which he had been working from before his appointment at Turin. It formed the basis of lectures he delivered at Cambridge during the Lent term in 1940 (January to March), entitled 'Peace and Liberty in the Ancient World.' But in wartime England the emphasis changed completely. Liberty, not peace, was where Momigliano sought his explanations: the failure of the Pax Romana was a failure of liberty. In May, when he offered a summary of the Cambridge lectures at Oxford, the title was changed to 'Freedom in Antiquity.'

And freedom in antiquity was, significantly, now defined in terms of religious freedom. 'The *pax romana* did *not* resolve the political problem because it did not resolve the religious problem.'[28] The problem of religious liberty as the key to the transformation of the ancient world: might there be a connection to the fact that Momigliano delivered these thoughts as an Italian Jew in exile in England because of religious persecution? (We know, from notes he made upon his arrival in England, that he used the example of Jew hatred to help explain the mechanics of historical explanation.)[29]

By war's end, the project, which Momigliano had planned to publish with Oxford University Press, had collapsed, and its two parts, on Greek and Roman history, were sundered. Tacitus was one of Momigliano's key souces on the breakdown of liberty in the Roman world, and as early as 1942 we find Momigliano turning his attention to him. By 1946, Momigliano was giving a course of lectures in London entitled 'The Political Ideas of Tacitus and Their Influence on the Formation of Political Thought.' And in 1947 they were reprised in Oxford as 'Conflicts of Political and Moral Ideas from Seneca to Tacitus.' The fusion of these projects was submitted to the Clarendon Press, with the title 'Aspects of Roman Political Thought from Seneca to Tacitus.' But an editorial review critical of its author's newly acquired English seems to have discouraged Momigliano from undertaking the necessary revisions.

Momigliano's turn to Tacitus during the Second World War had its precedents, as he was himself aware. In the lecture entitled 'Tacitus and "Il Tacitismo,"' Momigliano devoted two of its eighteen pages to Justus Lipsius, the editor of Tacitus in the dark years of the 1580s, who explicitly made the connection between the times explored by the historian and the Europe he and his sixteenth-century readers inhabited. The 'similitude of the times' – Lipsius's doctrine of *similitudo temporum* – was invoked by Momgliano speaking *in propria persona* at the conclusion of his lecture 'Tacitus' Political Opinions,' delivered at Oxford just after war's end, in July 1945: 'I have not studied Tacitus well enough to speak about him with any authority. There are several people in Oxford who could do it better than myself. But I may perhaps claim for myself a qualification to speak on Tacitus that other people have not. I have lived in a totalitarian regime for sixteen years, five months, one day and about eighteen hours.'[30]

The failure of these two projects, the one a product of his Italian past, the other of his English present, would seem to represent the breakdown of the intellectual rubrics, largely German, that Momigliano inherited with his Italian education. From this perspective, 'Friedrich Creuzer and Greek Historiography,' published in the *Journal of the Warburg and Courtauld Institutes* in 1947 but first drafted two or three years earlier, stands between Momigliano's past and future. As in his two essays on Hellenism and the Roman Empire, Momigliano went back to the overlooked beginning of an entire intellectual tradition that had gone a bit soft – in this case the value of Greek historians as teachers of modern historians – to recover for the future the purpose of history-writing. 'Ancient history,' he wrote, 'has now become a provincial branch of history. It can recover its lost prestige only if it proves again capable of offering results affecting the whole of our historical outlook. One of the ways is, quite simply, to regain contact with those writers of the past who treated classical subjects of vital importance to history in general. Creuzer produced a book of this kind.'[31] In this sense, Momigliano discovered in him a model. Creuzer's *Historische Kunst der Griechen* (1803) was an example, 'for the student of historiography is to find out the critical methods and the artistic proceedings whereby historians establish the facts in their own individuality and formulate the ideas which are behind the facts.'[32]

But the essay also fondly looks backwards – it now appears as a farewell song – to the 'old,' Germanocentric vision of methodological innovation of Momigliano's Italian formation. It is, after all, a return to the generation of 1800, to Humboldt and to Wolf, with Creuzer making three. What would come next for Momigliano reflects a whole new way of shaping the history of historiography. The German generation of poets and professors circa 1800 who formed the core of Momigliano's earlier essays gives way to the French, Italian, and Dutch erudites, some secular and some clerical, who dominated the world of learning circa 1700. And, pushed to the fore, really for the first time in the history of scholarship, were the antiquaries of early modern Europe. With this shift we find a wholly new appreciation – and centrality – for Edward Gibbon. How did Momigliano get from Creuzer to the Antiquaries?

That is the question Riccardo Di Donato and Anthony Grafton help us answer, Di Donato by looking into Momigliano's personal archive and Grafton into that of the Warburg Institute.[33]

Di Donato addresses the strange fact of the appearance of 'Ancient History and the Antiquarian' as if out of nowhere. He observes that there were few visible indications in the years 1946, 1947, 1948, and 1949 of the change of course embodied in the article.[34] Nor do the notebooks yield any good answers. There we find only chronological coincidence: one of those dated to around 1950 is given the working title 'Tacito, Antiquari' (N-f 58). But this just begs the question. Otherwise, the *Nachlass*, so abundant with detail, provides very little to hold on to. We do not find notebooks stuffed with drafts, or even wide reading notes. The preparations for 'Ancient History' seem either flimsy or none. It appears to be the fruit of old reading and new thinking.

The article was first given life as a lecture at the Warburg Institute in January 1949. It was published in December 1950. In between, there was revision and rethinking. There was also time for reflection. In his contribution to this volume, Di Donato presents some very important unpublished material from the summer of 1950, including the text of a lecture written in Italy for an Italian audience that is a 'supercommentary' on 'Ancient History and the Antiquarian.'

The lecture, given the title 'Antiquari e storici dell'antichità' ('Antiquaries and Historians of Antiquity') by Di Donato, begins by summarizing the main points of the article. It indicates as major themes the origin of the distinction between antiquaries and historians in deepest antiquity, Varro's invention of *antiquitates*, and the domination by antiquaries of research on ancient Greece and Rome in the fifteenth through seventeenth centuries. Momigliano then came to his longest and most significant point, the role of the antiquaries in the Pyrrhonian controversy. 'For the first time in the history of historical method, manuals were written to teach not only how one ought to write history rhetorically, but how one could and must distinguish probable from improbable facts ... Clarifying the concept of the "document," one naturally comes to give the antiquaries pride of place. The great part of their work was on inscriptions, statues, coins, and archival papers – all primary sources in the new conception.' The range of their evidence gave them confidence in their judgments, and even, or especially, in the view that material evidence of various sorts, ranged together, could prove more reliable than ancient literary sources. Far from being 'ancients,' the antiquaries 'affirmed also their superiority as modern scholars over ancient ones.' Out of the Pyrrhonian controversy came not only a new kind of historical method, but also a new notion of history – ours, really – in which material and literary evidence was to be sifted, compared, and combined. Moreover, in the eighteenth century, philosophical historians added the political interpretation of the historians to 'the cultural description of the antiquaries in the new idea of a history of civilization.' In fact, Momigliano continued, the philosophical historians actually 'replaced the antiquaries in cultural history,' though not in questions of method. What emerged was a new kind of history, embodied in the work of Winckelmann and, especially, Gibbon, that shaped the historiography of the nineteenth century.[35]

We have here all the main points of Momigliano's new theme. The era of the great methodological leap forward is pushed back into the seventeenth century and relocated, ironically, in the achievement of the most despised of historical drones, the antiquaries.

Grafton's essay, while ranging broadly across Momigliano's relationship with the Warburg Institute and its leading personalities, sheds particularly valuable light on Momigliano's isolation and his contacts as he worked through 'Ancient History and the Antiquarian.' First, his indifference to the small but splendid group of scholars who were working on English antiquaries and early modern historical thought: his colleague at Bristol David Douglas, Herbert Butterfield at Cambridge, and T.D. Kendrick at the British Museum. Momigliano took little notice of, and seems to have had little use for, their work. Grafton explores the consequences of this indifference for the relatively unsophisticated line Momigliano took on the uses and possible abuses of material culture. But Momigliano did feel that connection at the Warburg Institute, with its director Fritz Saxl and with Frances Yates and Gertrud Bing. Their surviving correspondence shows not only how the essay took its final form, but also how comfortable Momigliano was in an intellectual environment where his break with the received view of history's development was immediately recognized. It was also a place where, as Grafton shows, some people knew more about some aspects of cultural history than did Momigliano, a historian of the study of the ancient world just becoming a historian of history.

From 'Ancient History and the Antiquarian' to the Sather Lectures

Another tool we have at our disposal for understanding Momigliano's interpretation of antiquarianism is to look at what he published *subsequently*, through the re-elaboration of his thesis about antiquarianism in the Sather Lectures delivered in 1962 but begun a year or two earlier.[36] We find Momigliano actually building on the earlier essay throughout this period, moving towards the present with work on Gibbon, and back to the past with attention to Herodotus.

In 1954, Momigliano published his reassessment entitled 'Gibbon's Contribution to Historical Method,' which had been delivered as a lecture in 1950 and again in 1952.[37] Momigliano situates Gibbon in the midst of 'the 18th century conflict between the old-fashioned historical method of the *érudits* or antiquarians and the newfangled approach of the philosophic historians.'[38] Gibbon 'aimed at blending in himself the philosopher and the antiquarian' and by succeeding created a new kind of philosophical history that 'passed into the historical method of the 19th century together with Gibbon's synthesis of the philospher and of the antiquarian.'[39] It was this achievement that wrote the antiquaries out of the history of history. In a brilliant aside that he never pursued, Momigliano noted that the one other person who did something very like Gibbon was none other than Winckelmann. 'He too assimilated all the work of the antiquarians who had studied the artistic remains of Greece and Rome and interpreted them according to philosophic notions ... But [Gibbon] never showed (as far as I am aware) a marked interest in the man who was striving like himself to blend the philosopher with the antiquarian.'[40]

What is especially interesting about Momigliano's presentation is his emphasis on eighteenth-century historiography – enlightened historiography, or 'philosophical history.' Momiglano described its theme as civilization, or 'the progress of mankind as it was reflected in political institutions, religion, trade, custom.' Before Gibbon, there was Voltaire, Montesquieu, Hume, and Robertson, to name just the most influential. Momigliano gave them credit for overcoming the 'one-sided' view of history as kings and battles. 'In a way we modern students of history are all disciples of the philosophic historians. Every time we study the history of population, religion, education, commerce, we are treading in the steps of Montesquieu, Voltaire, Hume, Condorcet.'[41] But what Gibbon added was a familiarity with the tools for handling evidence honed by the antiquaries.

Gibbon helped Momigliano look from the eighteenth century to the future of historiography; Herodotus helped him catch a glimpse of its past. From the essays 'Herodotus in the History of Historiography,' 'Erodoto e la storiografia moderna' (both in the *Secondo contributo*), and 'Storiografia su tradizione scritta e su tradizione orale' (*Terzo contributo*), many of Momigliano's key ideas about the ancient practice of history that inspired the revolutionaries of the Renaissance were articulated through interpretations of Herodotus. It was he who had created the history of an event, like war, but also the history of the cultures that went to war. As important as his subject matter was his approach to it: the justification of the use of oral sources, study of alien peoples, and criteria for rejecting evidence as incredible. Thucydides followed him in the first and last – though in his insistence on a higher standard of verifiable truth he narrowed the historian's horizon to the most recent past. His critique of Herodotus was repeated by historians for centuries to come. During these long years, what we have come to think of as history, namely, the 'search for unknown facts about the past' through mastery of languages and documents, was left to the antiquarians – scholars considered beyond the pale of history, a field defined by the razor of 'relevance.'[42]

The antiquarian approach also left its mark on historians of religion. Momigliano was especially interested in the passionate use of 'antiquarian' learning by religious radicals of the fourth century, whether Christian or pagan. Here, Augustine was his guide. 'He fought the antiquarians, the sentimental and emotional pagans of his time – not the contemporary historians. The latter might be left to die from natural causes. But the former had to be fought.'[43] Eusebius represented the co-opting of the antiquarian tradition by the Church. The late antique interest in religion, borderlands, and peoples as the key to the future is described by Momigliano as the 'Herodotean element.'[44]

By May 1959, as Di Donato has learned, Momigliano had planned out the course of lectures he would deliver at Berkeley in the spring of 1962. But this synthesis, in which antiquarianism dominated – of the eight lectures planned, six dealt with biography, antiquarianism, and ecclesiastical history, both ancient and modern, and only two with political history – must not have felt right to Momigliano, because he never published the essays. Since they appeared only posthumously, and without the apparatus that Momigliano never provided, their impact has been muted. But they do offer Momigliano's most elaborate presentation of the pervasiveness of the antiquarian in the 'Herodotean' tradition, national history, and ecclesiastical historiography. What is more, in just a few compressed pages Momigliano sketched a history of the afterlife of the antiquarian, suggesting connections between the scholarship of the antiquaries and that of sociologists, anthropologists, art historians, and cultural historians.

For our purposes, the key chapter is 'The Rise of Antiquarian Research.' It begins with a confession that rings true – 'Throughout my life I have been fascinated by a type of man so near to my profession, so transparently sincere in his vocation, so understandable in his enthusiasms, and yet so deeply mysterious in his ultimate aims' – and then follows with a judgment that is questionable – 'the type of man who is interested in historical facts without being interested in history' – before continuing with a series of *aperçus* so evocative and provocative as to defy anything less than word-by-word exegesis: 'To find him [the antiquarian] one must go into the provinces of Italy or France and be prepared to listen to lengthy explanations by old men in uncomfortably cold, dark rooms. As soon as the antiquarian leaves his shabby palace, which preserves something of the eighteenth century, and enters modern life, he becomes the great collector, he is bound to specialize, and he may well end up as the founder of an institute of fine arts or of comparative anthropology.'

It is hard to miss the bitter caricature, still lingering on from the days of Chardin and Diderot, as well as the intuitive sense of the career paths that have evolved out of it, as if in a subsequent generation: art history and anthropology. Momigliano went on with an equally suggestive claim, that the antiquary has now himself become a subject of historical contextualization, has been historicized, which was precisely the sort of relativizing, interpretative scholarship he most feared and despised.[45]

In the next, long, paragraph, Momigliano adduced the Provençal antiquary Peiresc (1580–1637) as the living example – his word was 'archetype' – of this persona. Some of his facts here happen to be wrong, but no matter. What is more interesting is how Momigliano tried to explain Peiresc's activities. And here, again, we find Pyrrhonism doing the work, suitably modified for an appearance in the earlier part of the seventeenth century, *before there was a Pyrrhonist controversy*. 'Peiresc,' Momigliano averred, 'was a Pyrrhonist in so far as Pyrrhonists liked tangible things.' Momigliano then linked Pyrrhonism to the scientific revolution, via the experimental, documentary approach of the antiquary. In 'Ancient History' there was a hint about the coincidence of antiquarianism and science; it is now solidified. 'I have no doubt either that Gassendi and Peiresc and their friends were also trying to apply the

Galilean method of observation to their own antiquarian studies.'[46] Again, it is less the truth of the claim that is striking than the effort made to preserve an intellectual framework set out in terms of the eighteenth century for use in the early seventeenth. 'The new Pyrrhonism,' Momigliano concluded, 'turned against the reliability of ordinary historians. The antiquarians were in a stronger position.'[47]

Momigliano then moved back to discuss ancient antiquarianism. In antiquity, too, antiquarianism had flourished at a time of doubt; in antiquity, too, systematic handbooks were produced by antiquaries; and in antiquity, politics was also handled by a different branch of learning. In fact, he suggested that it was Thucydides's restriction of 'history' to contemporary politics that turned research on everything else into antiquarianism.

Momigliano then returned to the early moderns – perhaps the 're-vival' that in the initial plan was to be given a lecture of its own – and redefined the 'infamous' word 'Renaissance' in terms of antiquarianism. 'Something really was called back to life: the ancient erudite research as a discipline of its own, not to be confused with history. In the fifteenth century the term "antiquarius" acquired the meaning of "student of ancient objects, customs, institutions, with a view to reconstructing ancient life."'[48] Philology and antiquarianism went together in antiquity and were renewed, together, in the Renaissance. Momigliano was less sure about the ancient link between philosophy and antiquarianism, though noting that in the seventeenth and eighteenth centuries connections were more marked. But here, again, his gesture was to the Pyrrhonian controversy.

It is in looking towards the eighteenth and nineteenth centuries that Momigliano gives tantalizing hints of a story he never completed. He notes the impact of the antiquaries on Maffei's attempt to reform the Universities of Padua and Turin, and Schlözer's and Gatterer's incorporation of antiquarian skills into the auxiliary sciences at the dawn of history's professionalization. Elsewhere, however, the use of inscriptions, charters, coins, seals, and so on was rarely incorporated into historical scholarship, even in the early nineteenth century. And where historians did use non-literary sources – Momigliano identifying this most explicitly with antiquarianism – it was not to explore the kinds of questions dealt with by antiquaries, but just to get a new angle on the same old political and military narratives. 'The perfect fusion of antiquarian research and Thucydidean history might have seemed only a question of time,' Momigliano wrote, but it never happened.[49]

Momigliano's speculations as to why this fusion failed to occur are bound up with his sketch of the history of antiquarianism in the nineteenth century, after German classical philologists like August Boeckh had taken over their encyclopaedic, reconstructive approach to antiquity, and historians like Mommsen had begun to adopt a systematic approach to historical inquiry. Systematic presentation, Momigliano wrote, 'has now become a basic tenet of sociology, anthropology, and what is more vaguely known as structuralism.' This brought Momigliano to the last stage of the fortunes of the antiquary. 'I do not know enough about the history of sociology and anthropology,' Momigliano wrote, 'to be able to say to what extent antiquarian studies contributed to the origins of modern sociology and anthropology.' In some cases, the link between disciplines was actually biographical: Weber was an informal student of Mommsen and Durkheim a formal one of Fustel de Coulanges. But there was also another, genetic link: 'The rise of sociology is certainly connected with the decline of antiquarianism because sociology is the legitimate heir of antiquarian studies.'[50]

Di Donato has noted that the causality in this last sentence ('because ... is') was added by Momigliano in his 1976 revisions to the lectures. Why? The "Conclusion" to the lecture series, in which Momigliano returned to this relationship between antiquaries and sociologists, and which was not revised by him, does not clarify his meaning. Momigliano began by enumerating the three elements of the antiquarian achievement as the study of the remote past, the handling of original evidence, and interest in 'cultural history.' But then Momigliano emphasized only the third contribution: 'It was left to the antiquarians to organise the study of cultural history.'[51]

Again, as in his essays from the 1950s, Momigliano did not claim this as a victory for the antiquaries. On the contrary. 'Now in one sense the struggle between antiquarians and historians is over. The antiquarians are no longer needed as the custodians of cultural history and of archaeological remains.' Presumably, the explanation is the same as in 'Ancient History': antiquarianism had lost its mandate because it had been taken over by political history. But there was something that antiquaries *still* did better than historians: study the unchanging, or the slowly changing. 'As long as historians cannot produce a remedy for this deficiency,' Momigliano concluded, 'sociology will remain the refurbished form of antiquarianism which our age requires.'[52]

This ending certainly raises more questions than it answers. Why has Momigliano, for the first time, begun describing early modern antiquaries as cultural historians? Why would he describe the turn to cultural and material history by historians as a triumph of history over antiquaries, rather than, as seems more obvious, the reverse? Why would he persist in identifying sociology as the twentieth-century form of antiquarianism? And why, in a work compiled long after publication of Braudel's *La Méditerranée* would Momigliano suggest that historians still had no means of studying 'la longue durée'?

II. What Momigliano Did Not See

'Ancient History and the Antiquarian' and the 'The Rise of Antiquarian Research' lie at the centre of any examination of Momigliano, antiquarianism, and cultural history. Despite the fact that 'Ancient History' has become famous as *the* history of early modern antiquarianism, its vision is personal and any resemblance to the monographic is coincidental. 'Antiquarian Research' and the 'Conclusion' to the Sather Lectures, by contrast, have received almost no attention, yet even in their awkward, semi-finished state throw off fecund hints about what a history of antiquarianism in the *modern* age would look like. It is to these two problems, of what Momigliano did and did not say, that the remainder of this introduction is devoted.

'Ancient History and the Antiquarian' is an essay that has been read many times, but rarely critically. Ingo Herklotz, in this volume, suggests some of the reasons why: a small field with few investigators, many of them his students or colleagues, and all intimidated by him. In his contribution, Herklotz takes up the challenge, focusing on the contrast between what Momigliano said and what would need to be said to present a proper treatment of ancient and early modern antiquarianism.

First of all, Herklotz argues, Momigliano overemphasized the differences between antiquaries' synchronic and historians' diachronic accounts. He rejects the argument that the sixteenth-century theorists of history first ignored antiquarianism altogether and then declared it an imperfect, subordinate, kind of history. Momigliano's sharp distinction between history as presented in the sixteenth-century literature on the *ars historica* and antiquarianism has also come in for re-examination by Grafton, elsewhere. Although Momigliano knew of, and even wrote impressively about, the contributions of Bodin, Baudouin, Perizonius, and Niebuhr, he seemed strangely able to ignore the implications of their work for his own argument about a separation between structural and narrative historiographical practice.[53] Momigliano also orients the antiquary *against* the historian when, as Herklotz suggests, the proper pairing might be *with* philology – a union that persisted through the early modern period and that sheds much useful light on the meaning of early modern antiquarianism. (To be fair, in his unpublished essay of 1950 'Antiquari e storici dell'antichità' Momigliano does seem to emphasize just such a combination of antiquarian and textual skills.) Moreover, while the continuing importance of texts for antiquarianism should not be denied, neither can the turn to material evidence be dated to the end of the seventeenth century, when it flourished already a century and a half earlier. The insufficiency of literary sources as much as their unreliability had led antiquaries concerned with 'moeurs' to draw on visual and material evidence. Their comparison, which Herklotz signals with the contemporary term 'illustratione,' allowed for more secure conclusions.

Even if Momigliano had wanted to make the argument – though he never did – that the later seventeenth century was 'the age of antiquaries' because of the extraordinary proliferation of crowning projects, such as Graevius's and Gronovius's *Summae*, Ptiscus's *Lexicon antiquitatum Romanorum* (1713), and Fabricius's *Bibliographia antiquaria* (1726), the age of encyclopaedias – Minerva's flight – cannot also be an age of innovation. Finally, Herklotz notes pointedly that the late seventeenth century, far from being the triumphant antiquarian moment that Momigliano describes, marked instead a sharp decline in prestige. The Quarrel of the Ancients and the Moderns was, he suggests, only the most famous devastating comment on the antiquarian urge.

All these questions are different ways of asking why Momigliano focused on the late seventeenth and eighteenth centuries. This focus was not itself a revolutionary step, either. Eduard Fueter, for instance, in what was the classic treatment of the history of historiography in Momigliano's youth, also singled out the contribution of the generation of Tillemont and Mabillon to the method of the historian.[54] What Momigliano added was the insistence on Pyrrhonism as the motivating arch-problem of the age.

Why was Momigliano so focused on Pyrrhonism in 1949 and 1950? And why did he remain so committed to it as an explanatory paradigm, as in the Sather Lectures, when it led him into all sorts of difficulties? Recall that Momigliano described Peiresc, who died in 1637, as a Pyrrhonian because he studied material culture, when Peiresc was no Pyrrhonian, when the Pyrrhonian controversy didn't begin until decades later, and when Peiresc cannot be called a sceptic *because* he studied material culture.[55] What might have impelled the normally circumspect historian to go out on such a thin limb?

These questions are intimately bound up with Momigliano's biography and education and are explored in greater length in the final essay in this book. But there is evidence enough from unpublished materials brought to light by Di Donato that Momigliano equated Pyrrhonism with the intellectual breakdown that facilitated and accompanied the rise of Fascism and Nazism. The collapse of standards of proof under the barrage of propaganda amounted to a new *trahison des clercs*. This evoked for him – as it had for Paul Hazard in *La crise de la conscience européenne* (1935) – the challenge of Pyrrhonism, which he had been familiar with as an intellectual problem ever since his work on Tillemont. It led Momigliano to recall that erudite research was the late seventeenth-century answer to Pyrrhonism – again, as had Hazard.[56] But it also led him to overcome the conventional distinction between the history of historiography and the history of method: with Momigliano the tools of the historian were as important as his words.[57]

All this had become a matter of life and death for Momigliano in the 1940s with the murder of his parents, and would not lose its urgency during the rest of his life. Just a few weeks before his death he explained: 'A child of my times and preoccupied ... with the problems of my times (among others, to survive the organized persecution of the Jews by the Fascist government in the years 1939–1944), I posed to myself the historical problems suggested to me by my position within Italian and European civilization.'[58]

Momigliano's argument about the relationship between fascism and 'Pyrrhonism' – or something like it that is captured more or less precisely in the historical reference – and his sense that a return to antiquarianism was a defence of civilization against it, was actually the mirror image of what the extreme right-wing critics of that civilization thought. As early as 1909, Marinetti had explained that his goal was 'to liberate this country from the stinking gangrene of the professors, the archaeologists, the professional guides and the antique-dealers.'[59] Not surprisingly, the Nazis denounced learning that was not sufficiently politically motivated as 'schulmeisterlich,' or 'antiquarian.' But they also denounced cultural history and the cultural sciences, for the same reasons: as a pedant's withdrawal from the high calling of politics. The ever-increasing prominence of cultural history in the 'wilhelminischen Pseudoreich' was a manifestation of this decadence. One author drew a line from Burckhardt to 'Aby Moritz Warburg' and presented the latter as the most important contemporary promoter of his vision.[60] After the war, the unreconstructed but nevertheless rehabilitated Nazi Otto Brunner continued in this vein, arguing that the task of the historian was to marshall the past for the present 'but not to transmit dead antiquarian knowledge' ('nicht aber totes antiquarisches Wissen zu vermitteln').[61]

But even if Momigliano's intuition about antiquarianism as an antidote to Pyrrhonism was right about the twentieth century, was it also true for the seventeenth? Here, things are more complicated. Because if Momigliano had really been interested in antiquarianism as a form of historical scholarship with its own vitality, he would have had to study its flourishing *before* the Pyrrhonian controversy as well as *after* it. And even if one were to grant that Momigliano's method was always to study the ruptures and turning points rather than the continuities, if he were interested in the history of antiquarianism rather than in the impact of antiquarianism on history, then, as Herklotz notes in this volume, he should have had made the second half of the sixteenth and beginning of the seventeenth century his focus. For it was people like the heroes of the Farnese circle in Rome, from Ligorio and Panvinio through Chacón, Bosio, and their seventeenth-century Barberini heirs, Girolamo Aleandro, Cassiano Dal Pozzo, and their French counterpart Peiresc, who made the revolution in antiquarianism that was codified as 'method' half a century and more later by those Momigliano did study, Mabillon and Tillemont, Maffei and Muratori.[62] (And, of course, there were many others outside France and Italy who would be central to a proper 'history,' such as Camden, Ortelius, and Worm.) Only someone who had already decided that the only worthwhile aspect of antiquarianism was how it saved history from disgrace would have focused, as Momigliano did, on the later seventeenth and the eighteenth centuries.

Momigliano's history of antiquarianism, in short, is entirely oriented towards the history of the discipline of history – with the discipline now understood in terms of a shared method of handling evidence. Source criticism is what captured his attention, not questions asked and intellectual vistas opened up, because these tools were then bequeathed to historians. Momigliano always viewed antiquarianism in its relation to 'history.' Its byways were of little interest to him before the Pyrrhonian controversy, and once historians had taken over the tools of the antiquary, the antiquary again fades out of Momigliano's picture almost entirely – lost in the shadows of those dark palaces. And here is the paradox: that Momigliano, most responsible for bringing antiquaries back into scholarly conversation in the past fifty years, is also responsible for perpetuating their position as precursors in an old-fashioned teleology.

Thus his climactic judgment at the end of 'Ancient History,' that antiquarianism was dead because the old idea of political history – written from literary sources – was dead, seems to miss the much bigger point, in 1949, that political history was itself in the process of being killed off – or at least demoted – by the social and economic history represented by the *Annales d'histoire économique*, and that antiquarianism, mediated by its nineteenth-century heirs, had given its shape to Braudel's *La Méditerranée* – published in the same year that 'Ancient History' was first presented to a public.[63] Perhaps this was what Momigliano had in mind with his cryptic comment about the chances of antiquarianism's revival being brightest in France – but that is a matter for divination.

Because Momigliano never really took the measure of what antiquaries did when they weren't serving history, he gave eighteenth-century philosophical historians all the credit for broadening history to include subjects like trade, religion, law, clothing, or, generally, 'manners.' But these were areas of study first researched by the antiquaries of the sixteenth and seventeenth centuries. All he would give the antiquaries credit for was advances in rules for handling evidence. It is *Quellenforschung* that took him back to Gibbon in 1952 and gave him a role he did not have in 1936, but it also obscures the real importance of the antiquaries. In the Sather Lectures, as we saw, this same strange blindness clouds his conclusion.

Finally, Momigliano never was able to grasp the function of antiquarianism for life, as a philosophical exercise. He was aware of the connection between philosophy and antiquarianism in the ancient world, but when he came to the modern revival of antiquarianism, philosophy – certainly ethics – disappeared, occluded by the overarching problem of Pyrrhonism. There are occasional references to the 'ethics of the antiquarian,' such as the praise of Mabillon for having a 'coeur dégagé des passions' at the end of 'Ancient History,' and for the antiquary's love of learning. Momigliano's wide and deep reading in German neo-humanist scholarship would have brought him face to face with the raptures of philology.[64] Yet Momigliano himself showed no interest in exploring just what the philosophical implications of antiquarianism, or the antiquarian 'lifestyle,' might have been in the period before 1800. The start of 'Ancient History,' with its description of a 'new humanism' anchored in social life and open to an emotional relationship to the past, is presented almost as a kind of straw man, to be swept away by his immediately following revision of the meaning of the Age of Antiquaries: a revolution not in taste but in historical method. And yet, as Mark Phillips and others have shown, Momigliano was right about *both* revolutions, even though he could not be bothered to devote time to the former.[65]

These questions all point to ways in which Momigliano's account of early modern antiquarianism would need to be amended, revised, amplified, and expanded if it were to serve not as a proxy for a history of antiquarianism, as it has for the past half-century, but as a road-map or guide for inquirers of the future.

Momigliano's sketch of what antiquarianism turned into in the nineteenth century raises a different set of questions. The first challenge is its lapidary, even offhand character: just a few lines here and there in the Sather Lectures on which to base our argument. The picture that emerges is not very clear: the antiquary either was a cultural historian – and therefore may still survive, buried inside current practitioners of this approach (Sather Lectures) – or is the ur-local historian (Sather Lectures) evolved into the sociologist (both 'Ancient History' and the Sather Lectures), or has come back to life as the director of an institute of fine arts or comparative anthropology (Sather Lectures).

To make good this argument would require more space and talent than is represented by even the extraordinary collection of essays in this volume. We would need discussions about antiquarianism in the late seventeenth and the eighteenth centuries; about the relationship between the antiquarian interest in ancient peoples' daily life and the 'conjectural histories' developed in the natural law tradition; about the genealogy of the *Hilfswissenschaften* from Peiresc, Mabillon, and Muratori, whom Momigliano did write about, through to Gatterer and Fabri, whom he did not; of *Kulturgeschichte* in Germany before Burckhardt; of the relationship between antiquarianism, *Statistik*, and economic history – it was Schlözer who described history as *Statistik* in motion and *Statistik* as static history (*eine stillstehende Geschichte*); and between early modern and modern histories of religion. A case for the importance of some of these can, at least, be sketched out here. Other themes, such as the rich and complex afterlife of antiquarianism in nineteenth- and twentieth-century literature must await a later and separate investigation.

And yet, lest anyone assume that these holes render Momigliano's intuition less worthy of our attention, there are statements like this, in a letter to Gertrud Bing of 1956, uncovered by Grafton:

> Burckhardt was the first art historian to become a historian of a civilization as a whole – and this established a connection between visual studies and

the Renaissance [that] Warburg was to inherit. Then Warburg went beyond Burckhardt in emphasizing the irrational elements of the Renaissance, its anti-Flemish, anti-bourgeois reaction, its links with Antiquity through astrology and mythology. The method could be extended – it could be associated with the new trends in the psychology of the unconscious (from which it undoubtedly derived its strength) and with the new research on language. But, as far as I know, only in the study of the Renaissance the Warburg I. has produced something amounting to a re-interpretation or at least to a critical revision of a civilization. In other fields there have been contributions, suggestions, but not deep-going re-interpretations.

So Momigliano could have, if he had wanted to, written just the kind of history of cultural history through the lens of antiquarianism that we are talking about. But he chose not to.

In what follows, we will take up the challenge of these hints and try to reassemble, out of parts of the argument that Momigliano scattered among the *Contributi* and focused mostly on sociology, anthropology, archaeology, and history of religion, the rudiments of an account that would describe the relationship of early modern antiquarianism to these modern 'cultural sciences.'[66]

First, a word of explanation about this strange-sounding term. For there is no single English equivalent of *Kulturwissenschaft*, a word created at around the same time as the process Momigliano calls attention to in his essays: the flourishing of new approaches to the study of human culture in the second half of the nineteenth century. When Aby Warburg sought out a name for the new institute of art history and comparative anthropology that he founded in Hamburg around 1900, he chose 'Kulturwissenschaftliche Bibliothek Warburg,' presumably to indicate a breadth that went beyond fine art (*Kunstwissenschaft*) or any other single field. When Cassirer, Warburg's close friend and ally, offered a defence of liberal civilization in the midst of the Second World War, he called it *Logik der Kulturwissenschaften* – which was translated into English as 'Humanities,' a term giving all the wrong connotations (more like 'Geisteswissenschaften,' and little evoking the study of material culture and society that was equally part of the cultural sciences).

Why not just say that our question is about the relationship between antiquarianism and cultural history, then? Because, most imporant of all, Momigliano was not interested in cultural history. True, he was interested in Burckhardt, its 'father,' but mostly because of what Burckhardt's *Greek Cultural History* meant for the study of ancient history. In this sense, quite precisely, Momigliano was interested in cultural history for the same reasons that he was interested in all the other new approaches to studying the ancient world that came into being at around the same time, anthropology, sociology, and history of religion – just those 'cultural sciences.' In fact, Momigliano quotes Huizinga praising Burckhardt for precisely this ability to pursue these questions 'long before sociology and anthropology.'[67]

But there is a second powerful reason: Momigliano was formed in an intellectual culture shaped by the powerhouse that was early twentieth-century Germany. He grew up with the *Kulturwissenschaften*. And if this were not enough, when he came to England he found a second home, as Grafton has shown in this volume, at the Warburg Institute. The institution's name may have changed, but its library had not. There Momigliano the ancient historian would have found himself, as Cassirer the philosopher had two decades earlier, surrounded by books on religion, art, ethnography, and archaeology as well as history, philology, philosophy, and the more usual subjects. And even if Momigliano always thought of himself as an ancient historian, when he navigated the stacks of Warburg's library he passed from one division of the cultural sciences to another (as one still does today).

But before we turn to the main lines of an account of the modern transformations of antiquarianism as they exist within Momigliano's oeuvre, perhaps the clearest way of seeing just how a history of the cultural sciences built on the last of classical philology, like Momigliano's, might look different from one generated from within the discipline of history, is to compare it with an exactly contemporary 'history of cultural history,' lodged by Ernst Cassirer in the fourth volume of his *Problem of Knowledge*, written in his exile, in Sweden, between July and November 1940.

The two narratives are remarkably parallel. Like the early Momigliano, Cassirer began in Germany, with Herder, and then continued with Neibuhr, Ranke, and Humboldt through Taine, Mommsen, Burckhardt, and Lamprecht up to Fustel de Coulanges. He, too, pays some attention to the tension between historians and antiquaries and also, though only glancingly, to the history of their relationship.[68] Speaking of Mommsen, Cassirer wrote that 'compared with even the greatest of his forerunners he was the only genuine historian, as distinct from a mere antiquary. He may be called the first to deliver the history of government from its antiquarian isolation.'[69] Like Momigliano, Cassirer recognized the antiquary in Burckhardt but also saw that he was able to do with it things that no antiquary had ever accomplished.[70] And, also like Momigliano, Cassirer saw the 'end' of this historical revolution in the development of the scientific study of the history of religions in the last three decades of the nineteenth century.[71]

The parallels go deeper, and also wider. For, like Momigliano, Cassirer also looked back to Droysen for inspiration. For it was Droysen, in a letter to W. Arendt of 1857, who described 'the historical method as one of the three great forms of knowledge of Nature that our understanding makes possible, and it belongs to the world of Ethics, while the other two, the Physical and the Transcendental, may be philosophical or theological (dogmatic) speculation.'[72] Indeed, Cassirer's decision to include the history of historiography within the story of the human attempt to know the world exactly matches the later Momigliano's claim that the history of historiography offers us a picture of how human beings have striven for truth.

But precisely because of the similarities, the differences between the two accounts are all the more striking. There are two main reasons for the differences. First, Momigliano's fundamental narrative is about the nutritive role of the classics – philology and history – in generating all the new nineteenth-century research agendas. What did not emerge from classical philology, or what did not have its primary impact upon classical philology, was not essential to Momigliano's story. Hence the absence of Schopenhauer, the German tradition after Herder in general, and Lamprecht.[73] But, second, Cassirer had a very different view of where this all ended, in 'Historicism.' This is a subject that I will explore at greater length in the final essay in this volume, especially the way in which the problem of 'Historicism' revived interest in antiquarianism in the twentieth century. Cassirer, unlike Momigliano, did not perceive in it the threatening instability of facts. 'Historicism' represented to him, rather, the same explosion of knowledge characteristic of modern times and charted across the volumes of his magisterial survey. Momigliano, as we shall see, was so concerned by its implications that one could argue that his post-war oeuvre was shaped as a response to this threat.

In what follows we will try both to expand on Momigliano's hints and to make good his silences. Momigliano expressed surprise only at the antiquary's lingering for so long after the services he rendered to History had made him redundant. That was the view from where he stood. From where we stand, the surprise is at how vigorous was the antiquary's inspiration of the flowering of the cultural sciences in the nineteenth and early twentieth centuries. If, as Warburg prophesied, 'every age has the Renaissance of antiquity that it deserves,' then a question for others to ponder is what the flowering of these many new paths to the past can tell us about the later nineteenth century that we may not yet know.

Momigliano, less interested in the history of antiquarianism than in the history of historical method, does not explain how the antiquaries could so swiftly have gone from victors in the Pyrrhonian Controversy at the beginning of the eighteenth century to the vanquished in the salons of Paris by its middle. Momigliano's explanation focuses on the encounter between a philosophical history that had ideas but no method and an antiquarian tradition that had pioneered a method but had no ideas. In this equation, antiquarianism is the 'donor' and philosophical history the happy recipient. Eventually, this one-way trade had the effect of depleting antiquarianism's account, leading Momigliano to wonder not at its decline but at its survival.

Philosophical history in France, before Gibbon's arrival, had turned towards the kinds of questions antiquaries had asked of the past. Voltaire's *Essai sur les moeurs*, for example, or *Siècle de Louis XIV*, is often seen as blazing a trail away from political narrative towards 'civilization.' In the standard histories of historiography before Momigliano, cultural history began with Voltaire.[74] But did this newer version of the 'cultural turn' have a monopoly on the cause of progress or, alternately, reform? Marc Fumaroli's examination of Voltaire's contemporary the Comte de Caylus, the giant of mid-century French antiquarianism, helpfully complicates any simple-minded schema that identifies antiquaries with the ancients and, thus, with the cause of intellectual and aesthetic conservatism. In addition to showing how 'alive' antiquarian scholarship was in Gibbon's Paris, Fumaroli's essay sheds light on how the causes of antiquity and reform, far from being opposed, as the *philosophes* and their apologists would have it, could actually be conjoined.

Caylus was keen on rescuing art from the rococo. The connection between antiquarianism and the study of art is old and thick.[75] Fumaroli notes, of course, that Winckelmann is usually accorded the central role in this trajectory 'from the antiquarian to the art historian.' Momigliano himself had endorsed this germanocentric position as early as 1936 and reiterated it later in his parallels of Gibbon and Winckelmann.[76] This view, combined with the lingering success of the *philosophes*' attack on the idea of 'Erudition' and the person of Caylus, has worked to obscure the latter's activities.

But Caylus also recognized that art was not produced in a vacuum, and that artefacts could provide crucial information about how past peoples thought about themselves. Winckelmann became famous, through

Herder especially, as a historian of Greek liberty because of his study of Greek art, and later came to be seen as the founding father of art history, but Caylus was a much better historian. His attention to archaeological digs, for example, and to their stratigraphy and mapping is committed to realia in a way in which Winckelmann, as C.G. Heyne observed, was not.

Fumaroli's story, with its emphasis on Caylus – who, he notes, actually masterminded the French publication of Winckelmann's notes on the excavations at Herculaneum – challenges this familiar story. He suggests another route from the antiquary to the art history institute, one that remained in much closer touch with its origins. In this context, a history of 'Caylus-reception' could provide an alternative genealogy to the usual Berlin- and Vienna-centric histories of art history.

Moreover, focusing on Caylus lets us pick up still another of Momigliano's dropped threads, concerning the place of antiquarianism in the modern moral cosmos. For Caylus belongs, according to Fumaroli, to the same effort at finding in the ancient world an Archimedean point from which to criticize the critics, to outflank, as it were, the critics of society by showing the superficiality and flimsiness of their views. Caylus's strange bedfellows include Rousseau and, in a way, David. Fumaroli suggests an exhilarating point of contact not only between Momigliano and Leo Strauss, but also between Momigliano and Reinhard Koselleck. We emerge with the vertiginous realization that the alternative views of a 'pathogenesis' or 'dialectic' of enlightenment may have their origin in the antiquarian critique of the 'Moderns.'

But there is also a path from antiquarianism to philosophical history – or from Peiresc to Gibbon, to put a fine point on it – via jurisprudence. Momigliano had noted the preponderance of jurists among those French polyhistors of the sixteenth century who laid down the basis for historical criticism. But from Grotius onwards it was among the natural lawyers that interest in 'civilization' first took root, made necessary by the desire to know what things could really be supposed 'natural' to human beings, and not just a function of convention or environment. Many studies of tools, roads, clothing, religion, and calendars – in short, the rubrics that Momigliano assigned to 'philosophical' history – written from an explicitly comparative point of view, were the products of lawyers, and many of these discussions found their way into the tomes of the tradition that spilled from Grotius through Hobbes to Pufendorf, Barbeyrac, and on and on.

But even where facts were sparse, the need to explain the origins of institutions of such hoary age, like property, or language, or society, led to theoretical modelling of the archaic, or prehistoric, age of man. This 'loose' antiquarianism lies behind the approach known as conjectural history, for example, 'the state of nature' of seventeenth-century natural law treatises, or the 'four-stage theory' of eighteenth-century Scottish histories. According to Donald R. Kelley, one of the pioneering attempts to orient this form of history around the idea of culture was Isaac Iselin's *Geschichte der Menschheit*, or *History of Humanity* (1764). In Germany, as Jörn Garber has argued, Iselin's approach was immediately recognized as crucial by those who identified with the cause of 'culture,' as opposed to 'reason,' in debates about the meaning of Enlightenment. Before, but especially after, Herder, 'cultural history' (*Kulturgeschichte*) became widely practised.[77] (Kelley notes 20 titles with the term 'culture' appearing before 1800, 50 by 1820, and 100 by 1865.)[78] The impact of the antiquarian on this literature has not been examined.[79] Yet if we look at the ancestry of this cultural history, we find works like Johann Fabricius's *Bibliographia antiquaria* (1726; expanded ed. 1760), a bibliography of antiquarian writings divided by subject. The topics covered are so various, such as antiquities, ritual, weights and measures, and food ways, as to amount to an encyclopaedic presentation of ancient life. At this point, in a pattern recapitulated in Momigliano's own career, writing about antiquarian writing on past human culture evolves into a rudimentary form of cultural history – which was called *historia literaria* in the later half of the century. But it is also important to note that in this eighteenth-century ecology of encylopaedias, scholars became writers ('de scriptoribus'), writers were considered only as authors (index 'Authorum'), and antiquities were studied through books. Morhof's definition of the antiquary as a textual critic is a telling proof of this slimming down of antiquarianism as it passed into a literary history of culture.[80]

Historia literaria – histories of learning – stand between antiquarianism and cultural history in later eighteenth-century Germany. Michael C. Carhart observes that the project of gathering up all forms of human knowledge for study also had its beginning in that same circle of sixteenth-century French polyhistors to which Momigliano referred. He then sets out to explain how these encyclopaedias were constructed, the history of this genre in the eighteenth century, and its relation to the genre of *Kulturgeschichte* that emerged alongside it in the 1780s before becoming distinct and separate in the decades to come. Herder is usually located at the origins of *Kulturgeschichte*, but from the perspective of *historia literaria*, according to Carhart, it is J.G. Eichhorn who marks the junction with *Kulturgeschichte*. In 1796 he wrote that 'The history of arts and sciences, their origins, progress, and various transformations can never be separated from the history of the social conditions, for culture and literature are twin sisters, children of the same father, who continually provide support for each other. Culture, the firstborn, prepares the birth of her younger sister, and thereafter they live and work together, inseparable and unseparated, and also die together. Without the history of one the life of the other is incomplete and incomprehensible.'[81] Momigliano was able to ignore *historia literaria* because it had neither grown out of the study of ancient history nor had any impact on its subsequent study. Where Momigliano entered the German debates was with Herder – not even Winckelmann merited sustained treatment – and from there he moved directly to Humboldt and thence to Droysen or, alternatively, to Creuzer and then Bachofen.

But even with the two early essays, Momigliano's discussion of the German tradition was pointillist; for the narrative that filled in the connections between Humboldt, Boeckh, Schleiermacher, and Droysen we need to turn elsewhere, to Benedetto Bravo's extraordinary *Philologie, histoire, philosophie de l'histoire. Etude sur J.G. Droysen historien de l'antiquité* (1968).[82] At the centre of this inquiry is the increasingly philosophical tendency – or pretensions – of philology. On the one hand, there is pressure from the side of Hegel as it registered on his colleague in Berlin, Boeckh, underpinning the latter's critique of Wolf for being too superficial and not grasping the meaning of the Spirit that manifested itself in the external facts studied by the philologist. And Boeckh represented the wing of classical philology that *was* concerned with realia (*Sachphilologie*)! On the other hand, there was the new insistence of Humboldt on the crucial role of the empathy that the historian brought to his reading as the key to historical understanding. This subjective turn was followed up by Boeckh as the foundation of *his* notion of the process of understanding (*Verstehen*). According to Bravo, Boeckh's earlier familiarity with Schleiermacher's hermeneutical circle provided a framework for the assimilation of Humboldt's idea as a category for studying a past culture, not just a single text.[83] The notion that understanding the world began within, in the genius of the historian, was the cornerstone of the German celebration of German historians that continued through 1945, the elevation of the subjective that lay at the heart of *Historismus*. And in 1950, as I will argue in the final essay in the volume, this notion seemed to Momigliano to have evolved into the sloppy, generalizing, pseudo-intellectual posturing and misology that he identified with 'Pyrrhonism.'

For Bravo, Droysen, who was Hegel's student as much as Boeckh's, represented the apogee of this philosophizing tendency in history, displacing philology almost entirely. Karl Otto Müller, another student of Boeckh's – and also examined by Momigliano – likewise elevated the task of philology to a kind of philosophy, arguing that it could 'penetrate to the interior of the human spirit.'[84] And he too, following Humboldt, believed that this understanding was a matter of reproducing in oneself that which others had thought, for which one needed 'a special talent, a special state of the soul, let us say, too, a special initiation' ('ein eignes Talent, eine eigne Stimmung, ja eine eigne Weihe').[85] Where Müller parted company with Boeckh, and with Humboldt before him, was by insisting that the categories of research could emerge only from research itself and could not be imported from elsewhere. For Müller, the achievement of philology was a cultural history: 'to seize and render intelligible, with the aid of words and combinations of concepts, the life and spirit of these ancient peoples, however strange it is.'[86]

Droysen was for Momigliano a crucial figure, preparing the ground for a kind of Hegelian cultural history but then abandoning the project half-finished. (Later, Momigliano suggested that Droysen's own biography might have had something to do with this.) Müller's vision of philology as cultural history was left an even smaller torso by his early death in Greece. These stand as two 'dead ends' in Momigliano's history of cultural history, though it would seem only a short step from Müller's vision to Burckhardt's, with art history replacing philology as the tool that best unlocked the meaning of cultures' past.

In his only thrust through this period, the study of Creuzer, Momigliano was looking for something else. Thus, while he noted the dedication to Creuzer of Wilhelm Wachsmuth's *Entwurf einer Theorie der Geschichte* (1820), a pioneering treatise of cultural history (*Kulturgeschichte*), he left this thread hanging, too.[87] Yet Wachsmuth stood at the beginning of a fascinating translation of antiquarianism into anthropology and cultural history. He, and Gustav Friedrich Klemm, and the museum director Hans zu und von Aufsess are the most interesting representatives of a tradition of *Kulturgeschichte* that has been entirely lost, and with it the link connecting early modern antiquarianism and modern cultural history. Without them, too, Burckhardt's achievement appears both more original and more audacious. Without them we cannot understand, let alone answer, Fernand Braudel's challenge that 'it would be useful to see how far Jacob Burckhardt fits into the movement of German *Kulturgeschichte*, projected as early as Herder (1784–91) and popularized by the publication of Gustav Klemm's book (1843–52).'[88]

Yes, Momigliano's attention to the cultural historical impulse in nine-teenth-century historical practice is oriented on Burckhardt. But, tellingly, Momigliano's single set-piece treatment was occasioned by a new Italian translation of the *Griechische Kulturgeschichte*. As if Burckhardt's achieve-ment, had he only written on the Italian Renaissance, had he only shown how art could provide historians with evidence, would not have occa-sioned a study, so focused was Momigliano's attention on the ancient world.

Of course, Momigliano was acutely aware of the place of Burckhardt's kind of history in his history of historiography. He termed his own brief essay on Burckhardt and his Greek cultural history 'a further contribu-tion to the story of the relations between "antiquarianism" and "history"' ('un ulteriore contributo alla storia dei rapporti tra *Antiquitates* e *Historiae*').[89] He called Burckhardt's cultural history 'the new antiquari-anism' ('la nuova antiquaria'), but did not explain what that meant. Wilfried Nippel, more recently, has suggested that this had to do with its focus on private life, the systematic disposition of the material, and its accessible style.[90] Given how vehemently *Kulturgeschichte* was attacked in the 1850s by the historical establishment in Germany, Burckhardt's deci-sion not to publish the lectures makes sense. It also helps us appreciate that the designation of Burckhardt as an antiquary by the political historian and arch-antagonist of Lamprecht, Georg von Below, was not intended as a compliment.[91]

Already in the 1840s, like a weathercock, Burckhardt had insisted on the bankruptcy of philology, on its failure to adequately bring the past back to life, and its destiny as a mere auxiliary science, whatever its contemporary self-importance.[92] According to Momigliano, if in the eighteenth century antiquarianism lost ground because it failed to offer a philosophical vision of history, in the nineteenth it failed because its resolute rejection of narrative made it seem incapable of offering any-thing other than a static account of manners, customs, and practices – even though it was now clear that these were as conditioned by time as was any battle.[93]

Against this backdrop, Burckhardt's decision to write systematic rather than chronological narratives was quite daring. But the big difference between what Momigliano described as 'la nuova antiquaria' and old-fashioned antiquarianism was that whereas the latter stopped at the level of description without trying to penetrate its significance, Burckhardt sought to elucidate the 'Greek spirit' that animated institutions and that could emerge in visible form only from their systematic study.[94] Momigliano suggests that not only did Burckhardt make the quest for the spirit of the Greeks central to his *kulturgeschichtlich* approach, but that he erred in accepting it – from Winckelmann – and using it so uncritically.[95] The disputed question of Burckhardt's Hegelianism, insisted upon so forcefully by Ernst Gombrich and before him by von Below – though denied at the time by Burckhardt himself – seems to be seconded here by Momigliano, though as with Müller, there were other ways of thinking about total history.[96] Burckhardt himself distinguished between what he was doing and the thing historians did in the preface to the second edition of *The Age of Constantine the Great*, explaining that 'the objective in the mind of the author was not so much a complete historical account as an integrated description, from the viewpoint of cultural history.'[97]

Something about capturing the 'meaning' of the past through a survey of various linked aspects of it seems essential to the meaning of cultural history. In Momigliano's sense of development, Burckhardt stands between the early modern antiquary and the modern social scientist. That is what was meant in his description of Burckhardt's approach as an 'antiquarianism revised according to romantic notions of national genius and the organic state that in its way prepared for the sociological examination of the ancient world introduced afterwards by Max Weber.'[98]

In fact, when Momigliano wanted to think about the afterlife of the antiquarian, already in the 1940s he thought in terms of sociology. Max Weber, to whom Momigliano devoted no fewer than six essays – all subsequent to his appointment to the Committee on Social Thought at the University of Chicago – was the key figure. This view, which reaches its extreme in Momigliano's description of sociologists as 'armed antiquarians,' is mostly anchored in a study of Weber. But it reaches back, necessarily, to Weber's predecessor, Theodor Mommsen. Mommsen the historian's complex relationship with antiquarianism – dismissal of the phenomenon while recapitulating its success and its failures – is the subject of a close examination by Wilfried Nippel.[99] Mommsen himself dismissed the contributions of the antiquaries, but did much the same as they, using epigraphy to create a revolution, picking up where Gruter and Scaliger had left off. Yet he was clear that the philologist's tools only prepared the sources; the historian was the one who judged them. Momigliano's thoughts on the relationship between 'Philology and History' directly contradicted this sharp, schematic division.[100]

In his *Römische Geschichte*, Mommsen treated events in their succession *and* institutions in their structure. His *Staatsrecht* is an example of antiquarian systematicity. Mommsen's contemporaries were too overawed to note the continuity between his work and that of those who preceded him, except for the unflappable Jacob Bernays, who was quick to point this out – daringly – in his contribution to Mommsen's own *Festschrift*. Interestingly, as Nippel notes, Mommsen's critique of antiquarian scholarship on ancient Rome exactly paralleled K.O. Müller's critique of Wilhelm Wachsmuth's form of *Kulturgeschichte*. Weber's debt to Mommsen, finally, was both less and more than Momigliano suggested. The biographical connection was much weaker – he attended only one lecture of Mommsen's – and on substantive matters was influenced by many other scholars. On Roman questions, Weber did tend to follow the older man, but was disposed to a much broader form of comparatism, including the use of categories of his own devising.

'The Case of Max Weber' – to take one of Momigliano's titles – in fact represented the complete blurring of the differences between history and antiquarianism.[101] Weber's ideal type was intended as a solution to a problem that had always divided antiquarians from historians: the coordination of the synchronic and diachronic registers of historical time. 'In what precise relation Max Weber himself was putting history and sociology becomes a secondary problem once it is realised that there have always been two types of history, the history which pursues the fleeting event and the history which analyses permanent or long-lasting structures. Whether you call the second type of history, antiquarianism or "histoire de la longue durée" or anthropology or sociology or structural history is less important than the relation which at any given moment exists between these two types of history.'[102] This approach effectively repudiates, or rather replaces, the now classic dichotomy offered up by Momigliano in the 1950 article with one more nuanced and, indeed, less 'disciplinary.'

In the later years of his career, after his appointment at the University of Chicago, Momigliano began to discern others who emerged in Germany after 1870 and who, with a new interest in materialism and science, then shifted to art and religion and thence to problems of psychology, social organization, classification of data, and laws of evolution. Momigliano placed these new cultural sciences alongside the new cultural history, all born in the same decades from the same cause: the atrophy, or crisis, of classical philology.[103] 'Any great name of the cultural history so characteristic of the second half of the nineteenth century – whether Burckhardt, Taine, Dilthey or Comparetti – will confirm this independence from classical historiography ... The new disciplines of sociology and social anthropology were in a sense rooted in the works of Herodotus and Aristotle, but gained authority in a context of evolutionary theories unknown to the ancients.'[104] Of historians at work in the twentieth century, none was more highly praised by Momigliano as an exemplar of the new approach of the cultural sciences than Marc Bloch, and, by extension, the *Annales* school. 'But we live in the time of the *Annales*,' he wrote, 'and Marc Bloch's *Feudal Society* is the most beautiful book of history written in this century.'[105] What Momigliano seemed to have found most important was the way in which a historian had reclaimed the mantle of the antiquarian from sociology. 'Its true achievement is to render sociologists irrelevant by doing what sociologists do: doing it better, it is understood. Total history ['la storia completa'] makes sociology irrelevant.'[106]

In his only set-piece on *Annales* history, Momigliano saw Michel Foucault as standing foursquare in the tradition launched by Bloch. 'If M. Foucault appears, in theory, as a negator of historical movement' – this passage occurs in a discussion of structuralism and whether it implied stasis or mutability – 'his historical works suggest, instead, a profound and original sense of intellectual changes.'[107] This blending of the slowly and the quickly changing had undermined conventional divisions not so much between disciplines as between different ways of cutting up the past (namely, ideas versus instititutions). 'This is certainly the point which the astute Michel Foucault has grasped in trying to put across his new *archéologie du savoir* to replace *l'histoire des idées*,' Momigliano wrote elsewhere. Moreover, given both Momigliano's sympathy for Herodotus and his view of Herodotus-reception as a bellwether for changing historical sympathies and methodologies in the modern era, it is striking that it is to him that he likens Foucault. 'If Herodotus is the natural target for the sceptic about history, he is also the prototype of the creative historian, of the discoverer of new subjects within the ordinary human experience. Perhaps to connect the name of Herodotus with that of Michel Foucault, who until yesterday was the most original among our contemporary historians, is the best way to indicate what the Herodotean tradition can still produce.'[108] Whether Momigliano really understood Foucault is a different question.[109]

Momigliano may have come to anthropology later than to sociology – Di Donato has noted that all references to 'anthropology' and 'structuralism' were added to the Sather Lectures in Momigliano's 1976 revisions; prior to that he had mentioned only 'Sociology' – but, like sociology, he came to it through the study of ancient historians, in this case, Herodotus. 'It is true that professional historians now mainly work on written evidence. But anthropologists, sociologists and students of folklore are doing on oral evidence what to all intents and purposes is historical work. The modern accounts of explorers, anthropologists and sociologists about primitive populations are ultimately an independent development of Herodotus' *historia*.'[110] And yet, even though this passage is found in an essay that discussed the practice of early modern antiquaries, with their interest in travel, *moeurs*, and *autopsia*, Momigliano never drew the line from antiquarianism to anthropology, not even during his late immersion in Bachofen – except in that daring aside that the resurrected antiquarian might well be the director of an institute for comparative (should we read: historical?) anthropology.

Riccardo Di Donato has argued elsewhere, in the context of explaining the relationship between Durkheim and Mauss, that the latter's addition of history to the former's sociology created anthropology in France. Yet Momigliano himself, as in his comments on Marc Bloch, seemed keen on reclaiming the sociological approach from the sociologists. Bloch's *Les rois thaumaturges* was much more an anthropologist's book than a sociologist's, much more Mauss's than Durkheim's, yet this seems to have escaped Momigliano. Much misunderstanding and much 'unlearning' could have been avoided if Momigliano had drawn the connection. Yet these are distinctions Momigliano would have had to acquire much later in life; during the inter-war period, when he was 'formed,' French scholarship of the Durkheimians (including Bloch) was entirely unknown to him.[111] But by the mid 1960s he was aware and admiring of the cross-pollination occurring in the Ecole des Hautes Etudes en Sciences Sociales. Explicitly referring to it, he wrote that 'the first thing to do is to reinforce the study of ethnography, or comparative anthropology, and to connect it to ancient history ... One of the most promising aspects of current historical studies is this possibility of fruitful exchanges with anthropologists.'[112]

But this favour seems not to have been returned. For if Momigliano did not closely follow French debates about the 'sciences humaines' in the first half of the twentieth century, it is the French who did not pay attention to Momigliano's work in the second half. How else can we explain Lévi-Strauss's *exactly* reinventing the opposition between the Ancient Historian and the Antiquary in the guise of his distinction between 'Histoire et Ethnologie'? Or Jacques Le Goff's urging of anthropology upon the historian oblivious to Momigliano's story of how history became a discipline precisely by repressing the anthropological heritage of the antiquary?[113]

Peter Burke's essay in this volume surveys the whole world of fields that carried on the early modern antiquaries' attention to peoples and history. He conclusively links what the antiquaries did in the seventeenth century with what archaeologists, anthropolgists, and folklorists did in the nineteenth. And he demonstrates how the polymathy of the early moderns was continued in the imprecise disciplinary boundaries of eighteenth- and nineteenth-century scholars who pursued their quarry in areas that could alternatively be called ethnography, folklore, or archaeology. He also shows how eighteenth-century philosophical history – only gestured at by Momigliano – explored these 'lateral' connections with the concept of 'system.' Burke gives as an example the discovery of the 'feudal system.' Even as these coalesced into fields with their own research agendas in the nineteenth century, the conjunction 'Archaeology and Anthropology' lingered longest, reflecting these fields' common attention to the world before writing. These were also fields, as Suzanne Marchand shows, that were supported and encouraged by imperial vocations, both in Germany and in England. But unlike archaeology, anthropology by the end of the ninteenth century was able to break more decisively with the neo-humanist premise that the only Culture was Classical.

In a fascinating aside, Momigliano suggested that nineteenth-century classical scholars essentially recapitulated the achievements of the Renaissance: they read with the same sense of newness as did the fifteenth century, and likewise emerged with radical reinterpretations of antiquity.[114] But after 1850, Momigliano continued, the dynamic of research focused on developing these interpretations in new directions, often at the expense of the integrity of the classical sources themselves.[115] Some examples he gave were J.J. Bachofen's *Mutterrecht* and H.S. Maine's *Ancient Law* (both 1861); Fustel de Coulanges's *La cité antique* (1864); J.F. McLennan's *Primitive Marriage* (1865); Bachofen's *Sage von Tanaquil* (1871); L.H. Morgan's *Ancient Society* (1877); and W. Robertson Smith's *Kinship and Marriage in Early Arabia* (1885) and *Religion of the Semites* (1889).[116] We might wish to add Nietzsche's *The Birth of Tragedy* (1872).

Omitted from this list and, indeed, from the scope of Momigliano's nineteenth-century investigations was archaeology. Alain Schnapp has recently worked towards filling in this gap, and in this volume Suzanne Marchand speculates that perhaps Momigliano felt no need to comment on what may have seemed to him an obvious genetic link between antiquarianism and archaeology. Momigliano may also have been less interested, personally, in material culture, and more animated, as has already been suggested, by the problems of philology.

But as Marchand goes on to show in her careful study of Adolf Furtwängler (1853–1907), the line separating antiquarianism from archaeology was much blurrier than even Momigliano thought, and antiquarianism both more resistant to 'modern' practices and more adaptable than hitherto has been credited. In other words, the meaning of archaeology cannot simply be 'read off' the history of antiquarianism. Yes, the same hegemony of the philologist that damned the antiquarian had no time for the archaeologist either. But, as she shows, just because the archaeologist took up the tool-kit of the antiquarian didn't mean that he worked with the same mindset. And yet the persistence of antiquarianism in the modern discipline of archaeology suggests that from this perspective, too, Momigliano's assumption that decline and fall was the only scenario to be expected is unsustainable.

Antiquarianism not only survived as archaeological practice up until the end of the twentieth century, its reputation was actually burnished by the encounter with the sort of problems posed by the large-scale excavations of the last quarter of the nineteenth century. Proof from the field: Marchand presents Furtwängler as an antiquarianizing archaeologist. Proof from the page: Stark's *Systematik und Geschichte der Archäologie der Kunst* (1880) was described by Momigliano himself in 1950 as the best extant history of antiquarianism.[117] Nevertheless, as Marchand argues so convincingly, the late nineteenth-century archaeologist by no means necessarily repudiated the Winckelmannian hierarchy of arts and cultures – or Calylus's belief that the only way to better modern art was to study the best ancient art. In a way, the encounter with large-scale archaeology, rather than pushing archaeology towards the ethnographic, or social historical, actually propelled it backwards – as if in recoil – towards a Winckelmannian aesthetic of the masterpiece. The philologist's hostility at being dragged into middens by the archaeologist, in other words, may have been misplaced. The union of philology and archaeology – like that between Thucydidean and Herodotean history – was again to be deferred.

One of Momigliano's most absorbing interests in the last years of his life was the work of the Swiss Johann Jakob Bachofen. In the life of this one person, the connections between the different cultural sciences all come together. In Bachofen, one feels, judging from the extraordinary attention devoted to him in the 1980s, Momigliano felt he had found the prototype of the modern-day antiquary. But Bachofen was not always admired by Momigliano, so that changing taste in this local context can serve as a measure of the broader transformation of Momigliano's thought from the 1930s to the 1980s.[118]

What a difference fifty years makes! No fewer than three discrete articles on Bachofen emerged from the last *year* of Momigliano's life, and Bachofen was the subject of what turned out to be the last of Momigliano's seminars at Pisa on the history of scholarship. Beginning as a student of Savigny and Roman law, Bachofen turned, mysteriously, into a scholar of things for which there was as yet no name. That intrigued Momigliano.

For Bachofen, the crucial decade was the 1850s. Around 1855 or so, Bachofen's work crystallized into a project entitled *Das alte Italien*. This, in turn, bifurcated into the *Gräbersymbolik* (1859) and *Mutterrecht* (1861). Bachofen's weakness as an antiquarian imperilled the first; his strengths as a text reader salvaged the second. But scholars savaged both works, their attack made easier by Bachofen's vague justification of interest in the relationship between death, fertility, eternity, and women, and his reliance on Creuzer's *Symbolik* (1810–12), itself seen as a monument to an unacceptable form of etymology-as-history.[119] In his essay on Creuzer of 1944, Momigliano commented on the impact of his work by reference to its impact on Bachofen: 'Though soon dismissed by responsible philologists, it was greeted with enthusiasm by philosophers like Schelling, lastingly influenced the erratic genius of Bachofen.'[120]

Approaching Bachofen in 1986, Momigliano argued that he was best understood in the context of history of religion – indeed, that he understood himself to be working in that area. 'It was his deepest belief that religion determined history in those ages which really counted for the history of mankind.'[121] This reflected Bachofen's own view of religion as the best guarantor of tradition; that is to say, a 'religious attitude towards the past and the present' was the sine qua non of the historian.[122]

Bachofen realized that to understand Graeco-Roman religion – the antiquity of Europe – it had to be compared with other ancient societies. That was no great discovery. But Bachofen's corollary, that to understand Graeco-Roman religion you had to understand things that were not typically viewed as religion at all, such as deviant aspects of society, types of family organization, and patterns of cosmology – this was a huge step into the unknown.[123] 'Prima facie,' Momigliano argued, 'Bachofen in his mature work is the first of the giants who in the sixties and seventies of the last century created the new anthropology.'[124]

Another key figure in Momigliano's history of the development of anthropology – or of the anthropological perspective – out of classical philology was Hermann Usener, Professor at Bonn for many years. If the implied claim to encyclopaedic sovereignty made by classical philology at the beginning of the century, in the work of Wolf and Boeckh, provided the basic terms of debate for the rest of the century, several major turns can be discerned: Ritschl's rejection of a philosophical, or Idealist, construction of this sovereignty; Mommsen's concrete, archival response; and Usener's comparative cultural history, which used the concrete to ask questions about the philosophical. This led him beyond individuals, but also beyond intentionality, to issues of will and deep transmission.[125] Momigliano noted that 'the philology of the late nineteenth century was one of many ways of regaining the unconscious – or the non-documented.'[126] It is this approach that made Usener so attentive to questions of cultural survivals. The continuity of myths occupied one part of his researches, the survival of pagan ideas another.[127]

In this respect Usener was truly Aby Warburg's teacher. Here Momigliano endorses Gombrich's interpretation.[128] Although, as Grafton shows in this volume, Momigliano was at home at the Institute in London ('When I arrived in Oxford in 1939, it was enough to mention the word "idea" to be given the address of the Warburg Institute'), he did not devote a single essay to either Warburg or his influence on the history of classical scholarship.[129] Only in his necrology of Gertrud Bing does Momigliano come to grips most immediately with the Warburg tradition, through Bing, its 'custodian.'[130] In saluting her role, and that of Saxl, in preserving the institution during its founder's long convalesence, and then rescuing it from the catastrophe in 1933, Momigliano had occasion to turn to Aby Warburg himself.

But it was not Warburg's scholarship that attracted Momigliano's attention as much as his persona. Momigliano describes Warburg as uniting the 'cosmopolitan tradition of the Hamburg mercantile aristocracy' – hence his appreciation of Felix Gilbert's distinction between Hamburg and Berlin – and the 'religious anxiety of the enlightened Jew.' Momigliano described the K.B.W. as a centre 'of objective research on the encounters and collisions in the Western World between pagan ideas and emotions (equivalent for him to the primitive) and Judeo-Christian ideas and emotions.'[131] One wonders whether Momigliano saw in Warburg's swinging transmissions of knowledge from East to West to

East to West again something familiar, a kind of completion – if also translation – of Droysen's abandoned cultural historical perspective on the origins of Europe in the Hellenistic fusion with Eastern culture, producing Christianity. Nevertheless, Warburg, like Usener and Bachofen, was a *Kulturwissenschaftler* who chose for his vantage point the unmarked frontier between anthropology and history of religion.

Momigliano's insightful reading of Warburg against the history of religion – shared by Walter Benjamin and rediscovered by scholars only in the last decade – and, in general, his understanding of the history of religion, was very much informed by the questions asked by anthropologists.[132] Beginning in the seventeenth century, histories of religion, written by antiquaries, were among the first histories of culture. Lorenzo Pignoria's updating of Cartari's *Imagini degli dei de gli antiqui* (1615) and Selden's *De diis Syris* (1617) are among the best-known published antiquarian histories of religion.[133] At the heart of their approach was the redefinition of religion away from 'cult' and towards 'culture.' In the work of someone like Heyne, at Göttingen, history of religion took in history of mythology as well as *historia literaria*. Whatever the confessional imperatives that intervened in the next century, from Bachofen onwards through the twentieth century, cultural anthropology and history of religion were bound together.

The history of the study of the history of religion confirms Momigliano's insight even as it resists the chronological flow of his argument, for its modern form – or forms – is found complete and intact already in the seventeenth century.[134] Here, instead of tracing a continuity from the early modern to the modern, we can examine history of religion as in some sense paradigmatic for the whole antiquarian venture. In this way, the contributions of Guy Stroumsa and Moshe Idel are linked – linked in exploring Momigliano in the context of modern history, and historians, of religion; and linked also in seeing Momigliano's approach to history as prefigured, shaped, and even distorted by his attitude to religion-in-history.

Guy Stroumsa begins by examining Momigliano's fascination with the antiquarian discovery of the history of religion through the prism of his own writings on the history of religion. This perspective, so rare for a historian of the ancient world, Stroumsa traces back to Momigliano's own life and to his comfort in moving between the literatures of ancient Greece, Rome, and Israel. The vicissitudes of that life insisted to Momigliano even more strongly on the need to emphasize these connections and, especially, not to write the history of Israel, or Jews, *out* of the

historical narrative. This insistence, too, was tinged with present-day realities: the Jewish renunciation of so much of Greek culture was, he believed, what made possible the survival of Jews in history.

As Stroumsa argues, Momigliano's interest in the history of religion in the later part of his career cannot be separated from his interest in his own religion during those same years. Discussions of Jewish history and Jewish scholars became much more common. Stroumsa mentions Momigliano's relations with Elias Bickerman, with Leo Strauss, and with Gershom Scholem. It is this last that is the subject of Moshe Idel's contribution to this volume. With Idel, the biographical context alluded to by several of the contributors, especially Stroumsa, becomes the text, as he uses Momigliano's discussions of Scholem to probe the meaning of Judaism for Momigliano the historian.

Momigliano's 'Jewish Question' has been the subject of many essays dating from the last years of his life and since, his own, carefully re-presented and introduced by Silvia Berti, not the least.[135] But even a cursory survey of Momigliano's output shows that after his first book on the Maccabees, Jewish themes disappear from the published oeuvre, only to return in the 1960s. In his necrology for Gertrud Bing, cited just above, Momigliano seemed especially, perspicuously, attentive to Warburg's social condition as a hyphenated Jew – Momigliano's word was 'enlightened' – living in Hamburg in what Fritz Stern once described as 'the agony of assimilation.' It was in 'his personal explorations' that Warburg came to greater awareness 'of the pre-eminent position of Antisemitism among the passions of Western man.'[136] In 1964 no one was interpreting Warburg in this way; indeed, only recently has Warburg's Jewish dimension been treated as at all relevant to his intellectual make-up. Did this have anything to do with Momigliano's trip to Jerusalem in 1964 – his first to Israel – where he delivered two of the six Sather Lectures at the Hebrew University?[137]

Once Momigliano allowed himself to address questions of modern Jewishness, they formed the core of some of his most spectacular essays: 'Droysen between Greeks and Jews,' 'Jacob Bernays,' and 'The Jews of Italy.' Droysen's awkward inability even to mention that his wife and closest friends were converts from Judaism seems also to have made it impossible for him to address the position of ancient Judaism at the junction between the Greek and the Christian. His study of Hellenism remained unfinished, with monumental consequences, as we have seen, for the subsequent history of cultural history. Momigliano's brilliant portrait of Jacob Bernays explores many of the same issues from the perspective of the unassimilated Jew who studied the Hellenistic world *and* its greatest modern student, Joseph Scaliger. In his own auto-biogaphical writings, as Moshe Idel shows, Momigliano presents – intentionally or not – a picture of someone whose identity was hitched to the precarious condition of Jewish-European hybridity. Bernays was an alter ego, but from another age, to which Momigliano himself was denied access.

Momigliano became more self-consciously Jewish in his last decades. But there were tensions in his understanding of what was the best way to live Judaism in the modern world, and many of them emerge in his treatments of Scholem. On the one hand, Momigliano clearly admired Scholem, not only for his intellectual achievements but for the courage of his convictions (just as in 1954 he had admired Gibbon for his). Momigliano even went so far as to suggest a possible filiation to Scholem via Warburg (and hence to himself?) through the common influence of Usener, though he hastened to add that he had not yet found any explicit references to Usener in Scholem.[138]

On the other hand, Momigliano resisted the implications of the way Scholem lived that life. Central to these, according to Idel, was whether the 'core' or meaning of Judaism belongs to history or not, and whether its historians should be part of that history. Paradoxically enough, Momigliano the historian seems to have believed that the historical experience of Jews was extrinsic to the essence of Judaism, which he considered unchanging. This, perhaps, was what he meant when in his early discussion of the Jansenist origins of modern historiography he wrote of the difference between human and divine history that 'the answer, *also for me* [my emphasis], lies at the centre of [Bossuet's] *Discours.*'[139]

Scholem's history of the messianic eruption and its aftermath, and Scholem's own life, in which history erupted yet again, was a direct challenge. In 1937 – at a tense time, to be sure – Momigliano had argued strongly against Zionism and in favour of a Jewish-Italian identity. Momigliano's observation that when Kabbalists descend into the streets and make history (becoming Zionists) Jewish 'tradition' is at an end not only attacks Scholem, but also self-consciously, and perhaps a bit defensively, reflects his own life choices. For, as Idel observes, Momigliano's failure to carry on the beliefs of his grandfather was also the end of tradition, and he must have been aware of this on some level, too.

Scholem, though he began as the 'Catholic neo-Romantic' of Momigliano's somewhat mischievous characterization, became much more of a historicist over time.[140] And yet the young Momigliano seemed to view at least his scholarship on the Jewish tradition in much the same way as did the later Scholem: 'One may legitimately conclude that inasmuch as the history of the Maccabees is the history of religious and moral life, it is continued in the history of their own tradition ... And in our attempt to make a critical study of the Maccabean tradition and bearing in mind the spiritual force it established, we prolong that history.'[141]

But between this passage, written in 1931, and his essays on Scholem of the 1980s, Momigliano had his world turned upside down. 'Historicism' serves as the focus of the final essay in our volume because it enables us to understand why Momigliano was so afraid of Pyrrhonism and its discontents. The turn to antiquarianism that followed was a personal statement – a kind of credo – as much as it was a scholarly one. Scholem's friend Walter Benjamin – not a name generally mentioned in the same sentence as Arnaldo Momigliano, it is true – also sensed the danger in 'Historicism' and also responded to it with a turn to the antiquarian. Though the language he eventually chose to describe his rejection of 'Historicism' was the misleading one of 'historical materialism,' what Benjamin said about 'Historicism,' and how he went about creating a kind of historical scholarship that was intended as an exemplar of anti-Historicism, suggests that, if Momigliano had wished to read *Das Passagen-Werk* (*The Arcades Project*), he might have found in Benjamin a twentieth-century heir to Bachofen and, perhaps, a model antiquary for still another age of exploding canons.[142]

III. Conclusion

What Momigliano did not see, he was not looking for. He remained always a historian of the ancient world and of the historians of the ancient world. The tremendous range of his scholarship nevertheless stayed close to this centre: even where he strayed – as in his comments about Foucault – there was always some tangent that connected back to the study of the ancient world.

In this volume we have tried to show just how Momigliano's history of the study of the ancient world presents, all the same, the skeleton of a history of the development of the cultural sciences (largely because, as Momigliano so often noted, ancient history was for a long time the most innovative corner of the historical universe). Our attempt has involved, in some cases, taking Momigliano's argument apart, and in others, putting its pieces back together in a different shape. Because he was not trying to write a history of early modern antiquarianism, the picture of it that he did provide lacks the emphases, or 'hooks,' that would have made it easy for a reader to connect the 'early modern' and 'modern' parts of his own oeuvre. That Momigliano's later discussions of the subsequent development of research agendas in sociology, anthropology, and history of religion build on the efforts of the early modern antiquaries seems undeniable. And in the Sather Lectures, Momigliano authorized such a reading – we have, in fact, taken it as ours – but in such an offhand way, in a publication that appeared so long after most people had formed their impression of his notion of antiquarianism, that its call has not been heard, let alone heeded.

Momigliano assumed in 1950 that antiquarianism was finished – because political historians had finally mastered the synchronic – and that the only surprise was how long the patient lingered before being officially declared dead. By now, I think it is clear that the case is the opposite: antiquarianism as a methodological force 'disappeared' because it had conquered history. This perhaps seems clearer from the perspective of the beginning of the twenty-first century, when cultural history stands at the centre of the historical enterprise, taking in history of science as well as art, literature, philosophy, scholarship, and society, than it could have in the middle of the twentieth. All these cultural sciences are today part of the arsenal of the historian. Even the micro-history of the *Annales* and its adherents over the last fifty years documents this trend towards the cultural-historical; not against social or economic history, but, rather, building on that rebellion against the hegemony of the political while moving back towards recognizing, at the same time, the centrality of the individual.

Similarly, antiquarianism as an 'emotional' force remains alive and well. Nor should anyone be surprised at the staying power of the antiquarian. For the desire – no, the need – to reconstruct the past seems as basic and elemental an urge as the desire to bring the dead back to life. We find it at work 5,000 years ago in ancient Egypt, 2,000 years ago in China, and 500 years ago in Italy. The *yizker-bikher*, or encyclopaedic memorial volumes, published over the last fifty years by survivors of the destroyed Jewish communities of Eastern Europe, gather up documents and oral accounts of life in those communities. Like the early modern antiquarian studies of ancient Rome, they range across topography, demography, sociology, anthropology, folklore, history of religion, politics, and art history. Compiled by devoted amateurs rather than professional historians, they are shamelessly focused on detail and uncon-cerned with either theoretical cohesion or disciplinary integrity. For none was needed: every fact painstakingly recovered helped fill in a picture whose outlines were already known. Reading them we can understand how it was that antiquaries of the past could have pursued their work with such a sense of sacred responsibility. Reconstruction is as close as we get to resurrection.

The desire to put the past back together remains powerful today, even if the need is no longer answered by historians or recognized by any particular division of learning. Expelled from 'respectable' scholarship in the nineteenth century, the antiquarian 'longing,' as Nietzsche put it in his lectures on the study of antiquities, like a mighty river whose course is dammed at one point, has simply carved another channel for itself: in literature, and in reverence for the physical encounter with the past, whether in museums, historic places, or flea markets.

Momigliano, with the faith of his fathers, did not need to look in this direction. Others, without it, still put their faith in a past they can touch.

Notes

1 This account is obviously indebted to that in Ernst Gombrich, *In Search of Cultural History* (London, 1970); Felix Gilbert, 'Cultural History and Its Problems,' *Comité International des Sciences Historiques: Rapports*, vol. 1 (1960), 40–58; idem, 'Jacob Burckhardt's Student Years: The Road to Cultural History,' *Journal of the History of Ideas* 47 (1986): 249–74; Peter Burke, 'The Origins of Cultural History,' in his *Varieties of Cultural History* (Ithaca, 1997), 1–22; and, more broadly, Donald R. Kelley, *Faces of History from Herodotus to Herder* (New Haven, 1998); and idem, *The Fortunes of History from Herder to Huizinga* (New Haven, 2003). The most recent discussion of cultural history, Peter Burke, *What Is Cultural History?* (London, 2004), no longer tries to define its subject, only to anatomize its various forms.

2 Gerhard Oestreich, 'Otto Hintze's Stellung zur Politikwissenschaft und Soziologie,' in Otto Hintze, *Gesammelte Abhandlungen*, ed. Oestreich, 3 vols (Berlin, 1964), vol. 2, pp. 7*–67*; Felix Gilbert, 'Otto Hintze und die moderne Geschichtswissenschaft,' in *Otto Hintze und die moderne Geschichtswissenschaft*, ed. Otto Büsch and Michael Erbe (Berlin, 1983), 195–208; *The Historical Essays of Otto Hintze*, ed. with introduction Felix Gilbert, with the assistance of Robert M. Berdahl (New York, 1975), 3–30.

Sociology was also the rubric in which Eduard Fueter envisioned the comparative social scientific history of the future (*Geschichte der neueren Historiographie* [Berlin and Munich, 1911], 603–6). See Otto Gerhard Oexle, 'Geschichte als Historische Kulturwissenschaft,' in *Kulturgeschichte Heute*, ed. Wolfgang Hardtwig and Hans-Ulrich Wehler (Göttingen, 1996), 14–40.

3 Carlo Antoni, *Dallo storicismo alla sociologia* (Florence, 1940).

4 The richness and centrality of this archive for understanding Momigliano's work is best demonstrated in Di Donato's series of essays: Riccardo Di Donato, 'Materiali per una biografia intelletuale di Arnaldo Momigliano. I. Libertà e pace nel mondo antico,' *Athenaeum* 83 (1995): 213–44; idem, 'Materiali per una biografia intellettuale di Arnaldo Momigliano. II. Tra Napoli e Bristol,' *Athenaeum* 86 (1998): 231–44; idem, 'Materiali per una biografia intellettuale di Arnaldo Momigliano. III. Gli anni di Londra,' in *Arnaldo Momigliano nella storiografia del Novecento*, ed. Leandro Polverini (Rome: Edizioni di Storia e Letteratura, 1999) (Incontri perugini di Storia della storiografia IX, Spoleto, 31.5–2.6.1999), 125–36; idem, 'Nuovi materiali per una biografia intellettuale di Arnaldo Momigliano,' *Rend[iconti] [Classe di Scienze] Mor[ali, storiche e filologiche]. Atti della Accademia Nazionale dei Lincei*, s[er.] 9, vol. 11 (2000): 383–98.

5 These would include Riccardo Di Donato's edition of Momigliano's *Pace e libertà nel mondo antico. Lezioni a Cambridge: gennaio-marzo 1940* (Florence, 1996); Di Donato, 'La memoria e la storia: in ricordo di Arnaldo Momigliano,' *Archivio di storia della cultura* 2 (1989): 89–93; M. Gigane, 'Precisazioni sul rapporto Croce-Momiglano,' *Annali della Scuola Normale Superiore di Pisa*, ser. 3, vol. 17 (1987): 1045–60; Peter Brown, 'Arnaldo Dante Momigliano, 1908–1987,' *Proceedings of the British Academy* 74 (1988): 405–42; C. Dionisotti, *Ricordo di Arnaldo Momigliano* (Bologna, 1989); idem, 'Momigliano e il contesto,' *Belfagor* 42 (1987): 633–48; the introductory essays by Wilfried Nippel, Anthony T. Grafton, and Glenn W. Most in Arnaldo Momigliano, *Ausgewählte Schriften zur Geschichte und Geschichtsschreibung*, ed. Nippel, Grafon, and Most, 3 vols (Stuttgart, 2000); Carlo Dionisotti, 'Arnaldo Momigliano e Croce,' *Belfagor* 43 (1988): 617–41; Innocenzo Cervelli, 'Su alcuni aspetti della ricerca ebraistica di Arnaldo Momigliano,' *Studi storici* 29 (1988): 599–643; Luciano Canfora, 'L' "ellenismo" di Momigliano,' *Studi storici* 30 (1989): 53–8; Cervelli, 'L'ultimo Momigliano: costanti e variabili di una ricerca,' *Studi storici* 30 (1989): 59–104; L. Cracco Ruggini, 'Arnaldo Momigliano: Lo storico antico che ha trasformato le fonti in vita del passato,' *Studi storici* 30 (1989): 105–28; Giorgio Fabre, 'Arnaldo Momigliano: autobiografia scientifica (1936),' *Quaderni di storia* 21 (1995): 85–96; idem, 'Arnaldo Momigliano: materiali

biografici/ 2,' *Quaderni di storia* 27 (2001): 309–20; and the memorial volumes *Ancient History and the Antiquarian: Essays in Memory of Arnaldo Momigliano*, ed. M.H. Crawford and C.R. Ligota (London, 1995), with essays by T.J. Cornell, Anthony Grafton, Jean-Louis Ferrary, A.C. Dionisotti, C.R. Ligota, Christiane Kunst, and L. Capogrossi Colognesi; *Biblioteca di Athenaeum II. Omaggio ad Arnaldo Momigliano. Storia e storiografia sul mondo antico* (1989), with essays by E. Gabba, M.H. Crawford, G.W. Bowersock, and C. Pietri; and special issues of journals, *Storia della storiografia* 16 (1989), with articles by Emilio Gaba, Mario Attilio Levi, Livio Sichirollo, Karl Christ, Edward Shils, F. Parente, and Giuseppe Cambiano; *The Presence of the Historian: Essays in Memory of Arnaldo Momigliano, History and Theory* Beiheft 30 (1991), ed. Michael P. Steinberg, with essays by Karl Christ, Joanna Weinberg, G.W. Bowersock, Carlo Ginzburg, Oswyn Murray; and *Rivista storica italiana* 100 (1988), with essays by Carmine Ampolo, Silvia Berti, Karl Christ, Timothy J. Cornell, Furio Diaz, Carlo Dionisotti, Emilio Gabba, Giuseppe Giarrizzo, Carlo Ginzburg, Stuart H. Hughes, Oswyn Murray, and Evelyne Patlagean.

6 'Ancient History and the Antiquarian,' in *Contributo*, 102 n59. The nine volumes of Momigliano's *Contributi alla storia degli studi classici e del mondo antico*, published in Rome from 1955 to 1990, are referred to in short-title form here and in the notes below.

7 Ibid., 67–8.

8 Ibid., p. 69.

9 Ibid., p. 73.

10 Ibid., p. 75.

11 Ibid., p. 76.

12 Ibid., p. 79.

13 Ibid., pp. 85–6.

14 Ibid., pp. 88, 89.

15 Ibid., p. 91.

16 Ibid., p. 100.

17 Ibid., p. 102.

18 Ibid., p. 102.

19 'Genesi storica e funzione attuale del concetto di ellenismo,' in *Contributo*, 185.

20 '... si sente subito la vitalità del punto di partenza del Droysen e la sua legittimità' (ibid., 192). For the most recent traversal of this ground, see Wilfried Nippel, '"Hellenismus" – von Droysen bis Harnack – oder: Inter-disziplinäre Mißverständnisse,' in *Adolf von Harnack. Christentum, Wissenschaft und Gesellschaft*, ed. Kurt Nowak, Otto Gerhard Oexle, Trutz Rendtorff, and Kurt-Victor Selge (Göttingen, 2003), 15–28.

21 'Genesi storica e funzione attuale del concetto di ellenismo' (n19 above), 167.
22 'La formazione della moderna storiografia sull'impero Romano,' in *Contributo*, 123n62. For a different route to the same destination, see Bruno Neveu, 'Mabilon et l'historiographie gallicane vers 1700: érudition écclesiastique et recherche historique au XVIIe siècle,' in *Historische Forschung im 18. Jahrhundert: Organization. Zielsetzung. Ergebnisse*, ed. Karl Hammer and Jürgen Voss (Bonn, 1976), 27–81.
23 'La formazione della moderna storiografia sull'impero Romano,' in *Contributo*, 137.
24 'Note marginali di storia della filologia classica. Il contributo dell'autobiografia alla valutazione del Gibbon,' in *Contributo*, 379.
25 'Jacob Bernays,' in *Quinto contributo*, 152.
26 'La questione era se si dovesse presuppore per i fatti della storia profana lo stesso intervento puntuale e continuo di Dio, che era carattere della storia sacra. La risposta, *anche per me*, sta al centro del *Discours* ('La formazione della moderna storiografia sull'impero Romano' [n22 above], 116).
27 William Harris called attention to this obscured past in the *Times Literary Supplement* (12 April 1996; with replies on 3, 10, and 24 May and 14 and 28 June). Dionisotti answered decisively in *Belfagor* 42 (1987): 633–48. Di Donato described the biographical context in depth in 'Materiali I' (n4 above) and in his introduction to the the Italian edition of *Pace e libertà* (n5 above), 'Uno storico, un testo, un contesto.' This information has recently been used in a rather sad campaign of character assassination by Giorgio Fabre, 'Arnaldo Momigliano: autobiografia scientifica (1936)' and 'Arnaldo Momigliano: materiali biografici/ 2' (n5 above); and by Luciano Canfora in an interview in *La Repubblica*, 16 March 2001. But see Di Donato's reply of 29 March 2001, reprinted in *La Gazzetta di Pisa* 3, no. 7, 3 March 2001, p. 2, under the title 'Con i salvati e i sommersi.' The lies the unjustly persecuted may tell to save their skin are different from those told by the perpetrators to save theirs from justice. The ability to make such distinctions is also part of the pursuit of truth.
28 Momigliano, *Pace e libertà* (n5 above), xxv.
29 Ibid., xvi.
30 Di Donato, 'Materiali I,' 243
31 'Friedrich Creuzer and Greek Historiography,' in *Contributo*, 233.
32 Ibid., 239.
33 Di Donato's essay should be read alongside 'Materiali' I and II, Grafton's as the continuation of 'Arnaldo Momigliano e la storia degli studi classici,' *Rivista storica italiana* 107 (1995): 91–109.

34 As Grafton shows below, as of 1947, Momigliano had done no reading on the Etruscheria that would be a major part of the 1950 article.

35 Momigliano, 'Antiquari e storici dell'antichità' (title given by Di Donato), is found in Pisa, Archivo Arnaldo Momiliagno, N-f 56 13-25 and N-f 62 1-12r.

36 We know that individual lectures were delivered at Leiden and Amsterdam in 1961.

37 Another pendant is his 1956 essay 'Gli studi classici di Scipione Maffei,' in *Secondo contributo*, 255–72.

38 'Gibbon's Contribution to Historical Method, in *Contributo*, 196.

39 Ibid., 207.

40 Ibid., 203.

41 Ibid., 198–9.

42 'Herodotus in the History of Historiography,' in *Secondo contributo*, 32–3; 'Erodoto e la storiografia moderna. Alcuni problemi presentati ad un convegno di umanisti,' in *Secondo contributo*, 54–5; 'Storiografia sua tradizione scritta e su tradizione orale,' in *Terzo contributo*, 19.

43 'Pagan and Christian Historiography in the Fourth Century,' in *Terzo contributo*, 108–9; 'Popular Religious Beliefs and the Late Roman Historians,' in *Quinto contributo*, 76; 'Tradition and the Classical Historian,' in *Quinto contributo*, 17.

44 'L'età del trapasso fra storiografia antica e storiografia medievale (320–550),' in *Quinto contributo*, 59: 'Di qui le notazione di costumi, di aneddoti significativi, di qui l'abbondanza di *excursus* geografici e detnografici.'

45 Momigliano, *The Classical Foundations of Modern Historiography* (Berkeley and Los Angeles, 1990), 54.

46 The other reference by Momigliano to Peiresc also includes this same story: 'The Greater Danger – Science or Biblical Criticism?' in *Quinto contributo*, 1020.

47 Momigliano, *The Classical Foundations*, 57.

48 Ibid., 71. Momigliano repeated this claim in 'The Place of Ancient Historiography in Modern Historiography,' in *Settimo contributo*, 25.

49 Momigliano, *The Classical Foundations*, 74.

50 Ibid., 77–79.

51 Ibid., 155

52 Ibid.

53 See Anthony Grafton, 'The Identities of History in Early Modern Europe: Prelude to a Study of the *Artes historicae*,' in *Historia: Empiricism and Erudition in Early Modern Europe*, ed. Giana Pomata and Nancy G. Siraisi (Cambridge, MA, 2005) and, more extended, in his 2005 Trevelyan Lectures at Cambridge, 'What Was History? The Art of History in Early Modern Europe.'

54 Eduard Fueter, *Geschichte der neueren Historiographie* (n2 above), 307–12,
    especially 308.

55 For modern discussions of Pyrrhonism, see Markus Völkel, '*Pyrrhonismus
    historicus' und 'fides historica': die Entwicklung der deutschen historischen
    Methodologie unter dem Gesichtspunkt der historischen Skepsis* (Frankfurt am Main
    and New York, 1987); and, inflected towards its implications for political
    philosophy, Lorenzo Bianchi, *Tradizione libertina e critica storica. Da Naudé a
    Bayle* (Milan, 1988). Behind these lie the thesis of Richard Popkin, *The
    History of Scepticism from Erasmus to Spinoza* (Berkeley and Los Angeles, 1979)
    – but this story was not Momigliano's.

56 Paul Hazard, *La crise de la conscience européenne* (Paris, 1961; 1st ed. 1935),
    chap. 2, especially pp. 52–4.

57 Compare with Fueter: 'Die Geschichte der Historiographie hat sich mit der
    Geschichte der historischen Forschung und Kiritk an sich nicht zu befassen'
    (Fueter, *Geschichte* [n2 above], 330).

58 Quoted in Charles Pietri, 'A. Momigliano et l'historiographie française,' in
    Biblioteca di Athenaeum II. Omaggio ad Arnaldo Momigliano (n5 above), 53.

59 Quoted in David Ohana, 'The "Anti-Intellectual" Intellectuals as Political
    Mythmakers,' in *The Revolt against Liberal Democracy, 1870–1945: International
    Conference in Memory of Jacob L. Talmon*, ed. Zeev Sternhell (Jerusalem, 1996),
    97.

60 'Und weiter: nachdem die wissenschaftliche Stiftung Hamburgs sich verge-
    bens und nicht zufällig um den Kulturhistoriker Gothein bemüht hatte,
    sorgte Aby M. Warburg, ein Jude, der auch von Burckhardt ausging, dafür,
    daß der Geist der neuen Universität weitgehend kulturwissenschaftlich
    wurde; daneben schuf er in seiner kulturwissenschaftlichen Bibliothek eine
    Zelle, von der dann nach mannigfachen Richtungen hin Kulturwissenschaft
    sich ausbreitete' (Christoph Steding, 'Kulturgeschichte und politische
    Geschichte,' in *Reich und Reichsfeinde*, vol. 1 [Hamburg, 1941], 64). Steding
    tries hard to identify 'Kulturgeschichte' – as practice and consequences –
    with Jews, without, of course, glossing over Burckhardt's own anti-Semitic
    sentiments (66–7). The essay was delivered first as a lecture at the
    Deutschen Historikertag in Erfurt in July 1937.

61 Otto Brunner, 'Abendländisches Geschichtsdenken,' in his *Neue Wege der
    Verfassungs- und Sozialgeschichte* (Göttingen, 1968), 43.

62 This is terrain that has been mapped and anatomized in beautiful detail in
    Ingo Herklotz's magisterial study of, in equal parts, Cassiano Dal Pozzo and
    'archaeology in the seventeenth century.'

63 Of Braudel, in particular, Momigliano proclaimed himself an admirer
    ('Gli studi di storia antica,' in *Secondo contributo*, 350).

64 For example, Friderich Ast spoke for his age, as well as his profession, in
declaring that 'der Philologe soll daher "nicht bloßer Sprachmeister oder
Antiquar seyn, sondern auch Philosoph und Aesthetiker"' (quoted in
Hellmut Flashar, 'Die methodisch-hermeneutischen Ansätze von Friedrich
August Wolf und Friedrich Ast – Traditionelle und neue Begründungen,' in
Philologie und Hermeneutik im 19. Jahrhundert. Zur Geschichte und Methodologie
der Geisteswissenschaften, ed. Flashar, Karlfried Gründer, and Axel Horstmann
[Göttingen, 1979], 31). It was of precisely this putting on of 'airs' that the
young Jacob Burckhardt complained in a letter to a friend in 1843, quoted
in Momigliano, 'Introduzione alla Griechische Kulturgeschichte di Jacob
Burckhardt,' in Secondo Contributo, 283n.

65 Mark Phillips, 'Reconsiderations on History and Antiquarianism: Arnaldo
Momigliano and the Historiography of Eighteenth-Century Britain,' Journal
of the History of Ideas 57 (1996): 297–316; and his subsequent book Society and
Sentiment: Genres of Historical Writing in Britain, 1740–1820 (Princeton, 2000).

66 Obviously, this makes me more convinced than Benedetto Bravo of the
fundamental direction of Momigliano's argument, but his perceptive comments about where Momigliano put his emphases and where he did not
warrant serious reflection (Benedetto Bravo, 'Il libro postumo di Arnaldo
Momigliano sui fondamenti classici della storiografia moderna,' in
Athenaeum 70 [1992]: 244–50, especially 249–50).

67 'L'Agonale di J. Burckhardt e l'Homo Ludens di J. Huizinga,' in Sesto contributo,
326.

68 Momigliano, in admiring remarks on Cassirer's account of the development
of history in the seventeenth century, sought to put the emphasis on the
Jansenists rather than on Bayle, as had Cassirer ('Nuova storiografia
sull'imperio Romano,' in Contributo, 113).

69 Ernst Cassirer, The Problem of Knowledge: Philosophy, Science, and History since
Hegel (New Haven and London, 1950), 259.

70 Ibid., 280.

71 Ibid.

72 'Die historische Methode ist eine der drei großen Erkenntnisformen, die
der Natur unsrers Erkennens nach möglich sind, und ihr gehört die Welt
der Ethik, wie den beiden andern die der Physik und die transzendentale,
mag die Spekulation philosophisch oder theosophisch (dogmatisch) sein'
(Johann Gustav Droysen, Texte zur Geschichtstheorie. Mit ungedruckten
Materialien zur 'Historik,' ed. Günter Birsch and Jörn Rüsen [Göttingen,
1972], 82).

73 Again, that Momigliano knew this material is unquestionable – see the long
footnote on Schopenhauer and hermeneutics in 'La formazione della

moderna storiografia sull'impero Romano' (n22 above), 123 n6 – but its treatment is as something necessary to but also subordinate to classical philology.

74 Karl Brandi, *Geschichte der Geschichtswissenschaft*, 2nd ed., ed. Wolfgang Graft (Bonn, 1952); Georg von Below, *Deutsche Geschichtsschreibung von den Befreiungskriegen bis zu unseren Tagen: Geschichte und Kulturgeschichte* (Leipzig, 1916); Fueter, *Geschichte der neueren Historiographie* (n2 above).

75 Francis Haskell's *History and Its Images* (New Haven and London, 1993) is the obvious citation. But see also, for example, *Documentary Culture: Florence and Rome from Grand-Duke Ferdinand I to Pope Alexander VII*, ed. E. Cropper, G. Perini, and F. Solinas (Bologna, 1992); *Antiquarische Gelehrsamkeit und Bildende Kunst: Die Gegenweart der Antike in der Renaissance*, ed. K. Corsepius, U. Rehm, L. Schmitt, and A. Schreurs (Cologne, 1996).

76 'Ma il vero iniziatore è Winckelmann, che pone l'acento sull'arte invece che sulla politica, sulla Grecia invece che su Rome, e implicitamente evoca l'idea di genio nazionale che i suoi seguaci del periodo romantico, in specie in Germania, erigeranno a dogma fondamentale della filologia del sec. XIX. È Winckelmann che transforma in storia l'erudizione degli antiquari, ma è pure Winckelmann che pianta in questa storia un seme anti-storico destinato a straodinari sviluppi' ('L'eredità della filologica antica e il metodo storico,' in *Secondo contributo*, 473). Madame de Staël in 1810 saw A.W. Schlegel as doing for literature what Winckelmann had done for art ('German Romanticism and Italian Classical Studies,' in *Ottavo contributo*, 60).

77 Jörn Garber, 'Von der Menschheitsgeschichte zur Kulturgeschichte. Zum geschichtstheoretischen Kulturbegriff der deutschen Spätaufklaurung,' in *Spätabsolutismus und bürgerliche Gesellschaft: Studien zur deutschen Staats- und Gesellschaftstheorie im Übergang zur Moderne* (Frankfurt am Main, 1992), 409–33. See Béla Kapossy, *Iselin contra Rousseau: Sociable Patriotism and the History of Mankind* (Basel, 2006).

78 Kelley, *The Fortunes of History* (n1 above), 24.

79 Momigliano himself notes only the foundation of the Historical Institute at Göttingen in 1766 [*sic*] by Schlözer, with its institutionalization of some antiquarian practices as auxiliary sciences.

80 Daniel Morhof, *Polyhistor, Literarius, Philosophicus et Practicus*, 4th ed. expanded (Lubeck, 1747), V.ii.1, p. 930.

81 Quoted in Kelley, *The Fortunes of History*, 23.

82 See Momigliano's review in *Quinto contributo*, 898–902.

83 Bendetto Bravo, *Philologie, histoire, philosophie de l'histoire: Etude sur J.G. Droysen historien de l'antiquité* (Wrocław, Warsaw, Kraków, 1968; repr. Hildesheim, Zurich, New York, 1988), 93–6.

84 Quoted ibid., 114.

85 Quoted ibid., 117.

86 From a letter of 1833, quoted ibid., 119.

87 'Friedrich Creuzer and Greek Historiography' (n31 above), 234.

88 Fernand Braudel, 'The History of Civilizations: The Past Explains the Present [1959],' in his *On History* (Chicago, 1980), 186. I hope to write more about this story elsewhere.

89 'Introduzione alla *Griechische Kulturgeschichte* di Jacob Burckhardt' (n64 above), 293.

90 Wilfried Nippel, 'Von den "Altertümern" zur "Kulturgeschichte,"' *Ktèma* 23 (1998): 17–24.

91 von Below, *Deutsche Geschichtsschreibung von den Befreiungskriegen bis zu unseren Tagen* (n74 above), 72, quoted in Cassirer, *The Problem of Knowledge* (n69 above), 280.

92 'Introduzione alla *Griechische Kulturgeschichte*, (n64 above), 283n.

93 Ibid., 284.

94 Ibid., 285.

95 Ibid., 287–8.

96 Ibid.

97 Burckhardt, *The Age of Constantine the Great*, tran. Moses Hadas (New York, 1967), 12.

98 'Introduzione alla *Griechische Kulturgeschichte*, 285.

99 Nippel's essay here should be read alongside his 'Forschungen zur Alten Geschichte zwischen Humanismus und Aufklärung,' in *Die Präsenz der Antike im Übergang vom Mittelalter zur Frühen Neuzeit*, ed. Ludger Grenzmann, Klaus Grubmüller, Fidel Rädle, and Martin Staehelin (Göttingen, 2004), 161–76; 'Geschichte und System in Mommsens "Staatsrecht,"' *Geldgeschichte vs. Numismatik: Theodor Mommsen und die antike Münze*, ed. Hans-Markus von Kaenel, Maria R.-Alföldi, Ulrike Peter, and Holger Komnick (Berlin, 2004), 215–28; and, most recently, 'Der "Antiquarische Bauplatz." Theodor Mommsens *Römische Staatsrecht*,' in *Theodor Mommsen: Gelehrter, Politiker und Literat* (Stuttgart, 2005), 165–84.

100 Manfred Landfester, 'Ulrich von Wilamowitz-Moellendorff und die hermeneutische Tradition des 19. Jahrhunderts,' in *Philologie und Hermeneutik im 19. Jahrhundert*, ed. Flashar, Gründer, and Horstmann (n64 above), 158.

101 'Storiografia su tradizione scritta e su tradizione orale' (n42 above), 22.

102 'Two Types of Universal History: The Cases of E.A. Freeman and Max Weber,' in *Ottavo contributo*, 128.

103 'L'eredità della filologia antica e il metodo storico' (n76 above), 475; 'German Romanticism and Italian Classical Studies' (n76 above), 68.

104 'The Place of Ancient Historiography in Modern Historiography' (n48 above), 29.
105 Review of Paul Veyne, *Comment on écrit l'histoire*,' in *Sesto contributo*, 759.
106 Ibid. See also 'Gli studi di storia antica' (n63 above), 337.
107 'La storiografia del quindecennio 1961–1976,' in *Sesto contributo*, 390. Momigliano more fully explores the implications of this 'negation,' the denial of truth and lapse into relativism – though without mentioning the name of Foucault, with whom these are so often, and rightly, linked, in 'The Place of Ancient Historiography in Modern Historiography,' 32.
108 'History between Medicine and Rhetoric,' in *Ottavo contributo*, 24. For the innovativeness of Herodotus, and his exemplarity for modern explorers, anthropologists, and sociologists, see 'Herodotus in the History of Historiography' (n42 above), 44.
109 In a paper delivered to the conference on which this book is based, Glenn Most argued that Momigliano's marginal comments in his copies of Foucault's books, now in the library of the Scuola Normale Superiore in Pisa, reveal that he misunderstood some of Foucault's fundamental concerns.
110 'Herodotus in the History of Historiography,' 44.
111 'A Piedmontese View of the History of Ideas,' in *Sesto contributo*, 332.
112 'Prospettiva 1967 della storia graeca,' in *Quarto contributo*, 53.
113 'Surtout, l'histoire et l'ethnologie se distinguaient d'après les faits privilégiés par chacune. A l'histoire revenaient les classes dirigeantes, les faits d'armes, les règnes, les traités, les conflits et les aliances; à l'ethnologie, la vie populaire, les moeurs, les croyances, les rapports élémentaires que les hommes entretiennent avec le milieu. C'est au contact de l'ethnologie que les histoirens ont perçu l'importance de ces manifestations obscures et pour partie souterraines de la vie en société. En revanche, et du fait qu'elle renouvelait son champ d'étude et ses méthodes, sous le nom d'anthropologie historique, l'histoire allait être d'un grand secours aux ethnologues' (Claude Lévi-Strauss, 'Histoire et Ethnologie,' *Annales E.S.C.* [1983]: 1217–31, on 1217–18). The same call for a future history that has already come and gone, but with no knowledge of that story, is found in J. Le Goff, 'L'historien et "l'homme quotidien,"' in *Méthodologie de l'histoire et des sciences humaines*, 2 vols (Toulouse, 1976), vol. 1, pp. 227–43.
114 We find the same thought in Camille Jullian, *Extraits des historiens français du XIXe siècle*, 10th ed. (Paris, 1896), xxxvi, quoted in Kelley, *The Fortunes of History*, 142.
115 'The Place of Ancient Historiography in Modern Historiography,' 29.
116 'Foreword to N.D. Fustel de Coulanges, *The Ancient City*,' in *Settimo contributo*, 171.

117 *Contributo*, 69 and n3 – and just reprinted in facsimilie in 2005!

118 In his 1938 essay 'Tre figure mitiche: Tanaquilla, Gaia Cecilia, Acca Larenzia,' he dismissed Bachofen's *Sage von Tanaquil* as 'un lavoro di fantasia.'
'Importa a noi poco il significato di ripresa di un problema che fu centrale
per J. Bachofen.' Indeed, his conclusions had been 'polverizzatte' by the
next generation of scholarship. Momigliano's judgment was that 'le sue
teorie hanno già trovato facilmente nella nostra cultura il posto che loro
spetta' ('Tre figure mitiche: Tanaquilla, Gaia Cecilia, Acca Larenzia,' in
Quarto contributo, 463, 456).

119 'Bachofen tra misticismo e antropologia,' in *Nono contributo*, 776; 'Johann
Jakob Bachofen: From Roman History to Matriarchy,' in *Ottavo contributo*.

120 'Friedrich Creuzer and Greek Historiography' (n31 above), 233.

121 'Johann Jakob Bachofen' (n119 above), 91.

122 Ibid.

123 'From Bachofen to Cumont,' in *Nono contributo*, 595.

124 Review of Gossman, *Orpheus Philologus*, in *Ottavo contributo*, 410.

125 'H. Useners Standpunkt war der Standpunkt der vergleichenden Kulturwissenschaften. Für ihn erhielt die Philologie ihre Funktion im Rahmen
einer umfassenden Geschichtswissenschaft, deren Erkenntniszielen sie
dann auch verpflichtet war. Ziel der Geschichtswissenschaft war es, durch
empirische Vergleichung vorzudringen "zur Ergründung der allgemeinen
Gesetze, nach denen die einzelnen Lebensäußerungen der Völker sich
entwicklen und gegenseitig bedingen, zur Erkenntnis der menschlichen
Natur selbst." Dieser umfassenden Wissenschaft erscheinen "die einzelnen
Völkergruppen und Völker nur als verschieden Formen eines Organismen-
typus, dessen reguläre Konstitution und Lebensbedingungen sie erforscht,
während ihr die individuellen Besonderheiten derselben an sich gleichgül-
tig sind und nur als Korrektiv wichtig werden." Mit dieser Konzeption löste
sich H. Usener aus wesentlichen altertumswissenschaftlichen Traditionen,
denn ihm waren nicht mehr die großen individuellen Leistungen interes-
sant – das waren Produkte des Willens bzw. des Geistes und als solche
unwichtig – , sondern das "unwillkürliche, unbewußte Werden," das er aus
dem folkloristischen Material zu erschließen suchte. Diese Konzeption
hatte natürlich einen antiklassizistischen Effekt, wenn auch H. Usener
selbst ihn nicht betont hat; aber dieser Effekt lag im Ursprung der vergleichenden Kulturwissenschaften, die letzlich aus der Abneigung gegen die
Vorbildhaftigkeit der Antike entstanden waren' (Landfester, 'Ulrich von
Wilamowitz-Moellendorff' [n100 above], 161).

126 'Premesse per una discussione su Eduard Schwartz,' in *Settimo contributo*,
243.

127 Ibid., 209–10.

128 Ibid., 212.

129 What there is, is indirect: a sentence in a review of a book by Felix Gilbert praising the criticism of Gombrich's biography of the Institute's founder as 'the masterpiece of the volume,' and an anecdote about Warburg's answer to Bing's reproach about his wandering the streets of Rome on 11 February 1929 (Review of Felix Gilbert, *History, Choice and Commitment*, in *Sesto contributo*, 771; 'How Roman Emperors Became Gods,' in *Ottavo contributo*, 297, quoting Warburg: 'You know that throughout my life I have been interested in the revival of paganism and pagan festivals. Today I had the chance of my life to be present at the re-paganization of Rome, and you complain that I remained to watch it').

130 'Gertrud Bing,' in *Terzo contributo*, 837–41.

131 Ibid., 839. Momigliano's acute observation only accentuates the extraordinary repression that had to be involved for Gombrich, Warburg's *biographer*, to fail to discuss Warburg's identification of the pagan with the primitive, and the consequences he drew from this, in his own *The Preference for the Primitive: Episodes in the History of Western Taste and Art* (London, 2002).

132 For Warburg and the history of religion, see especially Roland Kany, *Die religionsgeschichtliche Forschung an der Kulturwissenschaftlichen Bibliothek Warburg* (Bamberg, 1989); for Benjamin's view, see the concluding chapter of this volume.

133 See Momigliano, 'Historiography of Religion: The Western Tradition,' in *Ottavo contributo*, 40; 'La nuova storia romana di G.B. Vico,' in *Sesto contributo*, 197–8.

134 See volume 3 of the *Archiv für Religionsgeschichte* (2001), a special issue entitled 'Das 17. Jahrhundert und die Ursprünge der Religionsgeschichte,' ed. Jan Assmann and Guy Stroumsa.

135 Momigliano, *Pagine ebraiche* (Turin, 1987); trans. as *Essays on Ancient and Modern Judaism*, ed. and introduction Silvia Berti (Chicago, 1987).

136 Nor was Momigliano oblivious to the different emphases of Warburg and his continuators: they were not interested in the permanence of these passion-demons, nor in the possibility of their eventual exorcism; pagan for them meant Plato, not primitive. 'Ma soprattutto tendevano a fare della iconografia un metodo di ricerca per la storia della cultura in generale. Se qualcosa andava indubbiamente perduto della profondità di visione di Warburg,' he concluded; the volumes of studies and the *Journal* have demonstrated the fecundity of their approach, too ('Gertrud Bing' [n130 above], 839).

137 For a description of Momigliano's first visit to the Old City of Jerusalem in September 1967, see Margherita Isnardi Parente, 'Arnaldo Momigliano, la VII epistola e l'autobiografia,' *Belfagor* 43 (1988): 245–54.

138 'Premesse per una discussione su Hermann Usener,' in *Settimo contributo*, 212.

139 'La questione era se si dovesse presuppore per i fatti della storia profana lo stesso intervento puntuale e continuo di Dio, che era carattere della storia sacra. La risposta, *anche per me*, sta al centro del *Discours*' ('La formazione della moderna storiografia sull'impero Romano' [n22 above], 116).

140 Momigliano treats him as yet another representative of turn-of-the-century German neo-Romantic philology. See 'Review of Luigi Canforma, *Ideologie del classicismo*, in *Settimo contributo*, 514.

141 Quoted in Joanna Weinberg, 'Where Three Traditions Meet,' in *The Presence of the Historian*, ed. Steinberg (n5 above), 15–16.

142 For the 'post-modern' fascination with antiquarianism, see, for example, Stephen Bann, *The Clothing of Clio: A Study of the Representation of History in Nineteenth-Century Britain and France* (Cambridge, 1984); P.J.A. Levine, *The Amateur and the Professional: Antiquarians, Historians and Archaeologists in Victorian England, 1838–1886* (Cambridge, 1986); and *Producing the Past: Aspects of Antiquarian Culture and Practice*, ed. Martin Myrone and Lucy Peltz (Ashgate, 1999). This body of scholarship is almost entirely focused on the eighteenth and nineteenth centuries and is on the whole oblivious of Momigliano's work and his early modern figures. Nor is it clear that he would have been entirely sympathetic to this enterprise – but he would surely have been fascinated by its existence.

chapter two

Arnaldo Momigliano from Antiquarianism to Cultural History: Some Reasons for a Quest

RICCARDO DI DONATO

In compliance with Momigliano's will and intentions, and with the consent of his family and of the late Anne Marie Meyer, the literary executor of Momigliano's work, I have gradually constituted and organized an archive of his papers in Pisa, the city of his happy homecoming. I am using this archive as a base for the publication of his unpublished texts, mainly within the series of the *Contributi*, and of the principal documents relating to him. These latter are being made available to the general public in a series of studies of the Italian scholar entitled 'Materiali per una biografia intellettuale' (Materials for an Intellectual Biography).

I have chosen this title not only in a formal display of modesty, but in order to stress some specific points of method that I have, with others, learned directly from and then read about and pondered in the writings of a master whose memory is dear to me. History is not made without documents or without their full interpretation. One does not practise historiography without thorough and direct knowledge of the themes or historical moments that are the subject matter of the work being studied. An incomplete mastery of the sources, combined with excessive closeness to the personality of the author one is studying, can give rise to inadequate or absurd judgments. These simple, basic truths are well worth stating at the outset.

My text, conceived as a contribution to a collective discussion,[1] belongs to a series of studies I have published on this topic, and which cannot be summarized here.[2] Like those previous studies, the present contribution is based on fresh examination of some texts and documents held in the Arnaldo Momigliano Archive in Pisa.[3]

The peculiar features and the importance of Momigliano's *Nachlass* call for a preliminary reminder. We are not dealing here with a collection intentionally assembled by the author for the perpetuation of his memory. The Momigliano Archive exists as the result of two opposing phenomena, not necessarily concomitant or consistent. On the one hand, for long periods of his life Momigliano kept and organized all his working papers and private correspondence. On the other hand, during the last ten years of his life his private correspondence was drastically destroyed, and after his death – and in compliance with his express wishes – whatever remained was returned to the senders. It is certain that many papers were involved in this latter operation.

As a result of Momigliano's preservation and organization, we have now an archive that contains an enormous quantity of handwritten and typed texts; a number of exercise books, block notes, and letter books; and, finally, an incredible bibliographical catalogue, constantly updated until the end of the 1970s.[4] The correspondence, on the contrary, is incomplete and very sparse. The bags Momigliano used in his last years were full of papers and letters, neglected at the end of every journey. Letters and cards filled the books and offprints in his library, today located in the Scuola Normale Superiore in Pisa. The preservation of all the other documents has been erratic and has come about by sheer chance.

I determined upon the current arrangement of the archive, after consultation with Anne Marie Meyer. As we agreed, a register was drafted and a provisional edition of it prepared in 1998.[5] Discoveries of significant new papers continued to occur in the years following the constitution of the archive, in various places: above all in London, including one very important discovery in July 1999;[6] in Chicago;[7] in Pisa; in Romagnano Sesia, in Carlo Dionisotti's home;[8] and in Turin, in Franco Venturi's home.[9] I cannot rule out further discoveries.[10]

Accounting for this material beyond merely compiling the register has not been simple. Aiming to supply the papers with their first interpretative context, I specifically chose to publish as 'Materials' the documents I judged unfit or inadequate for inclusion in the *Contributi*. For various reasons, other papers were published, in the form of separate volumes, for example the Sather Lectures and the Italian translation of the first version of 'Peace and Liberty in the Ancient World' (*Pace e libertà nel mondo antico*).

From a historiographical point of view, the material thus gathered is of varying relevance, but in each case it provides immediate answers to some primary biographical questions. First of all, besides bibliographical cards and work notes, the Archive presents us with an astonishing number of unpublished texts, hard to imagine given the vast published output. Naturally enough, I decided to concentrate my efforts, from the start, on these unpublished materials, and I continued to work on these papers while also seeing other major projects such as the Sather Lectures through the press. The choice of giving priority, in 1990, to the publication of the 1962 American lectures was made not only for scholarly reasons and out of an awareness of the importance of the text. There was also a contractual commitment – freely signed and repeatedly confirmed by Momigliano – that the publisher asked Anne Marie Meyer, in her capacity as literary executor, to honour.[11]

If it had been possible to wait a few more years, the edition would have benefited from a complete examination of the papers, and also of the bibliographical cards, that the Archive has gradually yielded.[12] The few unpublished texts included in the *Nono contributo*, which I edited, were all that at the time appeared to me to be of interest to the scholarly community at large and in a state fit for publication with a simple philological apparatus.[13] A different case was the publication, in my Italian translation, of the Cambridge lectures of January–March 1940, 'Peace and Liberty in the Ancient World,'[14] which in my opinion was the aptest response to the debate launched in April 1996[15] in the pages of the *Times Literary Supplement* on the inconsistency in Momigliano's notion of 'politics.' Other unpublished papers of varying length and scope will appear in larger numbers in the final volume, *Decimo contributo*, which has been in preparation for some time.[16]

The study of the texts relating to Hellenistic Judaism[17] and the series of lectures given in Chicago, which have been preserved in full,[18] will be dealt with at some time in the future. It is pointless, from a scholarly point of view, to consider publication of all the extant lectures, above all of those devoted to topics on which a publication by the author already exists. Nevertheless, some documents kept in the Archive retain their value and interest for specific inquiries.

In a letter to Sebastiano Timpanaro, written on 30 July 1967,[19] in answer to the review the younger scholar had written of his *Terzo contributo*,[20] Momigliano made a methodological statement of notable importance and drafted a rapid and problematic precis of his own intellectual biography:

If I had to define what I have been interested to find out in the study of history so far, I would say roughly three things: the influence of Graeco-Roman and Jewish historical thought on subsequent historical thought; the organization that the ancient political and social structures gave or didn't give to themselves to stabilize peace and to ensure freedom of decision and of discussion; the position of Jews and of Jewish civilization in the ancient world and after. I have a less specific interest in the organization of the Roman state, with its multi-national character ab origine and its dissolution due to – or concurrent with – the triumph of Christianity: less specific but nonetheless incessant. Not all these interests are clearly reflected in my *Contributi*, in fact, it is probably fair to say that they do not make up a noteworthy quantity. The first topic should stand out more clearly in the yet unpublished Sather Lectures. If I ever get round to writing the 'Greek Assemblies,' for which I have been collecting materials for many years, or if I ever get round to the even more remote sketch on ancient civilizations, for which I have a contract with Harper and Row, the second and third topics would be at the heart of it. However, one must recognize the danger that all this will be left in fragments and end up a mere ambition.[21]

In 1967, twenty years before his death, the Italian historian clearly saw as a possible problem the realization on his part – and, let me add, the interpretation by others – of his own intellectual work.

Leaving aside the three volumes of his early youth,[22] the risk of a fragmentary outcome appeared possible to Momigliano, in terms that sound very realistic today. The principal part of his work found its definitive end in the *Contributi*. The *Contributi*, however, even if internally articulated in thematic sections, do not always give a clear overview of the themes that were most central to Momigliano's own understanding of his research interests.[23] To return to the opinion expressed in 1967, none of the three books that in the letter are mentioned as essential for the elucidation of his work was ever published by Momigliano.

I shall come shortly to the first of these projects, the Sather Lectures; the second project, the 'Greek Assemblies,' a history of Greek political institutions, never, to my knowledge, went beyond the preparatory stage of collecting notes. As for the outline on ancient civilizations, a first draft is extant, consisting of some hundred pages relating to the history of Greece up until Hellenism. Momigliano used it in various ways to give lectures: it consists of twenty-two documents, handwritten or typed, starting with an introduction relating to 'principles of Historical Method.'[24] In the light of the documentary evidence relating to projects and long-term plans, the first forty years of Arnaldo Momigliano's intellectual career seem destined to complete oblivion.

If we return once again to the text of the letter to Timpanaro, we see that the three themes, plus the fourth on Roman state organization, appear to be identified with a certain conceptual and expressive difficulty. In any case, the first subject identified by Momigliano, the influence of Graeco-Roman and Jewish historical thought on subsequent historical thought, appeared, significantly, linked to a project that had not yet reached its final realization even though to some extent it had already been drafted in the lectures Momigliano gave in California five years earlier, in 1962.

Numerous hypotheses have been put forward concerning the nature of and reasons for this lifelong *parapraxis* in the intellectual life of Momigliano – I mean the failure to publish the American lectures, a project onto which Momigliano had obviously projected very strong intellectual aspirations.[25]

Our problem is now a historiographical one in the strictest sense of the word. We have a considerable number of texts and documents relating to Momigliano's activity for the period that interests us. This material has been left unpublished, for a series of rather complex reasons. How are we to interpret these documents, in addition to attempting to place them in significant relation to the rest of Momigliano's published output, so as to shed some light on the present inquiry? How are we to place Momigliano's research on specific subjects, such as his contribution on 'antiquarianism,' within the framework of research planned to follow the evolution of historiographical thought from the ancients to the moderns? What is the link between the studies on political history, conceived and carried out during the war, and the subsequent research into the origins and development of historiography? How far, in short, can we hope that these questions and the answers to them will eventually contribute to a comprehensive interpretation of Momigliano's intellectual biography?

I believe that some help in solving these problems may come from a reconstruction of the evolution of Momigliano's work from the end of the Second World War to the Sather Lectures. The material I am going to examine is limited, but it allows for the development of two specific pieces of analysis.

After the end of the war, in 1946 and 1947, a bulky manuscript occupied the desk used by Momigliano at the Ashmolean Museum in Oxford. Bearing the weighty title 'Aspects of Roman Political Thought from Seneca to Tacitus,' the text was the fusion of two university courses, held respectively in London in March 1946, 'The Political Ideas of Tacitus and Their Influence on the Formation of the Political Thought,' and in Oxford in January–March 1947, 'Conflicts of Political and Moral Ideas from Seneca to Tacitus.'

The Archive has preserved the scattered limbs of the volume (overall, twenty-six handwritten and typed papers), which I was able to reassemble, thanks to the presence of an index.[26] The Archive also holds all the handwritten papers for the two courses of lectures and, along with these, a series of notes and drafts in which we can see Momigliano taking the first steps in his inquiry into the relation between ancient historiography and its modern interpretations. They were clearly texts written as lectures intended for different audiences. The projected volume underwent unceasing revision; for example, the focus of Momigliano's interest kept shifting from Tacitus to Tacitism and back again. The volume was the first actual conclusion, on the Roman side, of the research on Graeco-Roman political thought, on which Momigliano had been concentrating ever since his first months in exile, under the general heading 'Peace and Liberty in the Ancient World.'[27] I will not return to themes about which I have already written, so limit myself to recalling a letter of Momigliano's dating from March 1940, cited by Dionisotti, in which, invoking a drastic alternative, he drew an explicit connection between the completion of the project on peace and liberty and the full realization of his goals: 'This is my path, success or failure.'[28]

At this point, let us take stock of a first important consideration: in 1947, Momigliano's research on ancient political thought, conceived unitarily, was already split in two, and the nature of the two parts, the Greek and the Roman, was very different. Only on the Roman side was Momigliano to produce simultaneously research on historical and historiographical topics, continuing along the path laid with the themes of peace and liberty. But the Tacitus book was never published, and for a reason that seems banal: the editing was unsuccessful.

That unsuccessful editing accounts for the eventual failure of the book project is obvious from an inspection of the handwritten draft, heavily corrected by the Clarendon Press editor, Dan Davin, who made various suggestions for improving or clarifying Momigliano's English style. Davin – as did all other Press officers – had the highest regard for the learning of the Italian historian, known to him also for his work, quick and substantial, as a contributor to the Oxford Classical Dictionary.[29] But the editorial undertaking appears poorly defined, and it is likely that the possibility of realizing the project slowly faded away.[30] As has been shown elsewhere, Momigliano returned at various times, and in a very different cultural context, to the theme of liberty in the Greek and

Eastern world up until his very late publication of a conclusion (in Italian in 1971 and in English in 1973)[31] in which the theme of the 'Greek Assemblies'[32] was also fused. Apparently, Momigliano gradually abandoned the project on Roman liberty as such.

A careful look in the Archive for notebooks and manuscripts relating to unpublished texts of the period 1947 to 1950, the year in which the essay on antiquarianism was published, gives rise to some useful observations. Unaccountably, the essays actually published in those years as separate articles occupy a totally marginal position in what we have reconstructed as Momigliano's own intellectual project. All the central texts of this period were to remain indefinitely as handwritten texts or else to re-emerge completely decontextualized at a subsequent moment. If we limit our research to papers and documents published in the course of 1947, we have just two very small and very learned papers about the reception of Tacitus. They have been included in the first *Contributo* (one had never been published previously) and reveal nothing about the large-scale research project for which they were first conceived.[33] In 1948, Momigliano published only some reviews.[34] In 1949, the 'Notes on Petrarch, John of Salisbury, and the Institutio Traiani'[35] appeared in the *Journal of the Warburg and Courtauld Institutes*. The manuscripts of these texts and the preparatory notes for them appear inseparable from the corpus of the 'Aspects,' which is in comparison great in both quantity and quality.[36]

A careful examination of the extant notebooks allows us to observe a second phenomenon of some interest. All the series, distinct in subject archivistically speaking, show continuous overlappings.[37] Accordingly, the studies for 'Aspects of Roman Political Thought,' those on humanism (also connected with Dionisotti's arrival in Oxford), and those on antiquarianism appear absolutely intertwined, as the product of a unique line of inquiry issuing forth in all these extant notes and papers. By comparison, the research on the Greek assemblies culminates in the 1947 draft of an index of the volume, after which it immediately disappears as a research theme.

Momigliano, who was during those years lecturer and then reader at Bristol, regularly commuted between Bristol, Oxford, where he then lived with his family, and London, where he came to be more and more involved in the activities of the Warburg Institute. Autumn 1947 saw the arrival of Carlo Dionisotti at Oxford as a University Lecturer; in November of the same year, Momigliano wrote to his *maestro*, Gaetano De Sanctis, about some lectures on Italian humanism taught jointly with this old friend, with whom he had been reunited.[38]

Two notebooks from the summer of 1950 have transmitted two copies each of two different texts.[39] These documents, couched in the form of personal statements, help us to understand the process of thought that led Momigliano to the essay on antiquarianism, which stands out in a sort of incomprehensible intellectual isolation among the published works that year.[40]

The first text, apparently a lecture for an Italian audience to be delivered at the end of the summer, is a sort of self-commentary on the research of antiquarianism. For its interest and its brevity it deserves a complete reading. It will appear in the *Decimo contributo* under the title 'Antiquari e Storici dell'antichita.'[41]

My research will appear complete, in English, in the *Journal of the Warburg and Courtauld Institutes* next December. I refer you to my study in the *Journal* for particular results. Here I wish to highlight the essential motives – historical and methodological – of the research.

1) First of all, it is interesting to note that the distinction between historians and antiquaries is practically coeval with the origins of Greek historiography. In the second half of the fifth century there are found in Greece, in addition to cultivators of *historia* such as Herodotus and Thucydides, cultivators of *archaeologia* such as Hippias of Elis, the Sophist. Naturally, it is not possible sharply to distinguish the scope of *historia* from the scope of *archaeologia.* But one can say in general that the historians collected traditions of the recent past and the archaeologists of the distant past; that the historians tended towards political interpretations, the archaeologists towards erudite collections concerning religion, manners, chronologies, etc.; that the historians preferred chronological order, the antiquaries systematic order.

This distinction between historians and antiquaries – the one with political interests, the other with an interest in describing manners, religion, institutions; the one interested in chronological order, the other in systematic order – is maintained in various forms from the 5th century B.C.E. to the 19th century C.E. It is something new in the historiography of the late 19th and 20th centuries that the antiquaries have lost the right to an independent existence.

2) Second, an important and not neglible phase, for our purpose, in the formation of the antiquaries' method is represented by Varro. At least according to what we know, no Greek or Roman antiquary before Varro conceived an idea similar to that reflected in the *Antiquitates Romanae* of Varro: a systematic description of Roman civilization seen in its historical roots. Moreover, the name, *Antiquitates*, is not found before Varro and could

have been invented by him. As far as we know, Varro broadened and made more precise the concept of antiquarian research and gave it its name. In the Middle Ages, St Augustine preserved a record of the complex structure of Varro's *Antiquitates*, but no one imitated it. Instead, it was imitated in the first half of the fifteenth century by Flavio Biondo. The *Antiquitates* of Varro are revived in the *Roma triumphans* of Flavio Biondo. Humanism sharpened the dualism of the chronological-political interpretation proper to the historian and the systematic-cultural description proper to the antiquaries. The Varronian concept of *antiquitates* – a systematic reconstruction of a people's civilization by means of all its documents, both literary and non-literary – is not known to me to be operative between the sixth and the fifteenth centuries.

3) Third, we must note a fact of no little importance. From the fifteenth to the seventeenth century, histories of Greece and Rome were almost never written; antiquarian books on Greece and Rome were widespread. Herodotus, Thucydides, Plutarch, Livy, Tacitus, Florus, Justin, and so on provide the political history of Greece and Rome. The classicizing prejudice prevented their being replaced. There are scholastic summaries of the history of Greece and Rome within the schemes of universal history, especially in the Protestant universities of the 16th and 17th centuries; and there are also collections of the biographies of emperors. But these did not replace the ancient historians. From the fifteenth to the seventeenth centuries there are antiquaries, not historians of antiquity. People who wrote the history of Rome and Greece at the beginning of the eighteenth century are fully aware of doing something new. Thus the Jesuits Catron and Rovillé in the preface to the *Roman History* of 1725: 'Until our day ... the serious savants exhausted themselves in research on the customs, *moeurs*, context, type of government, laws, etc.' In other words, they were antiquaries, not historians.

4) One understands, therefore, how these antiquaries, masters of the not merely philological study of the classical world through the end of the seventeenth century, occupied a position in the advance guard in the battle with Historical Pyrrhonism fought in the second half of the seventeenth century and lasting on into the beginning of the eighteenth. The reasons why history came into great discredit after the wars of religion and the rise of national histories are known. La Mothe le Vayer and Bayle give specific form to the sense of discredit that circulated throughout Europe with regard to historical works. In order to liberate themselves from the lack of trust in historians, the distinction between the primary and the secondary source, and between document and narration was deepened. For the first time in the history of historical method, manuals were written to teach not

only how one ought to write history rhetorically, but how one could and must distinguish probable from improbable facts. It is necessary, indeed, to inquire whether this casuistry of historical probabilism had direct or indirect connections with the theological casuistry of probabilism. In clarifying the concept of the 'document,' one naturally comes to give the antiquaries pride of place. The great part of their work was on inscriptions, statues, coins, and archival papers – all primary sources in the new conception. Moreover, the systematic character of their research (expressed in treatises on public law, the art of war, customs, etc.) naturally favoured the use of serial information, better documented than the isolated and fugitive. The antiquaries could justly congratulate themselves that the quantity and quality of the documents they used conferred on the knowledge of the past a greater certainty than that extracted from literary sources. They arrived at the point of asserting that information derived from medals and inscriptions was more secure than that derived from Livy and Tacitus: in affirming the superiority of their sources over literary sources, they also affirmed the superiority of modern scholars over ancient ones. As a typical example of the faith of the antiquaries, we could take the founder of modern numismatics, E. Spanheim. In 1672 he recorded the saying of Quintilian 'Historians disagree one with the other' and proposed a remedy: 'Nothing gives more certain support than ancient coins and inscriptions.' The Pyrrhonians could object that, after all, coins, inscriptions, and archival documents often come to be faked. One of them, F.W. Bierlingius, wrote in 1707: 'The art of interpreting inscriptions is so fallible, so uncertain ... the same doubts make coins hazardous ... You see, therefore, whoever indeed brings forward the sources of history and ancient monuments, all toil has its uncertainties.' But the objection of the Pyrrhonists did not take hold. Prevailing opinion maintained that the antiquaries stood on solid ground. Even a non-specialist writer like Addison could write, 'It is much safer to quote a medal than an author.' Paradoxically, in the great Quarrel of the Ancients and the Moderns, it came to be maintained that modern historians could be better than the ancients. Such was the opinion of Charles Patin, with whom agreed no less memorable a voice than Jacques Spon's, whose works on antiquarian method would merit reprinting. Similarly, Francesco Bianchini, an astronomer and antiquarian, in 1697 wrote *The Universal History Proved by Monuments and Illustrated with Symbols of the Ancients*, a general history founded more on monuments than on literary sources so that it would carry greater certainty. This same Bianchini, as we know, conceived a history of the origins of Christianity on the same basis, which appeared posthumously in 1752.

5) The Pyrrhonian crisis concluded, therefore, by making historians recognize the need for systematic use of non-literary sources. The use of literary sources and the confronting of literary with non-literary sources became two of the most important reasons why new ancient histories, which replaced Herodotus, Livy, and Thucydides, were written. From the crisis of Pyrrhonism emerged not only the new historical method but also, at least in part, the modern history of antiquity. Philologists and antiquaries operate together because literary texts have to be confronted with non-literary documents. Tillemont, discriminating among the literary sources, wrote the first history of the Roman Empire; with faith in coins, Vaillant composed the first histories of Ptolomy and the Seleucids. The French critics of the Academy of Inscriptions – and, based on them, de Beaufort – examined the documentary value of the traditions on the origins of Rome. To the work of the antiquaries is owed, in the end, that history of pre-Roman Italy that is the glory of eighteenth-century Italy, especially the history of the Etruscans – based on epigraphic and archaeological, not literary, material. It must be cautioned, however, that in other cases the new history of antiquity arose from a conscious revival of the political interpretation of ancient history, as in the history of the Roman revolutions by Vertot and, later still, the Greek history of Gillies. As one might expect, the antiquaries stimulated – to a considerable degree, though not exclusively – the formation of a historiography on the ancient world that was conscious of being superior to the historiography of the ancients themselves.

6) We know that with the advent of the philosophical history of the Enlightenment, the antiquaries and, in general, the erudites were bitterly attacked. *Philosophes* such as Voltaire agreed with the Pyrrhonists in discrediting the sources and the minute research [of the antiquaries], but against the Pyrrhonists found new certainty in schemes of providential reason. Moreover, they succeded in fusing the political interpretation of historians with the cultural description of the antiquaries in the new idea of the history of civilization. But the philosophical historians of the eighteenth century did not have a method of verifying facts to oppose to that of the despised erudites. They replaced the antiquaries in cultural history, but not in the method of checking facts. The scheme of providential reason that they implicitly opposed to Pyrrhonism could not help save individual facts. Combining the opposing needs of the *philosophes* and of the erudites was a manifest necessity. In the study of the ancient world, this combination was undertaken by Winckelmann and Gibbon. That they succeeded in bringing together the broad vision of the *philosophes* and the erudites' research criteria explains, at least part, their achievement. Winckelmann and Gibbon

directed eighteenth-century historiography towards what would be the master theme in nineteenth-century history-writing, in which philosophical interpretation and minute erudite research came together. The combination was naturally very clear to both men, and here it suffices to record the satisfaction with which Gibbon noted with reference to one of his predecessors a perfect 'blending of the antiquarian and of the philosopher.' With Winckelmann and Gibbon, the critical use of non-literary material, to the end of better stabilizing the value of the literary material, now became an essential part of historiography.

7) Two questions, then, present themselves: 1. Why, despite all this, did Antiquities remain for another century, until the end of the nineteenth, somehow distinct from history? 2. What can the methodological experience of the antiquaries teach us today?

To the first question it is not easy to give a simple answer. In part, in the nineteenth century, Antiquities – *Alterthümer* – was cultivated in the university as a mere offspring of an obsolete system of thought. In part, Antiquities came to be defended by certain theorists, above all German – first Friedrich August Wolf and later E. Meyer – with new arguments: historians (they alleged) examined facts in their becoming, antiquaries in their being; historians harvested the changing, antiquaries the static reality. It is evident from these definitions that Antiquities was defended in the nineteenth century on grounds analogous to those used by many scholars to differentiate sociology from history. The relations between the dying antiquarianism and the rising sociology are worthy of study.

To the second question – What can the methodological experience of the antiquaries teach us today?' – there is an implicit answer in the preceding exposition. One, such as the undersigned, who refuses to admit the existence of sociology (even if he were informed that something called sociology was expanding rapidly across the world) will also refuse to admit the existence of an antiquarian science distinct from historical science. On this point Gibbon had the last word. But this precisely because the method of the antiquaries – as a collection of critical experiences that helped vanquish the crisis of Pyrrhonism – is more relevant than ever. Today, as everyone knows, we are in a phase of scholarship in which too many historians, at least of antiquity, interpret the facts before being certain that the facts exist. Already we see, as if in reaction, a new Pyrrhonism of those weary of seeing scientific journals and books full of ill-founded conjectures. Extreme conjecturalism is inevitably accompanied by Pyrrhonism. Against conjecturalism and Pyrrhonism there is only the old remedy: the cautious and methodical examination of documents with all the skills that were developed in the collaboration of antiquaries and textual critics in the seventeenth and eighteenth centuries.

If this is true, various consequences for a future, modern *arte istorica* present themselves. I will limit myself to indicating one. In the decades between the last two wars, hermeneutics was discussed a great deal, especially in Germany. But by hermeneutics was understood that art of interpretation that Schleiermacher derived from theologians and introduced to philology. There exists a hermeneutic of the antiquaries, much more complex and more productive than that of the theologians, which merits attention in any future theory of the historical document.

What emerges clearly in every way from these pages is that Momigliano wrote his essay on antiquarianism not so much out of an interest in antiquarianism per se but with a particular purpose. He wanted to make a methodological statement (though his presentation of method is incomplete).

Our picture of Momigliano's methodological horizon at that stage becomes clearer if we move on to the second of the two texts, this one written in English and also to be published in the *Decimo contributo*, under the title 'Philology and History.' This text pre-dates by about twenty-five years the discussion of an essential part of the issue that we read in the text of 'Regole del giuoco' (Rules of the Game in the Study of Ancient History, 1974),[42] the most important methodological article the author wrote. If only in terms of Momigliano's biography, it is an important acquisition.

A problem is the starting point of any historical research. We mean by historical problem a situation which can be explained only with the help of some evidence which at the moment is not available to the historian, or if it is available is not fully clear. If all the evidence is available and perfectly interpreted there is nothing more to understand. The problem is non-existing because it is solved. The problem may be the Decline and Fall of the Roman Empire or may be the family history of the historian; it may be the evolution of post cards or the evolution of mankind.

Thus the historian looks for evidence. Eyewitnesses, historians of the past, archaeological remains, inscriptions are all documents of some kind – things which are suspected to provide the necessary evidence for the problem which is interesting the historian. How can he know that these documents are the evidence he needs? Strictly speaking he cannot decide until he has interpreted the documents. In practice his experience will save him time by addressing him in a direction rather than in another. If he studies the Decline and Fall he will go to a library where he thinks that there are ancient historians and inscriptions. But in any case the process of deciding which documents are relevant to one's own research coincides with the interpretation of these documents. By understanding what the documents say or mean or imply, the historian satisfies himself that they can or cannot throw light on his problem. Interpreting a document, thus, means a mental activity with at least two aspects: 1) the interpretation of a document conduces to the understanding of what the document is; 2) the interpretation of a document allows the historian to decide whether the document is relevant to his own research.

Let us examine both aspects. The understanding of what a document is implies the capacity of putting oneself into the position of the man who wrote a note or built a palace (or perhaps destroyed it), in order to attribute to it exactly that meaning that it had in the mind of its author. Interpreting an inscription means understanding what the author of the inscription wanted to say. Interpreting the ruin of a building means to understand the purpose of the building at least at one phase of its existence. If so, historical interpretation always means the understanding of what some people thought or did. The person we want to understand may of course be ourself at some moment of the past. We all know the difficulty of understanding what we really meant when we wrote a certain letter or made a certain drawing.

The mere fact of having understood the document already implies that the historian has already put himself in the condition of deciding whether the author of an inscription meant to tell the truth or the author of a chronicle was not a forger. A complete interpretation of a document – at least in the case of spoken or written words – is not only an interpretation of its language but also of the purpose of the speaker or writer. If that is so, interpretation is the effort of ascertaining through all the means at our disposal what was in the mind of the author of the document – including his bona fides.

This is, however, not all. By having understood the working of the mind of the author at the moment of producing the document, one has ascertained by implication whether he is honest, but one has not yet ascertained whether what he tells is true. This question arises, though very seldom, even in the case of buildings. It is true that they do not normally intend to convey information to other people or to the builder himself. But it is at least conceivable that a building should have been erected to deceive other people both about its functions and its style. The question of bona fides exists always, though it is much more relevant to written documents or statements of eyewitnesses than to anything else.

One then must pass from the stage of deciding that the man is sincere to the stage of deciding that the man tells the truth by collecting all the circumstantial evidence which may throw suspicion on the objective value of the evidence. The man may have misunderstood the language, may be a neuropath, etc.

So interpreting a document means to be able to say what the author of the document said and whether what he said can be considered true.

Having done that, we are in a position to consider the document from its second aspect: its serviceability for our research. We may discover, after a careful reading of the text, that it has nothing to do with our problem.

It follows that the interpretation of a document either leads to insertion of the document into the texture of our historical problem or to ascertaining that it has nothing [to do] with it.

If the former case is [not] in question, the interpretation of the meaning of the document can be said to coincide with its historical interpretation. What else can we say about a document except that it means that or that? If we really know what it means, we also know what it means for our problem. Indeed when we decide that a document throws light on our problem, we really imply that the problem has slightly or greatly changed [its] nature as a consequence of the discovery and interpretation of the document. Every researcher knows that by finding and understanding relevant documents, he modifies the original terms of his problem. When a document is recognized to be relevant, it helps to solve a problem by modifying the nature of the problem, narrowing it down, enlarging it, making it clearer, etc. On the other hand, the process can be closed by the admission that the document has nothing to [do] with our problem. In this case the interpretation of the document does not lead to historical conclusions. We know what it means, but we are unable or unwilling to make it part of a historical problem (unless we are working at two problems at the same time). We just leave it at that. We leave it at that before having decided whether the document tells the truth or not. It is generally enough to know what the author subjectively means to decide whether the document is relevant to our research or not. There may be exceptions. But, generally speaking, it seems clear that we decide the relevance of a document to our research by carrying the understanding of its content at most to the point of ascertaining the subjective bona fides of the author. When we know that the author means what he says, and that what he says has nothing to do with our problem, we do not have to worry about the factual truth of what he says.

Now, if we call philology the interpretation of a text as far as the stage of establishing its bona fides – but not the factual truth of what it tells – we can say that the philological process of interpretation becomes part of the historical process when we recognize that a document is relevant to research. When the document is rejected as irrelevant, the stage of philological interpretation remains isolated, and does not become part of the historical process.

We would therefore suggest that philology is that stage of interpretation of a document in which one has not yet decided whether the document is going to be relevant: when the decision is taken and is favourable to the document, philology becomes automatically a part of historical research; when the decision is taken but is negative, the philological stage remains concluded in itself. We can then talk of pure philological interpretation, meaning philology not absorbed into a historical interpretation.

If that is true, some consequences follow:

Croce argued that the basic distinction is between history and chronicles. History interprets the facts, the chronicle remembers the facts. He also argued, more recently, that philology is the activity of remembering facts properly, [and is] therefore basically identical with the activity of writing chronicles.

All that is not so certain. Men indeed put aside recollections of facts in various ways: monuments, inscriptions, chronicles, documents. The historian needs chronicles as [he needs] any other document. But he must interpret them just as much as any other document to make sure that they are relevant to his problem. The process of discovering, interpreting and checking the subjective bona fides of the documents is an essential part of historical work, even it leads to the conclusion that the document is irrelevant. If philology is this activity, philology is the basic part of historiography. Indeed, when the document is recognized to be relevant to the research, philology becomes ipso facto historiography. When, however, this process is not perfected, philology appears an autonomous activity which leads to the interpretation of a document. All the devices dictated by experience for interpreting a document and establishing its bona fides are an essential part of historical research. We can recognize that a document is relevant to our research only if we have made certain, by all the means available to science at the moment in which we write, that our interpretation of it is not misleading. Exactness is not irrelevant to the historical inspiration, it is indeed [an] essential part of it. The feat of historical inspiration can replace the fact that we are depending on both our interpretation of the document and on the *bona fides* of the document. Any historical research starts by understanding and checking evidence and concludes by making the evidence so checked a part of our living experience by telling how things happened and solving the problem. Historical experience is so given a widened maturity.

Mistakes are possible at any stage of the process of historical thinking, but experience teaches that the most dangerous ones – because the most difficult to contest – are the mistakes made at the philological stage of historical reasoning.

There are cases in which it is possible to determine the bona fides of a document only by establishing by independent evidence that what he [the historian] says is true and therefore he cannot have lied. But this means that the fact has already been proved to be true by independent evidence and that the new evidence, strictly speaking, adds nothing to what we already knew. Unless we are prepared to go back ad infinitum we must arrive at some evidence the bona fides of which, if examined, guarantees the truth without the need for establishing the truth by independent evidence.

Let me emphasize that the connection between the first and the second text is purely temporal: the notebooks in which the texts are preserved, written in succession, document a fact that would otherwise be difficult to deduce from a comparison of their contents. We know from the documentary evidence available to us that they belonged to the same sequence of thought, and this consideration allows us, indeed forces us, to try to establish links.

I would like to advance a provisional conclusion to this part of my argument. The direct connection between the two works of the summer of 1950, on antiquarianism and on the methodological link between philology and history, can help us gain a better understanding of the reasons behind, if not the contents of, the essay that appeared in December 1950 in the *Warburg Journal*. In particular it seems to me that the documentary context helps to fill the vacuum in which this essay stands within the production of this period. Antiquarianism – I repeat it – is not studied per se but inserted in a wider inquiry on historical knowledge.

I think it is important at this point to consider the interval between 1950 and the moment at which Momigliano returned to the same topic in the Sather Lectures. The primary fact to be borne in mind is the change brought to Momigliano's life and intellectual activity by his appointment to the London Chair of Ancient History in 1951. Momigliano suspended a great number of research projects in order to satisfy the obligations of this new engagement.[43] The chance to return with renewed enthusiasm to the issues we have followed in nascent state was deferred until Momigliano received an invitation to deliver the Sather Classical Lectures, for which he prepared for almost three years.

A letter dated 28 May 1959, which has come to my knowledge only in the last few months, presents us with a first scheme of the lectures in eight chapters, two of which are devoted to antiquarianism. It is worth noting Momigliano's chosen topics, keeping in mind the eventual organization of the lectures: 'I. The Birth of History; II. The Birth of Political History; III. The Birth of Biography; IV. The Birth of Antiquarian Studies; V. The Birth of Ecclesiastical History; VI. The Revival of Classical Political History and Biography; VII. The Revival of Antiquarian Studies; VIII. The Revival of Ecclesiastical History and Conclusion.'[44]

The first fact to strike us, in a comparison with the lectures as eventually delivered, is the presence of 'Biography' alongside 'Political History,' 'Antiquarianism,' and 'Ecclesiastical History.' In the end, biography was simply put aside, to be dealt with organically at a different moment.[45] What is also striking is the prominence accorded to antiquarianism – considered twice, in its origins and in its modern revival – together with the two distinct forms of history that constitute the main object of Momigliano's study. Also striking, finally, is the lack of an obvious continuity between the prominence now given to the theme 'Political Historiography,' which receives no further qualification in this list, and Momigliano's post-war concentration on Tacitus and Tacitism.

Here I put forward a hypothesis: that the partial fulfilment of his long-term research plan within the context of the Sather Lectures made Momigliano realize the need for wider foundations before the research could proceed any further. The studies on ancient biography and on the relationships between Jewish and other civilizations that culminated in *Alien Wisdom* may be interpreted as an attempt to satisfy this need. The introduction and the conclusion to the Sather Lectures, both dating to 1962, are intended to clarify and justify this work.[46] This is not only a hypothesis but also the anticipation of a theme that could better be handled in the future.

A study of the two unpublished papers of 1950 can make, I believe, a decisive contribution to this problem. The shift of interest from the history of antiquarian research to the methodological contributions that antiquarian research brought – *and could still bring* – to historical scholarship is particularly evident in the Italian explanatory memoir. This provides some link between the two studies of 1950, even in the absence of other evidence.

At a different level, that of the reconstruction of Momigliano's intellectual biography, this also helps explain the subsequent inclusion of 'Antiquarianism' among the lectures 'The Classical Foundations of Modern Historiography.' To some degree, the very theme and title of the

American lectures provides a *re*-unifying framework for the different themes handled here.

By way of an appendix to this conclusion, I feel it is appropriate to add another point relating to the analogous route taken by the Tacitus-Tacitism theme in the passage from the final years of the war through the immediate post-war period. The last point in this time sequence was a lecture at Oxford in 1978 in which Momigliano returned to Tacitus and tyranny.[47] Because of the at least residually ethical-political dimension of the theme, Momigliano's return to it needs to be seen as a choice, and therefore as a clue for the future biographer.

Every time Momigliano returned to his voyage of research on general history, he reconsidered the whole question in the light of the problem of the link between the history of the ancients and that of the moderns, which was for him a dominant question.

Considerations of space do not permit here a detailed exposition of the results of a complete collation of the 1962 version of the chapter on antiquarianism (certainly written in 1961, and related to the documents of the previous phase of Momigliano's research on this topic)[48] and the 1976 version, eventually published by the University California Press. A collation is now possible thanks to the availability of many copies of this chapter, both in the original version and in that used by Momigliano when he went back to work on the lectures, in 1976.[49] The results are quite surprising.

In the text on antiquarianism, all six paragraphs maintain the same structure and the same argumentative format, even if a number of small changes can be observed. More precisely, there are 12 changes in paragraph i, 16 in ii, 6 in iii, 11 in iv, 1 in v, and 14 in vi. They include:

a) minor English corrections
b) minor corrections of factual information
c) minor additions intended to clarify a point (never extending for more than one line)
d) inclusion of exact quotations, omitted in the 1961/2 version.

A few corrections, however, are worth discussing:

a) the insertion of the phrase 'the founder of modern scientific research on the antiquities of all the countries of Europe' referring to Flavio Biondo at the end of paragraph iv.[50]
b) the insertion of the sentence 'In Italy, Vico had somehow prepared

the way for a synthesis of philosophy and erudition,' which followed the mention of Voltaire and preceded that of Winckelmann and Gibbon in the first part of paragraph vi.[51]

c) the insertion of the sentence 'What Mommsen only implied has now become a basic tenet of sociology, anthropology, and what is more vaguely known as structuralism' after the beginning of the third from last paragraph.[52]

d) the systematic replacement of 'sociological' and 'sociology' with 'structural' and 'structuralism' in all passages of the last paragraph but one where these words occur (three times).[53]

e) the addition of 'Anthropology' next to 'Sociology' in the passage discussing poor knowledge of the history of sociology.[54]

f) the addition of the sentence 'Emile Durkheim was a pupil of N. Fustel de Coulanges, another forerunner of structuralism in his *Cité Antique*' after the sentence 'Max Weber was, and felt himself to be, a pupil of Mommsen.'[55]

g) the introduction of a causal connective and a change of the verb in the sentence 'The rise of sociology is certainly connected with the decline of antiquarianism *because* [added in 1976] sociology *is* [1962: *may even be*] the heir of antiquarian studies.'[56]

Two points of distinct interest seem obvious. In the first place, what needs emphasizing is that Momigliano maintained a constant line of argument that he evidently judged to be concluded and conclusive. He did not change the structure of his reasoning even with fifteen years' distance. In the second place, here one may observe Momigliano's new critical attention to French structuralism, which he presents as descending from the cultural line of the 'école sociologique,' in its turn seen as dating back to Fustel de Coulanges.[57] This point seems to have prompted him to take a more critical look at the hitherto privileged, even hereditary path from antiquarianism to sociology. The whole cultural route, from the phase immediately preceding 1948 until 1976, appears to be documented in every passage. The critique is enriched by details, but the substance of Momigliano's line of thought is unaltered. This vast cultural and historical project may perhaps be identified as the ultimate objective of Arnaldo Momigliano's lifelong research, in spite of various adjustments made along the road, and radical modification of every preceding project and personal resolution. If this identification is accurate, at least to some degree, then there are already the materials for biographical conclusions of some interest. In keeping with what I stated in my initial remarks, I would like to leave these further conclusions to whoever will come after me on this research path.

Appendix: 'Antiquari e storici dell'antichità'

La mia ricerca comparirà completa in inglese nel Journal of the Warburg and Courtauld Institutes il prossimo dicembre. Al mio studio in questo Journal io rimando per i particolari risultati. Qui desidererei accennare ai motivi essenziali – storici e metodologici – della ricerca:

1) Anzitutto interessa notare che la distinzione tra storici e antiquari è praticamente coeva con l'origine della storiografia greca. Nella seconda metà del sec. V a.C. si trovano in Grecia, oltre a cultori di ἰστορια, come Erodoto e Tucidide, dei cultori di ἀρχαιολογία, come Ippia di Elide, il sofista. Non è possibile naturalmente distinguere con rigore l'ambito di ἰστορια dall'ambito dell' ἀρχαιολογία. Ma si può dire in genere che gli storici raccoglievano tradizioni del passato recente, gli archeologi del passato lontano; gli storici tendevano a interpretazioni politiche, gli archeologi a raccolte erudite concernenti religione, costumi, cronologie etc.; gli storici preferivano l'ordine cronologico; gli antiquari l'ordine sistematico.

Questa distinzione tra storici e antiquari – gli uni con interessi politici, gli altri con interesse di descrizione del costume, della religione, delle istituzioni, gli uni a ordine cronologico, gli altri a ordine sistematico – si è mantenuta in varie forme dal V sec.a.C. al XIX secolo d.C. E' un fatto nuovo della storiografia del tardo sec. XIX e del sec.XX che gli antiquari perdono il diritto a una esistenza indipendente.

2) In secondo luogo una fase importante e non trascurabile al nostro scopo della formazione del metodo degli antiquari è rappresentata da Varrone. Almeno per quanto noi sappiamo, nessun antiquario greco o romano prima di Varrone concepì una idea paragonabile a quella delle *Antiquitates Romanae* di Varrone: una descrizione sistematica della civiltà romana vista nelle sue radici nel passato. Anche il nome – antiquitates – non si trova prima di Varrone e può essere stato inventato da lui. Per quanto sappiamo, Varrone allarga e precisa il concetto di ricerca antiquaria e le dà il nome. Nel Medioevo S.Agostino conserva il ricordo della complessa struttura delle Antichità di Varrone, ma nessuno le imita. Esse sono invece imitate nella prima metà del sec. XV da Flavio Biondo. Con la Roma Triumphans di Flavio Biondo rivivono le Antiquitates di Varrone. Con l'Umanesimo si acuisce il dualismo tra

la interpretazione cronologico-politica degli storici e la descrizione sistematico-culturale degli antiquari. Il concetto varroniano di Antiquitates – come ricostruzione sistematica della civiltà di un popolo per mezzo di tutti i documenti letterari e non letterari – non mi risulta operante tra il sec.VI e il sec. XV.

3) In terzo luogo è da constatare un fatto di non poca importanza. Dal XV al XVII secolo quasi non si scrissero storie di Grecia e di Roma; si scrissero prevalentemente libri antiquari sulla Grecia e su Roma. Erodoto, Tucidide, Plutarco, Livio, Tacito, Floro, Giustino e così via provvedevano la storia politica della Grecia e di Roma. Il pregiudizio classicistico impediva la loro sostituzione. Si hanno riassunti scolastici della storia di Grecia e di Roma entro gli schemi di storia universale comuni in specie alle università protestanti del XVI e XVII secolo; e si hanno anche raccolte di biografie di imperatori; ma essi non sostituiscono le storie degli antichi. Dal sec. XV al sec. XVII si hanno antiquari, non storici dell'antichità. Coloro che scrivono la storia di Roma e della Grecia al principio del sec. XVIII sono pienamente coscienti di fare qualcosa di nuovo. Così i gesuiti Catron e Rovillé nella prefazione alla Histoire Romaine del 1725: 'Jusqu'à nos temps .... les savants de profession s'étaient épuisés en recherches sur les Coûtumes, sur les Moeurs, sur le Milieu, sur le genre de Gouvernement, sur les Loix etc.' In altre parole: erano antiquari, non storici.

4) Si comprende allora come questi antiquari, padroni del campo nello studio non meramente filologico del mondo classico fino alla fine del Seicento, abbiano una posizione di avanguardia nella battaglia del Pirronismo storico combattuta nel secondo Seicento e ancora protrattasi nel primo Settecento. Le ragioni per cui dopo le guerre di religione e il sorgere delle storiografie nazionali la storia fosse venuta in grande discredito sono note. La Mothe le Vayer e Bayle danno forma precisa al senso di discredito che circola in tutta Europa nei riguardi delle opere storiche. Per liberarsi dalla sfiducia negli storici si approfondisce la distinzione tra fonte primaria e fonte secondaria, tra documento e narrazione. Per la prima volta nella storia del metodo storico si scrivono manuali per insegnare non più come si debba retoricamente scrivere la storia, ma come si possa e debba distinguere i fatti probabili dagli improbabili. Occorrerà invero indagare se questa casuistica del probabilismo storico abbia dirette o indirette connessioni con la casuistica teologica del probabilismo. Chiarendo il concetto di documento, si veniva naturalmente a metter in primo piano gli antiquari. Gran parte del loro lavoro si svolgeva intorno a iscrizioni, statue, monete, carte

d'archivio – tutte fonti primarie nel nuovo concetto. Inoltre il carattere sistematico della loro ricerca (espressa in trattati di diritto pubblico, arte della guerra, costumanze etc.) favoriva naturalmente l'utilizzazione della notizia ripetuta e quindi meglio documentata in confronto della notizia isolata. Gli antiquari potevano giustamente vantarsi che la quantità e la qualità dei documenti da loro usati conferiva alla conoscenza del passato una certezza maggiore di quella ricavata dalle fonti letterarie. Essi arrivavano al punto di asserire che le notizie derivate da medaglie e iscrizioni sono più sicure delle notizie derivate da Livio e Tacito: nell'affermare la superiorità delle loro fonti sulle fonti letterarie, affermavano anche la loro superiorità di studiosi moderni sugli studiosi antichi. Come tipico esempio per la fede degli antiquari può prendersi il fondatore della moderna numismatica E. Spanheim. Nel 1672 egli ricordava l'obiter dictum di Quintiliano: 'alii ab aliis historici dissentiunt.' Egli proponeva il rimedio: 'Non aliunde notis certius quam in nummis aut marmoribus antiquis praesidium occurrit'. I pirronisti potevano obiettare che dopo tutto anche le monete, le iscrizioni, i documenti d'archivio vengono spesso falsificati. Uno di essi, F.W. Bierlingius scriveva nel 1707: 'Ars inscriptiones interpretandi adeo fallax est, adeo incerta ... Numismata iisdem dubiis obnoxia sunt ... Vides ergo, quicumque demum proferantur historiarum fontes, et antiquitatis monumenta, omnia laborare sua incertitudine.' Ma l'obiezione dei pirronisti non faceva presa. L'opinione prevalente rimase che gli antiquari si erano posti su un terreno solido. Perfino un letterato non specialista come l'Addison poteva scrivere: 'It is much safer to quote a medal than an author.' Paradossalmente, nella grande Querelle tra antichi e moderni, vengono a sostenere che gli storici moderni possono essere migliori degli antichi. Tale è l'opinione di Charles Patin, col quale concorda voce non meno memorabile, Jacques Spon, i cui opuscoli di metodo antiquario meriterebbero di essere ristampati. Così pensa quel Francesco Bianchini, astronomo e antiquario, che nel 1697 scriveva la Istoria Universale provata con monumenti e figurata con simboli degli antichi, una storia generale fondata più che su fonti letterarie, sui monumenti, per raggiungere maggiore certezza. Lo stesso Bianchini, come è noto, concepì una storia delle origini cristiane con gli stessi criteri, che apparve postuma nel 1752.

5) La crisi del pirronismo si conclude dunque con il fare riconoscere agli storici la necessità di valersi sistematicamente delle fonti non letterarie. L'utilizzazione delle fonti letterarie e il confronto tra fonti letterarie e fonti non letterarie diventano due delle ragioni più importanti per scrivere nuove storie antiche le quali sostituiscano Erodoto, Livio,

Tucidide. Dalla crisi del pirronismo esce non solo il nuovo metodo storico, ma almeno in parte anche la moderna storia dell'antichità. Filologi e antiquari operano insieme perché i testi letterari devono essere confrontati con i documenti non letterari. Tillemont discriminando le fonti letterarie scrive la prima storia dell'impero romano; Vaillant compone sulla fede delle monete le prime storie dei Tolemei e dei Seleucidi. I critici francesi dell'Accademia delle Iscrizioni – e fondandosi su di loro il De Beaufort – esaminano il valore documentario delle tradizioni sulle origini di Roma. Al lavoro degli antiquari si deve infine quella storia dell'Italia preromana, in specie degli Etruschi, su materiale epigrafico e archeologico, oltre che letterario, che è la gloria del Settecento italiano. Deve però essere avvertito che in altri casi la nuova storia dell'antichità sorge da un conscio rinnovamento della interpretazione politica della storia antica, come nella storia delle rivoluzioni di Roma del Vertot e più tardi nella storia greca del Gillies. Come si potrebbe aspettare, gli antiquari stimolano – considerevolmente sì, ma non esclusivamente – la formazione di una storiografia sul mondo antico conscia di essere superiore alla storiografia degli antichi stessi.

6) E' noto che con l'avvento della storiografia filosofica dell'Illuminismo, gli antiquari e in genere gli eruditi sono duramente attaccati. I filosofi come Voltaire si accordano con i pirronisti nel discreditare le fonti e la ricerca minuta, ma contro i pirronisti trovano nuova certezza negli schemi della ragione provvidenziale. Essi inoltre riescono a fondere la interpretazione politica degli storici con la descrizione culturale degli antiquari nelle nuove idee della storia della civiltà. Ma gli storici filosofi del Settecento non hanno un metodo per l'accertamento dei fatti da opporre agli eruditi che essi disprezzano. Essi sostituiscono gli antiquari nella storia culturale, non nel metodo dell'accertamento dei fatti. Lo schema della ragione provvidenziale che essi implicitamente oppongono al Pirronismo non vale a salvare i fatti singoli. Si manifesta dunque la necessità di combinare le esigenze opposte dei filosofi e degli eruditi. Questa combinazione, nel campo degli studi del mondo antico, è operata da Winckelmann e da Gibbon. Che essi riuscissero a combinare la ampia visione dei filosofi con i criteri di ricerca degli eruditi spiega, almeno in parte, il loro successo. Winckelmann e Gibbon avviano la storiografia settecentesca verso quella che sarà la linea maestra della storiografia ottocentesca: dove la interpretazione filosofica si combina con la minuta ricerca erudita. La combinazione è naturalmente in entrambi ben conscia, e qui basterà ricordare la soddisfazione con cui Gibbon notava in taluno dei suoi predecessori il perfetto 'blending of

the antiquarian and of the philosopher.' Con Winckelmann e Gibbon l'utilizzazione critica del materiale non letterario, al fine anche di stabilire meglio il valore del materiale letterario, diventa ormai parte essenziale della storiografia.

7) Due questioni allora si pongono: 1) perché, nonostante tutto ciò, le antichità rimasero ancora per un secolo fino alla fine del sec. XIX qualcosa di distinto dalla storia. 2) che cosa oggi possa insegnare la esperienza metodica degli antiquari.

Alla prima domanda non è facile dare risposta semplice. In parte nel sec. XIX le antichità – Alterthümer – furono coltivate nelle università come mera eredità di un sistema di pensiero superato. In parte le antichità vennero difese da certi teorici soprattutto tedeschi – primo Federico Augusto Wolf e ultimo E. Meyer – con nuovi argomenti: gli storici (fu detto da costoro) esaminerebbero i fatti nel loro divenire, gli antiquari nel loro essere; gli storici coglierebbero il dinamismo, gli antiquari la staticità del reale. E' evidente da queste definizioni che le antichità furono difese nel sec. XIX con ragioni analoghe a quelle che portarono molti studiosi a differenziare la sociologia dalla storia. Le relazioni tra la morente antiquaria e la nascente sociologia sono degne di studio.

Alla seconda domanda – che cosa possa oggi insegnare la esperienza metodica degli antiquari – si è già implicitamente risposto con la esposizione precedente. Chi, come il sottoscritto, si rifiuta di ammettere l'esistenza della sociologia (sebbene sia informato che qualcosa chiamato sociologia si muove a passi rapidi nel mondo) si rifiuterà anche di ammettere la esistenza di una scienza antiquaria distinta dalla scienza storica. Su questo punto Gibbon ha detto l'ultima parola. Ma appunto perciò il metodo degli antiquari – come raccolta di esperienze critiche le quali contribuirono a vincere la crisi del pirronismo – è più che mai attuale. Oggi, come a tutti è noto, noi siamo in una fase degli studi in cui troppi storici, almeno dell'antichità interpretano i fatti prima di essere sicuri che i fatti esistano. Già si profila per reazione un nuovo pirronismo di chi è stanco di vedere le riviste scientifiche e i libri pieni di congetture mal fondate. Il congetturalismo a oltranza è inevitabilmente accompagnato dal pirronismo. Contro al congetturalismo e al pirronismo non c'è che il vecchio rimedio: l'esame cauto e metodico dei documenti con tutti gli avvedimenti che furono elaborati dalla collaborazione di antiquari e critici testuali nei secc. XVII e XVIII.

Se ciò è vero, si presentano varie conseguenze per una futura Arte Istorica modernamente intesa. A me basterà indicarne una. Nei decenni tra le due ultime guerre si è discusso molto, in specie in Germania, di ermeneutica. Ma per ermeneutica si intendeva quell'arte della interpretazione che Schleiermacher derivò dai teologi e introdusse nella filologia. Esiste una ermeneutica degli antiquari ben più complessa e più produttiva di quella dei teologi, che merita attenzione in ogni futura teoria del documento storico.

Notes

1 I wish to thank the institution that hosted the conference at which this paper was delivered, the William Andrews Clark Memorial Library, and the conference organizers, Professors Peter N. Miller and Peter Reill. An earlier version of part of the essay was delivered under the title 'Tra umanesimo e antiquaria,' in March 2002 in a seminar held at the Scuola Normale Superiore di Pisa, at the invitation of Carmine Ampolo. Many thanks to him and to my colleagues Michele Battini, GianBiagio Conte, Glenn Most, Giovanni Salmeri, Michela Sassi, and Salvatore Settis for their contributions to the discussion. For their friendly help, warm thanks to Rolando Ferri and Andrea Taddei.

2 I refer in these notes to the following works by Momigliano, to which I have contributed prefatory studies and annotations as editor of his books after 1987 (the short-title forms used are provided in brackets): *Saggi di storia della religione romana* (Brescia, 1988); *Nono contributo alla storia degli studi classici e del mondo antico* (Rome 1990) [*Nono contributo*]; *The Classical Foundations of Modern Historiography* (Berkeley 1990) [*Classical Foundations*]; *Le radici classiche della storiografia moderna* (Florence 1992) [*Radici classiche*]; and *Pace e Libertà nel mondo antico, Lezioni a Cambridge: gennaio marzo 1940 con un'appendice documentaria e ventuno lettere a Ernesto Codignola* (Florence 1996) [*Pace e libertà*].

I shall refer also to the following of my own articles: preface to the Italian edition in *Radici classiche*, vii–xii; 'Materiali per una biografia intellettuale di Arnaldo Momigliano. 1. Libertà e pace nel mondo antico,' *Athenaeum*, n.s. 83 (1995): 213–44 [*Materiali* 1]; 'Uno storico, un testo, un contesto,' introduction to *Pace e Libertà*, vii–xxxvi; 'Materiali per una biografia intellettuale di Arnaldo Momigliano. 2. Tra Napoli e Bristol,' *Athenaeum*, n.s. 86 (1998): 231–44. [*Materiali* 2]; 'Materiali per una biografia intellettuale di Arnaldo Momigliano. 3. Gli anni di Londra,' in *Arnaldo Momigliano nella storiografia del Novecento*, ed. Leandro Polverini (Rome: Edizioni di Storia e Letteratura, 2006) (Incontri perugini di Storia della storiografia IX, Spoleto, 31.5.–2.6.

1999), 125–36 [*Materiali* 3]; 'La polis e il supplice. Un inedito di Arnaldo Momigliano,' *Studi classici e orientali* 46:1 (1996 [1999]): 137–51; 'Nuovi materiali per una biografia intellettuale di Arnaldo Momigliano,' *Rendiconti Morali. Accademia dei Lincei*, ser. 9, vol. 11, fasc. 3 (2000): 383–98 [*Nuovi materiali*]. 'Leggere Momigliano,' in *Leggere e rileggere i classici. Per Livio Sichicollo*, ed. Marco Filoni (Macerata, 2004), 99–109; and 'Lo Jacoby di Arnaldo Momigliano,' in *Aspetti dell'opera di Felix Jacoby*, ed. Carmine Ampolo (Pisa, 2006), 31–45.

In addition, I shall refer to various earlier volumes of Momigliano's *Contributi alla storia degli studi classici e del mondo antico* (Rome, 1955–), in short-title form.

3 See Archivio Arnaldo Momigliano, *Guida all'Archivio e regesto delle carte*, ed. Giovanna Granata, foreword by Riccardo Di Donato, preprint (Pisa, 1998) [*AAM*], 346.

4 See G. Granata, 'Il catalogo della sezione bibliografica dell'Archivio Arnaldo Momigliano,' *Il Bibliotecario* 38 (1993): 179–88.

5 See n3 above. A new version with corrections and additions: *L'Archivio Arnaldo Momigliano. Inventario analitico*, ed. Giovanna Grenata, preface by Riccardo Di Donato (Rome, 2006).

6 See *Nuovi materiali*, 383–97.

7 Ibid., 397–8.

8 See *Materiali* 1, 217 and passim.

9 See *Materiali* 3, 125 n2.

10 I am certain that some of the most important family documents are still kept in London.

11 The documents in section D-b 10 of *AAM*.

12 See section P-c 34–5 of *AAM*.

13 I refer the reader to my introductory notes to the texts in the second part, 'Conferenze e lezioni inedite,' of *Nono contributo*, 459, 483, 503, 521, 531, 543, 563, 577, 593, 609.

14 See the 'Nota ai testi' in *Pace e libertà*, xxxv–xxxvi.

15 See W.V. Harris, 'The Silences of Momigliano,' *Times Literary Supplement*, 12 April 1996, pp. 6–7, and further interventions of O. Murray (3 May 1996); T.J. Cornell (10 May 1996); W.V. Harris (24 May 1996); C. Dionisotti (14 June 1996); and R.T. Ridley (28 June 1996).

16 Diplomatic transcriptions of other autograph documents, that is, the lecture 'Peace and Liberty in the Ancient World' (1940) and the monograph 'Aspects of Roman Political Thought from Seneca to Tacitus' (1947), will be included.

17 See G. Granata, 'La resistenza all'ellenizzazione. Il corpus di inediti momiglianei sul giudaismo ellenistico (1977–1982),' *Studi ellenistici* 12 (Pisa, 1999): 73–92.

18 In *AAM,* section P-e contains lectures of 1959; P-f of 1978; P-g of 1980; P-h of 1981; P-i of 1982; P-j of 1983; P-k of 1984; P-l of 1985; and P-m of 1986. Section P-n of 1987 is the only one never completed. This cycle overlaps with the series of lectures on Hellenistic Judaism, for which see n17 above.

19 I am planning to edit the entire correspondence, complete on both sides, thanks to the courtesy of M. Augusta Morelli-Timpanaro, for the Scuola Normale Superiore di Pisa press. I have published an anticipatory extract, covering the correspondence of 1967, in 'Filologia, marxismo, guerre e altro: dal carteggio Momigliano-Timpanaro,' in *La Gazzetta di Pisa* III, no. 7, 3 March 2001, pp. 2–3. The letter is translated in the text and cited in n21 below.

20 S. Timpanaro, review of A. Momigliano, *Terzo contributo alla storia degli studi classici e del mondo antico,* in *Rivista di filologia e istruzione classica* 96 (1968): 99–110.

21 'Se io dovessi definire che cosa mi ha interessato finora di scoprire nella storia, direi grossolanamente tre cose: l'influenza del pensiero storico greco-romano e giudaico sul pensiero storico successivo; l'organizzazione che gli organismi politici e sociali antichi si sono dati o non dati per stabilire pace e per assicurare libertà di decisione e di discussione; la posizione degli Ebrei e della civiltà ebraica nel mondo antico e successivo.

Meno precisa la mia preoccupazione sull'origine della organizzazione statale romana – con la sua caratteristica plurinazionale ab origine – e sulla sua dissoluzione per il – o in concomitanza del – trionfo del Cristianesimo: meno preciso ma pure costante.

Non tutti questi interessi hanno un chiaro riflesso nei miei Contributi, anzi è legittimo dubitare che vi compaiano in volume sufficiente da richiamare l'attenzione. Il primo interesse dovrebbe apparire più nitidamente nelle Sather Lectures ancora inedite. Se mai arriverò a scrivere le Greek Assemblies, per cui da tanti anni raccolgo materiali, e l'ancora più remoto schizzo sulle civiltà antiche, per cui ho contratto con Harper and Row, il secondo e il terzo interesse sarebbero al centro. Ma è da riconoscere il pericolo che tutto questo rimanga allo stato di frammento e perfino di velleità.'

22 A. Momigliano, *Prime linee di storia della tradizione maccabaica* (Roma 1930); *l'opera dell'Imperatore Claudio* (Florence, 1932); and *Filippo il Macedone. Saggio sulla storia greca del IV sec. a. C* (Florence, 1934).

23 An interesting attempt to propose a comprehensive interpretation of the evolution of Momigliano's work can be found in I. Cervelli, 'L'ultimo Momigliano: costanti e variabili di una ricerca,' *Studi storici* 30 (1989): 59–104. The elements of continuity and organic evolution in Momigliano's

work are stressed in the essays by E. Gabba now collected in *Cultura classica e storiografia moderna* (Bologna, 1995).

24 I have proposed an analysis in *Materiali* 3.

25 So G. Bowersock, 'Arnaldo Momigliano e la storiografia dell'antichità in USA,' in *Omaggio ad Arnaldo Momigliano. Storia e storiografia sul mondo antico*, ed. Clelia Cracco Ruggini (Como, 1989), 44.

26 See section P-b in *AAM*.

27 The most important texts are published, in Italian, in *Pace e libertà*.

28 C. Dionisotti, *Ricordo di Arnaldo Momigliano* (Bologna, 1989), 104.

29 Many autograph copies of articles written for the *OCD* can be found in section P-q of *AAM*.

30 Thanks to the friendly help of Oswyn Murray, I have been able to consult the Clarendon Press archives in Oxford. There are two mentions of the book, but no trace of a final agreement.

31 See 'La libertà di parola nel mondo antico,' *Rivista storica italiana* 83 (1971): 499–544; 'Empietà ed eresia nel mondo antico,' *Rivista storica italiana* 83 (1971): 771–91, repr. in *Sesto contributo*, 403–58; 'Freedom of Speech in Antiquity,' in *Dictionary of the History of Ideas*, vol. 2 (New York, 1973), 252–63; and 'Impiety in the Classical World,' ibid., 564–7. See also 'The Social Structure of the Ancient City' (with S.C. Humphreys), *Annali della Scuola Normale Superiore di Pisa*, ser. 3, vol. 4 (1974): 334–49, repr. in *Sesto contributo*, 459–76.

32 The outline for a book entitled 'Greek Popular Assemblies,' dated March 1947, is in N-b 42, along with the notebook containing the series relating to *Pace e libertà*. Only in N-b 46 (1970) does the heading 'Riassunti per assemblee' appear, with no explicit cross-references to the previous project.

33 'The First Political Commentary on Tacitus,' *Journal of Roman Studies* 37 (1947): 91–101, repr. in *Contributo*, 37–59; and 'Il "Tacito Espanol" by B. Alamos de Barrientos e gli "Aphorismos" by B. Arias Montano,' in *Contributo*, 61–6.

34 Six out of seven were published in *Rivista storica italiana*, a sign of Momigliano's intention to maintain a strong link with Italian culture.

35 Volume 12 (1949), 189–90, reprinted in *Contributo*, 377–9.

36 The corpus of 'Aspects' papers consists in *AAM* of the text of series P-b 1-26 and of the notes contained in the notebooks of series N-c 1-12. The entire set of papers deserves specific study; in particular we need to understand the relationship between the items eventually converging in the 1947 monograph, and those, like the Seneca texts, that were eventually separated from the rest of the book, during the 1950s. The index of the 'Aspects' has been

reproduced in my *Materiali* 1, 243–4, where also the contents and the
general structure of the book are interpreted.

37 I give just a few examples: N-f 47 contains reading notes for 'Friedrich
Creuzer and Greek Historiography' (1946); N-f 49 contains 'Appunti su
Homer' and 'Popular Assembly'; N-f 52 contains notes entitled 'History of
Classical Philology'; N-f 58 contains notes entitled 'Tacito e Antiquari'
and a fragment of the lecture 'La leggenda del cristianesimo di Seneca'
(1950).

38 The text of the letter (3 November 1947) is reprinted in *Materiali* 2, 238.

39 N-f 56 contains autograph texts of 'Philology and History' (pp. 1–12) and of
the Italian piece on antiquarianism (pp. 13–25); N-f 62 contains the Italian
piece on antiquarianism (pp. 1–12r) and a handwritten version by Beryl
Smalley of 'Philology and History' (pp. 72v–77), as well as handwritten texts
of 'Gibbon's Contribution to Historical Method' (1954) and 'Benedetto
Croce' (1950).

40 'Ancient History and the Antiquarian,' *Journal of the Warburg and Courtauld
Institutes* 13 (1950): 285–315, repr. in *Contributo*, 67–106.

41 The copyright of this and of the second of Momigliano's unpublished 1950
texts printed here is retained by the Archivio Arnaldo Momigliano, Pisa.
The full Italian text is found in the appendix to this chapter.

42 *Annali della Scuola Normale Superiore di Pisa*, ser. 3, vol. 4 (1974): 1183–92,
repr. in *Sesto contributo*, 13–22.

43 I have analysed Momigliano's first London period and the lectures he gave
as professor of ancient history at University College in *Materiali* 3. Very
significant in this context is the choice of topic for Momigliano's inaugural
lecture, 'George Grote and the Study of Greek History' (1952), reprinted in
Contributo, 213–31.

44 Neither this letter, nor the correspondence of which it is a part, is contained
in *AAM*.

45 See, obviously, *The Development of Greek Biography: Four Lectures* (Cambridge,
MA, 1971); and 'Second Thought on Greek Biography,' *Mededelingen der K.
Nederlandse Akademie van Wetenschappen*, Afd. Letterkunde, N.R. 34 (1971):
245–57, repr. in *Quinto contributo*, 33–47.

46 See B. Bravo, 'Il libro postumo di Arnaldo Momigliano sui fondamenti
classici della storiografia moderna,' *Athenaeum* 80 (1992): 243–50.

47 See section P-c 24, with handwritten notes by Anne Marie Meyer, who writes:
'Retyped 15.1. 1978 (revised). As read at Bangor and Oxford Jan. 78. The
original lecture title was *Tacitus and the Discovery of Imperial Tyranny*.' The
final treatment of the theme, as I have said, is the text published in 1990 by
the University of California Press.

48 See P-c 1, 7, 22, 36. In particular P-c 22 (with 'July 1961' written in pen) is the copy used by Momigliano at Berkeley while he was giving the Sather Lectures. P-c 7 is a copy of the same typewriting, arranged for lectures at Leiden and Amsterdam in December 1961, with corrections by Beryl Smalley and Anne Marie Meyer.

49 See P-c 27, carbon copy of typewriting in a 'folder' on which Anne Marie Meyer has written, 'TS copy of The Rise of Antiquarian Research.' The text does not contain Greek words, usually added handwritten, but has, typed, all the previous corrections added to the 1961–2 version.

50 *Classical Foundations*, 72.

51 Ibid., 75.

52 Ibid., 77–8

53 Ibid., 78–9.

54 Ibid., 78.

55 Ibid.

56 Ibid., 79.

57 See '*La città antica* di Fustel de Coulanges,' *Rivista storica italiana* 82 (1970): 81–98, repr. in *Quinto contributo*, 159–78.

chapter three

Momigliano's Method and the Warburg Institute: Studies in His Middle Period

ANTHONY GRAFTON

On 22 July 1955, the *Times Literary Supplement* welcomed the appearance of a new scholarly book with an enthusiasm rarely matched in its grey, closely printed pages. Pride of place, in those days, went not to the cover but to the so-called 'long middle' – a substantial review, which normally faced the correspondence columns. On this summer Friday, Peter Green wrote with phosphorescent enthusiasm of 'a trilingual collection of essays remarkable alike for their classical and humanistic erudition, their historiographical judgment, and a style equally graceful in Italian, German, or English': Arnaldo Momigliano's *Contributo alla storia degli studi classici*. This work, Green made clear, set a new standard for the history of ancient history.[1]

The fact that the *TLS* could feature a book printed in Italy, much of which was not in English, alerts us, if we need alerting, to a vital fact: Momigliano inhabited a world we have lost. Britain's grimy, bomb-damaged cities harboured poets, novelists, and scholars whose work dominated the intellectual life of the English-speaking world. British radio, British movies, British theatre, British literary criticism, British newspapers, British philosophy, even British natural science all put their American counterparts to shame, as no one confessed more eagerly than anglophile Americans. British universities, though as ramshackle and underfunded as British factories and cinemas, proved cosmopolitan enough to appoint dozens of European émigrés to prominent positions, where they not only formed English students but addressed the English public. Their presence made the English intellectual world at mid-century far livelier and more cosmopolitan than the international English-speaking intellectual world we live in, fifty years on. This rich environment not only fostered but partly shaped Momigliano's central historical work on the classical tradition.

Yet placing Momigliano in his London milieu is not simple, as an autobiographical anecdote will illustrate. In the spring of 1973, the Fulbright commission appointed me to a scholarship for study in England. The commission also arranged for my work to be supervised by Momigliano, then nearing the end of his time as professor at University College London. I planned to write a doctoral dissertation on Joseph Scaliger (1540–1609), the Huguenot philologist whose editions of texts and manuals of technical chronology had won him a prominent place in the pantheon of great past scholars, though no one – even Jacob Bernays or Mark Pattison, the authors of the last systematic treatments – seemed able to explain exactly what he had done, or why it mattered. My teachers at the University of Chicago, Eric Cochrane, Hanna Holborn Gray, and Noel Swerdlow, agreed that Momigliano could offer better guidance than anyone else in the world into this thorny and inaccessible part of the historical forest. In a long letter to him, I described my project and listed the works I had read to date. This song of innocence, happily, has vanished from my personal archive, and with luck it has also disappeared from that of my teacher. But I remember it all too vividly. I made clear that I had read not only Momigliano's 1950 essay 'Ancient History and the Antiquarian,' but a number of other studies by him and others which seemed to me to have expanded usefully on points and areas that he had touched on. I noted that the Warburg Institute, which had published so many of these studies and served as a research base for most of those interested in the history of scholarship, seemed the obvious place to do my work. And I asked for further advice.

A reply, in the form of a blue air letter, turned up some two weeks later in my mailbox in Hyde Park. It too has vanished – but its memory remains fresh. Momigliano paid me the compliment, as he always did, of treating my letter with absolute seriousness. But the compliments ended there. He pointed out that other scholars already working on Renaissance scholarship – above all, Sebastiano Timpanaro and Carlotta Dionisotti – had done work of the highest level on the history of the editing of texts: 'You could hardly compete with' them, he noted, unkindly but accurately. As to antiquarianism, he commented with more acerbity that I seemed to have indiscriminately studied works of very different level and value. Erna Mandowsky and Charles Mitchell's *Pirro Ligorio's Roman Antiquities: The Drawings in Ms XIII. B7 in the National Library of Naples*, published by the Warburg Institute in 1963, had fascinated me with its effort to separate Roman antiquarians of the fifteenth and sixteenth centuries into schools and generations, He dismissed it, citing his friend Carlo Dionisotti's swingeing review in the *Rivista storica italiana*.[2] Roberto Weiss's *Renaissance Rediscovery of Classical Antiquity* (Oxford, 1969) had offered me what looked like a plausible model for laying out the varied pursuits of early modern antiquaries, a model that I thought I might be able to emulate in my own work. It had also tickled my fancy by emphasizing the creativity and impact of the mad but brilliant forger Annius of Viterbo, whose invented Berosus and Manetho Scaliger had denounced with enough passion to show they mattered to him. Weiss's work received an even more withering dismissal: it did not even deserve invective. Momigliano warned that this solid-seeming book represented 'an outsider's first look at an unknown thing.' The authors of what I had taken as standard works were, in short, described by Momigliano as no help for navigating the unpathed waters that I hoped to explore. Their works had little or nothing in common with his, in origin or in method.

This letter caused me some surprise. To a young American, reading in the bright new Regenstein Library in Chicago, Momigliano's essays of the 1940s and 1950s, especially 'Ancient History and the Antiquarian,' and the later books and articles that had emerged from the same Bloomsbury circles had looked like a collaborative study of the antiquarians' world. A number of the books Momigliano dismissed began life, like his article, as lectures at the Warburg Institute. In style and scale, as well as content, his essays made a natural sequel to the lectures by the Warburg's first director in England, Fritz Saxl – lectures that traced the early development of antiquarian thought in Rome and Venice, and its varied relations to politics, art, and architecture, as well as historical writing. Mitchell, Weiss, and others, who analysed at length the works of Biondo and other antiquaries, which Momigliano had mentioned but not investigated at length, seemed to me to have laid out the detailed implications of his work with great clarity and interest. Momigliano, however, saw the matter quite differently. He noted such massive differences of method and substance that he could advise me only to ignore the secondary literature, head for the British Library, and plunge in.[3]

The year's research that followed – and the many years of attendance at Momigliano's lectures and seminars in Chicago, Oxford, London, and elsewhere that followed it – took me down many strange paths. The Scaliger whose life and work I reconstructed did not, in the end, look much like the protagonists of Mitchell and Mandowsky or Weiss. Like Momigliano's antiquaries, he grappled with the problems of historical method that concerned them: how to work between texts and inscriptions, for example, and how to assess the credibility, or *fides*, of attractive but wild historians like Herodotus. Like them too, he saw some curious connections between the methods of the new science of Copernicus and that of his own new science of chronology. Momigliano had mapped the field of antiquarianism from a great height. His articles provided a schematic London Underground map of the early modern world of learning, rather than an Ordinance Survey map of its details. But his cartography took me where I needed to go. Today, it still does.

This essay records a first effort to return to Momigliano's studies of antiquarianism and historical method in early modern Europe, and ask some questions about them. How did Momigliano himself arrive at the particular vision of the historical tradition that he espoused in these works? And how did he devise the particular form of narrative that they exemplified? What did he bring with him from Italy? What did he learn from the new environments he inhabited in Oxford, Bristol, and London – those smoky cities, gloomy and, Oxford apart, cratered – where Momigliano remade himself as scholar and teacher? What, if anything, did the Warburg Institute have to do with Momigliano's vision of the historical tradition? And why did he insist so strongly on the isolation of his own work?

First, some elementary facts. The history of the historical tradition that Momigliano articulated in the 1940s and 1950s arrived not in battalions but in single spies. It took the form of a series of articles, most of which began as lectures. Many, but not all, of them appeared together in 1955 in Momigliano's *Contributo* and reappeared in his 1966 *Studies in Historiography*. A bold red paperback edition of this book made Momigliano's work accessible to my generation of scholars in the United States. For once, the market's choice of materials was sound. The central texts include, roughly in order of original composition:

'Friedrich Creuzer and Greek Historiography' (1944)
'The First Political Commentary on Tacitus' (ca 1947)
'Ancient History and the Antiquarian' (1949)
'George Grote and the Study of Greek History' (1952)
'Gibbon's Contribution to Historical Method' (1954)
'Perizonius, Niebuhr, and the Character of Early Roman Tradition' (ca 1957)
'The Place of Herodotus in the History of Historiography' (1957)
'Mabillon's Italian Disciples' (1958)
'Pagan and Christian Historiography in the Third Century AD' (1958–9).[4]

Naturally, the list is not comprehensive. By no means all of Momigliano's studies on the history of scholarship reached print in the 1960s – or ever.[5] He continued to trace the threads he had begun to follow in these pieces for many years to come – for example, in several of his Vico studies of the 1960s, in his articles on the afterlife of Polybius in the early 1970s, and in the articles on Jacob Bernays, Hermann Usener, and other German scholars of the nineteenth century that occupied him from the 1960s until his death. He also wove all the strands together early in the 1960s in his remarkable Sather Lectures, the impact of which the Berkeley anthropologist John Rowe and others have evoked, though the final text, meticulously edited by Riccardo Di Donato, appeared only after Momigliano's death.[6] Nonetheless, the works in this group are clearly linked by a certain style and by their scope, themes, and methods. Momigliano continued to refer to the arguments he advanced in them over the years, as exemplary. And they represented something new in the history of historical thought and scholarship, as Green made clear in his prescient review.

All these articles, to begin with, worked dialectically between the present – of classical studies – and their past. Momigliano set out, consciously, to reinvigorate the study of the ancient world by connecting it to intellectual history, of a particular kind. He formulated his plan in the programmatic article on Friedrich Creuzer: 'Ancient history has now become a provincial branch of history. It can recover its lost prestige only if it proves again capable of offering results affecting the whole of our historical outlook. One of the ways is, quite simply, to regain contact with those writers of the past who treated classical subjects of vital importance to history in general.'[7] Ancient history – and classical scholarship more generally – needed to develop a rich sense of what it had been, and what its professional and amateur students had been, if it hoped, in the dull world of the 1950s and 1960s, to have any sort of a future. Green put the point eloquently when he praised Momigliano for 'having crystallised both past achievement and the contemporary predicament.'

From the start, however, Momigliano hedged his invitation to new forms of scholarship with stern warnings. One of them I have already cited: he saw the central task of the historian of scholarship as recovering the turning points in the development of the field. The historian had to identify and concentrate on those individuals and works that had made the greatest impact, both on specialists in classical studies and on the wider intellectual world. Momigliano's approach, at this stage, was only incipiently sociological. True, he noted that medical men were disproportionately represented among the antiquaries of the seventeenth century. But he did not, as yet, pay much attention to the outward and visible forms of disciplines. In the 1980s, after years of exposure to Edward Shils and other social scientists at the Universities of London and Chicago, he would examine the establishment of institutes, chairs, and programs in pedagogy and research.[8] In these early years, however, he took individual lives as the framework of most of his inquiries. Momigliano's history of scholarship, in its earliest phase, was vulnerable to the charge of cherry-picking – and if charged, he would have pleaded guilty. He taught, by precept as well as example, that the history of scholarship could not become profound except by concerning itself with profound scholars.

A second warning, equally heavy with meaning for Momigliano, he uttered implicitly in these articles and explicitly in a number of book reviews. The history of ideas was flourishing, at least in the United States. Even in Britain – where, as Momigliano famously pointed out in 1977, to mention the word idea was to be given the address of the Warburg Institute – Isaiah Berlin, Herbert Butterfield, and others were doing influential work on the history of political thought and of science. Partly under their influence, a number of younger scholars had begun to turn their attention to the work of philologists and historians. Momigliano found this development not praiseworthy but repellent. 'There are now plenty of people,' he warned in an otherwise favourable *TLS* review of Elizabeth Armstrong's *Robert Estienne, Royal Printer*, 'who write about the history of historiography without ever having done a piece of plain historical research. There is also an increasing number of students (especially in America) who find it easier to write about the history of classical scholarship than about classical texts. The fact that Mrs. Armstrong is so outstandingly successful in breaking the rules of the game should not encourage the mass of D.Phil. candidates.'[9] Momigliano saw the history of tradition as the preserve of a small group of classicists with broad interests and training – scholars at home both in the ancient sources and the current scholarly literature on them, and in the earlier periods in which influential interpretations and methods had taken shape. As he noted in his 'Piedmontese View of the History of Ideas,' he had little contact at this point with historians of science, and he apparently took no interest in the models that Butterfield, Kuhn, Medawar, and others developed in the 1940s and 1950s for re-creating the intellectual and discursive worlds of technical disciplines, any more than he did in most scholarly institutions.[10] In practice, though, he agreed with many scientists' belief that they are better equipped than historians of science to understand the past of their field: 'It is a good rule that historians should be judged by historians, classical scholars by classical scholars.'[11]

Momigliano's history crystallized in a particular shape – or a particular set of shapes. Episodic in substance, it would also be episodic in form. From the start of his time in Britain – at the torturous point, in 1940 and after, when he was largely unknown and his English still fragmentary, and he was treated with patronizing superiority by some of those who meant most to him in the English academic world, such as Hugh Last and Eduard Fraenkel – Momigliano chose the lecture as his characteristic genre.[12] He would begin, either with a story ('The name of Professor Friedrich Creuzer of Heidelberg University is associated with two of the most typical episodes of the Romantic period'; 'It was about twenty-five years ago that the name of Gower Street first impressed itself on my mind') or with a broad claim ('We shall not ask of Gibbon new methods in the criticism of sources'; 'When I want to understand Italian history I catch a train and go to Ravenna').[13] Then he would move, anecdote by anecdote and text by text, through a winding chain of narrative. He envisioned a public of listeners and readers who could recognize a vast range of names and milieux, possessed a broad familiarity with Western intellectual history from antiquity forwards, and would not be not put off by long quotations in Latin. Though these texts were continuously enlivened by Momigliano's irony and wit, he confined his rare rhetorical flights – and rarer ventures into pathos – to his conclusions ('Those who have known [Rostovtzeff] have known greatness. They will always cherish the memory of a courageous and honest historian to whom civilization meant creative liberty').[14]

Most important, Momigliano devised a highly distinctive analytical method. At a time when Watson, Crick, Franklin, and other scientists in Cambridge and London arranged the basic material of life on what turned out to be double helices, Momigliano laid out the history of scholarship along strikingly similar sets of double axes, like sets of genetic possibilities that determined what history could become (he himself later joked about Margoliouth, the Oxford Arabist who was thought to believe 'in the existence of thirty Indo-European Ur-jokes from which all the others derived').[15] He organized the possible modes of historical writing at a given time into two sets of possibilities and practices, and saw revolution as what took place when individuals or groups combined these. Thus he distinguished, in his most famous essays, between

The study of epic poetry and that of history
Famous German historians and forgotten antiquaries
Philosophic and erudite historians
Narrators and collectors of documents
Political and intellectual historians.

The Schlegels, Heyne, and Creuzer wed the first two, Mommsen and other nineteenth-century scholars melded the second, Gibbon managed to merge the third, Eusebius – of all people – connected the fourth set, and Grote brought together the fifth. By contrast, the oppositions between certain other possibilities – like history based on oral and history based on written tradition – proved so durable that they persisted in modern scholarship. Some double helices could never become single. Peter Green revealed his insight again when he called attention to the 'dualisms' that recurred in Momigliano's articles. Indeed, sometimes these dualisms outlived their heuristic usefulness – as when Momigliano found it hard to accept H.J. Erasmus's demonstration, in his 1962 study *The Origins of Rome in Historiography from Petrarch to Perizonius,* that a number of historians had found it possible in the sixteenth century to combine their pursuits and methods with those of the antiquaries.[16]

One pair of categories proved especially vital. From the start – and long before Hayden White and others had begun the revival of rhetorical analysis that amused and exasperated Momigliano in the 1970s and 1980s – he saw style as central to the history of scholarship. The antiquaries' style of collection and argument, Gibbon's prose, Eusebius's willingness to interrupt his narratives of the early Church to quote extensive documents, Muret's Tacitism – all these choices mattered, to Momigliano, as much as their choices of subject matter, and he paid direct and constant attention to them throughout the early part of his career as historian of scholarship (it seems that the appearance of White and others drove him to take less interest in such questions in later years, when he insisted that the critical use of evidence, rather than the construction of narratives, formed the core of history).[17] The antiquaries' passion for classification led them to create systematic treatises and museums; Gibbon's drive to combine reflection on causes with reflection on sources enabled him to devise the unique narrative architecture of the *Decline and Fall* – a textual Covent Garden, in which screaming Cockney vendors of macaroons and lemonade scurried about in the shadow of splendid, ornate arches and arcades.

Momigliano's essays rested on precise and exacting study of a great many texts. But he rarely allowed the formal research he had done to peep above the waterline of his trim vessels. He did so chiefly in the essays he wrote for classical journals – especially the studies of Tacitism and Perizonius that appeared in the *Journal of Roman Studies*. Even there, detailed analysis remained more exemplary than comprehensive.[18] In the ninth volume of the *Journal of the Warburg and Courtauld Institutes*, dedicated to articles by Italian scholars, Momigliano's study of Creuzer stood out partly because it did not essay the kinds of detailed textual reading on which his fellow authors, Fausto Ghisalberti, Alessandro Perosa, and Augusto Campana, concentrated. Momigliano's style, in sum, was as distinctive as his arguments.

How then did the scholarship of Momigliano's middle period take shape?[19] It is always dangerous – as it was during Momigliano's lifetime – to suggest that he was not familiar at any given time with any given written work, from any period, or its context. He seems to have been born with an encompassing memory and a powerful interest in the history of scholarship. By the time he reached his mid-twenties, he began addressing himself to the origins and development of modern historiography. Early essays investigated the development of the notion of Hellenism, taking a special interest in Droysen's passage from the student of the Greek spirit to the analyst of Greek and Macedonian politics; the development of Roman Imperial history from Tillemont and Bossuet onwards; the work of Gibbon and of Creuzer; the letters of Boeckh.[20] Already, as one footnote made clear, he urged his students to carry out similar kinds of study – and, already he insisted, with his customary irony, on his own incompetence as a student of modern intellectual history.[21] Momigliano arrived in Britain, as these early essays show, steeped not only in the previous two centuries and more of historiography – as well as in the larger intellectual background of Hegel and Romanticism – but already convinced that ancient historians needed to carry on some sort of dialogue with their predecessors.

He also worried already about the tendency of specialists in the modern world to try to assess the work of past scholars who concentrated on antiquity. With characteristic acerbity, Momigliano noted in 1937 that Meinecke did not grasp 'Gibbon's contribution to the formation of a new European historiography' – an observation he would develop in a characteristically mordant footnote in his essay on Creuzer: 'It is perhaps evident that F. Meinecke, *Entstehung des Historismus*, 1936, though of great importance for the historiography of the 18th century, does not describe the "Entstehung des Historismus," which is to be found in historians and philologists whom Meinecke does not consider,' and in his lifelong criticism of Meinecke's brilliant pupil, his own contemporary Felix Gilbert.[22]

Yet most of these early essays have little in common, in structure or method, with Momigliano's later work (that of 1933 on Droysen is the most prominent exception). Offering extensive textual paraphrases and stuffed with quotations, both of which dropped out of his later work, they did not adumbrate the sharp, allusive, fact-packed piece on Creuzer and its successors. More to the point, they did not anticipate Momigliano's later arguments. Steeped in the German language that he already wrote fluently, Momigliano was also steeped in a German conceptual apparatus. He believed wholeheartedly, at this point, in the German historical revolution of the early nineteenth century. The young Momigliano knew the Enlightenment well – well enough to criticize Cassirer for his failure to engage with Jansenism in the chapter on history of his book on the Enlightenment.[23] But he had not begun to examine, in an intensive way, some of the pre-modern students of the ancient world who would engage him most in later years. As late as 1947, Momigliano confessed in a letter to Fritz Saxl, 'I have not yet had the leisure to study the Etruscheria and the Vico tradition of the XVIII century.'[24] And he did not, at this point, even suggest what would become a central thesis of his later work: that 'pre-critical' scholars had not only created the historical tradition, but forged many of the essential tools that modern, critical scholars still used. That may explain why he added a note, in the *Contributo*, to his early essay on Gibbon, remarking that the reader would find a 'corrective' for it in his later piece 'Gibbon's Contribution to Historical Method.'[25]

The shock of expulsion from Italy in 1938 and the softer blow of internment in England reshaped Momigliano's thinking about many things. So did the period he spent lecturing to a tiny public at Cambridge and his intense contacts with a small but select group of unusually cosmopolitan British scholars – Hugh Last, Beryl Smalley, Isobel Henderson, Iris Murdoch, all of them set loose in the midst of world war, to read in Oxford's libraries, and talk in an open-air cafeteria, where scholars could take subsidized meals for very little, in that strange, febrile atmosphere so well evoked in the memoir of Oxford University Press's publisher, Dan Davin.[26] And so did his visits to the Warburg Institute, where Italian scholarship and culture enjoyed a respect and affection that Oxford did not always accord them – and where Fritz Saxl held open house, and an open purse, for European exiles of every sort.

During these years Momigliano learned and changed in many ways, enjoying direct contact with the German philological and historical tradition, as represented by his fellow émigrés, and learning in slow stages the terrible truth about the extinction of Continental Europe's Jews, including his own parents. Momigliano's eventual biographer will have to sort out how, in this cosmopolitan world, the ferocious Italian patriot became a hater of all absolute ideologies – and a committed, if ironic, Zionist.

My interest here is much more limited. The one-time believer in the German historical revolution now devoted himself to showing that forgotten antiquaries and philologists had really laid 'the foundations of future historical method.' And the one-time specialist on Greek and Roman history became – as the title of his collected essays proclaimed – the pre-eminent historian of his own discipline. In devoting himself to the history of European scholarship, Momigliano responded to – and in some ways sought to fill – the deep fractures that exile had caused in the tradition he came from. At a very general level, one could compare his enterprise to those of other European exiles, from those he admired (notably Gershom Scholem, Felix Jacoby, and Rudolf Pfeiffer) to those he did not: an epic adventure in the collection of fragments. But how, in particular, did Momigliano's first British years shape, and stamp, his new scholarship?

Momigliano, after all, did not lack models as he began to use the history of scholarship to teach lessons of methodology. But none of the established ones served his need. Naturally, he could not use the old compendiums of Conrad Bursian and J.E. Sandys as anything more than sources of information. Nor did he have much use for general surveys of what the classical tradition had meant in the past. Momigliano described A. Bernardini and G. Righi's *Il concetto di filologia e di cultura classica nel mondo moderno* (1949) as sterile, because it dealt only with abstract programs for the study of the ancients, not with the concrete details of what scholars had done to texts and monuments. Exceptionally, for someone who never listened to his own advice for eager reviewers, 'The cheapest way to get a book is to buy it,' he did not review the massive work of the scholar he dismissed as the 'compilatorio Bolgar': *The Classical Heritage and Its Beneficiaries from the Carolingian Age to the End of the Renaissance* (1954).[27] M.L. Clarke's tight and parochial studies of English classical scholarship, though the work of a real Hellenist, said little about the scholarly practices of their protagonists. Even Mark Pattison's classical essays and his life of Isaac Casaubon, which Momigliano cited with evident respect, generally avoided technical questions in the history of scholarship.[28] And though Jacob Bernays eventually came to have an almost talismanic value for Momigliano, his biography of Joseph Scaliger does not seem to have played a central role in Momigliano's thought in this period.

Nor did Momigliano's practices resemble those of the Italian specialists on the history of humanistic scholarship whom he most admired. Between the end of the Second World War and the early 1960s, Carlo Dionisotti, Alessandro Perosa, Giuseppe Billanovich, and Sebastiano Timpanaro created new models for a sophisticated internal history of philological practices. They analysed the methods that Renaissance, Enlightenment, and nineteenth-century scholars had created for assessing and collating manuscripts, editing critical texts, and explicating difficult passages. And they did so in much the same tightly focused way in which historians of science like Otto Neugebauer had long analysed the procedures of early mathematicians and astronomers. Their rigorous, detailed historical studies of scholarship became central both for the *Journal of the Warburg and Courtauld Institutes*, which printed Billanovich's first substantial analysis of Petrarch's scholarship, and for Billanovich's own new journal, *Italia medioevale e umanistica*. Momigliano eagerly read everything these men wrote, and he engaged in a lifelong and continually fruitful dialogue with Dionisotti. But as a historian of scholarship he went his own way.[29]

Moreover, Momigliano distanced himself deliberately from other intellectual possibilities and resources accessible in his new environment. When he studied antiquarianism – as he certainly knew – he entered territory that well-known British scholars were actively exploring. His Bristol colleague David Douglas, for example, had won the James Tait Black prize for biography in 1939 for a book entitled *English Scholars, 1660–1730*. Douglas dealt at length, and eloquently, with the polymathic Non-juror antiquaries and their successors, the men and women who forged the scholarly tools still used by everyone concerned with the British Middle Ages. The Cambridge historian Herbert Butterfield touched on similar matters in *The Whig Interpretation of History* (London, 1951) and *The Englishman and His History* (Cambridge, 1944), and he was already working on the studies of German scholarship in the eighteenth and nineteenth centuries that would culminate with the publication of his Wiles Lectures, *Man on His Past: The Study of the History of Historical Scholarship* (Cambridge, 1955).[30] In 1950, just before Momigliano joined the staff of another great institution in Bloomsbury and just after he had completed the final draft of 'Ancient History and the Antiquarian,' T.D. Kendrick of the British Museum published his eloquent and witty *British Antiquity* (London, 1950) – the first full analysis in English of how Renaissance antiquaries reconstructed and debated the British past and the texts and monuments that preserved it.

Momigliano referred to this body of work, but only to treat it as basically irrelevant to the story he had told. The British antiquaries were chiefly concerned with the past of the British Isles. Most of them had studied medieval rather than ancient history, and accordingly they had not made a sharp distinction between history, seen as elegant narrative, and antiquarianism, seen as endless compilation. Kendrick's book stood out from the rest for its interest in the Latin scholarship of the humanists. It emerged – as Kendrick stated – from a wider study of European antiquarianism in the Renaissance, based on the vast resources of the British Museum Library. But Momigliano seems to have felt little affinity for Kendrick, and couched his only explicit reference to *British Antiquity* in the key of irony. After arguing that the primary documents available did not support the story that the king had named John Leland his official Antiquary, Momigliano noted 'with pleasure' that Kendrick had arrived at the same conclusion – but also pointed out that 'Mr Kendrick does not discuss the texts mentioned above.'[31] In these cases, Momigliano probably saw himself as standing with the Warburg, in favour of a historical tradition that took the study of ancient history as its core, and that connected Britain with the Mediterranean – and against the modern British scholars' tendency to treat their predecessors in isolation from Continental developments, and their reluctance to enter into detailed analysis and discussion of the sources. In his powerful emphasis on the ethics of the antiquary, who 'rescued history from the sceptics, even though he did not write it,' Momigliano treated the work of the early modern scholars as part of a great tradition, one that combined erudition with integrity and that the twentieth century had almost exterminated. Of the British scholars who worked on antiquarianism, only David Duncan shared something of his interest in this dimension of past scholarship.

The decision to take this stand limited Momigliano's work in certain ways. Kendrick showed that the antiquaries' turn to material evidence did not by any means put an end to controversy or shore up the credibility of history. They regularly disagreed – in fact, they regularly flailed one another mercilessly – about what they had seen in a given church or castle and what it meant. Their disagreements showed that no drawing, woodcut, or engraving could perfectly reproduce the style and content of a site. The conventions of the artist, the assumptions of his scholarly informant, and the simple liability of humans to interpret when they mean to reproduce an object or a text all hung between the scholars and the monuments like a scrim, which no form of lighting could make transparent. For all Momigliano's belief that the study of material remains had been intimately connected with the resolution of history's sceptical crisis, he did not pursue these problems. In the end, he left the creation of a fuller and more detailed panorama of early modern antiquarianism to Francis Haskell, whose learned, depressing *History and Its Images: Art and the Interpretation of the Past* (New Haven and London, 1991) praised Momigliano even as it subverted parts of his work.

In both form and content, Momigliano's works stood out sharply from those of his contemporaries. First of all, there was his commitment to the lecture – and, in consequence, to the biography and the episode, as the central genre of history of scholarship.[32] Here the Warburg Institute certainly played a role, and not only in the sense, obvious from 'Ancient History and the Antiquarian,' that it provided him with a magnificent body of primary and secondary literature, available in the open stacks – an accessible source base that had no parallel on the Continent. Since the 1920s, when Saxl and Warburg made the original Hamburg library into a new kind of intellectual institution, lectures had played a central role in its life. They served as the occasions for polyglot international meetings and discussions; they yielded articles and monographs for the library's publication series; and they gave its programs of research and publication a unique form, one that united the concrete with the conceptual.[33] Warburg scholars analysed specific texts and images in order to reveal the intellectual and emotional orders that underlay them, and visitors rapidly absorbed their method – as Ernst Cassirer notoriously found himself doing, almost involuntarily, in his Hamburg years. Momigliano joined eagerly in the library's yearly lecture series, organizing one of them and participating in others. And he regularly highlighted the role that discussion with an international circle had played in his work, in footnotes that confessed his intellectual debts.[34] The contemplative, systematic, and argumentative thinker of the 1930s transformed himself, in these new circumstances, into an eager and intensive conversationalist as well as a more concrete and powerful writer. The Momigliano who loved to learn from others' lectures – even as he read books during them – seems to have been born in the Imperial Institute, then the Warburg's London home.[35]

In concentrating on lectures that explored dualities and contrasts, moreover, Momigliano adopted one of the Warburg Institute's house styles. From the 1930s onwards, Panofsky and Saxl began to formulate some of the Warburg scholars' major findings about the classical tradition for an English-speaking public. They found themselves at once impoverished and stimulated. Bereft of the precise but abstract German vocabulary in which they had learned to write, they had to address a public far less knowledgable and specialized than the German one – sometimes, indeed, one that included what Panofsky called 'Chinchilla-Damen,' who found his lectures as painful to listen to as the Wagner they squirmed through in his presence at the Metropolitan Opera House.[36] Yet they continued to pose and answer complex historical questions, and to insist even in their new environment on the close connections between scholarship on the one hand, art, politics, and letters on the other. They too used dualisms as narrative armatures, following Warburg – and simplifying him – as they devised sharp dilemmatic ways to present the possibilities of expression within the classical tradition. Panofsky and Saxl, for example, formulated the principle of disjunction – according to which classical form was severed from classical content in medieval art and reunited with it in the Renaissance – to make the Warburg tradition of research on the classical tradition accessible and coherent to audiences in New York, Princeton, Philadelphia, and London. Panofsky, in fact, generalized the principle, treating it as the core of Rennaissance culture. They too, moreover, told stories – often ones familiar to a German or European public but virtually unknown in English – and drew implicit morals from them.[37]

The Warburg Institute, finally, stood for a particular approach to the classical tradition – one that applied all the tools forged by the German philologists of the nineteenth and twentieth centuries, but that emphasized continuities rather than breaks. Well before Momigliano began to write for the *Warburg Journal*, it had published what became classical studies by Fritz Saxl, on the ways in which Renaissance scholars and artists had interpreted classical inscriptions and rituals, and by Rudolf Wittkower, on the millennial tradition in Western ethnographic writing that placed monstrous races of Cynocephali and Sciapods on the edge of human habitation, in India.[38] No wonder, then, that Saxl reacted with such delight to Momigliano's essay on Creuzer. He liked it precisely because he knew the traditional accounts, and he saw its value at once: 'It is a very unexpected contribution. I had no idea of Creuzer's importance in this respect.' Yates, in the same way, immediately recognized the

greatness of 'Ancient History and the Antiquarian': 'The article is magnificent – a most deep and rich and at the same time polished and
elegant piece of scholarship.'[39] The Warburg circle was one of the few
groups of scholars – if not the only one – in a position to appreciate and
welcome the novelty of Momigliano's approach to the history of scholarship, and the revisionist character of many of his findings.

The new path that Momigliano would follow looked clear enough to
him, by the late 1940s, when he announced, at a 'traumatic meeting'
with Dan Davin of Oxford University Press, 'that he had found a new
theme for research, to which he intended to devote himself – the history
of historiography.'[40] In fact, however, his decision to devote himself to
this new field – and the form his devotion took – had a certain element
of contingency. Momigliano's early dealings with the Warburg Institute,
and his exchanges with Saxl, Yates, and Bing, helped him to find his
intellectual and even his stylistic way. The documents that record these
discussions also make clear how early he decided not to follow certain
paths as a scholar – a decision vital to understanding the nature of his
enterprise as a whole.

Saxl, as Oswyn Murray has shown, first brought Momigliano into
contact with the Warburg Institute in the 1930s, and Momigliano submitted his article on the Ara Pacis to the *Journal* in 1942. Wittkower, after
taking some time to read the manuscript, accepted it with enthusiasm,
and it appeared in the same year. But it was the Institute's subsequent
decision to produce 'a volume of the *Journal* which will consist entirely of
contributions from our Italian friends,' in the hope of rebuilding intellectual relations between the two countries, that set Momigliano on what
became his definitive way. As early as July 1945, Wittkower asked him to
contribute to this project.[41] Momigliano agreed with alacrity, offering
either a paper 'on the study of Roman history during the Risorgimento'
in Italy or one on a classical topic.[42] Wittkower, expecting the volume to
'have a strong Renaissance bias,' preferred the piece on the Risorgimento,
which he thought might serve as a good coda.[43] Again and again, through
1945, 1946, and early 1947, Wittkower and Yates pressed Momigliano to
deliver his article.[44] Answer came there none. Finally, on 20 March 1947,
a higher authority intervened. Saxl made a direct appeal to his laggard
author. The Italian manuscripts had now 'come in,' he wrote, 'and they
make quite a good number, but there is very little of outstanding merit.'
A piece by Momigliano would raise the quality of the whole enterprise.
Without one, Saxl feared, 'it will not serve the purpose, which so many
people have tried to achieve.'[45]

Momigliano could not resist this entreaty, but he professed his doubts about what exactly he should contribute to the *Journal*. For some time he had been badly overworked, since he was both 'lecturing and tutoring like an ordinary don (though not paid like an ordinary don!)' and trying to complete two books. These primary occupations had left him little time for articles. At this point, moreover, he simply did not know enough about Vico and the eighteenth century to produce a solid piece on the Risorgimento. His work on Tacitism in Spain, France, Italy, and England, though more advanced, had stalled temporarily, until he could study manuscripts in England and Spain and clear up a number of bibliographical and textual puzzles. But he did have one old paper on a somewhat unexpected theme that he thought might serve Saxl's purposes, when revised: 'I have looked also among my mss to see whether there is anything there which I could bring together for the Journal. Two or three years ago, I wrote a paper on the pre-symbolistic phase of Creuzer – when he founded the modern study of Greek historiography. What I wrote is perhaps not unimportant, but must be re-written, because style and disposition are faulty. Besides, the subject is not Italian. If you want to see the ms, I am always happy to discuss a point with you. But you will concur with me about the necessity of re-writing it.'[46] Saxl invited him to submit the manuscript, and Momigliano duly did so, in a fair copy that he wrote himself, since he had failed to find a typist. He was still uncertain that he had done enough research, or that the work deserved publication as it stood: 'I may say that I feel that I ought to expand the introductory remarks of #2 [#3 of the paper as published]. For obvious reasons German philology and historiography of the XVIIIth century is practically non-existing in Oxford, and I never had the leisure to complete my research in the B.M. Another spell of good sleep will do no harm to my old friend Creuzer. So it does really not matter if you cannot utilize my paper in its present form.' In the event, Saxl accepted the article on 1 May, with enthusiasm.[47]

But he also asked Momigliano to provide it with a different kind of lead-in. Evidently, the first section of the paper, as Momigliano submitted it, was the second section of the paper as printed. This begins 'Friedrich Creuzer's *Historische Kunst der Griechen in ihrer Entstehung und Fortbildung* is now read in the second edition of 1845 ...'[48] Saxl found this plunging *in medias res* a bit forbidding and mysterious, at least for the *Journal*'s local readership, and urged a change:

There is one thing which I feel about it. The number of English people who know the name of Creuzer is, I suppose, very small, and if they know him they know him with regard to theories of mythology. You will remember that you begin the article by saying 'We are used to reading Creuzer in the second edition', and I wonder how this sounds to English ears because hardly anybody reads Creuzer either in the first or the second edition. So what I would suggest is that we type the manuscript out as it stands and have it printed. But there ought to be an introduction giving some indication of Creuzer's work to those who are quite unfamiliar with this part of German philology. I do not expect that this would give you much trouble, but I think it will help readers towards a better appreciation of the article.[49]

Momigliano saw Saxl's point. On 11 May he replied, enclosing a new introduction – section 1 of the paper, as it finally appeared. He declined to say anything about Creuzer's most famous work, his study of ancient mythology: 'I should not like to have to say much more on his *Symbolik* at the present, because I have been collecting materials for the history of mythological studies for many years. When I come to it, I must do it in full.' But he began the paper with a story that would grab any reader's attention – that of Caroline von Günderode, who committed suicide out of unrequited love for Creuzer, despite his notorious ugliness. He briefly described some of Creuzer's accomplishments as a scholar. And in a second lapidary paragraph, quoted in part above, he made clear that he now saw the study of the history of scholarship as a way to renew the study of antiquity itself. It was in this indirect and partly collaborative way that Momigliano created what would become the distinctive intellectual style of his middle period.[50]

The story of Momigliano's contacts with the Warburg did not, of course, end here, and it sheds a new light on the limits, as well as the origins, of the historigorophical studies that preoccupied him in this period. At 5:30 p.m. on Monday, 10 January 1949, Momigliano gave a lecture at the Institute, 'Ancient History and the Antiquarian.' His ensuing discussions with the members of the Warburg delighted him, and he submitted a revised and enlarged text of the lecture to the *Journal* at the end of 1949, to Frances Yates's great pleasure.[51] The correspondence that ensued, which lasted through 1950, shows two great scholars in their prime.[52] Only a reader with a heart of stone could fail to enjoy the lesson on copy preparation that Yates offered her brilliant author, in the hope that he would write often for the *Journal*,[53] or to be amused by Momigliano's description of his heroic efforts to verify his references,[54] or to savour his assessment, in a letter to Yates, of the 1950 Paris Congress on Historical Studies: 'The atmosphere was very pleasant, and the hosts were charming. But the present decline in historical research was made only too obvious. I felt like writing a ballade des historiens du temps jadis.'[55]

The correspondence went well beyond editorial details and witty travel notes. Yates recognized that Momigliano's story posed a challenge to traditional versions of the origins of art history, and urged him to follow it through into the eighteenth and nineteenth centuries: 'I very much hope you will find time one day to continue this fascinating story right into the 19th century when, if I understand it rightly, the Hegelians come into it in Germany and begin to claim that the Spirit of the Age can be deduced most safely from visual documents. Does not this development start already with Winckelmann?'[56] Momigliano, who always insisted on his amateur status as a student of monuments, did not take up this challenge, leaving it to Francis Haskell, Thomas Kaufmann, and others to do so two generations later.[57] This seems a pity – especially as Momigliano, in the years to come, would read and think intensively about the intellectual filiation between Jacob Burckhardt's form of cultural history and Aby Warburg's version of art history.[58] Yates's query revealed an acute sense of one of the ways in which Momigliano's story needed – and needs – to be filled in.

Another of Yates's editorial letters asked formally for a small but meaningful revision. Momigliano, in his discussion of the antiquaries and the history of ancient religions, noted – a little ironically – that Athanasius Kircher, S.J., had found 'even the Trinity' in Egypt. Yates, in a long, learned, and deeply intelligent letter, pointed out that efforts of this kind long preceded Kircher. The Neoplatonists of the fifteenth and sixteenth centuries had taken a serious interest in 'exotic religions,' even though they knew less about them than did the polymaths of the age of Kircher and Witsius, and a full study of these studies in comparative religion would have to trace their growth over several centuries.[59] Momigliano found what Yates called an 'admirable' solution for the specific problem to which she called attention.[60] He reformulated the sentence in question to read 'The Jesuit A. Kircher satisfied himself that the *Mensa Isiaca* provided evidence for an Egyptian belief in the Trinity (1652).'[61] But though he did further work on 'the discussions of the XVIII century in Italy and France between antiquarians and theologians,'[62] he did not take up the larger challenge Yates offered – that of making clear, in precise terms, exactly how the highly technical work of the seventeenth-century antiquaries differed from, and how far it grew from, the less professionalized studies of the fifteenth- and sixteenth-century humanists. Only in the last decade have Ingo Herklotz, in

Cassiano dal Pozzo und die Archäologie des 17. Jahrjunderts (Munich, 1999), and other scholars begun to pose this question systematically once again. One must regret that Momigliano did not return to these problems at greater length, as Yates clearly hoped he would. But this decision – like his early one not to write on the history of archaeology and art history – is entirely understandable, in the light of the way he came to these subjects. Momigliano did not see himself as a member of the Warburg Institute, though he joined its committee of management, constantly advised on appointments and fellowships, worked closely with its students and younger staff, and held his own celebrated seminars there. Rather, he was, as he had always been, a professor of ancient history, who hoped that his own field could regain the richness and cultural standing it had once enjoyed by returning to selected moments in its own tradition. The Warburg offered him a way to publish these investigations, and its members helped him find an idiom in which to couch them, so effectively that scholars in a great many fields seized upon them and made them into classics. But Momigliano never meant his work to amount to a survey of the historical tradition.

In recent years, younger scholars have begun to fill in the empty spaces and amend the contours of Momigliano's great map of the historical tradition. They have begun to criticize not only the details of his work, but also, to some extent, his larger methods.[63] It seems only appropriate, then, to raise the sorts of question that Momigliano himself would have asked first about a predecessor whom he took seriously enough to argue with: to ask, that is, how Momigliano himself came to his subject, and to set his published work into its biographical and intellectual contexts. By doing so, we can learn what chances of renewal a great scholar's masterpieces may hold for the dull, provincial scholarship of our own sad time. More particularly, we can also see that Momigliano came to the history of scholarship at a particular moment and in a particular context. He regarded his salient contributions to the history of classical studies not as parts of a general survey of the historical tradition, but more modestly as 'works on historical method' aimed at fellow practitioners of his own field.[64] Wide and deep though his knowledge of historiography was, he resisted many temptations, and some well-informed invitations, to invade fields outside his own. Criticism of Momigliano's work – and nothing could be more in his spirit than criticism, whether based on a renewed close reading of the sources he used or on wider research – can hit the mark only if it takes account, as he would have, of what the record shows.

Appendix 1: Frances Yates to Arnaldo Momigliano, 9 October 1950

Warburg Institute Archive, Journal Correspondence, typescript. Momigliano's reply is not in the archive. But Yates's letter to him of 10 November 1950, accepting his revision of the sentence on Kircher, indicates some of its contents (and reveals Momigliano's characteristic alertness to new publications of interest): 'I must read the book by Schwab [*La Renaissance Orientale* (Paris, 1950)], which you mention, which sounds most important. It certainly would be a splendid idea if we could one day have a Warburg symposium on the lines you suggest. I will mention it to the Director.' See also the letter from Momigliano to Yates printed as Appendix 2 below.

Dear Professor Momigliano,

Thank you for your letters which have been unanswered for so long because I was in Italy, whence I have just returned, and where I had – of course – a wonderful time. I am very sorry to hear of your fall, and hope that you are by now quite recovered from it. You seem to have got through a great deal of work in spite of it. I am very interested to hear that you have collected material on eighteenth century controversies between antiquarians and theologians – certainly a rich field waiting to be worked.

The various corrections to your article which you mention can certainly all be worked into the page proofs, and the point which I wanted to discuss with you would only involve a tiny adjustment somewhere about p. 309 – that is if you consented to make it.

When you say (p. 309) that Kircher found 'even the Trinity in Egypt' perhaps it could be indicated that this is a sixteenth century tradition (Gyraldi, Ficino, Tyard etc.). You have indeed guarded yourself by mentioning in the next sentence that there was 'nothing unusual or unorthodox in the view that some pagans had known the truth', but even so one is rather left with the impression that Kircher invented the 'Trinity in Egypt' idea.

It seemed to me, when trying to wrestle a little with this subject when reading for my *French Academies*, that the sixteenth century had – though in a vague way – the principles of comparative religion and had no fear of including any number of exotic religions into its scheme, though the *knowl-edge* of such religions which it possessed was often limited to remarks in Plutarch, or the Fathers. See for example the insistence in the sixteenth century on the truth that God is light being known to the Brahmans (quoted in my *French Academies*, p. 90) which seems to have rested on a remark in Origen. I have wondered whether, when increased knowledge of oriental religions came into the possession of scholars in the seventeenth and eighteenth centuries, the first step in their minds (so to speak) may not have been to fit their new discoveries into the framework already provided by the sixteenth century syncretistic tradition. Perhaps one could follow such a process by taking one line – for example Zoroastrianism – and tracing it through from the vague enthusiasms of Ficino and disciples for the 'wise Magi' to Anquetil Du Perron. Academic debates might well provide a major source for such a study.

That the Deists seize on comparative religion as a weapon had also, of course, a pre-history. Toland derives from Giordano Bruno, who in turn derives – with only a very slightly bolder twist – from Ficino – Pico. Was it only after the Council of Trent that comparative religion began to become a badge of revolt?

But you are only touching on comparative religion in your amazingly rich and inspiring article. Please forgive this long letter, the only practical point in which is to suggest that some tiny modification of the sentence on Kircher and the Trinity on p. 309 might be made.

Yours very sincerely,

Appendix 2: Arnaldo Momigliano to Frances Yates, 20 March 1951

Warburg Institute Archive, Correspondence of Frances Yates, manuscript. Written on the occasion of the death of Frances Yates's sister Hannah, this letter also sheds light on the development of his studies in the history of scholarship. The interest in Yates's own work and in Renaissance studies more generally that appears here is documented elsewhere in the correspondence as well: for example, Momigliano to Yates, 6 April 1950, and Yates to Momigliano, 18 April 1950, Warburg Institute Archive, Journal Correspondence.

Dear Miss Yates,

I was very sorry to hear that your sister and companion died. Rubinstein who was here last week told me that you were having great anxieties. Though you are fortunate in being able to put so much of yourself into your work, there is unfortunately no remedy for personal losses. I hope you will find it possible to carry on your research on the Italian Academies which looked so promising. I was thinking of you while reading in the essay on G. Naudé by Sainte-Beuve that he gives a list of the Italian Academies in his *Mascurat*.

I am still ruminating antiquaries in my free moments and hope to elaborate into an article a paper on Gibbon which I have lately read to a 'classical' audience in Reading. But it will of course take much time.

I wonder whether a review-copy of Liebeschütz's John of Salisbury would be available for the Rivista Storica Italiana. The medieval section of it is edited by my colleague Giorgio FALCO, Facoltà di lettere, Università, via Carlo Alberto, Torino, to whom any communication should be addressed. I read the book with great interest in the copy so charmingly presented to me by the author, and I should like to see the book noticed and discussed by my Italian friends who are qualified to do so.

Yours very sincerely,
Arnaldo Momigliano

Notes

This essay develops arguments put forward much more briefly in Grafton, 'Arnaldo Momigliano e la storia degli studi classici,' *Rivista storica italiana* 107 (1995): 91–109, at 106–9, and 'Einleitung,' in Arnaldo Momigliano, *Ausgewählte Schriften zur Geschichte und Geschichtsschreibung*, vol. 2, *Spätantike bis Spätaufklärung*, ed. Grafton, trans. Kai Brodersen and Andreas Wittenburg (Weimar and Stuttgart, 1999), vii–xx. My thanks to Michael Crawford, Carlotta Dionisotti, Joseph Levine, Christopher Ligota, Anne Marie Meyer, Glenn Most, Wilfried Nippel, Joanna Weinberg, and, above all, Peter Miller for many years of conversation on the topics discussed here; to J.B. Trapp for a critical reading of an earlier draft and for the letter from Yates to Momigliano that appears in appendix 1; and to Dorothea McEwan and her colleagues in the Warburg Institute archive, Susanne Meurer and Claudia Wedepohl, who enabled me to use the documents discussed here in the most pleasant imaginable working conditions. Finally, my thanks to the members of the New York Seminar in Intellectual History, especially Samuel Moyn, Jerrold Seigel, and Will Stenhouse, who discussed the paper with me, to my great profit.

1 Peter Green, 'Ancient History and Modern Historians,' *Times Literary Supplement* [*TLS*], 22 July 1955, p. 412. In what follows, references to secondary sources have been kept to a minimum.

2 Carlo Dionisotti, review of Mandowsky and Mitchell, *Pirro Ligorio's Roman Antiquities, Rivista storica italiana* 75 (1963): 890–901. Dionisotti's critique, though characteristically erudite and pointed, was overstated. Mitchell's introduction to this work offered a stimulating survey that retains some value even now.

3 For a more detailed account of this meeting and its consequences, see Grafton, 'Arnaldo Momigliano: A Pupil's Notes,' *American Scholar* (Spring 1991): 235–41.

4 For these articles, see Momigliano, *Contributo alla storia degli studi classici* (Rome, 1955), 233–48, 37–54, 67–106, 213–31, 195–211; *Essays in Ancient and Modern Historiography* (Oxford, 1977), 231–51; *Studies in Historiography* (New York, 1966), 127–42; *Essays in Ancient and Modern Historiography*, 277–93, 107–26.

5 Thus, on 3 November 1947, Momigliano wrote to Gaetano De Sanctis, while riding a train from Bristol to Oxford, that 'oggi pomeriggio devo far lezione a Oxford per un corso di Storia dell'Umanesimo italiano, in cui siamo Dionisotti, io e altri'; so far as I know he did not publish this text. The note-books that he kept during his time in Bristol, 1948–51, include 'un riassunto del saggio sull'antiquaria' in Italian. See Riccardo Di Donato, 'Materiali per una biografia intellettuale di Arnaldo Momigliano. 2. Tra Napoli e Bristol,' *Athenaeum* 86 (1998): 231–44, at 241 n40.

6 Momigliano, *The Classical Foundations of Modern Historiography*, ed. Riccardo Di Donato (Berkeley, 1990). Cf. John Rowe, 'Ethnography and Ethnology in the Sixteenth Century,' *The Kroeber Anthropological Society Papers* 30 (1964): 1–19.

7 Momigliano, *Contributo*, 234.

8 See, for example, Momigliano, 'History in an Age of Ideologies [1982],' in *Settimo contributo alla storia degli studi classici e del mondo antico* (Rome, 1984), 253–69; and 'The Introduction of History as an Academic Subject and Its Implications [1985],' in *Ottavo contributo alla storia degli studi classici e del mondo antico* (Rome, 1987), 161–78. Cf. the wonderful passage on Harnack and Estienne in Momigliano, review of Elizabeth Armstrong, *Robert Estienne, Royal Printer: An Historical Study of the Elder Stephanus, TLS*, 25 February 1955, p. 124: 'It requires a great deal of worldly wisdom to get things done by other people.' Of course, Momigliano referred occasionally to such institutions as the Italian academies in his early work, and his lecture on Mabillon's Italian disciples, delivered in 1958 but not published until 1966, showed a profound understanding of the Maurists' world of learning as well as of the rather different ones that flourished in the Italy of Bacchini and Muratori.

9 Momigliano, review of Armstrong, *Robert Estienne, Royal Printer*. Note also the remarks that led up to these: 'No criticism of Mrs. Armstrong is implied if it

is observed that, being neither a classical nor a biblical scholar, she is less effective in assessing Robert Estienne's contribution to scholarship. She probably never intended to provide a complete assessment ... She has prepared the way for any future study of Robert Estienne as a biblical and classical scholar. But a warning should be added even if it may seem pretentious.' See also his review of A. Bernardini and G. Righi, *Il concetto di filologia e di cultura classica nel mondo moderno* (1949), in *Contributo*, 393–5; his review of Domenico Maffei, *Alessandro d'Alessandro giureconsulto umanista (1461–1523)* and *Gli inizi dell'umanesimo giuridico* (1957), in *Secondo contributo alla storia degli studi classici* (Rome, 1960), 418–21; and his review of Jürgen von Stackelberg, *Tacitus in der Romania* (1963), in *Terzo contributo alla storia degli studi classici e del mondo antico* (Rome, 1966), vol. 2, pp. 775–6. These concerns still inspired his later series of Pisan seminars on the history of historiography, on which see Giuseppe Cambiano, 'Momigliano e i seminari pisani di storia della storiografia,' *Storia della storiografia* 16 (1989): 75–83.

10 Cf. Momigliano, *Essays*, 6–7: 'When I became a professor at University College London more than twenty years ago, it did not take me long to realize that the best historians of ideas in the place were two practising scientists, J.Z. Young and Peter Medawar. But the fact that they talked about sciences I did not know not only paralyzed me in regard to them (which is easy to understand) but also paralyzed them in regard to me or anybody else in my position. That is, they lacked the potential public necessary for developing their scientific ideas in an historical context.' In fact, this was no longer true of Medawar, at least, by the 1960s.

11 Momigliano, review of Armstrong, *Robert Estienne, Royal Printer.*

12 For Momigliano's reception in England and the impact of his teaching, see Carlo Dionisotti, *Ricordo di Arnaldo Momigliano* (Bologna, 1989); Peter Brown, 'Arnaldo Dante Momigliano,' *Proceedings of the British Academy* 74 (1988): 405–42; Oswyn Murray, 'Momigliano e la cultura inglese,' *Rivista storica italiana* (1988): 422–39, revised as 'Arnaldo Momigliano in England,' in *The Presence of the Historian: Essays in Memory of Arnaldo Momigliano*, ed. Michael Steinberg, *History and Theory* Beiheft 30 (1991): 49–64; and Michael Crawford, 'L'insegnamento di Arnaldo Momigliano in Gran Bretagna,' in *Omaggio ad Arnaldo Momigliano: storia e storiografia del mondo antico*, ed. Lellia Cracco Ruggini (Como, 1989), 27–41.

13 Momigliano, *Contributo*, 233, 213, 195; *Secondo contributo*, 191.

14 Momigliano, *Contributo*, 354.

15 Momigliano, *Essays*, 6.

16 Momigliano, *Terzo contributo*, vol. 2, pp. 769–74. More than one reviewer of *The Classical Foundations of Modern Historiography* called attention to the dualistic schemes that persisted there: see the review essays by David

Konstan (*History and Theory* 31 [1992]: 224–30) and Ernst Breisach (*Clio* 23 [1993]: 81–91). In later years – after he had laid down the durable foundations of his work on historiography – Momigliano showed a liking for triangular schemas. See, for example, Momigliano, 'History between Medicine and Rhetoric [1985],' in *Ottavo contributo*, 13–25. But dualistic schemas persisted as well.

17 The locus classicus is Momigliano, 'The Rhetoric of History and the History of Rhetoric: On Hayden White's Tropes [1981],' in *Settimo contributo*, 49–59.

18 I have not seen the volume by Momigliano on Seneca and Tacitus, eventually rejected by Oxford University Press, described by Riccardo Di Donato, 'Materiali per una biografia intellettuale di Arnaldo Momigliano,' *Athenaeum* 83 (1995): 213–44, at 242.

19 For the general development of Momigliano's work in this field, and its context, see Karl Christ, 'Arnaldo Momigliano and the History of Historiography,' in *The Presence of the Historian*, ed. Steinberg (n12 above), pp. 5–12. A more detailed chronology is offered by Di Donato, 'Materiali' (nn 5, 18 above)

20 Momigliano, *Contributo*, 263–74, 165–94, 107–64, 379–82.

21 Ibid., 165 n1. Momigliano's letter to D.M. Pippidi of 24 December 1933 shows him mastering these materials, with his customary speed: 'E stato per me un periodo molto interessante quello che ho potuto dedicare alla lettura del pensiero dei proto-romantici (Humboldt, Wolf, Niebuhr, Boeckh etc.) che mi hanno precisato la radice del pensiero del mio Altvater Droysen (non vorrei però danneggiare presso di Lei la "purezza" di Droysen dandogli dei discendenti semitici!).' Published in Momigliano, 'L'epistolario con D.M. Pippidi,' *Storia della storiografia* 16 (1989): 15–33, at 17–18, and quoted by Di Donato, 'Materiali' (n18 above) 220.

22 Momigliano, *Contributo*, 380, 245 n32; *Essays*, 312.

23 Momigliano, *Contributo*, 112–13.

24 Momigliano to Saxl, 24 March 1947, Warburg Institute Archive, Journal Correspondence.

25 Momigliano, *Contributo*, 379 n*.

26 See especially Murray, 'Arnaldo Momigliano in England'; and Dan Davin, *Closing Times* (London and New York, 1975). For the role possibly played by Davin in the rejection of Momigliano's book on Tacitus by Oxford University Press, see Di Donato, 'Materiali' (n18 above), 242.

27 See Momigliano, review of R.M. Ogilvie, *Latin and Greek* (1964), in *Quarto contributo alla storia degli studi classici e del mondo antico* (Rome, 1969), 657 (itself in some ways a curious document). Perhaps he felt that his friend Dionisotti had said what needed to be said in 'Tradizione classica e

volgarizzamenti,' *Italia medioevale e umanistica* 1 (1958): 427–31, repr. with an additional note and a massive further study of the general topic in Carlo Dionisotti, *Geografia e storia della letteratura italiana* (Turin, 1967), 103–44 (for Bolgar, see 103–9).

28 Cf. Grafton, 'Mark Pattison,' *American Scholar* (1983).

29 See Sebastiano Timpanaro, *The Genesis of Lachmann's Method*, ed. and trans. Glenn Most (Chicago, 2005), especially Most's 'Introduction,' 20–2.

30 On Butterfield, see, most recently, Nick Jardine, 'Whigs and Stories: Herbert Butterfield and the Historiography of Science,' *History of Science* 41 (2003): 125–40.

31 Momigliano, *Contributo*, 104 n61. For Momigliano's reading of Kendrick, see his letter to Frances Yates, 17 September 1950, Warburg Institute Archives, Journal Correspondence: 'I have also to add at least one reference to T.D. Kendrick, *British Antiquity* – just appeared – in connection with Leland's title Antiquarius.'

32 For Momigliano's gradual decision after the Second World War to abandon the monograph for the public lecture, and its relation to his new environment, see especially Carlo Dionisotti, 'Commemorazione di Arnaldo Momigliano,' *Rivista storica italiana* 100 (1988): 348–60, at 356–7; and *Ricordo di Arnaldo Momigliano*, 21.

33 See Giorgio Pasquali's essay of 1930, 'Aby Warburg,' in *Pagine stravaganti di un filologo*, 2 vols, ed. Carlo Ferdinando Russo (Florence, 1994), vol. 1, pp. 40–54, at 40.

34 Momigliano's acknowledgments, unlike most people's, were anything but routine, and normally reflected actual discussions. In 'Ancient History and the Antiquarian,' for example, he thanked Felix Jacoby and Carlo Dionisotti, among others, for their help. In fact, he had asked Jacoby 'to read the first pages on the Greeks' in the spring of 1950 (Momigliano to Yates, 6 April 1950, Warburg Institute Archive, Journal Correspondence), and in the fall he wrote to Frances Yates, 'Personally I have finished with the page proofs, but I should like them to be seen by Dionisotti, whose keen eyes will certainly catch flaws' (Momigliano to Yates, undated but after 21 September 1950, Warburg Institute Archive, Journal Correspondence).

35 On Momigliano's Warburg Institute seminar, see the fine characterization in Crawford, 'L'insegnamento,' 28–9.

36 Panofsky to Gertrud Bing, 3 March 1935, in Erwin Panofsky, *Korrespondenz*, vol. 1, ed. Dieter Wuttke (Wiesbaden, 2001), 812–13.

37 See especially Fritz Saxl, *Lectures*, 2 vols (London, 1957); and Erwin Panofsky and Saxl, 'Classical Mythology in Mediaeval Art,' *Metropolitan Museum Studies* 4 (1932–3): 228–80.

38 Fritz Saxl, 'The Classical Inscription in Renaissance Art and Politics,' *Journal of the Warburg and Courtauld Institutes* 4 (1941): 18–46; Rudolf Wittkower, 'Marvels of the East: A Study of the History of Monsters,' *Journal of the Warburg and Courtauld Institutes* 5 (1942): 159–97.

39 Saxl to Momigliano, 1 May 1947; Yates to Momigliano, 4 January 1950, Warburg Institute Archive, Journal Correspondence.

40 Murray, 'Arnaldo Momigliano in England,' 53–4.

41 Wittkower to Momigliano, 6 July 1945, Warburg Institute Archive, Journal Correspondence (including the description of the project quoted in the previous sentence).

42 Momigliano to Wittkower, 22 July 1945, Warburg Institute Archive, Journal Correspondence.

43 Wittkower to Momigliano, 26 July 1945, Warburg Institute Archive, Journal Correspondence.

44 Wittkower to Momigliano, 1 October 1945; Wittkower to Momigliano, 26 November 1946; Yates to Momigliano, 1 January 1947, Warburg Institute Archive, Journal Correspondence.

45 Saxl to Momigliano, 20 March 1947, Warburg Institute Archive, Journal Correspondence.

46 Momigliano to Saxl, 24 March 1947, Warburg Institute Archive, Journal Correspondence,

47 Saxl to Momigliano, 27 March 1947; Momigliano to Saxl, 16 April 1947, Warburg Institute Archive, Journal Correspondence.

48 *Journal of the Warburg and Courtauld Institutes* 9 (1946 [1947]): 153.

49 Saxl to Momigliano, 1 May 1947, Warburg Institute Archive, Journal Correspondence.

50 It is not surprising that Momigliano was so willing to learn from Saxl, whom he greatly respected. See, again, his review of Elizabeth Armstrong, *Robert Estienne, Royal Printer*: 'The modern reader may be reminded of the skill with which Fritz Saxl got his Warburg Institute out of Germany.' And cf. Momigliano to Gertrud Bing, 8 May 1957, Warburg Institute Archive, General Correspondence: 'Dear Bing, as you happen to mention the fact that I did not contribute to the Saxl volume, the quite simple explanation is that I was not invited. As Gordon is a friend of mine, there is no evil intent behind the exclusion. The probably explanation is that the contributors were chosen among British subjects – *or* I may just have been forgotten.'

51 Momigliano to Gertrud Bing, 12 January 1949; Warburg Institute Archive, Lecture Correspondence; Yates to Momigliano, 4 January 1950, Warburg Institute Archive, Journal Correspondence.

52 On Yates's intellectual life and scholarly career, see J.B. Trapp, ed., *Frances S.*

Yates, 1899–1981: In Memoriam (London, 1982); and Patrizia Delpiano, '"Il teatro del mondo." Per un profilo intellettuale di Frances Amelia Yates,' *Rivista storica italiana* 105 (1993): 180–245.

53 Yates to Momigliano, 18 May 1950, Warburg Institute Archive, Journal Correspondence: 'As we all hope that you will let us have more articles for the Journal in the future, I trust you will not mind if we humbly ask you next time (a) to send us a top copy rather than a carbon; (b) to double-space your footnotes; and (c) not to continue them on the back of the page? Please forgive these petty remarks.'

54 Momigliano to Yates, 17 September 1950, Warburg Institute Archive, Journal Correspondence: 'I am now back from Italy, and have checked again almost all the bibliographical references and quotations on the original texts (I cannot say that I have become very popular either at the Vittorio Emanuele in Rome or in Bodley here where I performed the operation). I have discovered a considerable number of petty mistakes which usually involve only one letter or syllable. But half a dozen of them imply the addition or deletion of a word and would be better removed in the galley proofs stage. If my article is still at that stage, I should be glad to have it back. Otherwise I think we can wait for the page proofs.'

55 Momigliano to Yates, 17 September 1950, Warburg Institute Archive, Journal Correspondence.

56 Yates to Momigliano, 18 May 1950, Warburg Institute Archive, Journal Correspondence.

57 Momigliano to Saxl, 16 May 1942, Warburg Institute Archive, Journal Correspondence: 'Io sono non dico un dillettante – una parola che a orecchie italiane ancora suona complimento! – ma un ignorante in materia archaeologica.'

58 See Momigliano to Bing, 24 July 1956, Warburg Institute Archive, General Correspondence: 'Burckhardt was the first art historian to become a historian of a civilization as a whole – and this established a connection between visual studies and the Renaissance Warburg was to inherit. Then Warburg went beyond Burckhardt in emphasizing the irrational elements of the Renaissance, its anti-Flemish, anti-bourgeois reaction, its links with Antiquity through astrology and mythology. The method could be extended – it could be associated with the new trends in the psychology of the unconscious (from which it undoubtedly derived its strength) and with the new research on language. But, as far as I know, only in the study of the Renaissance the Warburg I. has produced something amounting to a re-interpretation or at least to a critical revision of a civilization. In other fields there have been contributions, suggestions, but not deep-going re-interpretations. The

future will probably qualify this picture, but so far the Renaissance studies have rightly been associated with the Warburg I. in the minds of the outsiders.'

59 Yates to Momigliano, 9 October 1950, Warburg Institute Archive, Journal Correspondence, given in full in appendix 1.

60 Yates to Momigliano, 10 November 1950, Warburg Institute Archive, Journal Correspondence.

61 *Journal of the Warburg and Courtauld Institutes* 13 (1950): 309.

62 Momigliano to Yates, 17 September 1950, Warburg Institute Archive, Journal Correspondence.

63 See Mark Phillips, 'Reconsiderations on History and Antiquarianism: Arnaldo Momigliano and the Historiography of Eighteenth-Century Britain,' *Journal of the History of Ideas* 57 (1996): 297–316; and his subsequent book *Society and Sentiment: Genres of Historical Writing in Britain, 1740–1820* (Princeton, 2000). Phillips's work, which is excellent on its own terms, sheds considerable light on eighteenth-century historiography and the larger development of the historical tradition. But he does not attend to the context and documented intentions of Momigliano's studies, and this detracts from the usefulness of his imporant critique. William Stenhouse, 'Georg Fabricius and Inscriptions as a Source of Law,' *Renaissance Studies* 17 (2003): 96–107, incisively revises Momigliano's work in one crucial aspect. For further substantive discussion and criticism, see Robert Gaston, 'Merely Antiquarian: Pirro Ligorio and the Critical Tradition of Antiquarian Scholarship,' in *The Italian Renaissance in the Twentieth Century*, ed. Allen J. Grieco, Michael Rocke, and Fiorella Gioffred Superbi (Florence, 2002), 355–73; and Ingrid Rowland, 'Antiquarianism as Battle Cry,' in *The Italian Renaissance*, ed. Grieco et al., pp. 401–11.

64 Note the way in which, in a letter to D.M. Pippidi of 25 January 1950, Momigliano described the widest-ranging and most influential of all his studies in the field, 'Ancient History and the Antiquarian': 'Sono venuto pubblicando lavori di metodo storico – tra cui uno su "Ancient History and the Antiquarian" destinato a uscire a fine d'anno nel Journal of the Warburg Institute' (Momigliano, 'L'epistolario con D.M. Pippidi,' 31).

chapter four

Arnaldo Momigliano's 'Ancient History and the Antiquarian': A Critical Review

INGO HERKLOTZ

To dedicate a critical review to an article that appeared more than half a century ago might seem paradoxical. What scholarly contribution would not be out of date at that age? Momigliano's 'Ancient History and the Antiquarian,' however, presents a rather unique case in point.[1] First published in 1950, and reprinted several times thereafter, it still enjoys the splendid reputation not only of having made a ground-breaking contribution in its day, but of remaining fundamental for the study of antiquarianism up to the present. Apart from the expression of some minor doubts, a general review of its considerations on antiquarianism and historiography has never been ventured.

The reasons for this silence seem twofold. First, antiquarian research did not attract much attention until some ten or fifteen years ago, when the history of the humanities finally became a popular field of investigation and renewed an interest in early modern forms of scholarship. More significant, however, is the nature of the article itself. Digressing far beyond the borders of *Altertumswissenschaft* into early Etruscology, biblical studies, Church history, and comparative religion, and thus covering various areas of learning with seeming expertise and over the broadest period of time (from the fifth century BCE to the twentieth century CE), the author was able to intimidate most of his readers. And to say it from the outset, nor does the present writer feel competent to address many of the issues touched upon. One wonders, however, whether it is necessary to do so in order to raise some critical reflections about the kernel of the argument – Momigliano's notion of ancient and early modern antiquarianism. The discovery that antiquarian learning of the Renaissance and Baroque periods is rooted in the classical past was indeed one of Momigliano's most valuable contributions. In what follows, it will be shown that this relationship was even more comprehensive than he had recognized. On the whole, however, the impression can hardly be avoided that 'Ancient History and the Antiquarian' was a premature and in several respects erroneous synthesis of various fields that by Momigliano's day had not yet received sufficient preparatory work. In this paper Momigliano's major shortcomings will be highlighted against the results of research carried out over the last decades.

I. Antiquarianism and History

The objection that Momigliano overstressed the intellectual gap between the antiquarian and the historian has been made by earlier readers.[2] Nevertheless, it may be further amplified. Although his basic distinction between the antiquary, who dealt with institutions, customs, and topography, and the historian, who was concerned with past events – the *histoire événementielle* in modern terminology – is correct, the clear-cut difference claimed for the presentation of the material, that is, the systematic or topical survey of the antiquarian as opposed to the chronological order of the historian, oversimplifies the matter. Even the seemingly most systematic of all such systematic arrangements from classical times, Varro's famous *Antiquitates rerum divinarum et humanarum,* resists such a generalization.[3] Too little is known of this highly fragmentary work for us to conclude that within his individual classes of Roman civilization Varro paid no attention to historical change. The notion that Roman society developed from the better to the worse is present in his *De vita populi Romani* and in his *De lingua Latina.*[4] Why then should the *Antiquitates* have been indifferent to a chronological approach?

As a matter of fact, a sort of compromise between the linear *histoire événementielle* and the rather static description of customs and institutions can be encountered in numerous ancient and early modern authors. To single out but a few: Aristotle's *Athenaíōn politeía,* written between 328 and 325, is centred on the Athenian constitution of his time (see chaps. 42–69). What precedes, however, is an analysis of how the present state of social organization came about, in other words, a chronological presentation of Athenian constitutions, the first of its kind, from Epimenides to Pythodoros. This history, as we may indeed call it, does not ignore the decisive events and historical personalities that provoked the numerous changes in the legislation of the city-state.

Social institutions are likewise called upon in the *Origines* of M. Porcius

Cato (234–149 BCE), a work no one would classify as anything but history. Fragmentary though it is, there can be little doubt that the *Origines* presented the history of Rome from the mythical beginnings down to Cato's times and that the Roman state was continuously compared with the rival tribes of the Apennine peninsula.[5] This was not political or military history modelled on Thucydides. In Cato's tale, Roman and foreign institutions figure prominently, and it is the aetiological model, all too frequent in both Greek and Roman historiography, that sets a chronological framework for the introduction of socio-political renewal. Attention is paid to law and juridical practice. Far from being centred on public institutions alone, however, Cato's account also describes the daily life of ordinary people, their eating habits and their clothes, women's bijoux and the hairstyles of the past – in other words, topics we would tend to associate with the antiquary, not the historian.

The approach of the *Origines* proved of particular relevance when the archaic period of Rome was at issue. Accordingly, the city's religious institutions, temples, statues of the gods, rites of purification and sacrifice, *ludi magni*, and so forth are discussed in another history of early Rome, the *Archaiologia* of Dionysios of Halikarnassos (late first century BCE).[6] Such observations, comparing religious life in Rome with that in Greece, are meant to demonstrate the Greek author's basic ethnogenetic assumption that the origins of the Roman population should be traced to Greece, whence it migrated across the sea to Italy.

The kind of cultural history we encounter in Cato and Dionysios, but also in Varro's *De vita populi Romani*, in Livy, and in the anonymous fourth-century *Origo gentis Romanae*[7] was renewed only in the eighteenth century. It would be a great exaggeration, however, to conclude that chronological approaches were completely absent from the antiquarian writings of the preceding centuries. In their investigations of ancient magistrates, to mention a field that enjoyed particular popularity from the 1420s onwards, modern antiquaries simply had to follow Dionysios, Livy, or Plutarch's *Life of Romulus*, the better preserved of their ancient predecessors, in order to find out that such offices as that of the *tribunus celerum*, the *quaestores*, the *praefectus urbi*, and the *interreges* already existed in the alleged period of the kings, but that the situation changed radically during the Roman Republic.[8] Then the consuls acquired what came close to a royal power, though they later delegated some of it to the tribunes, the censors, and the praetors, whose increased number from one to six brought about further shifts of responsibility. Keeping to Livy only, the introduction of some of these magistrates could be linked with concrete data; accordingly, the appearance of the first censor seems to have been in 310 AUC, and so on.

Even dedicated Varronians, such as Biondo in his *De Roma triumphante* or Ioannes Rosinus in the *Romanae antiquitates,* did not refrain from occasionally putting aside their usual taxonomic arrangements. Biondo, for instance, presented his final chapter on Roman triumphs in annalistic terms.[9] On the other hand, Rosinus's book VIII on Roman legislation starts off with some legal fragments attributed to the kings.[10] There follows a lengthy discussion of the Twelve Tables, which mark the beginning of a new era. The subsequent analysis of the Republican period is classified according to sacred, civil, and public law, but allows for a chronological sequence within individual classes (*De legibus agrariis, De legibus sumptuariis,* etc).

Further examples illustrating the fusion of subject taxonomy with chronology could certainly be traced elsewhere. It might appear more important, however, that there was one branch of antiquarian learning in which chronological patterns played a most decisive role throughout. The reference is, of course, to numismatics, the antiquarian discipline that no doubt was the most widespread and popularized owing to the thousands of professional and amateur collectors.[11] Whereas collections and publications of Greek coins were mostly presented topographically, that is, according to their cities of provenance, and those of the Roman Republic tended to be classified by mint master families, there was little alternative to chronology when it came to Imperial Rome – which provided the bulk of the material. Ever since Andrea Fulvio's *Illustrium imagines* (1527), the sequence of emperors and Imperial families had been used as the most important principle of arrangement. Much discussion was devoted to chronology within the same reign.

If a closer look reveals that antiquarian and historical approaches diverged less than Momigliano had thought, the same holds true for the underlying scholarly purposes. In Momigliano's opinion the political historian wrote for the instruction of politicians, whereas the antiquary accumulated knowledge for its own sake or for his personal pleasure. Although this statement might be true for the modern period, its relevance for antiquity should certainly be questioned. Cato left no doubt that by highlighting the modest customs and harsh living conditions of the forefathers he intended to evoke a model for the present, a present he felt much in danger of the moral corruption he did not cease to attack while consul and censor. After all, it was he who vigorously opposed the abolishment of the famous Lex Oppia, with its severe restric-

tions on luxury (195 BCE). The *mos maiorum*,[12] as opposed to the decadence of the late Republic, stands likewise as a glorious ideal behind
Varro's *De vita populi Romani*, and one may wonder whether the same
spirit informed Varro's *Antiquitates*. While we know nothing of the
Antiquitates' improvement of contemporary morals, its impact on religious life seems obvious. Augustus's reintroduction of numerous forgotten cults, those same cults St Augustine later ridiculed for their
insignificance, seems hardly imaginable without the scholarly ground
paved by Varro.[13] Such instances should caution us not to wholly deprive
antiquarian research of its social relevance or of that very exemplary
function as *magistra vitae* that we prefer to attribute to historiography.

   However, a more fundamental question needs to be raised at this
point. Some overlapping of antiquarian and historical interests notwithstanding, did the antiquary really think of himself as being either subservient or in opposition to the historian, as Momigliano implied? In other
words, was historiography the primary point of reference for his discipline? It seems that at least as good a case can be made for a crucial
relationship between antiquarianism and philology.[14] Once again, the
history of this relationship starts in antiquity.

II. Antiquarianism and Philology

Detecting the meaning of words was an essential task for every antiquarian. Prior to, or at least parallel to, the rise of independent antiquarian
treatises, antiquarian learning figured prominently in various kinds of
philological scholarship. Textual criticism is one of the literary genres
here to be considered.[15] Once more, it seems that the work of Aristotle,
in particular his *Aporémata homeriká,* played an essential role for the
development of the antiquarian commentary dedicated to the writings
of older authors.[16] Homer's historical reliability was unquestioned, and
Aristotle explained all those objects of material culture, those rites and
ways of human behaviour that were no longer obvious to his contemporaries. Illuminating remarks are therefore centred on Homeric measure-
ments and weights, on the Greeks' use of their arms, and on a semi-ritual
performance like that of Achilles dragging the corpse of Hector around
the walls of Troy. Two hundred years later the *Techné* of Dionysios Thrax,
an early attempt to establish a code of grammar and philology, defined
the explanation of the epic's contents as the main task of the grammar-
ian, right next to the analysis of the poets' archaic or unusual wording.[17]

   A longer and more continuous tradition of textual criticism can be traced, at least in lacunar shape, within the literary history of Rome.[18] As early as the second century BCE, Varro's teacher Aelius Stilo dedicated a commentary to the archaic Chants of the Salians that combined textual exegesis with the history of religion.[19] Stilo dated these texts, sung by the priests of Mars and Quirinius, to the period of Numa Pompilius and believed them to provide the earliest literary specimen of the Latin language. Varro himself published a commentary on Plautus, now lost.[20] Plautus and Terence, the masters of early Roman comedy, attracted considerable philological attention even under the Empire.[21] But another author was soon to become the champion of textual exegesis, Virgil.

Having absorbed much antiquarian knowledge itself, the *Aeneid*, Rome's national and most popular epic, must have provoked extensive commentary soon after its author's death.[22] Little of this commentary has survived from before the turn from the fourth to the fifth century and the famous Indian summer of Rome's pagan aristocracy.[23] To this final glowing of the classical tradition we owe the commentary of Servius, which became the authoritative model for all early modern commentators. Servius alone has permitted modern scholars to draw a complete sketch of Roman religion covering both private rites, to be held on the occasion of wedding, motherhood, and death, and public religious practice, including accounts of individual gods, priests, sacrifices, games, augurs, and haruspices.[24] Much attention is paid to the instruments and insignia used by those responsible for the correct execution of religious ceremonies. Time and again one feels that Servius's investigation is informed by the same ideal that stood behind the Republican writers on archaic history, since throughout his commentary it is the sadly lost *mos maiorum* he wants to describe.

Beginning in the fifteenth century, textual commentaries on the model of Servius flourished again.[25] Lorenzo Valla's treatise on the Constantinian Donation (1440), although concerned with a medieval text, might be looked upon as an early but nevertheless remarkably successful case in point.[26] It was not only Valla's expertise in Latin, but also his familiarity with ancient material culture, that enabled him to prove the alleged Imperial document a post-classical fake. After all, the author of the Donation was not aware that the Imperial diadem was a decorated stripe of linen or silk, rather than a ring of gold, as were medieval crowns. Speaking of *imperialia sceptra*, the suspicious writer had forgotten that the Roman emperor never used more than one sceptre. As to senatorial insignia, he names nothing but the characteristic shoes, and not, as one would have expected with Valla, the much more prominent *laticlavus*.

From the turn to the sixteenth century, bulky commentaries, on occasion several times as long as the ancient texts they intend to illuminate, abound. Whoever dedicates some reading to the *Cornucopie* that Niccolò Perotti attached to the epigrams of Martial (published posthumously in 1489) or to Filippo Beroaldo's edition of Apuleius's *Metamorphoses* (1500) will soon be overwhelmed by genuine antiquarian discourse that goes far beyond the already abundant annotations on linguistic devices and etymology.[27] Beroaldo's most significant contribution is to the cult of Isis, which had not been discussed as fully during the early Renaissance. Perotti, on the other hand, gets involved in numerous antiquarian problems. One hundred and nineteen columns in the folio edition of 1501 are subsumed under the title *De amphitheatro,* with the Flavian Colosseum, which Martial had celebrated in no more than eight verses, taken as a starting point. The exaggerated length of such digressions is due, on the one hand, to the fact that rather trivial and obvious terms receive a great deal of attention, and, on the other, to Perotti's almost uncontrolled etymological associations. Departing from the lemma *Pyramide* the author introduces two dozen words with the prefix *pyr,* ranging from the Pyrenees and the solar horse Pirous, over the *pyratae* (= *piratae*), the funeral *pyrae,* and the *pyrgus* used for playing dices, to the *pyrites* stone and the *pyretra* herba, the dragon herb.[28] Obviously, Martial's poems have become a key for opening the door to an independent lexicographical compilation and enabling Perotti to present a cornucopia of his own erudition. The model for Perotti's farrago seems to lie in classical lexicography, where authors like Pollux, Varro, and Verrius Flaccus had already combined topical with etymological approaches. Before we turn to these, one branch of textual exegesis requires special mention, legal commentary.

From the early explanations of the Twelve Tables that can be traced back to the second century BCE to the definitive legal codification under Justinian, the interpretation of older textual evidence belonged to the daily business of ancient jurisprudence.[29] The legal experts had a twofold aim. Beyond the philological and antiquarian understanding of their material, they wanted to adapt it for practical use in their own time. In both respects a solid knowledge of older language and customs was indispensable. As Sextus Caecilius put it, 'Longa aetas verba atque mores veteres oblitteravit, quibus verbis moribusque sententia legum comprehensa est.'[30] Specific glossaries for legal history, such as C. Aelius Gallus's lost *De verborum quae ad ius civile pertinent significatione,* seem to have contributed to overcoming such difficulties – which did not, however, prevent terms from older laws from provoking lengthy controversies.[31]

Fifteenth-century Italian antiquarians scanned the Codex for ancient magistrates and their respective competences.[32] A far more comprehensive legal humanism, however, was developed in sixteenth-century France, where the adherents of the *mos gallicus* aimed at a radical historicization of Roman law, which was no longer thought of as a model for the application of individual *tituli*, but rather studied for its underlying philosophical and logical principles.[33] An analysis of Guillaume Budé's annotations to the Pandects (1508), often considered the foundational work of the new French jurisprudence, would suffice to demonstrate that legal commentaries shared both the strengths and the weaknesses of contemporary commentary on classical poetry.[34] Their exhaustive, or even associative approach, showing off a vast reading on the ancient world, went far beyond what was necessary for an understanding of the legal document in question, adducing instead information on multiple aspects of ancient life. The work that eventually became the standard commentary on the Digest and was used as such in most law schools, Denys Godefroy's apparatus of 1584 (with many editions to follow), had to severely prune his predecessor's excesses. Basic historical and antiquarian information was nevertheless preserved.[35]

The legal background deserves our attention all the more since many of the most outstanding sixteenth- and seventeenth-century antiquarians, such as Pinelli, Panciroli, Aleandro the Younger, Pignoria, Peiresc, and Dal Pozzo, had been educated in civil law, which at that time still meant Roman law. It was probably through their legal sources that these scholars first came into contact with the civilization of the classical past.

One of the natural outcomes of textual criticism was lexicography. Important classical contributions to it came from Varro himself (*De lingua Latina*), from Verrius Flaccus (*De verborum significatione*, first century CE), and from the Greek orator Pollux (*Onomastikón*, second century CE).[36] Here, too, terms were analysed not only etymologically but, in particular when dealing with archaic language, with regard to their historical content. It seems significant that only Verrius Flaccus arranged his material in an albeit not too strict alphabetic order, whereas Varro and Pollux preferred a taxonomic division, allowing for etymological associations only as a secondary criterion. The lexicographers drew heavily on the antiquarian tradition. Accordingly, some of the testimonies for Varro's *Antiquitates* derive from Verrius Flaccus, and some from Varro's own *De lingua Latina*.

No doubt classical lexicography, too, was renewed by the humanists, whose obsession with good Latin was proverbial. Lorenzo Valla's *Elegantiarum libri*, written during the 1430s, soon became the canonical manual of Latin style produced by the Quattrocento.[37] Although correct grammatical forms and the semantic differences of similar terms and idioms were meant to instruct Valla's readers in the language of Cicero and Quintilian, the author's aim had to be based on a deeper comprehension of classical usage. To understand the difference between *iocus* and *ludus*, *pompa* and *spectaculum*, or *munimenta* and *monumenta*, to grasp the significance of the *pugillares*, long out of use by the Renaissance, or of specific Roman offices, depended after all on knowledge of ancient customs, institutions, and material culture. As in ancient lexicography, linguistics and antiquarianism tend to fuse. The encyclopaedias of the later Renaissance, such as those of Charles Estienne and the giant unpublished corpus of Pirro Ligorio, stripped themselves of the stylistic ambitions of earlier manuals in order to become pure *Realenzyklopädien*.[38] Nevertheless, even here the philological element is omnipresent. Hardly any lemma is introduced without some consideration of its etymology.

A third literary genre from classical times, intimately linked with philological research, was revitalized during the Renaissance more or less simultaneously with the new type of antiquarian commentary on literature and law: the collection of miscellaneous treatises. Following the *Noctes Atticae* by Aulus Gellius, which was the sole survivor of what must have been an extensive branch of ancient Roman writing, Politian's *Miscellanorum centuria* of 1489 inaugurated an overwhelming sequence of *Variae lectiones*, *Emendationum libri*, *Comentarii*, and *Electorum libri* soon to be published by Celio Rhodiginus, Domizio Calderino, Alessandro D'Alessandri, Francesco Robortello, Pier Vettori, Sigonio, Agustín, Muret, Lipsius, and others.[39] The short tracts gathered in these compilations rarely cover more than three to five pages in print, and are not necessarily too long but rather too incoherent among themselves to be published in a commentary on a single classical text. However, like the contemporary commentaries, most of these tracts betray the technique of the commonplace book. In these notebooks, textual scholars used to assemble the findings of their readings under certain *loci communes*, that is, historical, ethical, or philological headings, expanding their lists with every new author they read.[40] Accordingly, catalogues of parallel or contrasting quotations were produced that aimed to help illuminate obscure or corrupt passages in ancient literature and law. In their most comprehensive form, as represented by D'Alessandri's *Genialium dierum libri sex* of 1522, the extent of classical civilization covered in the miscellaneous collections could be as exhaustive as Biondo's *De Roma triumphante*.[41] What these miscellanies did not aim for, however, was Biondo's organizational rigour. Indeed, they never tried to overcome their loose and coincidental character.

It should be emphasized that within the commentaries, the lexicographic volumes, and the *variae lectiones*, the analyses of literary evidence completely overshadowed non-literary sources. Nevertheless, the antiquarian's relationship to philology might explain that turn towards material remains that seems so typical of his intellectual achievement.

III. Literary and Non-Literary Sources

In Momigliano's opinion, the new emphasis on non-literary sources can be noted from the late seventeenth century. He believed it was a response to the crisis brought about by a historical Pyrrhonism that seriously questioned the reliability of ancient historians, opposing their personal and biased views to that of the more trustworthy *monumenta publica*, such as coins, inscriptions, and statues.[42] But Momigliano failed to prove his point. First, because his main apologists for the consideration of such evidence, Spanheim, Spon, and Bianchini, were not historians but antiquarians and thus part of the very discipline that had been accustomed to working with non-literary material for at least a century and a half. Second, because his main test field for the alleged new approach, pre-Roman Italy, was a historical area exceptionally devoid of accessible literary information and had to be approached by different ways *faute de mieux*.[43] In view of the fortune that Momigliano's thesis about historical Pyrrhonism has enjoyed within modern scholarship on the history of the humanities, several misunderstandings need to be set right.

First, the antiquarian's use of non-literary evidence was by no means self-evident, and even less a *conditio sine qua non* for the definition of antiquarianism.[44] In this, my own understanding of antiquarian research agrees with Momigliano's definition of antiquarianism as a discipline that was dedicated to all those aspects of antiquity that were not, or not primarily, concerned with *histoire événementielle*. It is obvious not only from the philological and legal work referred to above, but also from genuine antiquarians like Biondo (*De Roma triumphante*) and Rosinus, whose use of non-literary sources was remarkably limited, that such an aim could be pursued by the investigation of texts alone. Although the literary type of antiquarian continued to survive throughout the seventeenth and eighteenth centuries, the desire to explore material objects did not originate in the late seventeenth but in the mid-sixteenth century. In particular, it was a group of outstanding scholars working at or close to the Roman court of Cardinal Alessandro Farnese, including Pirro Ligorio, Onofrio Panvinio, Alonso Chacon, and Fulvio Orsini, who brought about the 'iconic turn.'[45]

Second, the consideration of non-visual evidence was by no means solely a matter of philosophical credos; it was equally conditioned by academic logistics. If we look at two scholars like Ioannes Rosinus (Rosfeld) and Cassiano Dal Pozzo, who, following Varro and Biondo, both intended to present a *corpus antiquitatum* covering – according to the by now established pattern – religious, public, military, and private life, we find that their approaches differed considerably.[46] Rosfeld, who never set foot on Italian soil, worked in German provincial places like Regensburg, Wickerstadt, and Naumburg. His book of 1583, which soon became a classic of its kind, relied on an almost exclusively literary base, with only few illustrations of coins and minor objects. Dal Pozzo, on the other hand, while living in Rome and having numerous artists in his service, acquired more than 2,000 drawings of ancient material culture, reliefs, statues, and paintings, which were then supposed to be coordinated with classical texts, a project unfortunately never completed. Do we really have to assume that such a difference of method was due to the advancement of historical Pyrrhonism? One would suspect that availability and money were far more decisive. Dal Pozzo significantly made some of his documentation available to the contemporary Paduan school of antiquarians, Pignoria, Liceti, Johannes Rhode, Giacomo Filippo Tomasini, and Ottavio Ferrari, who did not share his advantage of being surrounded by the physical remains of antiquity.

Third, the antiquarian's plea for non-literary evidence was never a plea for material objects instead of, but rather in addition to, literary sources. It is precisely this point that made coinage such a pleasurable field of study. Here text and image appear in perfect harmony.[47] Although from the early seventeenth century onwards statements in favour of material and visual documents abound also among students of customs and institutions, these scholars rarely explain what the advantage of such non-literary sources might have been. It seems, however, that at least in dealing with ancient material culture, which was crucial for their investigations, the archaeological objects brought to light by excavations, and their visual reproduction through ancient statues, reliefs, and paintings, were felt to provide more immediate access than did verbal description. Interestingly, natural historians expressed the same concern. As Ulisse Aldrovandi, who confronted the same problem when it came to understanding the writings of classical zoologists and botanists, put it in 1581: 'Se gli antichi havessero fatto ritrare e dipingere tutte le cose, che hanno descritte, non si trovarebbe tanti dubbi et errori infiniti appresso i scrittori ... e Dio volesse che gli antichi Principi et Monarchi come fu Alessandro Magno, et tanti altri scrittori, come Aristotele, Teofrasto et Cratina, tanto amico del nostro divino Hippocrate, havessero fatto dipingere le piante et animali, che da loro descritte furono, che certo non ci sarà hoggi tanta difficolta in conoscerli.'[48]

Antiquarians concerned with rites and customs – during the seventeenth century the dominant field of classical studies – would have subscribed to Aldrovandi's preoccupation. Their desire for visual material was by no means rooted in a sceptical distrust of biased ancient authors, but rather in the awareness that the literary tradition more often than not proved insufficient. As early as 1529, Francesco Guicciardini lamented the fact that writers from the past – with no regard for later generations – would not report on what was evident to them, and he enumerates the classic fields of antiquarian research among those topics treated with too much neglect in ancient historiography.[49] Pier Vettori intended to overcome this very difficulty by consulting Greek sources on Roman civilization, since, being strangers, the Greeks might have recorded what seemed superfluous to the Latins.[50] Still another way of closing the awkward gap between past and present knowledge was proposed by Claude Saumaise in 1635. Although he was an eminent philologist, and not without reason Scaliger's successor in the classics at the University of Leiden, his suggestion offers a revealing insight into the meaning of antiquarian method. *Joindre la pratique à la théorie* is the essence of his methodological plea, and his argument sounds reasonable:

La pluspart de nos scavants n'ayant exercé que l'une des parties, et s'estant contenté de scavoir ce que les livres leur en pouvoient apprendre, qui n'est rien au prix de ce que les choses mesmes nous enseignent lorsque nous venons à les mettre sous nostre veue, les tenir et manier dans nos mains. Je scais bien moi mesme a quoi m'en tenir, et je n'ai que prou essayé par ma propre expérience, combien est fautive et fallacieuse la science que j'en pesche dans les anciens auteurs qui ne traitent jamais à escient, et de propos délibéré de ces matières, qui leur estoient connues et triviales, non plus que nous ne faisons aujourd'hui en nos escrits de nos vestements et ustancilles, lesquels aussi eux ne touchent qu'en passant, comme parlant de choses connues, et à des gens qui connoissoient sans ce soucier si après leur siècle il en suivroit d'autres, qui se serviroient d'autres termes, que ceux qui estoient lors usités parmi eux.

His own experience seemed to prove him right:

Pour example, nous n'eussions jamais compris la facon de calculer des anciens, si nous n'eussions veu l'Abacus, sur lequel ils calculoient, et la forme de leurs jettons. Cependant, y a-t-il rien dont les auteurs fassent plus de mention en leurs escrits, tant les grecs que les latins? Ainsi de tout le reste, et principalement des habits antiques Togae, Pallia, Chlamydes, Saga. Combien me suis-je de fois rompu la teste, et travaillé en vain à expliquer et éclaircir ce que j'en rencontrais chés les autheurs, et n'en fusse jamais venus à bout, sans avoir vu de mes yeux, le portrait des choses que je ne pouvois me figurer telles par la lecture seule des livres.[51]

In other words, the banalities of ancient life, too self-evident for any contemporary author to explain in greater detail, made the investigation of its monuments worthwhile.

The point at issue therefore is the use of non-literary evidence where literary sources prove inadequate or non-existent. Reciprocally, monuments and texts shed light upon each other. A key term applied throughout the seventeenth century to describe such scholarly procedure is *illustratione*. The 'illustrative' effect could have a twofold direction. *Libri vistisi … per haver facilità nell' illustrar' anticaglie* is the heading of a list of books that Dal Pozzo had read for commenting upon his drawings.[52] Here, then, texts would 'illustrate' monuments. Dal Pozzo's brother Carlo Antonio wrote about the same collection of graphic records, 'v'è raccolta assai generale e curiosa per illustratione di poeti e prosatori antichi'; and elsewhere, '[questi disegni] possono esser d'aiuto all'intelligenza e chiarezza di diversi buoni autori.'[53] In his phrasing it obviously worked the other way round: the archaeological material illuminated the ancient authors. *Illustratione* thus indicates an antiquarian method of combining text and image or object and was meant to provide a means of overcoming the inevitable limitations of written evidence.

It might suffice to quote just one further spokesman for the same method, one who may appear somewhat unexpected in this context, not only because of his late date but because he is famed as an apologist of ancient art as art, as against those of the antiquarian tradition, who had used classical sculpture and paintings for the purpose of historical documentation. Yet in his introduction to the *Monumenti antichi inediti* of 1767, published three years after his seminal *Geschichte der Kunst des Altertums*, Winckelmann defined the purpose of his new book in terms of its utility for classical philology and antiquarian studies: 'corregere ed illustrare un gran numero di passi degli antichi scrittori ... per poter fare delle nuove scoperte intorno ai costumi degli antichi.'[54] The polemical digression that follows emphasizes that past textual criticism, which had made use of written evidence alone, had brought the discipline to a hopelessly dead end. Such a credo, however, was deeply rooted in the seventeenth-century antiquarian approach to art.

The search for non-literary evidence had one further dimension still, and here again it is difficult to see any effect of Pyrrhonism. Once again the pattern of reasoning derives from Greek historiography, which on occasion had tried to combine knowledge of the past with information from contemporary ethnography. The essential idea, which was shared by Thucydides, Aristotle, and Dionysios of Halikarnassos, consisted of the conviction that non-Greek barbarian tribes had conserved archaic customs that the Greeks themselves had abolished as their society became more civilized.[55] The early modern comparison juxtaposed Western Europe on the one hand with the rest of the world on the other. It received particular stimulus through the discovery of America and the increasingly numerous reports on the Red Indians. The sixteenth-century publications of Bartolomé de Las Casas and José de Acosta opened the way to studying antiquarian and ethnographic material in comparison and to relating the world of the American Indians to that of pre-Christian Europe.[56] Their work found its most important successor in the early eighteenth century when the Jesuit Joseph-François Lafitau, who had himself lived as a missionary in the New World, came out with his *Moeurs des sauvages amériquains comparées aux moeurs des premiers temps* (1724). The type of cultural comparison here at work was no doubt supported by the fact that the investigation of *mores et instituta* so close to the heart of several generations of antiquarians had stood in the centre of ethnography ever since Herodotus's founding works in the fifth century BCE.[57]

The notion of the survival of antiquity outside European civilization must have been familiar to many antiquarians indeed, even though they had never left their European homelands. As Peiresc with almost programmatic conviction wrote to Dal Pozzo in 1634, 'Li popoli più barbari et più sylvatici hanno conservato molto più ostinatamente per così dire i riti degli antiqui, si come si va ogni dì scuoprendo nelli deserti così del settentrione, come dell'Africa, dove con il paganesimo si conservano le superstitioni, habiti, e maniere di vivere più celebri ne' tempi antiqui.'[58] Much in line with the same principle, Peiresc's friend Lorenzo Pignoria searched the New World for traces of the ancient Olympus. In his eyes, the pose and costume of the Mexican Homoyoca clearly derived from the Egyptian Osiris, and the Japanese mother-goddesses holding their babies had a classical ancestor in Isis holding the Infant Horus.[59] Dal Pozzo himself disposed of a vast collection of ethnographic documentation, which he studied side by side with the classical monuments.[60] He knew about strigils used by contemporary Turks, which had to derive from those of ancient Rome, and he claimed that for the sake of chastity a Turkish sect called 'Calandar' had preserved the use of infibulation rings, formerly applied to Roman slaves. More than this, he was able to discover residues of antiquity among the peasant population of Western Europe. During his journeys through southern France and Spain he noted musical instruments among the natives similar to those one saw on Dionysiac sarcophagi. To be sure, the underlying scholarly assumption here at work can be traced far beyond Dal Pozzo and Lafitau. After all, it was his interest in ancient serpent rituals that stimulated the young Aby Warburg to visit the North American Indians in 1895.[61]

IV. Competing Parties

If it were correct that in the late seventeenth century the antiquary with his knowledge of non-visual material became a sort of paradigm for classical studies and history altogether, as insinuated by Momigliano, antiquarian scholarship would have enjoyed the height of its prestige only from that time on. That, however, was by no means the case. Although a conspicuous tide of antiquarian publications continued to flood the world of learning throughout the eighteenth and nineteenth centuries, it is obvious that already during the seventeenth century, and more so in the Age of Enlightenment, the wind started to blow sharply in the antiquary's face. Abundant testimonies of the rather hostile attitude have recently been presented and do not need to be repeated at this point.[62] The particular seventeenth- and eighteenth-century trends that might have worked against the antiquarian should be sketched briefly, however. As far as I can see, at least four developments, less distinct from than supporting each other, seem relevant to this discussion.

First, the 'Querelle des Anciens et des Modernes' questioned the paradigmatic value of antiquity as such by emphasizing the achievements of the modern age instead and requiring an intellectual commitment to the present and the future.[63] Such self-confidence was fostered by the awareness, which became increasingly widespread over the course of the seventeenth century, that the knowledge of the ancients had its limitations. Modern geography was able to improve upon Strabo, experimental medicine could demonstrate the mistakes of Galen and Celsus, and empirical observation of nature could lead to better results than reading Aristotle and Theophrastes. To those convinced that man's destiny was the construction of a new society, the retrospective antiquary, who would never go beyond his reproducing what had been thought and done many centuries before, was no more than a *singe antiquaire* without creativity of his own.[64]

Second, it was the antiquarian's pedantry, his obsession with the minute details of ancient material culture, that throughout the seventeenth century met with increasingly less tolerance. Once again, such criticism was rooted in antiquity. Seneca and Aulus Gellius had launched polemical utterances against the scholarly aims of contemporary philology.[65] In his *Dell'arte historica* of 1636, Agostino Mascardi appears as an early follower of their protest, questioning the purpose of studying ancient customs and institutions.[66] According to Mascardi, such investigations contributed at best to the understanding of classical authors, but had already been sufficiently realized. What he suggested, instead, was a reading of the classics for exemplary human behaviour, and the development of a historiography that while shedding light on past models directly served the needs of the present. The humanist idea of history as *magistra vitae* is all too apparent in this strategy, and the same raison d'être was to underlie many eighteenth-century works on ancient history. As an inevitable counterpart of such an idealistic mission, the irrelevance of the antiquarian's results remained the kernel of all polemics against his professional species.

Third, the general epistemic shift from the seventeenth to the eighteenth centuries, informing both the humanities and the natural sciences, has long been recognized as one from the synoptic table to linear chronology.[67] Occasional overlappings of history and antiquarianism notwithstanding, even during the eighteenth and nineteenth centuries antiquarian discourse proved remarkably immune to the general trend of *Verzeitlichung*. If antiquarianism had ever enjoyed the reputation of being an avant-garde discipline, this reputation had long been lost. Despite some new attempts at compromise – witness the *corpus antiquitatum* of Montfaucon (1719) subdividing the conventional taxonomic classes by chapters on Egyptian, Greek, Etruscan, Roman, and Gaulish civilization[68] – systematic organization survived against the general predominance of chronology in other fields of research. It might be understood as an answer to such resistance, however, that during the eighteenth and nineteenth centuries a new type of ancient cultural history was born that absorbed some of the questions previously tackled by the antiquarian.[69]

Fourth, the aesthetic revolution of the eighteenth century was able to free the study of ancient art from its subservient role as a philological and antiquarian *Hilfswissenschaft* and to establish ancient art history instead. It was the Comte de Caylus, a personality paradoxically more often than not looked upon as an old-fashioned antiquarian, who expressed this concept with programmatic insight at an early point. As he explained in the famous preface to his *Recueil* in 1752, works of art gave witness to the progress of the arts, a fact the antiquarians, while applying such artefacts *comme le supplément & les preuves de l'histoire*, had continuously ignored.[70] In the end it was, to be sure, not Caylus who first demonstrated the progress of the arts, but Winckelmann, when he published his *Geschichte der Kunst des Altertums* twelve years later (1764).

In reviewing such adversarial tendencies, one must agree with Momigliano that we have to wonder how antiquarianism could survive. It has survived, longer than he foresaw. Even if his diagnosis that 'the idea of "antiquitates" is now dead' had been true in 1950, antiquarianism experienced a miraculous rebirth during the second half of the twentieth century that has had lasting effects on the present. The primacy of political history has long been questioned again. During the last decades, the *Annales* school and historical anthropology have inquired into the living conditions and the material surroundings of the lower strata of past societies. Classical archaeology has likewise found its way back from the history of style to the analysis of ancient material culture. Although modern anthropological historians and archaeologists pay more attention to chronology and historical change than did their seventeenth-century predecessors, the field of investigation addressed in such successful works as Duby and Ariès's *Histoire de la vie privée* (1985–7) and Salvatore Settis's *Civiltà dei romani* (1990–3) stands conspicuously within the tradition of antiquarian research. Topical arrangement (religion, sports, daily life, death, etc.) of ancient works of art, albeit primarily of the 'minor' arts, can likewise be encountered in many modern museums, where artefacts continue to function as *preuves de l'histoire*. Obviously, the antiquarian has left his stamp.

Notes

1 The following discussion is based on the first edition, which appeared in the *Journal of the Warburg and Courtauld Institutes* 13 (1950): 285–315. The collection of articles *Ancient History and the Antiquarian: Essays in Memory of Arnaldo Momigliano*, ed. M.H. Crawford and C.R. Ligota (London, 1995), elaborated some of Momigliano's ideas, but generally refrained from taking critical positions. Most of the sources cited in the present paper are discussed within a broader context by Ingo Herklotz, *Cassiano Dal Pozzo und die Archäologie des 17. Jahrhunderts* (Munich, 1999.) The same volume contains an extensive bibliography of modern studies on ancient and early modern antiquarianism, to which can be added *Ciriaco d'Ancona e la cultura antiquaria dell' umanesimo. Atti del convegno internazionale di studio (Ancona 6–9 febbraio 1992)*, ed. G. Paci and S. Sconnocchia (Reggio Emilia, 1998); M.M. McGowan, *The Vision of Rome in Late Renaissance France* (New Haven and London, 2000); *L'idea del bello. Viaggio per Roma nel Seicento con Giovan Pietro Bellori* (Rome, 2000); *Dell'antiquaria e dei suoi metodi. Atti delle giornate di studio*, ed. E. Vaiani (*Annali della Scuola Normale Superiore di Pisa. Serie IV. Quaderni, 2, 1998*) (Pisa, 2001); *Art History in the Age of Bellori: Scholarship and Cultural Politics in Seventeenth-Century Rome*, ed. J. Bell and T. Willette (Cambridge and New York, 2002).

2 G. Huppert, 'The Renaissance Background of Historicism,' *History and Theory* 5 (1996): 48–60, especially 58–60; A. Schnapper, *Le géant, la licorne et la tulipe. Collections et collectionneurs dans la France du XVII siècle*, vol. 1, *Histoire et histoire naturelle* (Paris, 1988), 119; C. Ginzburg, 'Ekphrasis and Quotation,' *Tijdschrift voor Filosofie* 50:1 (1988): 3–19; M.S. Phillips, 'Reconsiderations on History and Antiquarianism: Arnaldo Momigliano and the Historiography of Eighteenth-Century Britain,' *Journal of the History of Ideas* 57 (1996): 297–316.

3 The fragments of this work are in need of a modern edition. For the time being, see P. Mirsch, 'De M. Terentii Varronis Antiquitatum rerum humanarum libris XXV,' *Leipziger Studien zur classischen Philologie* 5 (1882): 1–144; and B. Cardauns, *M. Terentius Varro. Antiquitates rerum divinarum* (Wiesbaden, 1976). A useful introduction to Varro's antiquarian work is provided by

E. Rawson, *Intellectual Life in the Late Roman Republic* (London, 1985), 236–46. Recent monographs are those by Y. Lehmann, *Varron théologien et philosophe romain* (Brussels, 1997); and B. Cardauns, *Marcus Terentius Varro. Einführung in sein Werk* (Heidelberg, 2001). For general studies of ancient Roman antiquarianism, see M. Fuhrmann, 'Erneuerung als Wiederherstellung des Alten. Zur Funktion antiquarischer Forschung im spätrepublikanischen Rom,' in *Epochenschwelle und Epochenbewußtsein*, ed. R. Herzog and R. Koselleck (Munich, 1987), 131–51; Herklotz, *Cassiano Dal Pozzo* (n1 above), 187–203, 241f; B. and M. Sehlmeyer, 'Die Anfänge der antiquarischen Literatur in Rom. Motivation und Bezug zur Historiographie bis in die Zeit von Tuditanus und Gracchanus,' in *Formen römischer Geschichtsschreibung von den Anfängen bis Livius. Gattungen – Autoren – Kontexte*, ed. U. Eigler et al. (Darmstadt, 2003), 157–71.

4 The fragmentary *De vita populi Romani* is available in B. Riposati's edition, *M. Terentii Varronis De vita populi Romani. Fonti, esegezi, edizione critica dei frammenti* (Milan, 1939). The better preserved *De lingua Latina* has appeared in various editions.

5 Modern editions are provided by M. Chassignet, *M. Porcius Cato: Les origines. Fragments* (Paris, 1986); and H. Beck and U. Walter, *Die frühen römischen Historiker*, vol. 1, *Von Fabius Pictor bis Cn. Gellius* (Darmstadt, 2001), 148–224. For Cato, see the bibliography in *Lo spazio letterario di Roma antica*, vol. 5, *Cronologia e bibliografia della letteratura latina*, ed. G. Cavallo, P. Fedeli, and A. Giardina (Rome, 1991), 239–41; and, most recently, M. Gotter, 'Die Vergangenheit als Kampfplatz der Gegenwart. Catos (konter)revolutionäre Konstruktion des republikanischen Erinnerungsraumes,' in *Formen römischer Geschichtsschreibung*, ed. Eigler et al. (n3 above), 115–34. The particular tradition of a broader history of civilization, to which Cato's work can be attributed, was elaborated parallel to political history. Momigliano himself later recognized the importance of this alternative; see, for instance, his *Classical Foundations of Modern Historiography* (Berkeley, Los Angeles, London, 1990), 29–53.

6 For Dionysios, see E. Gabba, *Dionysius and the History of Archaic Rome* (Berkeley and Los Angeles, 1991); and, most recently, N. Luraghi, 'Dionysios von Halikarnassos zwischen Griechen und Römern,' in *Formen römischer Geschichtsschreibung*, ed. Eigler et al. (n3 above), 268–86.

7 For this little-known text, see P.L. Schmidt's contribution in *Restauration und Erneuerung. Die lateinische Literatur von 284 bis 374 n. Chr.*, ed. R. Herzog (Munich, 1989), 184–6. See also the new edition *Origo gentis Romanae – Die Ursprünge des römischen Volkes*, ed. M. Sehlmeyer (Darmstadt, 2004).

8 I am following here C. Sigonio, *De antiquo iure civium Romanorum libri duo*

(Venice, 1560), 134–40. Much antiquarian research on ancient magistrates is dealt with in Herklotz, *Cassiano Dal Pozzo*, passim (see index, s.v. 'Magistrate'); for the modern founding work of this tradition, Andrea di Domenico Fiocchi's *De Romanorum magistratibus*, see M. Laureys, 'At the Threshold of Humanist Jurisprudence: Andrea Fiocchi's De potestatibus Romanis,' *Bulletin de l'Institut Historique Belge de Rome* 65 (1995): 25–42. Fiocchi's and several other treatises of its kind were reprinted in P. Scriverius, *Respublica Romana ... honori urbis aeternae* (Leiden, 1629).

9 In the Italian edition, *Roma trionfante* (Venice, 1544), 356r–373r. A detailed study of Biondo's book is provided by M. Tomassini, 'Per una lettura della Roma triumphans di Biondo Flavio,' in *Tra Romagna ed Emilia nell'umanesimo: Biondo e Cornazzano*, ed. M. Tomassini and M. Bonavigo (Bologna, 1985), 9–80.

10 I. Rosinus, *Romanarum antiquitatum libri decem* (Basilea, 1583), 316–75. Rosinus is much in need of a modern monograph; for biographic basics, see *Neue deutsche Biographie* 29 (1889): 237–9.

11 The best modern introduction is J. Cunnally, *Images of the Illustrious: The Numismatic Presence in the Renaissance* (Princeton, 1999); other recent studies include Schnapper, *Le géant* (n2 above), 133–64; *Medals and Coins from Budé to Mommsen*, ed. M.H. Crawford, C.R. Ligota, and J.B. Trapp (London, 1990); and *Numismatische Literatur 1500–1864: die Entwicklung der Methoden einer Wissenschaft*, ed. P. Berghaus (Wiesbaden, 1995).

12 For the importance of this concept, see C. Gizewski, 'Mores maiorum, regimen morum und licentia. Zur Koexistenz catonischer und plautinischer Sittlichkeitsvorstellungen,' in *Festschrift Robert Werner zu seinem 65. Geburtstag dargebracht von Freunden, Kollegen und Schülern* (Constance, 1989), 81–105; and two recent collections of essays, *Mos maiorum. Untersuchungen zu den Formen der Identitätsstiftung und Stabilisierung in der römischen Republik*, ed. B. Linke and M. Stemmler (Stuttgart, 2000); and *Moribus antiquis res stat Romana. Römische Werte und römische Literatur im 3. und 2. Jahrhundert v. Chr.*, ed. M. Braun, A. Haltenhoff, and F.-H. Mutschler (Munich and Leipzig, 2000).

13 Augustus's religious reform has attracted much scholarly attention; see, for instance, P. Zanker, *Augustus und die Macht der Bilder* (Munich, 1987), especially 107–69.

14 To this complex and all too obvious problem, Momigliano, 'Ancient History' (n1 above), 289 n6, did not dedicate more than a footnote.

15 For Greek textual criticism, R. Pfeiffer, *History of Classical Scholarship from the Beginnings to the End of the Hellenistic Age* (Oxford, 1968), remains fundamental. See, further, *La philologie grecque à l'époque hellénistique et romaine*, ed.

F. Montanari (Geneva, 1994); and, for ancient commentary on Homer, most recently, T. Schmit-Neuerburg, *Vergils Aeneis und die antike Homerexegese. Untersuchungen zum Einfluß ethischer und kritischer Homerrezeption auf imitatio und aemulatio Vergils* (Berlin and New York, 1999).

16 The best edition of the surviving fragments is that by O. Gigon, *Aristotelis opera: Librorum deperditorum fragmenta* (Berlin, 1987), Fr. 366–404.

17 *La grammaire de Denys le Thrace*, ed. J. Lallot (Paris, 1989), 40, 77–9.

18 F. Della Corte, *La filologia latina dalle origini a Varrone*, 2nd ed. (Florence, 1981), especially 31–91; Rawson, *Intellectual Life* (n3 above), 117–31, 267–81.

19 *Grammaticae romanae fragmenta*, ed. H. Funaioli (Leipzig, 1907), 57f; Varro, *Lingua Lat.*, VII. 2f, 26f.

20 *Grammaticae Romanae fragmenta*, ed. Funaioli, 58f.

21 H. Bardon, *La littérature latine inconnue*, 2 vols (Paris, 1952–6), vol. 1, p. 298; vol. 2, pp. 116, 184–8, 269, 286.

22 S. Timpanaro, *Per la storia della filologia Virgiliana antica* (Rome, 1986); see also the bibliography in *Lo spazio letterario*, ed. Cavallo et al., vol. 5 (n5 above), 359f.

23 See the bibliography in *Lo spazio letterario*, vol. 5 (n5 above), 360–2, to which should be added Schmidt's contribution in *Restauration und Erneuerung*, ed. Herzog (n7 above), 148–54.

24 See the old but still illuminating study by J.F. Holstein, *Rites and Ritual Acts as Prescribed by the Roman Religion According to the Commentary of Servius on Vergil's Aeneid* (New York, 1916); and, more recently, M. Mühmelt, *Griechische Grammatik in der Vergilerklärung* (Munich, 1965), 18–27.

25 The *Catalogus translationum et commentariorum: Medieval and Renaissance Latin Translations and Commentaries: Annotated Lists and Guides*, ed. P.O. Kristeller et al. (Washington, 1960–), intends to provide a complete inventory of these commentaries including those transmitted by manuscript only. See also the bibliography in P. Petitmengin and B. Munk Olsen, 'Bibliographie de la réception de la littérature classique du IXe au XVe siècle,' in *The Classical Tradition in the Middle Ages and the Renaissance*, ed. C. Leonardi and B. Munk Olsen (Spoleto, 1995), 199–274. On the great range of methods applied in these writings, further information is provided both by specialized works on commentaries and in more general works dealing with Renaissance philology, much studied in recent years. See, for instance, D.C. Allen, *Mysteriously Meant: The Rediscovery of Pagan Symbolism and Allegorical Interpretation in the Renaissance* (Baltimore and London, 1970); *Der Kommentar in der Renaissance*, ed. A. Buck and O. Herding (Boppard, 1975); J. Jehasse, *La renaissance de la critique. L'essor de l'humanisme érudit de 1560 à 1614* (Saint-Etienne, 1976); A. Grafton, *Joseph Scaliger: A Study in the History of Classical Scholarship*, 2 vols

(Oxford, 1983–93); idem, *Defenders of the Text: The Traditions of Scholarship in the Age of Science, 1450–1800* (Cambridge, MA, 1991); idem, *Commerce with the Classics: Ancient Books and Renaissance Readers* (Ann Arbor, 1997); *Commentaries. Kommentare*, ed. G.W. Most (Göttingen, 1999); *Die Praktiken der Gelehrsamkeit in der Frühen Neuzeit*, ed. H. Zedelmaier and M. Muslow (Tübingen, 2001); and *Philologie und Erkenntnis. Beiträge zu Begriff und Problem frühneuzeitlicher, Philologie*, ed. R. Häfner (Tübingen, 2001).

26 L. Valla, *De falso credita et ementita Constantini donatione*, ed. W. Setz (Weimar, 1976). Setz also published the fundamental analysis of this text; see his *Lorenzo Vallas Schrift gegen die Konstantinische Schenkung* (Tübingen, 1975).

27 N. Perotti, *Cornucopie nuper emendatum a Domino Benedicto Brugnolo ...* (Venice, 1501) (the edition I used); see also the new edition by J.-L. Charlet and M. Furno (Sassoferrato, 1989–). Perotti's philological method is discussed in M. Furno, *Le Cornu copiae de Niccolò Perotti: Culture et méthode d'un humaniste qui aimait les mots* (Geneva, 1995); and, more recently, in Johann Ramminger, 'Auf dem Wege zum Cornu copiae. Niccolò Perottis Martialkommentar im Vaticanus lat. 6848,' *Neulateinisches Jahrbuch. Journal of Neo-Latin Language and Literature* 3 (2001): 125–44. For F. Beroaldo, *Apuleius cum commento Beroaldi* (Venice, 1500), and other editions, see K. Krautter, *Philologische Methode und humanistische Existenz. Filippo Beroaldo und sein Kommentar zum Goldenen Esel des Apuleius* (Munich, 1971); for the same author's further contributions, see A. Rose, *Filippo Beroaldo und sein Beitrag zur Properz-Überlieferung* (Leipzig, 2001).

28 Perotti, *Cornucopie* (n27 above), 4–6.

29 M. Bretone, *Storia del diritto romano*, 4th ed. (Bari, 1995), provides a useful survey on ancient juridical learning. The antiquarian implications of legal history were also pointed out by Fuhrmann, 'Erneuerung' (n3 above), 142f.

30 Quoted in Aulus Gellius, *Noc. Att.*, XX.1.6.

31 *Iurisprudentiae anteiustinianae reliquiae ...*, ed. P.E. Huschke, 6th ed. E. Seckel and B. Kuebler, 2 vols (Leipzig, 1908–11), vol. 1, pp. 37–9.

32 D. Maffei, *Gli inizi dell'umanesimo giuridico*, 3rd ed. (Milan, 1972); J.-L. Ferrary, 'Naissance d'un aspect de la recherche antiquaire. Les premiers travaux sur les lois romaines: de l'Epistula ad Cornelium de Filelfo à l'Historia iuris civilis d'Aymar du Rivail,' in *Ancient History*, ed. Crawford and Ligota (n1 above), 33–72; Laureys, 'At the Threshold' (n8 above).

33 See the articles reprinted in D.R. Kelley, *History, Law, and the Human Sciences* (London, 1984); and also H.E. Troje, *Graeca leguntur. Die Aneignung des byzantinischen Rechts und die Entstehung eines humanistischen Corpus iuris civilis in der Jurisprudenz des 16. Jahrhunderts* (Cologne and Vienna, 1971).

34 Herklotz, *Cassiano Dal Pozzo* (n1 above), 213; for a somewhat different view,

see D.R. Kelley, 'Guillaume Budé and the First Historical School of Law,' *American Historical Review* 72 (1967): 807–34.

35 Troje, *Graeca Leguntur* (n33 above), 183–90.

. 36 For Varro, see Della Corte, *La filologia latina* (n18 above), 149–216; and Rawson, *Intellectual Life* (n3 above), 237–42; for Verrius Flaccus, known through an extract by Pompeius Festus, see *Lo spazio letterario*, ed. Cavallo et al., vol. 5 (n5 above), 486–8; for Pollux, R. Tosi, 'La lessicografia e la paremiografia in età allessandrina ed il loro sviluppo successivo,' in *La philologie grecque*, ed. Montanari (n15 above), 143–97.

37 L. Valla, *Elegantiarum libri*, in his *Opera omnia*, with an introduction by E. Garin, 2 vols (Turin, 1962), vol. 1, pp. 3–235. Garin's introduction is useful. See also *Poliziano nel suo tempo. Atti del VI Convegno internazionale (Chianciani–Montepulciano 18–21 luglio 1994)*, ed. L. Secchi Tarugi (Florence, 1996).

38 C. Estienne, *Dictionarium historicum ac poeticum ...* (Paris, 1561). The manuscripts of Pirro Ligorio are preserved at the Biblioteca Nazionale at Turin. A pioneering study on Ligorio's antiquarian method was published by E. Mandowsky and C. Mitchell, *Pirro Ligorio's Roman Antiquities. The Drawings in Ms XIII.B.7 in the National Library at Naples* (London, 1963). A more recent bibliography is compiled in A. Schreurs, *Antikenbild und Kunstanschauungen des neapolitanischen Malers, Architekten und Antiquars Pirro Ligorio (1513–1583)* (Cologne, 2000). The encyclopaedic genre at issue is surveyed in G. Tonelli, *A Short-Title List of Subject Dictionaries of the 16th, 17th and 18th Centuries as Aids to the History of Ideas* (London, 1971).

39 Several smaller collections are reprinted in J. Gruterus, *Lampas, sive Fax artium liberalium, hoc est Thesaurus criticus ...* (Frankfurt, 1602–5). For the literary genre, see Grafton, *Joseph Scaliger* (n25 above), vol. 1, pp. 17–22; and M. Marangoni, *L'armonia del sapere: i lectionum antiquarum libri di Celio Rodigino* (Venice, 1997).

40 A. Buck, *Die Rezeption der Antike in den romanischen Literaturen der Renaissance* (Berlin, 1976), 83–9; A. Moss, *Printed·Commonplace-Books and the Structuring of Renaissance Thought* (Oxford, 1999).

41 For D'Alessandri, see the entry in *Dizionario biografico degli Italiani*, vol. 31 (Rome, 1985), 729–32, with further bibliography.

42 Reservations as to both Momigliano's periodization and the effect of Pyrrhonism were expressed by Ginzburg, 'Ekphrasis' (n2 above); and M. Völkel, *'Pyrrhonismus historicus' und 'fides historica': Die Entwicklung der deutschen historischen Methodologie unter dem Gesichtspunkt der historischen Skepsis* (Frankfurt, Bern, New York, 1987), 342–4. It should also be mentioned that the significance of one of Momigliano's main witnesses for the new historio-

graphic approach of the late seventeenth century, Jean Mabillon's *De arte diplomatica* of 1681, has recently been seriously questioned; see L. Deitz, 'Die Scarith von Scornello. Fälschung und Methode in Curzio Inghiramis "Etruscarum antiquitatum fragmenta" (1637),' *Neulateinisches Jahrbuch. Journal of Neo-Latin Language and Literature* 5 (2003): 103–33, especially 117f.

43 A detailed sketch of this chapter of historiography has recently been outlined by M. Raskolnikoff, *Histoire romaine et critique historique dans l'Europe des Lumières: La naissance de l'hypercritique dans l'historiographie de la Rome antique* (Strassburg, 1992), 99–161, 668–85, and passim. Useful material is also provided in M. Cristofani, *La scoperta degli Etruschi. Archeologia e antiquaria nel '700* (Città di Castello, 1983); and *L'Accademia etrusca*, ed. P. Barocchi and D. Gallo (Milan, 1985).

44 This latter view was taken by the otherwise highly illuminating book of A. Schnapp, *La conquête du passé: Aux origines de l'archéologie* (Paris, 1993), 39f, 62, 275f. Concentrating on prehistoric excavations in northern Europe, this author, too, moves in fields where literary documentation was remarkably rare.

45 F. Haskell, *History and Its Images: Art and the Interpretation of the Past* (New Haven and London, 1993), 14–20, rightly emphasized the importance of the 1550s for numismatics. For the Farnese circle, see Herklotz, *Cassiano Dal Pozzo* (n1 above), 214–26; for Ligorio, see, further, Schreurs, *Antikenbild* (n38 above).

46 For Rosinus's *Antiquitates* (n10 above), see Herklotz, *Cassiano Dal Pozzo*, 247f; for Dal Pozzo, ibid., passim.

47 See the citations in Schnapper, *Le géant* (n2 above), 138.

48 See 'Avvertimenti del dottore Aldrovandi all' Ill.mo e R.mo Cardinal Paleotti sopra alcuni capitoli della Pittura' (1581), in *Trattati d'arte del Cinquecento fra Manierismo e Controriforma*, vol. 2, ed. P. Barocchi (Bari, 1961), 511–17, especially 513f.

49 F. Guicciardini, *Ricordi*, ed. R. Palmarocchi (Bari, 1933), 316: 'Parmi che tutti gli storici abbino, non eccettuando alcuno, errato in questo, che hanno lasciato di scrivere molte cose che a tempo loro erano note, presupponendole come note; d'onde nasce che nelle istorie de' Romani, de' Greci e di tutti gli altri, si desidera oggi la notizia in molti capi; verbigrazia delle autorità e diversità de' magistrati, degli ordini del governo, de' modi della milizia, della grandezza delle città e molte cose simili, che a' tempi di chi scrisse erano notissime e però pretermesse da loro. Ma se avessino considerato che con la lunghezza del tempo si spengono le città, se si perdono le memorie delle cose, e che non per altro sono scritte le istorie che per conservarle in perpetuo, sarebbono stati più diligenti a scriverle, in modo

che così avessi tutte le cose innanzi agli occhi chi nasce in una età lontana, come coloro che sono stati presenti, che è proprio il fine della istoria.' On this passage, see also Tomassini, 'Per una lettura' (n9 above), 17.

50 P. Vettori, *Explicationes suarum in Ciceronem castigationum* (Venice, 1537), 14r (on Cicero, *Fam.*, VIII.11): 'apud Graecos Romanarum historiarum auctores, qui cum externis gentibus scriberent, quae Romanos ritus ignorabant, diligentius, minutiusque haec pertractarunt quae latini scriptores, ut passim, vulgoque praeteribant.' See also Grafton, *Joseph Scaliger* (n25 above), vol. 1, p. 56, with n60.

51 Letter to Peiresc, 1 June 1635; published in *Les correspondants de Peiresc*, vol. 1 (Geneva, 1972), 232f. For Saumaise, see A. Bresson's introduction to N.-C.F. de Peiresc, *Lettres à Claude Saumaise*, ed. Bresson (Florence, 1992), viii–xx.

52 Herklotz, *Cassiano Dal Pozzo*, 265, 407–9.

53 Ibid., 265.

54 J.J. Winckelmann, *Monumenti antichi inediti* (Rome, 1767), I, (XV)–(XVI). The rather conservative spirit of the *Monumenti*, in particular when compared to the *Geschichte*, was pointed out by Herklotz, *Cassiano Dal Pozzo*, 299.

55 The fundamental study of this historiographic pattern is W. Nippel, *Griechen, Barbaren und 'Wilde'. Alte Geschichte und Sozialanthropologie* (Frankfurt, 1990); for Aristotle, see also Pfeiffer, *History of Classical Scholarship* (n15 above), 69f.

56 M.T. Hodgen, *Early Anthropology in the Sixteenth and Seventeenth Centuries* (Philadelphia, 1964), 296f, 332–43; Nippel, *Griechen*, 30–55; D.A. Lupher, *Romans in a New World: Classical Models in Sixteenth-Century Spanish America* (Ann Arbor, 2003), 236–317.

57 For the history of ethnographic studies, Hodgen, *Early Anthropology*, remains an excellent survey; for ancient investigations of the field, see also K.E. Müller, *Geschichte der antiken Ethnographie und ethnologischen Theoriebildung von den Anfängen bis auf die byzantinischen Historiographen*, 2 vols (Wiesbaden, 1972–80).

58 N.-C.F. de Peiresc, *Lettres à Cassiano dal Pozzo (1626–1637)*, ed. J.-F. Lhote and D. Joyal (Clermont-Ferrand, 1989), 128. For Peiresc, see, most recently, P.N. Miller, *Peiresc's Europe: Learning and Virtue in the Seventeenth Century* (New Haven and London, 2000), with extensive bibliography. The importance of the passage quoted was recognized earlier by C. Rizza, *Peiresc e l'Italia* (Turin, 1965), 101.

59 See Pignoria's addenda to V. Cartari, *Le vere e nove Imagini de gli Dei Antichi …* (Padua, 1615), part 2, pp. vi, lxiii.

60 For Dal Pozzo's ethnographic interests see Herklotz, *Cassiano Dal Pozzo*, 287f; for similar views within Dal Pozzo's circle, see idem, 'Jean-Jacques Bouchard (1600–1641): Neue Spuren seines literarischen Nachlasses,' *Lias* 29 (2002): 3–21, especially 5.

61 A.M. Warburg, *Schlangenritual. Ein Reisebericht*, ed. U. Raulff (Berlin, 1988).
62 See C. Kunst, *Römische Tradition und englische Politik: Studien zur Geschichte der Britannienrezeption zwischen William Camden und John Speed* (Hildesheim, Zürich, New York, 1994), 48–50, 137–41; A. Assmann, 'Der Sammler als Pedant,' in *Sammler – Bibliophile – Exzentriker*, ed. Assmann (Tübingen, 1998), 261–74; Herklotz, *Cassiano Dal Pozzo*, 295f; Miller, *Peiresc's Europe* (n58 above), 33–6, 64, 69, 125, and 203 n130.
63 Recent contributions on the Querelle include J.M. Levine, *Between the Ancients and Moderns: Baroque Culture in Restoration England* (New Haven, 1999); and *La Querelle des Anciens et des Modernes XVIIe–XVIIIe siècles*, ed. A.-M. Lecoq (Paris 2001). The seventeenth-century shift away from historical learning in French salon culture has been emphasized by Miller, *Peiresc's Europe* (n58 above), 148–60; the negative effect of the Querelle on classical learning is described by A.-B. Renger, 'Frankreich in wissenschaftsge-schichtlicher Perpektive: Ausgrenzung und Einbindung der Philologie in Institutionen des Grand Siècle,' in *Disciplining Classics = Altertumswissenschaft als Beruf*, ed. G.W. Most (Göttingen, 2002), 1–38. The Enlightenment criticism of antiquarian studies is rooted in opposition and satire voiced against humanist learning and methods since the sixteenth century. See W. Kühlmann, *Gelehrtenrepublik und Fürstenstaat: Entwicklung und Kritik des deutschen Späthumanismus* (Tübingen, 1982), 288–319; A. Stäuble, '*Parlare per lettera*': *Il pedante nella commedia del Cinquecento e altri saggi sul teatro rinascimentale* (Rome, 1991), especially 9–130; and G.E. Grimm, *Letternkultur, Wissenschaftskritik und antigelehrtes Dichten in Deutschland von der Renaissance bis zum Sturm und Drang* (Tübingen, 1998), especially 34–43, 162–236.
64 The *singe antiquaire* is the subject of a famous painting by Simon Chardin of 1740 that was quickly reproduced and circulated in engravings; see the catalogue by P. Rosenberg, *Chardin 1699–1779* (Paris, 1979), 221–4. K. Pom-ian, *Collectionneurs, amateurs et curieux. Paris, Venise: XVIe–XVIIIe siècle* (Paris, 1987), 195, suggested that this was a shot at the Comte de Caylus.
65 Seneca, *De brev. vitae*, 13; Aulus Gellius, *Noc. Att.*, XIV.6. Earlier criticism had been voiced against Alexandrian philology; see Pfeiffer, *History of Classical Scholarship* (n15 above), 97f; and R. Kassel, *Antike Kritik an Philologie und Philologen* (Berlin and New York, 1974).
66 A. Mascardi, *Dell'arte istorica libri cinque*, ed. A. Bartoli (Florence, 1859), 190f; also quoted in Haskell, *History and Its Images* (n45 above), 94.
67 The reference is, of course, to M. Foucault, *Les mots et les choses: Une archéo-logie des sciences humaines* (Paris, 1966); see also W. Lepenies, *Das Ende der Naturgeschichte: Wandel kultureller Selbstverständlichkeiten in den Wissenschaften des 18. und 19. Jahrhunderts* (Munich, 1976).

68 B. de Montfaucon, *L'antiquité expliquée et représentée en figures* ... (Paris, 1719–24); on which see, most recently, Herklotz, *Cassiano Dal Pozzo*, 302–4.

69 This, to be sure, was emphasized by Momigliano; but see Raskolnikoff, *Histoire romaine* (n43 above).

70 A.-C.-Ph. de Tubière Comte de Caylus, *Recueil d'antiquités égyptiennes, étrusques, grecques et romaines* (Paris, 1762), i–xiv. The most recent contribution on this author is *Caylus, mécène du roi: Collectionner les antiquités au XVIIIe siècle*, ed. I. Aghion (Paris, 2002), with further bibliography.

chapter five

Arnaldo Momigliano et la réhabilitation des 'antiquaires': le comte de Caylus et le 'retour à l'antique' au XVIIIe siècle

MARC FUMAROLI

Dans les livres qui font autorité, on apprend que la Querelle des Anciens et des Modernes, cette dispute qui a vivement ému la République des Lettres à partir de 1687, a pris fin en 1700. On lui accorde un bref ressac, la Querelle d'Homère, terminée net en 1716. Deux assauts entre gens de lettres et érudits qui ne doivent pas divertir l'attention de la grande 'crise de la conscience européenne,' où combattirent les géants Bossuet et Spinoza, Malebranche et Locke. Dans le français courant, l'expression 'Querelle des anciens et des modernes' a perdu son ancrage historique, elle désigne l'éternel retour du conflit des générations opposant les vieux *laudatores temporis acti*, vaincus d'avance, aux jeunes modernes qui ont la vie, l'avenir et le progrès pour eux. Ce sens courant et général de l'expression rejaillit rétrospectivement l'interprétation de la 'Querelle,' au sens strict et historique.

C'est l'un des mérites d'Arnaldo Momigliano et de Leo Strauss, chacun à sa manière, chacun dans son ordre, que d'avoir remis en question pour nous le préjugé, pour ne pas dire l'illusion trompeuse, selon laquelle la Querelle des Anciens et des Modernes lancée en fanfare à Paris en 1687 aurait, assez vite et définitivement, donné raison aux Modernes, comme il sied aux 'jeunes' bousculant les 'vieux' et les poussant dans la tombe et l'oubli. Avec des arguments et selon des prémisses différentes, le philologue et le philosophe ont montré que cette Querelle, inaugurale en effet du conflit entre la modernité et ses ennemis, loin d'avoir été définitivement tranchée par une prétendue défaite des 'Anciens' et par le triomphe sans partage des Encyclopédistes au XVIIIe siècle, est restée ouverte et disputée jusqu'à nos jours, tant les 'Anciens' de la Querelle ont réussi au cours du XVIIIe siècle à opposer à une modernité où ils dénonçaient avec pugnacité une figure de la Décadence un 'retour à l'antique' réparateur ou régénérateur.

1. Décadence et Progrès: le contrepoint du sentiment européen du temps historique

Chacun de son côté, le philologue italien et le philosophe politique germano-américain se sont montrés 'Anciens' parmi les Modernes, arrachant l'étude de l'Antiquité classique à la spécialisation universitaire et lui restituant le sens philosophique, moral et civil que lui avait donnée la Renaissance: distance prise vis-à-vis des 'vaines disputes scolastiques' et de la 'barbarie gothique' (la modernité décadente d'alors), mais aussi assise demandée à l'Antiquité pour une 'renaissance' ou une 'régénération' de la vieille Chrétienté déchirée par le Grand Schisme. Dans une crise générale analogue, ces deux grands esprits ont répété au XXe siècle le mouvement des humanistes du XVe siècle revenant aux 'sources antiques' pour guérir l'Europe de sa maladie mélancolique, ou encore, trois siècles plus tard, celui des 'antiquaires' du XVIIIe siècle, du philosophe du 'retour à la nature et à l'antique,' Rousseau, de l'historien de l'Art dans l'Antiquité Winckelmann, de l'historien du *Decline and Fall of the Roman Empire*, Gibbon, qui eux aussi firent de l'Antiquité classique le socle sur lequel prendre appui pour s'arracher aux sables mouvants des Lumières. Régulièrement depuis le XVIIIe siècle, 'vieillesse,' 'crépuscule,' 'maladie de l'âme,' 'corruption,' 'dissolution,' toutes les métaphores mises en œuvre par les 'Modernes' se réclamant contre les 'Anciens' du progrès, de la jeunesse, de la printanière et féconde nouveauté, de la santé de l'esprit nettoyé de la 'rouille' des naïves illusions et des vieilles erreurs, ont été retournées contre eux par les 'Anciens,' accusant la modernité de n'être qu'un décadence décrépite et fardée, une sinistre vieille de Goya posant à la jeune et attrayante beauté.

Ce contrepoint ne s'est pas interrompu avec la Révolution française. Le 'retour aux antiquaires' d'Arnaldo Momigliano et le 'retour aux Anciens' de Leo Strauss obéissent à une récurrence (Vico dirait un *ricorso*) de l'esprit européen divisé contre lui-même, qui oscilla plus que jamais au XIXe siècle entre deux mélancolies, celle d'une modernité qui se croit bridée dans son essor par les rémanences d'un grand âge aveuglé et celle d'une anti-modernité qui demande à un état antique et originaire de l'esprit le remède à ses maux tardifs et à son vieillissement modernes. Tour à tour, un Auguste Comte et un Ernest Renan ont fait valoir le caractère destructeur et négatif de ce que Comte appelle 'la

doctrine critique' et Renan 'l'art critique' de la Réforme et des Lumières, négateurs assez efficaces pour miner les assises religieuses et morales
de l'Église romaine et de l'Ancien régime politique, mais impuissantes à
remplacer les liens sociaux qu'ils avaient critiqués et dissous par d'autres
plus inattaquables.

Cette ombre projetée par les Lumières avait été décrite dès 1802 par
la nouvelle de Chateaubriand, *René*, 'preuve à l'appui' de son *Génie du
Christianisme*: c'était le portrait allégorique, sous les traits paradoxaux
d'un jeune homme vieilli et paralysé moralement avant l'âge, de la
mélancolie ou de l'ennui engendrés par la critique des Lumières, corro-
sifs des liens sociaux naturels aussi bien que de la foi religieuse qui les
sacralise.

Cette 'critique de la critique' philosophique a été récapitulée en 1959
par Reinhart Koselleck, dans son *Kritik und Krise*[1]. Koselleck appelle à
témoigner les 'philosophes' du XVIIIe siècle eux-mêmes, et avec eux
leur maître à tous, l'auteur du *Dictionnaire historique et critique*, Pierre
Bayle. Dans leurs moments de suprême lucidité, les 'rois de la critique'
des Lumières, libérateurs et pourfendeurs infatigables de dogmes, de
mythes, de superstitions, de légendes, de traditions, mais prudemment
conservateurs en politique, ont reconnu à quel désarroi ils condam-
naient une humanité réduite à des négations, et à quelle autorité intolé-
rante montait leur critique en exigeant la tolérance entre systèmes de
croyance qu'elle avait tous, au préalable, vidés de sens et d'autorité. Il est
arrivé à Bayle dans son *Dictionnaire* de décrire les méfaits de l'extension,
hors du 'secret' aristocratique de la République des Lettres, du procès
de tous contre tous, voire de la guerre civile, que les 'critiques' avaient
déclenchés entre eux, et cela en des termes qui préfigurent le diagnostic
de Chateaubriand en 1802 sur l'homme moderne, déboussolé dès ses
premières années par la critique généralisée des 'préjugés':

> En un mot [écrit l'auteur du *Dictionnaire*] le sort de l'homme est dans une si
> mauvaise situation que les lumières qui le délivrent d'un mal le précipitent
> dans un autre. Chassez l'ignorance et la barbarie, vous faites tomber les
> superstitions, et la sotte crédulité du peuple si fructueuse à ses conducteurs,
> qui abusent après cela de leur gain pour se plonger dans l'oisiveté et la
> débauche: mais en éclairant les hommes sur ces désordres, vous leur inspi-
> rez l'envie d'examiner tout, ils épluchent et ils subtilisent tant, qu'ils ne
> trouvent plus rien qui contente leur misérable raison.[2]

Dans une addition à son *Dictionnaire philosophique*, en 1771, Voltaire en
vint lui aussi à stigmatiser la vulgarisation du jugement critique souverain

qu'il avait lui-même pratiqué, mais en croyant pouvoir le réserver, en toute sécurité, aux seuls princes de l'esprit: 'Il n'y a pas un seul de ces critiques qui ne se croie juge de l'univers et écouté de l'univers'[3].

Comte avait à l'esprit cet état de révolution et guerre civile permanentes ouverts par la raison critique lorsqu'il préconisait, pour le 'troisième état' de l'histoire de l'esprit, le rétablissement d'un 'pouvoir spirituel' étayant les progrès de la science, mais faisant contrepoids au naufrage de toute certitude et de toute norme partagées dans un monde de crise où la vérité toujours en devenir condamne toutes les vraisemblances provisoires à s'annuler les unes les autres. Renan parvint à des conclusions analogues dans ses *Dialogues* et ses *Drames philosophiques*, où il ne voit plus d'avenir pour le caractère 'brahmanique' et 'aristocratique' de la science que dans la reviviscence d'une religion du cœur qui recrée une conscience morale, restituant le sens du sacrifice que demande une vérité scientifique en marche, mais inachevée, encore lointaine et largement cachée. Après Chateaubriand prônant un *revival* de l'ancienne foi chrétienne, Comte et Renan ont donc repris à Rousseau, qui avait perçu mieux que quiconque le caractère destructeur et négatif de la critique de la religion par les Lumières, son apologétique de l'acte de foi religieux comme pierre angulaire de toute société, même et surtout régénérée.

Rousseau avait en effet inclus dans l'utopie de la société reconstruite du *Contrat social* une esquisse de 'religion civique,' sacralisant le lien social naturel retrouvé; dans son *Émile*, la 'Profession de foi du Vicaire savoyard' avait demandé à l'évidence intime du cœur, plus persuasive et universelle que les arguments de la raison théologique ou de la critique athée, la régénération de la conscience morale et de la foi religieuse dans un monde moderne privé de l'une et de l'autre par l'anticléricalisme des Lumières parisiennes.

2. Retour à l'antique et retour aux sources de la foi: conjonction et dissociation

Cette négation de la négation et cet appel à la positivité d'un 'retour du refoulé' religieux et moral sont structurellement analogues à la foi dans l'Antiquité qui inspirait les travaux des 'antiquaires' du XVIIIe siècle, indifférents à la critique et au dédain dont ils étaient l'objet de la part des philosophes des Lumières. À première vue cependant, on n'aperçoit pas le rapport entre le 'retour à l'Antique' et le retour à l'acte de foi que préconisèrent, chacun à sa manière, un Vico et un Rousseau, le premier en attribuant le premier éveil de la conscience proprement humaine à la crainte des dieux et au culte des morts, l'autre préconisant le retour à la 'religion du cœur' naturelle à tous les hommes. Le 'retour à l'Antique' n'est-il pas d'essence 'païenne,' et l'acte de foi d'essence biblique et chrétienne ? Si contradiction il y a, elle n'était que latente chez les humanistes du XVe siècle, et déjà chez Pétrarque, pour lesquels le 'retour à l'Antique' procédait du même mouvement régénérateur de la Chrétienté que 'le retour à l'Église des premiers siècles et à ses Pères,' grecs et latins, indemnes de la 'gothicisation' consécutive aux invasions barbares. Ce mouvement ne dissociait pas le retour de la foi chrétienne à ses 'sources' patristiques de la réappropriation par les chrétiens modernes du fonds gréco-romain dans lequel les Pères de l'Église avaient fait pénétrer les lumières de la Révélation. Exaspéré par la Réforme et la Contre Réforme, ce mouvement de 'retour aux sources' a pu engendrer dans le catholicisme français une véritable 'archéolâtrie' de l'Église des premiers siècles et des Pères[4], portée à l'extrême par l'augustinisme doctrinaire de Port-Royal[5]. Plus fidèle au mouvement originel et refondateur de la Renaissance, 'l'art critique' des Bénédictins de Saint-Maur se proposa, pour la vivifier, de purifier la tradition catholique des accrétions légendaires ou superstitieuses accumulées dans les siècles 'gothiques' aussi bien qu'à mieux connaître, à travers les documents figurés et les inscriptions, comme s'y emploie *l'Antiquité expliquée* du mauriste Bernard de Montfaucon, le fonds religieux de l'Antiquité païenne que la Révélation chrétienne a pénétré, purifié et éclairci.

Les 'antiquaires' laïcs du XVIIIe siècle, il est vrai, se préoccupent fort peu, contrairement à leurs prédécesseurs de la Renaissance italienne, d'un 'retour aux sources' patristiques. Même Vico, qui fait exception parmi eux par son souci d'apologétique catholique, la construit indirectement sur une anthropologie: la raison critique moderne atrophierait l'esprit humain et l'égarerait si celui-ci se coupait des sources du connaître qui l'ont éveillé à lui-même, la religion et la poésie. Le plus ardent des 'Anciens' du XVIIIe siècle, Rousseau, est étranger, voire hostile au monde des 'antiquaires': il s'en éloigne d'autant plus que son anthropologie ne se contente pas de recommander un retour conjugué 'à la nature' et 'à l'antique,' elle préconise un retour à la religion naturelle, et même à la forme la plus transparente au cœur, le christianisme, pourvu qu'il se soit purifié des aliénantes 'lumières' de l'érudition et de la controverse théologiques. En revanche, un 'antiquaire' de plein exercice tel que Edward Gibbon est d'autant plus tenté, comme Machiavel, d'attribuer au christianisme une vocation ruineuse de tout ordre politique solide et durable, que cette religion d'esclaves a déjà contribué au *Decline and Fall* de l'Empire romain. La révérence de Gibbon, historien de l'Antiquité tardive, s'adresse à l'Empire romain tel que l'ont célébré les Grecs Polybe et Aelius Aristide, et non à la Rome républicaine dont Lucain et Tacite pleuraient la chute et dont Rousseau avait exalté les vertus civiques pour faire honte aux vices des sujets des grandes monarchies modernes. L'anatomie de la décomposition de l'Empire que propose Gibbon est à la mesure de l'admiration qu'il porte à l'aristocratie administrative et militaire des Flaviens et des Antonins, indemne encore des révolutions de palais, des religions orientales, du christianisme et des lâches concessions aux barbares. Le *Decline and Fall* (1776) propose d'avance un miroir et un avertissement pour l'Empire britannique du XIXe et du XXe siècles. Kipling réécrira Gibbon au présent.

Ce que les 'antiquaires' du XVIIIe siècle se contentent en général de demander à Antiquité grecque et romaine, c'est une forme noble et désintéressée du savoir historique. Mais les plus ambitieux sont entraînés plus loin: ils demandent à l'Antiquité mieux connue les principes d'une régénération des arts et du goût modernes: leurs fouilles ardentes et patientes dans le sol de la Romanité, héritière de la Grèce, leur appel à reprendre pied sur ce fonds ancien, quoi qu'ils ne les justifient plus comme les humanistes du XVe siècle par la réceptivité providentielle du monde gréco-romain à la Révélation chrétienne, n'en supposent pas moins de leur part un acte de foi dans les vigoureuses lumières naturelles du génie antique, oubliées, affaiblies et affadies chez les modernes. Cet acte de foi dans une Antiquité supposée avoir exercé dans sa plénitude la lumière naturelle à l'homme les opposent aux 'philosophes' des Lumières modernes, et les rapprochent, sans qu'ils s'en doutent, de Rousseau, le nouveau Diogène qui calomnie les arts et qui n'est point des leurs. C'est que le recours de Rousseau à la lumière naturelle encore intacte dans l'Antiquité implique une régénération radicale de l'homme (l'*Émile*) et de la société modernes (le *Contrat social*) alors que les 'antiquaires,' même les plus ambitieux, sont aussi conservateurs en politique que les 'philosophes,' et ne songent, par le retour à la nature et à l'Antique dont ils croient leur science susceptible, qu'à remédier à la 'corruption du goût' et des arts modernes.

La critique d'art de Diderot, l'ex-ami de Rousseau, est le meilleur témoin de la fusion qui s'est produite en France entre les deux conceptions du 'retour à l'antique,' celle des 'antiquaires' et celle de Rousseau. Cette fusion, dont la 'peinture d'histoire' de David après 1785 est largement tributaire, a fourni l'un de ses ingrédients explosifs à la 'révolution' prophétisée, espérée et redoutée, dès 1763, par l'auteur de l'*Émile*. Reste que, radical ou conservateur, ami ou ennemi du christianisme, le point de vue des 'Anciens' du XVIIIe siècle, hanté par le sentiment d'une décadence, d'une amputation, ou d'une aliénation modernes, s'est opposée avec un succès surprenant au point de vue des 'Modernes,' inspiré par une confiance euphorique dans la supériorité de l' 'esprit du temps' et de son 'progrès.'

3. Les Contre-Lumières et Rousseau

Arnaldo Momigliano, en réhabilitant les 'antiquaires' du XVIIIe siècle et en prenant le parti de Gibbon contre Diderot, a rendu possible une relecture plus profonde et moins naïve du siècle des Lumières. De son côté, en réhabilitant contre la philosophie moderne et critique la pensée classique des anciens philosophes et historiens, Leo Strauss a demandé lui aussi à un 'retour à l'antique' la guérison de l'esprit moderne du relativisme général hérité des Lumières et la restauration d'assises classiques dont la modernité politique à la dérive est dépourvue. À certains égards, ces deux penseurs du XXe siècle recoupent, par leur 'critique de la critique,' l'anti-modernité de Nietzsche, et comme lui, ils se retournent vers le sol antique, quoi que ce ne soit pas pour y réveiller Dionysos ni Zarathoustra. Ils rejoignent plutôt Comte et Renan dans une essentielle conviction commune: la modernité est fille sans boussole d'une critique en dernière analyse délétère, qui ne l'a délivrée de la foi que pour la mieux la précipiter dans le nihilisme et l'irrationalisme. Un 'progrès' qui prétend éclairer les hommes en les amputant de leur vocation au sacrifice, à la beauté, à l'admiration, dément la raison dont il se réclame et condamne l'humanité à un rabougrissement moral sans précédent. Tout en se proposant de sauver 'l'avenir de la science' en l'arrimant à une religion qui rende au peuple le sens du sacrifice, Renan ne pouvait s'empêcher de douter de cette greffe qu'il souhaitait, car au bout de la science, 'la vérité est peut-être triste.'

Le doute moderne s'est ainsi révolté et retourné à plusieurs reprises contre la modernité qui l'a imprudemment généralisé. Fille d'une critique qui feignit longtemps d'épargner la société et l'État, la crise moderne a si bien attaqué toutes les assises de la société et de l'État qu'elle a suscité, de génération en génération, avec des diagnostics répétés de décadence, de nouvelles tentatives de guérir la maladie moderne par le retour aux principes d'une ancienne santé.

Le talent et la propagande des 'Encyclopédistes' français ont réussi à convaincre, bien au delà de leur public initial, que les 'Modernes' de la Querelle étaient les seuls à avoir eu raison et à l'avoir pour jamais. Les 'philosophes,' Voltaire à leur tête, ont réussi à faire passer en axiome que leur modernité critique avait un avenir illimité et qu'elle pouvait se passer de mémoire. La 'doxa' critique et sceptique des Lumières s'est voulue paradoxalement la dogmatique d'une modernité irréfutable et irrésistible, adoratrice du progrès qui la dévore, rejetant tout frein, résistance et objection dans le camp de l'archaïsme ridicule ou pervers. Dans l'*Émile*, il arrive à Rousseau de tourner en dérision l'Académie des Inscriptions, mais ses citations constantes de faits et de textes antiques prouvent à quel point l'Antiquité est vivante pour l'*homo naturalis redivivus* qu'il prétend être et qu'il veut encourager à croître chez son élève. Aucun 'Ancien' de la Querelle n'a mieux défini que lui en quoi l'Antiquité, temps de l'homme encore éclairé naturellement, est à jamais le recours contre les temps décadents où l'homme est aliéné de sa propre nature par le poids même de ses contradictoires lumières:

> En général, Émile prendra plus de goût pour les livres des anciens que pour les nôtres; par cela seul qu'étant les premiers, les anciens sont plus près de la nature, et que leur génie est plus à eux. Quoi qu'aient pu dire Houdart de la Motte et l'abbé Terrasson, il n'y a point de vrai progrès de raison dans l'espèce humaine, parce que tout ce qu'on gagne d'un côté on le perd de l'autre; que tous les esprits partent toujours du même point, et que le temps qu'on emploie à savoir ce que d'autres ont pensé étant perdu pour apprendre à penser soi-même, on a plus de lumières acquises et moins de vigueur d'esprit. Nos esprits sont comme nos bras exercés à tout faire avec des outils, et rien par eux-mêmes.[6]

Aussi les Lumières dont son siècle est si content semblent-elles à Rousseau l'état d'aliénation ultime et moderne de la lumière naturelle, une guerre civile de l'esprit contre lui-même qui conjugue à un scepticisme et à une critique universels un dogmatisme arrogant et intolérant:

> Fuyez ceux qui, sous prétexte d'expliquer la nature, sèment dans les cœurs des hommes de désolantes doctrines et dont le scepticisme apparent est cent fois plus affirmatif et dogmatique que le ton décidé de leurs adversaires. Sous le hautain prétexte qu'eux seuls dont éclairés, vrais, de bonne foi, ils nous soumettent impérieusement à leurs décisions tranchantes et prétendent nous donner pour les vrais principes des choses les inintelligibles systèmes qu'ils ont bâtis dans leur imagination. Du reste, renversant, détruisant, foulant aux pieds tout ce que les hommes respectent, ils ôtent aux affligés la dernière consolation de leur misère, aux puissants et aux riches le

seul frein de leurs passions; ils arrachent du fond des cœurs le remords du crime, l'espoir de la vertu, et se vantent encore d'être les bienfaiteurs du genre humain. Jamais, disent-ils, la vérité n'est nuisible aux hommes. Je le crois comme eux, et c'est à mon avis une grande preuve que ce qu'ils enseignent n'est pas la vérité![7]

Du fait de cet aplomb de la 'critique' qui a intimidé la postérité plus encore que le public des Lumières, qui a lu Rousseau avec passion, des pans entiers du XVIIIe siècle ont été laissés dans l'ombre et censurés comme moucherons négligeables incapables d'arrêter le char de la modernité en marche. C'est seulement depuis quelques années que l'on a commencé à surmonter ce strabisme rétrospectif. Soudain se sont multipliés des livres impensables voici dix ans seulement, mesurant l'étendue, invisible auparavant, de la résistance du XVIIIe siècle aux Lumières dont on l'avait cru envahi et investi[8].

Au centre de ce tableau des Contre-Lumières se dresse la figure formidable de Rousseau, traditionnellement enrégimenté parmi les Docteurs de l'*Aufklärung*, alors que ce *Janus bifrons* est aussi, et peut-être surtout, l'ennemi le plus déterminé et le plus prophétique de la modernité critique telle que la célébraient et la pratiquaient les Lumières. Dès le *Discours sur les origines de l'inégalité*, Rousseau, oppose Fabricius, le citoyen antique et sa grandeur d'âme héroïque prêt au sacrifice pour la Cité, au bourgeois moderne, délivré de Dieu aussi bien que des idoles et jalousement rapetissé à la jouissance de ses droits et libertés privées. Dans l'*Émile*, il ne se contente pas d'opposer 'l'homme de la nature' en possession de tous ses dons au rabougrissement de l'individu moderne, 'l'homme de l'homme,' aliéné de sa propre nature; il invite l'homme rendu par exception à sa nature, rené 'Ancien' parmi les 'Modernes,' à délivrer la terre des hommes aliénés et dégénérés:

C'est par le désordre du premier âge que les hommes dégénèrent, et qu'on les voit devenir ce qu'ils sont aujourd'hui. Vils et lâches dans leurs vices mêmes, ils n'ont que de petites âmes, parce que leurs corps usés ont été corrompus de bonne heure; à peine leur reste-t-il assez de vie pour se mouvoir. Leurs subtiles pensées marquent des esprits sans étoffe, ils ne savent rien sentir de grand et de noble; ils n'ont ni simplicité ni vigueur; abjects en toutes choses, et bassement méchants, ils ne sont que vains, fripons et faux; ils n'ont même pas assez de courage pour être d'illustres scélérats. Tels sont les méprisables hommes que forme la crapule de la jeunesse; s'il s'en trouvait un seul qui sût être tempérant et sobre, qui sût au milieu d'eux, préserver son cœur, son sang, ses mœurs, de la contagion de l'exemple, à trente ans il écraserait tous ces insectes et deviendrait leur maître avec moins de peine qu'il n'en eut à rester le sien![9]

Heurtant de front l'anticléricalisme violent et facile des Lumières, Rousseau exalte le sentiment, qui fait croire, au dessus de la raison, qui fait douter, et il célèbre la fécondité d'une religion du cœur supérieure à la sécheresse stérile et ricanante de 'l'esprit' exclusivement critique. Il va jusqu' à écrire, décrivant d'avance sur la Terreur de 1793 et les Terreurs qui nous sont contemporaines:

Bayle a très bien prouvé que le fanatisme est plus pernicieux que l'athéisme, et cela est incontestable; mais ce qu'il n'a eu garde de dire, et qui n'est pas moins vrai, c'est que le fanatisme, quoique sanguinaire et cruel, est pourtant une passion grande et forte, qui élève le cœur de l'homme, qui lui fait mépriser la mort, qui lui donne un ressort prodigieux, et qu'il ne faut que mieux diriger pour en tirer les plus sublimes vertus; au lieu que l'irréligion, et en général l'esprit raisonneur et philosophique, attaché à la vie, efféminé, avilit les âmes, concentre toutes les passions dans la bassesse de l'intérêt particulier, dans l'abjection du moi humain, et sape ainsi à petit bruit les vrais fondements de toute société: car ce que les intérêts particuliers ont de commun est si peu de chose qu'il ne balancera jamais ce qu'ils ont d'opposé.[10]

Dans la *Lettre à d'Alembert*, anticipant sur les rébellions et répulsions aujourd'hui dirigées contre l'anti-société 'globalisée' du spectacle et de la consommation, Rousseau se livre à un assaut impitoyable contre la 'société des loisirs' de son temps, qui préfigurait en effet, en Angleterre et en France, celle de l'*entertainment* d'aujourd'hui où les individus distraits, décentrés, ennuyés, dépolitisés demandent à la 'culture' massifiée, qui a digéré les arts, d'occuper leur vacance. 'Ancien' réapparu parmi les 'Modernes,' il a discerné dans la modernité philosophique et morale du XVIIIe siècle anglais et français l'esquisse déjà très poussée de 'notre modernité,' et il l'a condamnée par avance en adoptant le point de vue éloigné, surplombant, et violemment ironique du 'retour à l'antique et à la nature.' Rousseau n'a certes rien d'un 'antiquaire,' mais sa lecture des poètes, des moralistes et des historiens anciens rejoint celle de Mme Dacier vantant la simplicité et la grandeur du monde de l'*Iliade*, contemporain de celui de la Bible, à un public sollicité par les 'Modernes' de ne voir dans le poème homérique qu'archaïsme, grossièreté et vulgarité. La révolte de Rousseau contre les sophismes des Lumières au nom de la nature et de l'Antiquité est parallèle au combat que les 'antiquaires' du parti des 'Anciens' menaient contre la décadence moderne des arts et des mœurs, résumée à leurs yeux dans le poudroiement des couleurs et la mollesse du dessin des peintres d'alcôve, flatteurs du goût 'corrompu' du public moderne, les François Boucher ou les Carle van Loo.

Vint un moment en France où les parallèles se rejoignirent, et où la révolte morale et politique de Rousseau coïncida avec le combat des 'antiquaires' pour une régénérescence du goût. L'héritier génial et éloquent des 'antiquaires' du XVIIIe siècle, Winckelmann, est à sa façon 'rousseauiste' lorsqu'il construit l'édifice de son Histoire de l'art chez les Anciens sur le schème pathétique du *Traité du sublime* du Pseudo-Longin, opposant à la grandeur et à la liberté héroïques des républiques antiques, mères de la grâce et du sublime dans les arts, l'affaissement physique et moral du monde 'dénaturé' du XVIIIe siècle.

En Angleterre, le *Decline and Fall* d'Edward Gibbon, qui porte un jugement beaucoup moins 'romantique' sur l'Europe contemporaine, cherche au contraire dans l'Empire romain à son zénith un modèle à imiter et méditer pour les Européens décidés à perpétuer, étendre et défendre une civilisation que la Renaissance a réveillée, dont ils sont désormais responsables devant toute l'humanité et à laquelle ils se doivent de croire.

Si la révolution française de 1789 a été, selon la vulgate marxiste, une révolution 'bourgeoise,' la 'bourgeoisie' jacobine qui l'a poussée vers les extrêmes s'est voulue 'citoyenne à l'antique' et 'sublime,' au sens du Fabricius de Rousseau, et non pas 'bourgeoise,' au sens du Mondain moderne de Voltaire ou du 'philosophe' père de famille dont Diderot a fait son porte-parole dans le *Neveu de Rameau*. Les jacobins français avaient parfaitement assimilé le véhément anti-bourgeoisisme qui éclate dans les deux *Discours*, dans l'*Émile* et dans le *Contrat social* de Rousseau, et qui fait de la 'vertu' du citoyen à l'antique l'ennemie plébéienne aussi implacable de l'hypocrisie bourgeoise que des vices de l'aristocratie. Il est revenu à un disciple de Leo Strauss, Allan Bloom, de signaler le premier qu'il faut chercher chez Rousseau, à qui il est arrivé par ailleurs de se montrer fort indulgent envers l'aristocratie de naissance et en sympathie avec ses vertus chevaleresques, le principe de l'horreur 'romantique' du bourgeois, et la meilleure définition qui ait été donnée de l'hypocrisie de l'homme 'moderne': Celui, qui dans l'ordre civil, veut conserver la primauté des sentiments de la nature, ne sait ce qu'il veut. Toujours en contradiction avec lui-même, toujours flottant entre ses penchants et ses devoirs, il ne sera jamais ni homme ni citoyen; il ne sera bon ni pour lui, ni pour les autres. Ce sera un de ces hommes de nos jours, un Français, un Anglais, un bourgeois: ce ne sera rien[11].

4. Vico, les philosophes des Lumières et l'antiquariat du XVIIIe siècle

L'autodidacte Rousseau est au fond le cas le plus conséquent, le plus extrême de la réaction dont est capable un esprit qui décide d'adopter le point de vue de l'Antiquité et de la Nature pour juger la modernité des Lumières bourgeoises. Dans les années qui ont suivi sa mort, et qui ont précédé la révolution, c'est Rousseau le prophète, parlant au nom de l'Antiquité et de la Nature, et non plus les 'Modernes' Voltaire, D'Alembert ou Diderot, qui a enflammé la jeune génération des Bonaparte et des Chateaubriand. C'est lui qui a inspiré l'héroïsme néo-classique et républicain de David 'peintre d'histoire.' Il n'est donc pas surprenant que l'auteur de l'*Émile* ait été l'objet, de son vivant, de la part des 'philosophes' et de Voltaire, d'une formidable campagne de dénigrement et de dénonciation[12]. L'ironie noire de Rousseau envers le progrès des Lumières était le revers d'un enthousiasme pour l'Antiquité et la Nature dont la radicalité gênait une critique philosophique refusant de voir le caractère destructeur de sa modernité.

Mais même dans son type classique et conservateur, l'antiquaire du XVIIIe siècle, héritier de la tradition humaniste du lettré regardant son temps à la lumière de l'Antiquité, fut l'objet du soupçon et du dénigrement persévérants de la part des Encyclopédistes. C'est l'*Encyclopédie* qui a introduit la confusion entre antiquariat et pédantisme passéiste, confusion devenue depuis un lieu commun de la modernité. Dans un article qui a fait date[13], Arnaldo Momigliano a eu la tranquille audace de remettre en cause ce poncif et de renouer avec la Renaissance italienne, pour laquelle l'antiquaire et le philologue étaient au contraire les agents d'une régénération de l'Europe chrétienne. L'Italie du XVIIIe siècle demeura la terre élue de l'antiquariat: Venise, Padoue, Florence, Cortone, Parme, Rome, Naples, leurs antiquaires (le plus souvent aussi amateurs et collectionneurs d'art), leurs académies, leurs fouilles, leurs publications monumentales tinrent en haleine l'Europe émerveillée, comme l'avaient fait au XVe et au XVIe siècles les premières découvertes à Rome et dans le Latium des 'grottes' peintes et les statues antiques. L'Italie des Lumières eut aussi son philosophe et philologue de la décadence moderne, Giambattista Vico, que découvriront à la fin du siècle les premiers 'philosophes de l'histoire' allemands. Sur le paradigme de la romanité et de ses trois âges, Vico a construit une interprétation cyclique du procès de civilisation, où la décadence ne figure pas comme une fin, mais comme un retour aggravé, et gravide d'un recommencement, à la féconde barbarie originelle. Cette civilisation dévoyée en décadence, que Rome a connue au IIIe siècle et qui portait en germe la Chrétienté féodale et médiévale, se répète dans l'Europe moderne de la 'critique' et des 'Lumières.' Vico la définit comme une 'barbarie de la réflexion,' formule que Chateaubriand reprendra à son compte dans ses *Mémoires*, lorsqu'il évoque les 'barbares de la civilisation' sévissant dans le Paris de la Terreur, ou lorsqu'il prévoit les effets moraux encore à venir de la décomposition sociale de l'Europe post-révolutionnaire. Mais Vico avait déjà parlé, au passé comme au futur, de guerres civiles

transformant les cités en forêts, où vont se cacher dans des repaires ceux qui furent des hommes; ainsi de longs siècles de barbarie viennent recouvrir de leur rouille des esprits devenus pervers à force de subtilités, et certes la barbarie de la réflexion les avait rendus plus cruels et plus inhumains qu'ils ne l'avaient été au temps de la première barbarie, qui n'atteignait que les sens: celle-ci était en effet une férocité généreuse dont celui qui était attaqué pouvait se défendre par le combat ou par la fuite; celle-là au contraire est à la fois cruelle et vile, au moment où elle s'attaque à la vie et aux biens de proches et d'amis, sous les flatteries et les caresses.[14]

Le retour dans l'Europe du 'troisième âge,' celui de la civilisation, d'une 'barbarie de la réflexion' qui annonçait son entrée en décadence, répétant ce qui s'était passé au IIIe siècle à Rome, Vico l'avait diagnostiqué dès 1707 dans son discours 'Sur la méthode des études de notre temps': l'éducation des Lumières, qui tarit le sentiment, l'imagination et la foi des adolescents par leur exposition prématurée à la raison analytique et critique de Descartes, les prive du développement naturel qui récapitulerait celui des trois âges de la société humaine (barbare et poétique, religieux et héroïque, humain et rationnel) et les pousse du côté de la 'barbarie de la réflexion.' L'aliénation de 'l'homme de la nature' en 'homme de l'homme,' selon le Rousseau de l'*Émile*, est fort analogue à cette amputation, chez l'homme moderne et exclusivement calculateur, dénoncée par Vico comme le principe même de la déca-

dence, des puissances poétiques, religieuses et courageuses dont sura-
bondait l'homme antique.

5. Momigliano, Gibbon, Caylus et le retour aux 'antiquaires'

Mais c'est en France, théâtre de la Querelle des Anciens et des Moder-
nes, et non en Italie restée sur la lancée de la Renaissance et de la
Réforme catholique, que la question de la décadence prit au cours du
XVIIIe siècle prit le tour le plus âpre, la critique des 'philosophes'
prenant le relais de celle des 'Modernes,' et la 'critique de la critique' de
Rousseau prenant ensuite le relais de la critique de la 'corruption du
goût moderne' par les 'Anciens.' En pleine Querelle des Anciens et des
Modernes, les 'Anciens' s'étaient pourvus d'une citadelle par la création
en 1701, à l'initiative de l'un des leurs, l'abbé Bignon, de l'Académie
royale des Inscriptions et Belles Lettres. L'Académie française était alors,
à chacune ou presque de ses élections, le champ de bataille où chacun
des deux camps cherchait à marquer des points.

La haine persévérante dont le maître d'œuvre de l'*Encyclopédie*, Denis
Diderot, devenu aussi l'un des persécuteurs de Rousseau, poursuivit le
plus prestigieux et influent des 'antiquaires' français, le comte de Caylus,
membre de l'Académie des Inscriptions depuis 1742, n'est qu'un épi-
sode de cette bataille acharnée des 'philosophes' français contre les
'antiquaires.' L'épigramme que Diderot fit circuler sur la tombe du
comte de Caylus en 1765 a néanmoins suffi pour compromettre durable-
ment la mémoire de cet 'antiquaire' et retarder jusqu'à ces dernières
années l'évaluation équitable de son rôle et de son œuvre.

Pourtant, dans sa correspondance avec Diderot, le grand sculpteur
Falconet, interprète du monde des ateliers et des vrais connaisseurs,
avait pris avec feu en 1766 la défense du comte et de son action sur les
arts français[15]. Et dès 1761, Edward Gibbon, qui avait été témoin de la
campagne haineuse de Diderot contre Caylus, prit hautement et publi-
quement le parti de l'antiquaire dans son *Essai sur l'étude de la littérature*.
Caylus, dans un billet joint à une lettre de Mallet adressée au futur
historien du *Decline and Fall*, lui en marqua sa reconnaissance:

> Je parle comme si M. Gibbon ne m'avoit pas loué, et même un peu trop fort.
> J'ai lu le livre d'un citoyen du monde, d'un véritable homme de lettres, qui
> les aime pour elles-mêmes, sans exception ni prévention, et qui joint à
> beaucoup d'esprit le bon sens plus rare que l'esprit, ainsi qu'une imparti-
> alité qui le rend juste et modeste, malgré l'impression qu'il a dû recevoir des

auteurs sans nombre qu'il a lus et très bien lus. J'ai donc dévoré ce petit ouvrage, auquel je désirerais de bon cœur une plus grande étendue et que je voudrais faire lire à tout le monde.[16]

Gibbon, pourvu de lettres de recommandation, avait vu à Paris 'trois ou quatre fois,' un Caylus qu'il décrit dans ses Mémoires comme «un homme simple, uni, bon, et qui me témoignait une bonté extrême.' S'il n'a pu le fréquenter davantage, c'est que le genre de vie du comte, dévoué aux artistes dans la journée, renfermé chez lui pour ses propres travaux après six heures du soir, l'en a empêché[17].

Telle a été l'autorité posthume en France de Diderot, de Marmontel et des Encyclopédistes qu'une relative *damnatio memoriae* a frappé Caylus malgré les tentatives de réhabilitation esquissées au XIXe siècle par les frères Goncourt et par plusieurs érudits, Nisard, Rocheblave et Fontaine.

Je dois à Arnaldo Momigliano, lors d'un séminaire au Warburg Institute en 1980[18], d'avoir attiré mon attention sur la défense de l'antiquariat et en particulier de l'antiquaire Caylus, par Gibbon. Encouragé par Francis Haskell, j'ai consacré en 1994 mon enseignement au Collège de France à ce personnage méconnu du siècle des Lumières, et je prépare, depuis, un livre qui sera consacré à sa pensée et à son action, décisives dans le mouvement français de 'retour à l'antique.' Depuis cette date, une jeune génération d'historiens de l'art et de la littérature se passionne pour cette figure longtemps restée dans l'ombre, et plusieurs travaux et publications de textes sont actuellement en gestation.

Par une rencontre qui n'est pas due au hasard, c'est un disciple indirect de Momigliano, Alain Schnapp, qui a de son côté réveillé l'intérêt scientifique pour Caylus. Dans un livre publié en 1994, *La Conquête du passé*, aux origines de l'archéologie, il a montré que Gibbon avait raison de prendre la défense de Caylus: l'antiquaire français était très en avance sur son temps dans sa manière méthodique et concrète de concevoir les fouilles archéologiques et d'étudier leurs résultat. Schnapp a combattu ainsi un autre préjugé de Diderot, depuis endossé par les marxistes: quoique aristocrate, et à ce titre 'condamné' par le progrès historique, un grand seigneur comme Caylus ne pouvait avoir d'autre point de vue que 'réactionnaire' et obscurantiste. Pour ma part, j'avais été très tôt guéri de ce préjugé par un autre de mes aînés, Raymond Aron, qui le premier avait démontré qu'un autre aristocrate, Tocqueville, avait pu se montrer sur l'avenir des sociétés modernes au moins aussi perspicace que le roturier Karl Marx. Il peut arriver aux prétendus 'vaincus de l'Histoire en marche' de voir plus clair et plus loin que ses très provisoires vainqueurs.

6. Un magistrat de la République des Lettres et des Arts

Le comte de Caylus, né en 1692 en quelque sorte sur les marches du trône de France, fils d'une nièce de Mme de Maintenon et d'un descendant d'une ancienne famille féodale du Sud-Ouest, ami de tout ce qui comptait à la Cour de Louis XV, était bien loin d'être au XVIIIe siècle un 'vaincu' au sens où pouvait l'être au siècle suivant Alexis de Tocqueville, né en 1805, dans une famille noble, décimée et dépouillée de ses privilèges par la Révolution. Néanmoins, tout en appartenant de fait à la noblesse de Cour, et en se montrant passionnément attaché à la monarchie, Caylus, après 1714, date à laquelle il mit fin à sa brève et brillante carrière militaire, ne servit plus ni le gouvernement ni l'administration royales. Dédaigneux du faste et du pouvoir, il confondit, en un même idéal de vie, le loisir de 'l'honnête homme' né noble qui 'ne se pique de rien' et celui du magistrat de la République des Lettres et des Arts qui veille, en 'Amateur' désintéressé, dévoué et généreux, à la bonne intelligence de la communauté et à la meilleure éducation de ses concitoyens artistes. On a pu avec beaucoup de finesse comparer cet idéal de vie, choisi par un laïc résolument agnostique, libre d'esprit et de mœurs, mais élevé par une mère fénelonienne et par un oncle paternel, l'évêque d'Auxerre, résolument port-royaliste, à celle d'un prélat *in partibus*, pratiquant par 'amour pur,' sans espoir de récompense, sans même compter sur les consolations de la grâce efficace, cette charité éclairée et universelle dont il a défini lui-même les présupposés moraux et sociaux dans sa conférence sur l'Amateur lue devant l'Académie de Peinture et sculpture en 1748: 'les mœurs douces, le savoir, la politesse, le goût pour la bonne compagnie, les ornements et les agréments de l'esprit'[19].

Le comte de Caylus ne devint pas du jour au lendemain, en 1714, au sortir de sept années de service actif dans les armées royales, au cours de la guerre de Succession d'Espagne, ni l'Amateur influent des années 1747–51, ni l'Antiquaire respecté dans toute l'Europe des années 1751–65. Contrairement au grands antiquaires des siècles précédents, un Scaliger, un Pirro Ligorio, un Peiresc, un Saumaise, tous nés dans des familles d'humanistes et enfants prodiges de la philologie, le jeune gentilhomme destiné par les siens à la carrière des armes n'avait reçu qu'une formation sommaire et tôt interrompue. À contre-courant de la mode mondaine et moderne, ce gentilhomme d'épée s'imposa lui-même une seconde éducation sévère sous les meilleurs maîtres de l'heure, dans les arts du dessin et de la gravure auprès d'Antoine Watteau et de Pierre-Jean Mariette, rencontrés à l'hôtel Crozat dès 1711 et dans les disciplines littéraires auprès d'un ami de sa mère, l'abbé vénitien Antonio Conti, un polymathe résolument du parti des 'Anciens' et d'Homère dans la Querelle. Plus tard, il bénéficiera de la collaboration d'un grand numismate et helléniste, l'abbé Barthélémy.

Initié de l'intérieur au monde des ateliers d'artistes et à celui du système de commandes privées et publiques qui régit leur production, initié aussi bien de l'intérieur à la théorie académique des arts et à ses fondations littéraires et érudites, Caylus se donna les moyens d'exercer une médiation active entre les deux univers. Il mit sa naissance, son rang, ses rentes, ses amitiés et ses relations à la Cour, la position qu'il en vint à occuper dans deux Académies royales, au service de la vie des arts, et de plus en plus résolument, et de leur 'retour à la nature et à l'antique,' dont il escomptait une redressement du goût du public, du talent et du métier des artistes, et de la fécondité des institutions littéraires et artistiques de la monarchie.

Dès 1714, il entreprend une série de voyages d'étude en Italie, en Méditerranée orientale, puis en Hollande et en Angleterre. Il étudie sur les lieux et en présence des 'monuments' les arts de la Rome et de la Grèce antiques et ceux de l'Italie moderne. Il se lie aux amateurs et aux antiquaires italiens, Zanetti à Venise, Gaburri à Florence, et aux princes hollandais et anglais de la République des Lettres, à Londres, un Richard Mead, à La Haye un Basnage de Beauval.

En 1731, il est élu au titre d' 'amateur honoraire' à l'Académie de Peinture et Sculpture. Il n'exercera vraiment cette magistrature qu'à partir de 1747, année où son ami le peintre Charles Coypel devient Directeur de l'Académie et Premier peintre du roi et où tous deux s'emploient à rétablir les 'conférences' dans la vie académique et à réformer le système d'éducation des jeunes artistes. C'est cette année-là que, de l'extérieur des cercles académiques, et à propos de l'exposition du Salon du Louvre, Lafont de Saint-Yenne publie ses *Réflexions sur quelques causes de l'état présent de la peinture en France*, où il formule en public ce que Caylus, Coypel, Mariette pensaient tout bas entre eux, mais selon de tout autres prémisses: les arts français sont sur la pente du 'déclin,' et 'tout nous conduit nécessairement au décri et à la ruine de ce qui est pensé fortement et inutilement'[20]. En 1749, le même auteur, se réclamant d'un zèle de 'citoyen,' approfondit et élargit son portrait de la décadence des arts du royaume dans une brochure intitulée: *L'Ombre du Grand Colbert, le Génie du Louvre et la Ville de Paris*, dialogue, où le 'déclin' du système académique des arts royaux depuis la Régence est opposé au 'grand goût' dans tous les ordres dont il s'était montré capable, sous Louis XIV et Colbert, suscitant l'admiration de toute l'Europe pour le génie de la nation. Cette vive polémique 'patriotique,' qui connut un grand écho[21], reprenait et amplifiait les thèses soutenues en faveur de l'administration de Colbert par Charles Perrault en 1687, dans son poème *Le Siècle de Louis le Grand*, déclencheur de la Querelle des Anciens et des Modernes. Prenant pour emblème du 'grand goût' la colonnade du Louvre conçue par Claude Perrault, Lafont de Saint-Yenne préconisait dans l'abstrait et dans un esprit tout 'moderne' un 'retour à Louis XIV' sous Louis XV.

Caylus, à qui sa mère avait dicté des *Souvenirs de la cour de Louis XIV*, que publiera en 1770 Voltaire, auteur lui-même dans le sillage du succès de *L'Ombre du Grand Colbert*, d'un panégyrique 'philosophique' du Siècle de Louis XIV, n'était certainement pas insensible à cette nostalgie du 'Grand siècle' et du 'grand goût.' Mais comme Coypel et Mariette, il savait que les choses de l'art n'étaient pas si simples. Le 'grand goût' de l'Académie colbertienne avait été travaillé par la Querelle du dessin et du coloris, opposant 'poussinistes' et 'rubénistes,' sur fond du grand débat du XVIe siècle italien entre Florence et Venise. Caylus avait été l'ami du peintre Antoine Watteau, le génie du 'rubénisme.' Il était l'ami du sculpteur Edme Bouchardon, le sculpteur que l'Italie avait salué comme un 'Ancien' réapparu parmi les modernes. La vraie réponse au 'zèle' oratoire de Lafont de Saint-Yenne ne pouvait être un pur et simple 'retour à Louis XIV' moderne et franco-français, mais un travail de longue haleine à l'intérieur de l'Académie et auprès de ses professeurs, une refonte de l'éducation des jeunes artistes, et la réappropriation de ce qui avait rendu classique le génie de la Renaissance italienne: l'étude de la nature et des Anciens, le métier probe et savant, les grands sujets. Il ne s'agit pas de répéter le 'siècle de Louis XIV,' mais d'inventer un 'siècle de Louis XV' qui soit classique de son propre chef.

En 1742, Caylus avait été élu au titre d' 'Amateur honoraire' à l'Académie des Inscriptions. Il s'y montra si assidu et il y prononça un si grand nombre de conférences qu'il apparut comme le successeur du Bénédictin Bernard de Montfaucon. En 1717–21, dans les volumes illustrés de son *Antiquité expliquée*, ce Bénédictin avait publié une somme de documents visuels et d'inscriptions étayant ou complétant la connaissance du monde gréco-romain tirée des seuls textes littéraires. Montfaucon était un immense érudit, mais aveugle pour les qualités intrinsèques des œuvres d'art qu'il 'expliquait' et pour la fiabilité graphique de leurs reproductions, le moindre de ses soucis étant les leçons de technique ou les modèles formels que les artistes contemporains pouvaient éventuellement trouver dans ces reliques d'une civilisation disparue. Graveur lui-même et habitué des ateliers d'artiste, Caylus avait collaboré chez Pierre Crozat à l'élaboration techniquement impeccable d'un Recueil de reproductions gravées de tableaux et de dessins de maîtres italiens du XVIe siècle, figurant dans les collections du roi, du duc d'Orléans ou de Crozat lui-même, grand connaisseur. Il avait gravé et publié, avec le même souci d'exactitude et de goût, un recueil de caricatures attribuées à Léonard, en possession de Mariette qui avait écrit la préface de l'ouvrage. Son entrée à l'Académie des Inscriptions avait été préparée par sa réputation de voyageur en Grèce et en Turquie, et par la publication en 1750 d'un *Recueil des pierres gravées de la collection du roi*, illustré de gravures de Caylus, d'après des dessins 'au trait' de Bouchardon, illustrant le *Traité des pierres gravées* de Mariette. Ce monument répondait au souci d'éduquer l'œil des artistes et des amateurs sur les témoignages les plus fiables et intacts de l'art antique de la composition et du dessin. À partir de 1747, Caylus s'employa à faire passer dans ses nombreuses conférences à l'Académie de Peinture et Sculpture et dans ses publications à l'usage des artistes, le meilleur de son expérience des techniques et du sentiment des formes qui avaient rendu supérieurs les artisans et les artistes antiques, avant tout les Grecs, et qui avaient nourri les maîtres de la Renaissance italienne.

Ce dessein de régénération de l'École française, embrassé et poursuivi avec une extraordinaire ténacité sur plusieurs registres à la fois, se substitua de plus en plus à la vie sociale de 'virtuose' qui l'avait long-temps occupé, mais aussi dispersée. Bon connaisseur de l'ennui et du divertissement pascaliens, Mme du Deffand eut un jour ce mot: 'Caylus grave de peur de se pendre.' L'abbé Le Blanc, dans l'éloge funèbre qu'il fit de son ami et confrère à la mort de celui-ci en 1765, décrit de façon plus enveloppée cette facette morale du comte:

> Ennemi des affaires, le comte s'en fit une de tous les amusements de la vie. Il s'occupa de musique, de dessin, de peinture. Il écrivit, mais ce n'étaient que des jeux et des caprices de société auxquels il ne donna jamais plus de soin qu'ils n'en méritaient. Étincelant de feu et de gaîté, jamais il ne s'asservit à la correction du style, il ne se proposait d'autre perfection en ce genre que le divertissement de ses amis. Il attendait tout de la nature et elle le servait à son gré. Pour juger des ouvrages de l'Art, il possédait ce goût, cet instinct supérieur à l'étude, plus sûr que le raisonnement, plus rapide que là réflexion. Son premier coup d'œil le trahissait rarement, il saisissait sur le champ les beautés et les défauts.[22]

L'espèce de conversion à l'*otium studiosum* qu'il connut dans la compagnie des plus savants antiquaires de France, il l'a décrite lui-même dans la préface du premier volume de son *Recueil d'Antiquités*, adressée à ses confrères de l'Académie des Inscriptions: 'Avant que vous ne m'eussiez fait la grâce de m'admettre parmi vous, je ne regardais que du côté de l'art les restes de l'antiquité savante arrachée à la barbarie des temps. Vous m'avez appris à y attacher un mérite infiniment supérieur, je veux dire celui de renfermer mille singularités de l'histoire du culte, des usages et des mœurs de ces pays fameux qui, par la vicissitude des choses humaines, ont disparu de la surface de la terre, qu'ils avaient rempli de leur nom'[23].

7. Caylus, Bouchardon et le 'retour à l'antique' dans les arts français

Qu'est-ce qui a poussé Caylus, non content de devenir un 'pont' entre les divers mondes où il était chez lui, celui des 'bonnes compagnies' parisiennes, où se rencontraient d'éventuels clients, français et étrangers, pour les artistes qu'il protégeait, celui de l'Académie de peinture et des artistes, celui enfin des antiquaires des Inscriptions, à pencher personnellement de plus en plus du côté de l'antiquariat, prêtant par ce choix un poids et un prestige insolites à une vocation en elle-même modeste et austère. Pourquoi, lui qui avait 60 000 livres de rentes et qui était doué pour tous les plaisirs, s'est-il détourné de Watteau et de l'art rocaille, pourquoi s'est-il même détaché des agréments de la vie sociale parisienne et pourquoi, non content d'avoir accumulé avec ses savantes conférences aux deux Académies, une œuvre en soi monumentale, a-t-il consacré ses dernières années à l'immense entreprise de son *Recueil d'Antiquités*, dont le septième volume parut après sa mort? La clef de cette extraordinaire activité réformatrice, littéraire et savante est à chercher dans son affiliation précoce au parti des Anciens de la première Querelle et de la Querelle d'Homère qui lui fit suite. Les 'Anciens' et les partisans d'Homère ont vu dans les thèses 'modernes' le symptôme d'une décadence qu'il fallait à tout prix combattre. L'auteur en 1731 de *Trois essais sur la corruption du goût*, Toussaint Rémond de Saint-Mard, excellent interprète de cette angoisse, avait fréquenté le cercle qui se réunissait autour de Mme de Caylus et de l'abbé Conti, dans la petite maison proche du Luxembourg où la comtesse vécut entre 1715 et 1728 en compagnie de son fils. Dans cette compagnie, où furent conçus les *Souvenirs de la cour de Louis XIV* de la comtesse, le regret du 'Grand siècle' ne prenait pas le caractère étroitement patriotique et moderne que lui donnera Lafont de Saint-Yenne. On y goûte la musique italienne, on y lit Fénelon et Gravina, on s'y intéresse à la querelle entre Newton et Leibniz. L'abbé Conti et ses amis académiciens des Inscriptions, tous du parti des 'Anciens,' ouvrent largement au jeune Caylus l'horizon européen de la République des Lettres. À l'hôtel Crozat, où reste vivant le souvenir de Roger de Piles, et où fréquentent académiciens des Inscriptions, peintres académiciens, comédiens érudits de la troupe italienne de Luigi Riccoboni, le même Caylus échappe à la rétraction nationale et à l'italophobie des 'Modernes': l'horizon là aussi est européen, c'est celui de Paris capitale de la République des arts, mais qui sait avoir encore beaucoup à apprendre de la mère-patrie de la Renaissance, de la Rome antique et de la Grèce.

Bien avant que le dessein du *Recueil d'Antiquités* se soit formé dans son esprit, il avait pu mesurer la différence entre l'art de son ami Antoine Watteau, autodidacte de génie dont la formation avait mûri devant les Rubens du Luxembourg et les Vénitiens de la collection Crozat, et celui des maîtres de la Renaissance et du XVIIe siècle qui s'étaient formés à l'étude de l'antique. Il s'était peu à peu détaché de ce moderne 'art rocaille' auquel la Régence avait fait fête, et qui avait rompu avec le 'grand goût' classique dont s'étaient réclamé Charles Le Brun et les sculpteurs de Versailles. Un symptôme de ce virage, dont il fera la confidence indirecte dans la *Vie de Watteau* lue devant l'Académie de Peinture et Sculpture en 1748, c'est l'amitié et la collaboration qui le lièrent dès 1733, au retour d'Italie de l'artiste, à Bouchardon, génie ancien qui avait naturellement retrouvé à Rome la forme antique. Dans l'éloge funèbre du grand sculpteur qu'il lut en séance de l'Académie en 1762, il fit le portrait d'un artisan français de génie dont les mœurs et le goût de la perfection font revivre les auteurs grecs et romains de pierres gravées: 'Modeste dans ses habits et dans son domestique, il conserva toujours des mœurs simples. La droiture de son cœur le rendait incapable d'aucune brigue et d'aucune cabale; vivant retiré, il ne connut jamais l'intrigue … Sa vie était réglée et modérée, ses délassements domestiques ne causaient aucun préjudice à la perfection du travail dont il était sans cesse occupé; au contraire, sans le perdre de vue, il le laissait reposer, ou plutôt il s'en éloignait pour se reposer lui-même et le voir avec des yeux plus frais'[24].

Il s'employa à valoir à cet artiste 'à l'antique' par ses mœurs comme par son génie des commandes royales à la mesure de ses capacités, notamment pour le décor du Bassin de Neptune à Versailles, que Louis

XV et sa Cour avaient regagné après la mort du régent. Il réussit à obtenir pour Bouchardon la commande d'une statue équestre de Louis XV, qui fut achevée par Pigalle après la mort de l'artiste et détruite à la Révolution. Dès 1737, Caylus fournissait à Bouchardon les sujet, empruntés à l'épopée antique, de grands dessins dramatiques qu'il grava lui-même, et qui recueillirent un vif succès. Dans les années 1755-8, fort de cette expérience, il publia plusieurs recueils de descriptions de tableaux d'après les scènes majeures de l'*Iliade*, de l'*Odyssée*, de l'*Énéide*, et de la *Légende d'Hercule*, afin d'encourager les peintres ignorant les langues anciennes à traiter de grands sujets classiques et leurs commanditaires à les leur proposer.

Une fois qu'il eut perçu les 'faiblesses' de l'art rocaille, Caylus déploya tout son entregent et ses multiples talents à rendre le système académique français capable de pourvoir le 'siècle de Louis XV' d'un grand art qui n'ait rien à envier à celui du 'siècle de Louis XIV,' mais qui soit une création originale inspirée directement par la souche-mère de la Renaissance: les arts antiques mieux connus, mieux compris, mieux étudiés du point de vue de l'art. Dès que l'occasion devint favorable, en 1747, il s'employa, avec Charles Coypel, à redresser l'enseignement dispensé aux jeunes peintres, n'épargnant pas son argent pour doter de bourses, créer des prix et fournir des commandes, en France et en Europe, aux élèves les mieux disposés à entrer dans ses vues. Les nombreuses disciplines qui avaient fait la force des Académies d'art du XVIe et du XVIIe siècles, et qui avaient toutes pour objet l'étude approfondie du corps héroïque et de l'expression des passions de l'âme, furent remises à l'honneur dans l'atelier des artistes qu'il protégeait. À partir de 1747 et jusqu'en 1764, Caylus s'est montré un infatigable éducateur de ses confrères artistes de l'Académie de Peinture et Sculpture, lisant devant eux quinze Vies d'artistes français du XVIIe et du XVIIIe siècles dont il fait valoir 'les beautés' et les 'défauts,' et douze essais sur des points concrets du métier et de la poétique des arts. En 1761, il fonde un Prix de têtes et de l'expression en 1763, un Prix de perspective, et en 1764, un Prix d'Ostéologie, afin d'encourager les élèves à se rendre maîtres de la représentation, dans les tableaux d'histoire, de la grâce et de la grandeur du drame humain, à contre courant du *far presto* et de la 'manière' décorative de l'art rocaille, appropriés aux seuls délices de la vie privée.

Les ateliers de ses protégés, peintres et sculpteurs, Bouchardon, Jean-Marie Vien, Lagrenée, Vassé, devinrent dès les années 1750, les foyers d'un 'retour à l'antique' dans les commandes royales et même dans le décor ou le mobilier 'à la grecque' des demeures privées. Il attribue à

Bouchardon en 1763, dans la Vie qu'il dédie à sa mémoire, une devise qu'il avait faite sienne: 'S'approprier le talent des Anciens et le retrouver sur la Nature.'

8. Caylus antiquaire et la connaissance technique et esthétique de l'art antique

La logique de cette action sur les arts royaux, menée d'abord en s'appuyant sur l'Académie de peinture et sculpture, l'a conduit à s'engager de plus en plus profondément et exclusivement, avec cette fois le soutien et la collaboration de l'Académie des Inscriptions, dans l'étude comparée des textes et des monuments de l'art grec, étrusque, égyptien et romain. Le fait qu'il ait ajouté à ces recherches, par lesquelles il rivalise avec les travaux des 'antiquaires' vénitiens, florentins, romains et napolitains, des explorations archéologiques portant sur la Gaule celtique et romaine et sur la France mérovingienne, atteste qu'une passion nationale le guidait aussi. Sa génération avait été marquée par le grand traité d'esthétique du parti des Anciens, les *Réflexions sur la poésie et la peinture* de l'abbé Du Bos, publiées en 1718. Caylus connaissait l'abbé Du Bos, qui fréquentait l'hôtel de Pierre Crozat. Historien d'une science et d'une stature exceptionnelles, l'abbé avait établi dans ses *Origines de la monarchie française*, que le royaume médiéval n'avait pas été, comme le soutenait Boulainvilliers, une création *ab ovo* des envahisseurs germains mais une continuation locale de l'administration et de l'armée romaines malgré la dislocation de l'Empire d'Occident, mais avec la bénédiction obtenue par Clovis de l'Empire d'Orient. Pour Caylus lecteur de Du Bos, et comme lui partisan des 'Anciens' dans la Querelle, le 'retour à l'antique' dans les arts royaux n'était pas seulement une reprise du 'grand goût' classique des Académies de Louis XIV, c'était une remontée aux origines et à l'essence romaines de monarchie gallicane, la remise en lumière de la souche-mère inépuisable qu'elle partage avec l'Italie et l'Europe civilisée.

En 1754, geste typique de sa méthode de ressourcement de l'invention moderne dans la mémoire de l'antique, Caylus utilise le canal des deux Académies pour faire connaître sa redécouverte, longuement élaborée avec la collaboration de chimistes et de philologues, de la peinture à l'encaustique des Anciens. À l'Académie de peinture, il lit pendant plusieurs séances un mémoire sur la 'Peinture des Anciens,' et à l'Académie des Inscriptions, il présente et explique un 'tableau peint à la cire sur bois,' exécuté par son protégé Vien, et figurant une tête de Minerve.

Diderot publia aussitôt un libelle pour tenter de détruire l'effet produit par cette redécouverte d'une antique technique oubliée. La peinture à l'encaustique allait néanmoins devenir une technique souvent employée pour les décors néo-classiques.

Typique et topique, elle aussi, avait été la publication en 1750 du *Recueil des pierres gravées de la collection du roi*: dans cette oeuvre de remémoration érudite, Caylus et Bouchardon inventent ou réinventent la technique du 'dessin au trait' qui aura la faveur des artistes néo-classiques, de Flaxman à Girodet. De son côté, le *Traité des pierres gravées* de Mariette, rappelait que depuis la Renaissance, c'est dans ces figures confiées aux pierres dures que les grands artistes modernes ont retrouvé, plus intact que dans d'autres supports plus friables, le sens des contours, l'art de composer en fonction du sujet et l'exécution parfaite des Anciens. Les deux amis travaillent de concert à une seconde Renaissance.

Cette Renaissance, ils ne la conçoivent qu'en collaboration étroite avec l'Italie, où leurs amis le Vénitien Zanetti, et surtout les grands antiquaires florentins Gaburri et Venuti tiennent en haleine l'Europe lettrée par leurs publications monumentales: le *Museum Florentinum*, le *Museum Etruscum*, diffusés dans toute l'Europe par souscription. Dès 1715, Caylus avait été témoin oculaire des premières fouilles tentées sur le site d'Herculanum par l'ambassadeur de France. Depuis la reprise des fouilles sur le même site par Charles III et la découverte de peintures antiques jalousement transportées et gardées dans la Villa royale de Portici, l'intérêt passionné de tous les antiquaires européens était tourné vers Naples; la curiosité du public était éveillée, ce qui allait dans le sens du 'retour à l'antique' auquel travaillaient Caylus, Mariette et leurs amis. En 1757, pour protester contre le secret qui entourait encore les découvertes d'Herculanum, et obliger les autorités napolitaines à porter très haut les critères de la publication, par l'Académie d'Herculanum créée par le roi de Naples, des peintures antiques retrouvées, Caylus fait reproduire à ses frais en un petit nombre d'exemplaires, avec les exigences philologiques du 'Recueil Crozat,' un ensemble de dessins à la gouache de Pietro Santi Bartoli reproduisant eux-mêmes des peintures antiques retrouvées au XVIIe siècle dans des 'grottes' romaines et dans d'autres sites du Latium, mais effacées entre temps. En 1764, il fait traduire par Michel Huber et publier à ses frais à Paris les *Sendschreiben von den herculanischen Entdeckungen, an den Reichsgraven von Brühl*, du jeune Winckelmann, alors basé à Dresde où Caylus avait un correspondant attitré, comme dans la plupart des capitales européennes. Cette publication parisienne inaugura la réputation internationale de l'inconnu, qui protestait lui aussi contre l'attitude des autorités napolitaines, contraire au devoir de communication de règle dans la République des Lettres et des Arts.

En décembre 1749, Caylus avait présenté à l'Académie des Inscriptions un livre de dessins représentant des vases antiques et provenant de la bibliothèque de Nicolas Peiresc, marquant ainsi sa filiation avec le grand polymathe aixois et la tradition française d'antiquariat. Ses nombreuses conférences lues devant l'Académie des Inscriptions et publiés dans les célèbres *Mémoires* de cette Académie portent aussi bien sur l'interprétation de passages de Pline l'Ancien, sur le grand débat de la Querelle d'Homère sur le Bouclier d'Achille, que sur des relevés de découvertes archéologiques récentes dans le sol gallo-romain qui lui étaient transmises, selon un protocole établi par ses soins, par les ingénieurs des Ponts et Chaussées de l'administration de Trudaine. Il forme le projet, aidé par ses correspondants avignonnais le marquis de Clavière et l'abbé Esprit Calvet, de reconstituer l'ensemble des relevés de monuments romains de Provence dessinés sur l'ordre de Colbert par Nicolas Mignard, et de les publier selon l'intention du ministre de Louis XIV. Cette reconstitution d'un ensemble divisé se révéla très difficile et incomplète. À la mort de Caylus, Mariette reprit le flambeau, mais il mourut lui-même trop tôt pour mener à bien l'entreprise.

Les études et les communications de Caylus, réservées de plus en plus exclusivement aux Inscriptions, prennent à partir de 1751 un nouveau caractère: elles sont destinés, avec les notices scientifiques des pièces antiques de sa propre collection de travail, à figurer dans le *Recueil d'Antiquités* dont il mènera à bien sept volumes, avec l'aide de plusieurs de ses confrères, dont le grand helléniste Jean-Jacques Barthélémy.

Chacune des pièces antiques de sa collection de travail, beaux objets d'usage courant plutôt que chefs d'œuvre exceptionnels, dont il publie la ou les gravures établies avec soin, y est décrite et commentée avec une extrême précision, sous l'angle matériel et technique, mais souvent aussi sous l'aspect esthétique, donnant une leçon rétrospective aux articles et aux planches de l'*Encyclopédie*, qui s'étaient bornées dans l'ordre des arts visuels à un inventaire des pratiques de l'Académie et de l'industrie contemporaine. Caylus ne se borne donc pas à enrichir à l'intention des seuls antiquaires leur 'corpus' iconographique, il veut pourvoir les artistes et les amateurs de témoignages authentiques et concrets du *modus operandi* des artistes et des artisans antiques. Les pièces qu'il publie, il les a pour la plupart tenu en sa possession, il a pu les examiner et les analyser lui-même, avec la collaboration de chimistes; aussitôt publiées, il les a données à la Bibliothèque du roi pour faire place à d'autres. Outre celles qui proviennent de fouilles récentes faites en France, beaucoup lui sont envoyées d'Italie, mais aussi du Levant ou de Marseille, par ses correspondants, mais aussi par des inconnus et par des admirateurs. Son interlocuteur le plus assidu et son fournisseur le plus avisé fut le grand antiquaire théatin Paolo Paciaudi. Leur correspondance, publiée par Charles Nisard en 1850, est l'équivalent en plein XVIIIe siècle de celle de Peiresc avec Cassiano dal Pozzo, et elle nous ouvre les coulisses de la mise en œuvre du *Recueil.* On ne saurait surestimer le rôle que celui-ci a joué dans l'invention des ébénistes, bronziers, ornemanistes, bijoutiers, et décorateurs des différents styles du néo-classicisme jusqu'à l'Empire. Le *Recueil,* souvent cité par Quatremère de Quincy avec les conférences de Caylus aux Inscriptions, fut l'ouvrage de référence pour la conception des *Antiquités étrusques grecques et romaines* de Pierre-Hughes d'Hancarville (1766–76), pour celle de *l'Histoire de l'art dans les siècles obscurs* de Seroux d'Agincourt (1821), et il le resta pour les travaux des Sociétés d'antiquaires et d'archéologues qui se multiplièrent en France au XIXe siècle.

9. Le singulier destin du 'retour à l'antique' français

Quand Caylus meurt en 1765, il est au sommet de sa réputation et de son influence en France et en Europe. Il a eu le temps de voir s'esquisser autour de lui un retournement du goût de la Cour et du talent artistique de la Ville en faveur de cette Antiquité qu'il avait si bien servie. Dès 1750 pointe la mode du mobilier, des vases, du décor, des tableaux 'à la grecque' qui rivalise à Paris avec la persistance du goût rocaille. Caylus a pu être témoin, aux Salons de 1761 et 1763, du succès remporté par son protégé, le peintre Jean-Marie Vien, que Girodet appellera 'le Nestor de l'École néo-classique,' et par son sculpteur de prédilection, après Bouchardon, Vassé. Il a pu s'amuser d'apprendre que son ennemi et celui des 'antiquaires,' Diderot, en 1763, s'enthousiasmait dans la *Correspondance littéraire de Grimm* pour *La Marchande d'amours* de Vien, directement inspirée, très probablement à l'instigation du comte et à l'insu du critique, d'une peinture antique reproduite dans le t. I, planche VIII, des *Pitture antiche d'Ercolano,* enfin publié en 1759 et parcimonieusement distribué par les autorités napolitaines. Vien, pour composer d'autres figures féminines gracieuses 'à la grecque,' les quatre Saisons, Glycère, Une prêtresse sacrifiant (Salon de 1762), s'était déjà inspiré des gouaches d'après l'antique de Pietro Santi Bartoli publiées à compte d'auteur par Caylus en 1757. Infatigable, dès 1755, le comte avait incité les peintres, dans une brochure, à préférer la grâce 'à la grecque' à la grâce moderne et 'rocaille': 'Si l'on veut des images simplement riantes, les tableaux des filles de l'Isle Sacrée et des filles de Sparte fourniront des groupes aussi délicieux qu'intéressants. L'habillement simple des Filles Grecques, la noblesse de leurs attitudes, l'élégance de leurs tailles, la beauté de leurs traits, tout cela joint aux recherches nécessaires du Costume, fera valoir infiniment l'esprit et le mérite du Peintre, dans l'un et l'autre sujet'[25].

Dans le registre de la grandeur, où le 'rocaille' était par définition décevant, les recueils de 'sujets' antiques (l'*Iliade*, l'*Odyssée*, l'*Énéide*, la *Légende de l'Hercule thébain*) narrés et commentés à l'usage des peintres, et que Caylus publia en 1755–7, figurèrent dans les ateliers des peintres d'histoire de la jeune génération, et fournirent leur sujet à plusieurs 'tableaux d'histoire' néo-classiques de Gavin Hamilton, du jeune David et d'autres peintres français et étrangers.

Dans la préface parue après sa mort du t. VII de son *Recueil d'Antiquités*, Caylus était en droit de se féliciter, en termes qui se souviennent des *Géorgiques* de Virgile, de la sérénité et de la plénitude qu'il avait trouvées dans ses longs travaux de 'labourage' et de 'semailles' d'antiquaire: il avait vu croître la première moisson. À cette patiente fécondité il oppose l'agitation vaniteuse, jalouse et desséchante de la critique introduite dans la République des Lettres et des Arts par les 'philosophes.' On trouve dans la *Vie de Bouchardon* de 1762 la même ironie fustigeant 'le brillant, le sublime métaphysique' dont se parent les ignorants qui se piquent de trancher dans les choses de l'art.

Le pire lui a donc été épargné. Le pire, c'eût été pour lui de voir le mouvement français de 'retour l'antique' dans les arts visuels, qu'il avait souhaité et préparé avec une extraordinaire persévérance, changer de sens, et de réformateur du goût devenir sinon le ferment, du moins le reflet d'une révolution politique. À bien des égards pourtant, le Directeur des Bâtiments royaux de Louis XVI, le comte d'Angiviller aura été l'exécuteur testamentaire de Caylus, achevant vigoureusement la restauration des disciplines de la peinture d'histoire dans l'enseignement académique, et passant commande à Jacques-Louis David de 'tableaux d'histoire' à sujet antique. C'est dans l'atelier du peintre le plus cher à Caylus, et à qui il avait fait d'emblée partager ses vues réformatrices, Joseph-Marie Vien, que David avait été formé. Avec David, l'École française pour laquelle l'auteur des Tableaux tirés de l'*Iliade* et de l'*Odyssée* avait rêvé une Renaissance toute à l'honneur de Louis XV, trouva un maître qui mit le 'retour à l'antique' au service de la Sparte jacobine et de la Rome impériale napoléonienne.

Entre 1765, date de la mort de Caylus, et 1785, date du Salon où fut exposé le *Serment des Horaces* de David, le 'retour à l'antique' dans l'Académie royale de Peinture et Sculpture, et dans l'Académie de France à Rome avait insensiblement cessé d'être le mouvement réformateur des arts de la monarchie dont Caylus avait voulu être l'âme. Toute l'œuvre et toute l'action du comte avaient tendu à répéter dans la France de Louis XV la réforme académique 'sur l'antique et sur la nature' qui avait régénéré l'École bolonaise, puis romaine, sous l'impulsion d'Annibal Carrache à la fin du XVIe siècle, et l'École française du XVIIe siècle sous l'impulsion de Le Sueur, de Poussin et de Le Brun. David, élève du protégé de Caylus, était avec sa génération, un lecteur de l'*Émile* de Rousseau, détesté de Caylus, mais aussi de *l'Histoire de l'Art chez les Anciens* de Winckelmann, que le comte mourut trop tôt pour pouvoir la détester. Chez ces deux auteurs, le sublime, moral pour l'un, moral et artistique pour l'autre, pour lequel les Anciens étaient merveilleusement doués, n'avait brillé dans leurs mœurs et dans leurs arts que dans leurs époques de liberté républicaine. Serve et artificielle, la société moderne interdisait de retrouver le secret vivant de ce sublime autrement que comme un objet de désir et de deuil lacérant, ou comme la récompense de sa régénération radicale, sur une table rase délivrée des siècles de servitude et de leurs décombres. La logique française du 'retour à l'antique,' dans les mœurs ou dans les arts, ne pouvait se contenter de réformes, académiques ou politiques: elle conduisait soit à une Terreur soit au Romantisme.

En 1785, avec le *Serment des Horaces*, commandé par le Directeur des Bâtiments du roi, peint dans la Rome des papes et exposé au Salon de l'Académie royale, David commençait à rompre avec l'esprit de réforme que Caylus avait enseignée à son protégé Vien: il créait l'icône mâle du sublime républicain 'à l'antique,' selon Rousseau et Winckelmann, en rupture non seulement avec la manière de Boucher et de Van Loo, mais même avec la grandeur 'à l'antique' que Caylus et D'Angiviller attendaient des artistes de l'Académie royale réformée. David posait ainsi la première pierre angulaire de son propre néo-classicisme jacobin, puis impérial, dont l'Académie ne serait plus celle d'un roi, mais celle d'une France régénérée par sa révolution politique, rendue à la 'liberté des Anciens' et au civisme héroïque, et se reconnaissant spartiate ou romaine dans les 'tableaux d'histoire' forgés dans son atelier et par ses élèves.

La Querelle des Anciens et des Modernes, dont Arnaldo Momigliano et Leo Strauss nous ont appris à ne pas ignorer la faille béante sous l'apparent consensus du salon des Lumières, tourna si bien au cours du XVIIIe siècle à la victoire des 'Anciens' qu'elle réussit à faire ressurgir à Paris, dans les arts comme dans la vie, tour à tour l'Athènes du *Voyage du jeune Anacharsis* de l'abbé Barthélémy (1788), la Sparte lycurgienne et la Rome républicaine du *Discours sur l'inégalité* de Rousseau (1790–4), puis l'Empire romain d'un nouveau César (1804–15).

Notes

1 Voir la traduction française, *Le Règne de la critique* (Paris, 1979).

2 Cité par Koselleck, trad. et éd. citées, p. 91.

3 Ibid., p. 100.

4 Voir Jean-Louis Quantin, *Le catholicisme classique et les Pères de l'Église, un retour aux sources (1669–1713)* (Paris, 1999).

5 Voir Bruno Neveu, 'Archéolâtrie et modernité dans le savoir ecclésiastique du XVIIe siècle,' *XVIIe siècle*, n° 131, 1981, p. 169–223; et 'L'érudition ecclésiastique du XVIIe siècle et la nostalgie de l'Antiquité chrétienne,' *Religion and Humanism* (Oxford, 1981), p. 195–223.

6 *Émile ou de l'éducation*, éd. L'Aminot-Richard (Paris, 1992), L. IV, p. 428–9.

7 Ibid., p. 387.

8 Voir Lionello Sozzi, ed., *Ragioni dell'anti-illuminismo* (Alessandria, 1992); Didier Masseau, *Les ennemis des philosophes: l'antiphilosophie au temps des Lumières* (Paris, 2000); Darrin M. MacMahon, *The French Counter Enlightenment and the Making of Modernity* (Oxford, 2001).

9 *Émile*, éd. cit., L. IV, p. 419. Cette page et celle qui suit proposent un véritable portrait-robot prémonitoire du 'leader' révolutionnaire jacobin, ou de sa version militaire, qu'incarnera Bonaparte.

10 Ibid., p. 386.

11 Ibid., L. I, p. 10.

12 Voir Henri Gouhier, *Rousseau et Voltaire: portraits dans deux miroirs* (Paris, 1983).

13 A. Momigliano, 'Ancient History and the Antiquarian,' *Contributo alla storia degli studi classici* (Rome, 1955).

14 Cité par Julien Freund, *La Décadence, histoire sociologique et philosophique d'une catégorie de l'expérience humaine* (Paris, 1984), p. 103.

15 Voir l'excellent article de Jean-Louis Jam, 'Caylus, l'amateur crépusculaire,' *Les divertissements utiles des amateurs du XVIIIe siècle*, p. 36–7.

16 *The Miscellaneous Works of Edward Gibbon, Esq. with Memoirs of His Life and*

Writings Composed by Himself and Illustrated with Occasional Notes and Narrative by the Right Honourable John, Lord Sheffield, 5 vol. (Londres, 1814), t. 2, p. 42.

17 Voir *Mémoires de Gibbon. Suivi de quelques ouvrages posthumes et de quelques lettres du même auteur, recueillis et publiés par Lord Sheffield, traduits de l'anglais par M. Marignié*, 2 vol. (Paris, An V), t. 1, p. 159.

18 Les Actes de ce colloque ont été publiés dans la revue *XVIIe siècle*, n° 131, 1981, où figure, p. 149–68, le texte de la communication qui avait été l'occasion de cet échange avec A. Momigliano: 'Temps de croissance et temps de corruption: les deux Antiquités dans l'érudition jésuite française du XVIIe siècle.'

19 Cité par Jean-Louis Jam, art. cit., p. 30.

20 Voir Lafont de Saint-Yenne, *Œuvre critique*, éd. Étienne Jollet (Paris, 2001).

21 On peut en effet dater de la campagne de brochures menée par Lafont de Saint-Yenne le mouvement étudié par Colin B. Bailey chez plusieurs éminents collectionneurs parisiens sous Louis XV, dans son livre *Patriotic Taste: Collecting Modern Art in Pre-Revolutionary Paris* (New Haven et Londres, 2002).

22 Voir cet éloge dans *Histoire ... avec les Mémoires ...*, op. cit., t. 34, p. 221–32; et aussi *Recueil d'Antiquités*, t. 7.

23 Cette épître dédicatoire, qui figure en tête du t. 1 du *Recueil d'Antiquités*, a été reprise par L.-J. Jay, *Recueil de lettres sur la peinture, la sculpture et l'architecture* (Paris, 1817), p. 591–3.

24 Voir André Fontaine, *Comte de Caylus, Vies d'artistes du XVIIIe siècle, Discours sur la Peinture et la Sculpture, Salons de 1751 et de 1753, Lettre à Lagrenée* (Paris, 1910), p. 25.

25 Cité par Thomas Gaethgens et Jacques Lugand, *Joseph-Marie Vien (1716–1809)*, p. 79.

chapter six

Historia Literaria and Cultural History from Mylaeus to Eichhorn

MICHAEL C. CARHART

Textbooks by definition are far from revolutionary. Neither was Michael Denis's *Introduction to the Study of Books* in 1777. A conventional textbook for a conventional course required of all first-year students in German universities, Denis's two volumes laid out the development of all human knowledge from earliest antiquity to the present day. Moving easily from German to Latin and adding a smattering of Greek, Denis began with the invention of writing in the ancient Near East and the codification of oral traditions in the poetic age of Homer and the Old Testament. He described the golden ages of Greece and Rome down to Constantine, the overrunning of the western empire by his students' Germanic ancestors, the preservation of ancient knowledge in the cloisters, and the rise of liturgy and theology. The last occurred as the Arab world experienced its golden age, through which the works of Aristotle, then lost, would be rediscovered and translated. The fall of Constantinople and the flight of its refugees westward inaugurated the modern age in Europe. The classics were cultivated in Italy and brought north by intellectual pilgrims. Finally, Descartes, Newton, Leibniz, and others represented the latest age, which understood nature in mathematical and mechanical terms. This story was as familiar then as it is to any student of Western civilization now.[1]

The second volume covered the same ground but from a different point of view. Rather than developing a comprehensive narrative that explained the whole of human society functioning as an integral unit, the second volume proceeded topically, by discipline. Theology, Law Philosophy, Medicine, Mathematics, History, and Philology were treated in isolation, the development and state of the art of each described. The first volume was a narrative. The second was a reference work. The value of Denis's work, and what set it apart from mediocre contemporary works, was the way it illustrated the origin and development of the disciplines rather than simply listing titles. Every title was cited with a view to the higher purpose of explaining the development of the human spirit. On account of its clarity and brevity, his work was widely held to be a joy to read. Largely owing to the success of this textbook, Denis, a scholar of Germanic poetry and the translator of Ossian into German, was promoted to the position of chief custodian of the royal imperial library.

The *Introduction to the Study of Books* was a form of *historia literaria*. I use the Latin phrase to avoid confusion that might result from its translation as 'literary history' or 'the history of literature.' Those imply poetry or belles-lettres whereas Denis's phrase *Literaturgeschicht* designated all of human knowledge, the arts and sciences, crafts, history, religion, governance, agriculture – every form of knowledge created by human beings. Although Denis's title indicates a preoccupation with formal book-learning, the genre in which he wrote encompassed learning in all its forms, whether written or not. Denis stated that historia literaria was synonymous with the history of the human spirit, that is, the depiction of the origin and progress of human knowledge.

Like most textbooks, the *Introduction to the Study of Books* was compiled from lecture notes. Since the early 1760s, Denis had taught his bibliographic survey as an elective course to the young nobility enrolled at the Kaiserin Theresa Gymnasium in Vienna. Similar courses were taught at gymnasiums throughout the German-speaking world, and they were generally required of first-year students at German universities. Such courses generated a substantial textbook market. Denis tried to instil in his students a love of books, citing their ancient peers as examples: Alexander the Great kept his Homer in a golden chest and slept with it under his pillow during his Asian campaigns; Scipio Africanus read Xenophon at night; Alphonse of Aragon would rather have lost his treasury than his books; and Francis I, according to Sleidan, was accustomed at breakfast and dinner to speak only of books and literature. Denis cited Austrian bookworms also. Perhaps more important than a true love of reading was a knowledge of books in order to avoid the embarrassment of the French courtier who thought Seneca lived in the sixteenth century because he found a translation dedicated 'au Roi Henri IV.' Or the English nobleman who travelled to Frankfurt to see the hoofed golden bull; the priest who turned the Capuchin Valerianus Magnus into Valerius Maximus; or the librarian who catalogued a treatise *De missis dominicis* under ritual, thinking it addressed the Sunday mass.

Through his lectures and textbook Denis tried to give his students a sense of the intellectual lay of the land. Scholarship was a journey undertaken by students, who could choose which roads to follow and even where their ultimate destination lay. At the beginning of the journey it was useful for students to know where they were headed and how to get there. Historia literaria was the road map. Denis's northern contemporary Christoph Meiners wrote that ideally students would know the general geography of the disciplinary provinces even before they reached the gymnasiums. That way, from the beginning, students would be able to plot their intellectual journey rationally.[2] In Dresden the lexicographer J.C. Adelung offered grammar-school students just such an introduction in his *Short Conception of Human Finishing and Knowledge.*[3]

Denis found a novel way of organizing the disciplines, one that could not have been invented before the mid-eighteenth century. He classified them. On the model of Linnaeus's biological taxonomy, he assigned each branch of knowledge to either order, genus, or species. The seven disciplines (Theology, Law, Philosophy, Medicine, Mathematics, History, and Philology) constituted the Ordines; major divisions within those disciplines were called Genera (e.g., the Genera of Philology were historia literaria, bibliography, archaeology, criticism, linguistics, rhetoric, poetics, semiotics, epigraphy, and polymathia); each of the Genera was further divided into two to five Species. Polymathia was alive and well at the end of the eighteenth century.

By the time of Denis, European scholars had been investigating the rise and progress of intellectual and social traditions for centuries. What was new in the late eighteenth century was the articulation that historia literaria was the history of culture; as Denis himself put it in 1777, 'Historia literaria is both the history of the human spirit and the description of the origin of human knowledge.'[4] That is to say, encyclopaedism (the compilation and organization of human knowledge) was put to a new purpose in the second half of the eighteenth century, and that new purpose was to explain the progress of the arts and sciences, of the human spirit, and of European society as a whole. To put it another way, by what process did Europeans arrive at their happy position of Enlightenment? Enlightenment was a new term. Culture was a new term. But the investigation of rise-and-progress was not new at all. Historia literaria as a genre originated in the sixteenth century as part of a specific northern European humanist ideology of social renewal and transformation, and if historia literaria survived (itself renewed and transformed) until the end of the Old Regime, then so did those literary strategies called 'humanism.'

Although the taxonomy of the disciplines was a novelty characteristic of the eighteenth century, the intellectual tradition in which Denis wrote extended back through the Middle Ages to antiquity.[5] Historia literaria can also be viewed as an early modern form of the ancient *de viris illustribus*, as in St Jerome's eponymous work, Plutarch's *Lives*, and the history of philosophical schools by Diogenes Laertius.[6] The distinctly modern form of historia literaria began in the sixteenth century in response to a perceived social, moral, and intellectual crisis. To contemporary eyes, the arts of history, medicine, and law appeared to be suffering most from social turmoil and moral decay. As usual, the humanists appropriated ancient rhetoric to describe their own predicament. Justus Lipsius emphasized the 'similitudo temporum' of his own day to that of Tacitus, saying that one could read Tacitus 'as a theater of contemporary life.'[7] Lack of political support for schools, scholarship, and education; war and economic depression; moral depravity and defective pedagogy all were conspiring to bring European scholarship to its knees.[8] Erasmus feared that if the 'honestae disciplinae' were lost, Europe would be reduced to a state of barbarous tyranny similar to that of the Turks.[9] Melanchthon spoke of the need for 'solida doctrina' for the 'bene constituta civis.'[10] The Latin language had languished under barbaric manners for a thousand years, and now the very arts and sciences themselves were in danger of being lost.

These were not idle fears. At the beginning of the sixteenth century, Beatus Rhenanus found a manuscript of Valleius Paterculus in an Alsatian monastery at Murbach. He published an edition in 1520, and subsequently the manuscript was lost.[11] Simon Grynaeus discovered a manuscript containing most of the first pentad of Livy's fifth decade (books 41–5) in the Lorsch monastery near Worms and published an edition in 1531.[12] Four years later, in 1535, Beatus Rhenanus and Sigismund Gelenius published a second edition of the Lorsch manuscript and added part of Livy's fourth decade from manuscripts discovered at nearby Worms and Speyer. Those two manuscripts, from Worms and Speyer, were subsequently lost too.[13] Ancient knowledge was literally slipping away. How much more had been lost in the middle age between antiquity and the Renaissance?

Clearly a systematic and disciplined inquiry into human knowledge was required simply for the preservation of human knowledge, to say nothing of the advancement of learning. The fear of continued decay motivated several humanists, like Juan Luis Vives, who compiled a bibliography of the disciplines in twenty books, to compose a more precise and disciplined inquiry into human knowledge. As a part of what Cassirer called 'a thoroughgoing reform in educational method,' Vives used polyhistorical learning to determine exactly what knowledge humanity possessed, what had been lost, and what knowledge could be saved by collecting the fragments of history and poetry that remained from antiquity.[14] And not just antiquities. Vives advocated also direct experience and observation as ways of confirming scholarship and urged his students to consult farmers, artisans, shepherds, and hunters, to cultivate plants, and to study meteorology.[15] That is, erudition should be supported by the scholar's own personal observation and experience. This combination of philological erudition with modern empirical observation would be the hallmark of *Kulturgeschichte* at the end of the eighteenth century.

Mylaeus

Well into the eighteenth century, the compilers of works of historia literaria looked to the standard set in the mid-sixteenth century in Christophorus Mylaeus's *Five Books on the History of the Universe of Things* (1555). Mylaeus had composed a narrative history, encyclopaedic in scope and modelled on the universal histories of the Middle Ages and antiquity, that was designed to show the *rerum primordia, progressiones, incrementa, inclinationes, et exitus*. Ideas, Mylaeus believed, could be properly understood only when seen in the context of the entire world, not in isolation like limbs torn from a body. The only way to grasp the process of human improvement was to observe the whole world at once, to inquire into its 'many causes and reasons.' Mylaeus called it *literaturae historia*, the history not just of fine literature but of all things known to humanity and recorded in writing.[16]

His first book, 'natural history,' worked its way up the chain of being from the elements and the heavenly spheres to the physical condition of humanity in the context of the kingdoms of minerals, plants, and animals. The other four books considered, from different points of view, the kinds of knowledge humanity produced: practical knowledge (*historia prudentiae*, books II and III) such as agriculture, technology, and government; and contemplative knowledge (*historia sapientiae*, books IV and V) including astronomy, the liberal arts, and the higher faculties of law, medicine, and theology. Books two and four discussed the individual subjects in turn, topically. Readers accordingly saw the developments within each discipline from the earliest ages to the present. Books three and five rehearsed the same material – in different form – but in strictly chronological order. Readers now saw the way the disciplines interacted and the influence each had on the others. In treating the same material in two ways (topically and chronologically) Mylaeus established the analytic and synthetic methods of historia literaria. His method of emphasizing the close connection among the disciplines, society, and nature established the model of historia literaria that would remain in place down to the end of the eighteenth century.

Daniel Morhof (1639–91) and His Followers

For reasons of space I shall omit the historia literaria of the seventeenth century – Alsted, Vossius, Lambeck, Jonsius – and leap ahead 170 years to the early eighteenth century.[17] Towards the end of the seventeenth century, the ideas and methods of historia literaria and polymathia that had developed over the preceeding century and a half came together in one of the most influential works of historia literaria in the early modern period, Daniel Morhof's *Polyhistor.*[18] More than a thousand pages in quarto, the first volume, 'Polyhistor literaria,' introduced the pathways that opened access to knowledge: bibliography and codicology, languages ancient and modern, grammar and literary genres, oratory, and poetry. The other two volumes, which discussed in detail the histories of the different disciplines, were much shorter, barely six hundred pages in all. The second volume, 'Polyhistor philosophicus,' covered the history of philosophy from the Pythagoreans to the scholastics, the philosophy of nature and the behaviour of natural bodies, magic, mathematics, and metaphysical logic. The third volume required only 120 pages to discuss the development of the practical disciplines: ethics, politics, economics, history, theology, law, and medicine.

Morhof did not live to see his monumental work in print. In fact, 'Daniel Morhof' is little more than a figurehead hiding the collaborative effort of a later generation of scholars. At the time of his death in 1691, Morhof had produced only the first two books of the first volume. But his work was considered to be of such significance for teaching and reference that for twenty years scholars in northern Germany collaborated to complete the work in Morhof's name. The *Polyhistor* was printed as a whole for the first time in 1714. New editions were brought out, still under Morhof's name, in 1732 and 1747.

The cohort that completed Morhof – a generation of Pietist scholars active in the first quarter of the eighteenth century – reshaped historia literaria to serve their own eclectic and pedagogical purposes. Their contributions came in two principal forms: compendiums of scholarship similar to Morhof's; and serial publications, most of them lasting only a few years and composed in their entirety by a single scholar. None of the German serials begun in the mood of Pietist eclectic historia literaria were as enduring and varied in terms of their contributors as, for example, the French *Journal des sçavans*. Nevertheless, their goals were similar to those of the *Journal des sçavans*, that is, to keep track of new developments in scholarship, including discussions, sometimes lengthy, of recent publications, obituaries of recently deceased scholars, and news of interest to the academic community.

Some of the eighteenth-century German serials began as grandiose plans by their authors, who abandoned them shortly after they were begun. One of the more influential of these was Nicolaus Hieronymus Gundling's *History of Moral Philosophy* (1706), of which only the first volume, in 115 pages, ever appeared.[19] Gundling compiled a selection, more detailed than Morhof's, of philosophical sects and doctrines, which he explained for the benefit of beginners. He marketed his work as an introduction for those who did not own books and a guide for those who did. Not a complete survey of all knowledge, Gundling's history of philosophy was an introduction to only one discipline. Nor did the first (and only, as it turned out) volume cover all of history, but only the moral philosophy of the Egyptians, Chaldeans, Persians, Arabs, Indo-Chinese, ancient Germanic peoples, Hebrews (the longest section), and Phoenicians. What made Gundling's work a form of historia literaria rather than a history of philosophy as its title indicated was his method of treating these national philosophies: instead of discussing them he offered a guide to the existing literature *about them*.[20] In the text of his work Gundling summarized what was available on a given subject. His footnotes were much more extensive, including analysis and extracts from the available texts. Some of the footnotes even had footnotes of their own. As an introduction for beginners, the work was overwhelming. The Latin was not easy, and Greek and Hebrew phrases were scattered liberally in the footnotes, alongside occasional paragraphs in French. Gundling's *History of Moral Philosophy* was not so much an overview as a guide to the literature. Although Gundling produced only the first volume of what was intended to be a series, in the opinion of many of his contemporaries he had the right idea.[21]

Gundling's second influential contribution to the genre was a *Sketch of Historia Literaria*, a sort of blueprint of a project that he or someone else might fill out at a later date.[22] He included chapters on palaeography in both Germany and Europe as a whole, chapters on manuscripts as artefacts organized by nation, reviews of authors and their books, and finally, sections on the three university disciplines of civil law, Lutheran theology, and philosophy.[23]

Much easier, and longer, was Christoph August Heumann's *Acta philosophorum*, which appeared ten years after Gundling's history of moral philosophy.[24] Writing in easy German, Heumann acknowledged that there were already several such histories of philosophy both ancient and modern, but that he (and his publisher, who also produced Gundling's work) saw a need for a history of philosophy 'mit einem Teutschen Kleide.' Not simply a reference work, Heumann intended his book to be read from cover to cover. To that end, he issued it serially and in small pieces, which he considered more likely to be read than a single large work. The name *Acta philosophorum* was a conscious adaptation of the seventeenth-century *Acta eruditorum*. Organized neither chronologically nor topically, Heumann's *Acta philosophorum* was a collection of book reviews and articles on specific aspects of the history of philosophy. In the first three issues of the series, Heumann wrote a seven-part introduction to the history of philosophy. He was particularly interested in reviewing the work of his predecessors in the historiography of philosophy and literature, including Thomas Stanley,[25] George Horn,[26] and Gundling.[27]

By the time Heumann was writing the *Acta philosophorum*, in the second decade of the eighteenth century, historia literaria had become a small industry in Protestant German academia. Heumann himself helped to define the genre once and for all in a short book that became the eighteenth-century standard for histories of European scholarship. Heumann's first edition (1718) of the *Conspectus Reipublicae Literariae* was a thin volume that sketched the parameters both of what historia literaria had been and what it ought to become.[28] For the rest of his life Heumann revised the book, and, like the works of Vossius, Morhof, and, as we shall see, Gundling, Heumann's work continued to be expanded and revised under his name long after his death in 1764.

The most influential introduction to European scholarship of the eighteenth century, the *Conspectus* went through eight editions between

1718 and 1791. In this work Heumann presented a thorough yet intentionally shallow picture of the history of scholarship from antiquity to the present. Standard works of historia literaria, such as those of Vossius, Morhof, Gundling, and Fabricius, read like lengthy annotated bibliographies, informing the reader where to turn for detailed information on (ideally) any part of the collective human memory. Heumann's *Conspectus*, by contrast, was a bibliography of those bibliographies.

Intended as a first reference for young students, Heumann's title promised to chart a course through what Morhof had called the 'ocean of scholarship.'[29] In the *Conspectus*, Heumann defined the parts that a complete historia literaria would have: chapters on how to read manuscripts (*de arte scribendi*), on the development of scholarship from antiquity to the present (analytic, or diachronic), and on the development of the disciplines considered independently (synthetic, or synchronic); a bibliography of reviews of specific books; and a bibliography of reviews of particular scholars. These five topics were intended to cover the whole of human knowledge. From 1718, Heumann's method would serve as the model for historia literaria for the rest of the century.

Heumann supplied the organization. He also articulated the methodology.[30] In all of historia literaria there were essentially two manners of proceeding, analytically and synthetically. Juggling all the disciplines at once, the author of an analytic work tried to describe the progress of the human spirit in all areas of knowledge and society simultaneously. This is what Mylaeus had done in his fifth book, 'Historia de literatura.' Gundling had discovered how difficult that task was when he completed only the first volume of what was intended to be a much longer work. Several attempts at a chronological account of the history of scholarship had been made in the seventeenth century, with varying degrees of success. The synthetic method, by contrast, proceeded one discipline at a time, as Mylaeus had shown in his fourth book, 'Historia de sapientia.' The synthetic method was conceptually easier to write, but it lacked the broad vision of the whole of society and scholarship.

When Momigliano distinguished between history and antiquarianism, he did so in part through the diachronic and synchronic methods. The historian's business was narrative, strung together by a chain of events that brought the reader from Time A to Time B. The antiquarian was less interested in historical process than in the reconstruction of a static configuration through the collection and juxtaposition of artefacts. To Heumann's mind, ideally the author of historia literaria would write both history and antiquarianism: a diachronic narrative that depicted the whole of society and knowledge operating in concert; and also a synchronic examination of the several component parts that comprised human knowledge. For the rest of the eighteenth century, the authors of works of historia literaria consciously followed Heumann's method. That is why Michael Denis wrote his *Introduction to the Study of Books* in two volumes, analytic and synthetic. Eyring used the same analytic and synthetic methodology in the posthumous eighth edition of Heumann's own *Conspectus* (1791). In the early nineteenth century Eichhorn wrote his *Litteraturgeschichte* in two volumes, the first analytical (i.e., chronological) and the second synthetic (i.e., by discipline and much longer). As late as 1920, Sigmund von Lempicki organized his literary history 'synthetically' rather than 'analytically,' as he would have done had his chief interest been philology rather than literature.

The Later Historia Literaria

The period from 1690 to 1730 marks the high point of historia literaria – so at least the recent German historiography would have us believe. Morhof, together with G.J. Vossius and Peter Lambeck, inspired the movement. The generation that completed Morhof's work after 1700 was the same that produced Fabricius's *Entwurff*, Struve's *Introductio*, Reimmann's *Einleitung*, Stolle's *Historia eruditionis*, and Heumann's *Conspectus*. That second generation, just after 1700, so the story goes, marks the *Blütezeit* of historia literaria, which thereafter changed very little and eventually dwindled into irrelevance. By the time Lessing wrote a satire in the 1740s about a young scholar who learned seven languages at the university and described himself as a polymath but upon returning home could not carry on a meaningful conversation with the sexton at his church, historia literaria was out of date.[31]

In the 1730s and 1740s, historia literaria underwent a change, and that change is generally perceived as the end of the historia literaria movement. But historia literaria neither disappeared nor became irrelevant.[32] On the contrary, around 1740 a new generation of scholars built on the work of their teachers, adding new rigour and thoroughness to the *Precursors, Introductions, Overviews*, and *Sketches* of the first quarter of the eighteenth century. The innovations of the generation of the 1730s and 1740s were principally of two kinds. On the one hand, the younger Fabricius (Johann Andreas, not to be confused with Fabricius the elder, Johann Albert, author of the *Bibliothecae Graecae* and *Latinae*), C.F. Hempel, J.J. Brucker, and J.F. Zedler put flesh on the skeletons that Heumann and

Gundling had created, actually realizing parts of their projects. Heumann lived until the 1760s and continued modestly to revise his own work, not changing the text but simply expanding the notes. In the name of the deceased Gundling, though, Hempel did not just reproduce the metabibliography that Gundling had written thirty years earlier. Instead he restructured the work according to Heumann's model, and filled out the notes with every work he could find on every aspect of European scholarship. The 'new Gundling' appeared in five volumes, filling more than 7,700 pages in quarto.[33] The new Gundling used the same division into seven chapters that Heumann had used.[34] What Heumann accomplished in twenty pages required over a thousand in the new Gundling. In the name of the long deceased Morhof, Fabricius the younger re-edited the *Polyhistor*, small in comparison to the new Gundling but still a formidable 1,200 pages. Brucker produced a five-volume history of the discipline of philosophy, the standard upon which all modern histories of philosophy are based.[35] Zedler organized the first modern alphabetical encyclopaedia in sixty-four volumes, beating to press the *Encyclopédie* of d'Alembert and Diderot by a decade.[36]

The textbook project continued as well.[37] M. Denis updated historia literaria for the young nobility at the Kaiserin Theresa Gymnasium in Vienna by classifying the disciplines in a Linnaean taxonomy. In Dresden, J.C. Adelung wrote an overview of the disciplines for Realschule students, followed by a sequel that he very self-consciously termed a 'cultural history.'[38] Heumann's *Conspectus* was updated posthumously by a Göttingen scholar in the 1790s.[39]

Also in Göttingen, J.G. Eichhorn set aside his cutting-edge biblical scholarship in order to pursue historia literaria in two separate projects. In one, he organized a team of scholars to write exhaustive histories of their disciplines since the Renaissance in a projected ninety-two volumes. Not limited to scholarship but presenting scholarship in the context of European culture as it had developed over the previous three hundred years, Eichhorn's company of scholars promised to emphasize the citizen in his city, the farmer in his hut, the noble in his castle, the merchant in his shop, and what they enjoyed 'in the bosom of their families.' That is, he intended to discuss *das Volk* – its condition, relative happiness, and relationship to the whole of society and the state. Eichhorn's historian was to write total history: 'His view should be directed simultaneously towards all parts of history, and he must often despair of the wealth of material he has to work with; everywhere he must meet and fully develop the true causes of spiritual changes, of the origin, progress, arrest, and decline of literature.[40] Eichhorn himself wrote a two-volume *Litteraturgeschichte* (a companion to a two-volume *Weltgeschichte*), one volume describing the progress of the arts, sciences, and culture analytically and a second treating the disciplines in isolation synthetically. With minimal updating every few years, Eichhorn's *Litteraturgeschichte* and *Weltgeschichte* textbooks reliably supplied his bank account with funds until his death in 1828.

Eichhorn's program of showing the farmer in his hut was not new. In the *Advancement of Learning* (1605, 1623), Bacon had outlined a history of learning and the arts in all ages and in all places from the earliest human memory to the present. Historia literaria would be the history of the most important authors, books, schools, students, academies, societies, colleges, and orders and would describe the origin, progress, decline, destruction, rebirth, and migration of the sciences in different places and at different times, as well as the events that caused them.[41] Bacon and then Eichhorn believed that through the history of learning (*historia literaria*) one could trace human knowledge to its early stages, shortly after the development of writing. But in the seventeenth and, especially, the second half of the eighteenth century, students of antiquity began to acknowledge that the invention of writing came relatively late. How then was the original genius of a nation to be discovered? And, more generally, how could one probe the earliest conditions of human development given that there were no written records? Archaeology was the most familiar way back. That is where the antiquarian came in: he could collect material artefacts that predated writing. As other essays in this volume have pointed out, the 'study of the old' became systematic and analytical in the seventeenth and eighteenth centuries. But the careful textualist could also gain access to the primitive mind: through mythology.

Myth and Memory: Christian Gottlob Heyne

If one wanted to reconstruct the history of humanity, taught the Göttingen philologist C. G. Heyne, one could do so – for the prehistoric periods – only by studying myth. Through a career spanning a half-century beginning in the 1760s, Heyne repeated to his audiences and students that the history and the philosophy of the first peoples was contained in their mythology.[42] Though myth a people remembered events or ideas in a form that was historical and at the same time characterized by a rich pictorial and imaginative manner of thought and expression. Myths preserved remnants of the expressions and figures of speech of a nation in its preliterate, prehistoric stages. By the time myths were written down in the form received by posterity, in Homer, Hesiod, Pindar, and pseudo-Apollodorus, the myths were already in a late form. Myths emerged long before writing, and for generations, perhaps centuries, they were handed down through the oral medium of song and poetry. By studying figures of speech, one could learn about the literary and linguistic style of the early Greek poets before the development of writing.

Myths concealed (or better, carried) the judgments, opinions, ideas, and sensibility of ancient peoples. The task of the philologist was to uncover the hidden core of mythology in order to discover the character of the nation that produced it. Each nation or people (*Volk*) had its own body of myth that had existed from the earliest beginnings of the nation. Contained within the national mythology were stories about the birth of the world or the origin of the nation, that is, the ideas that gave the nation a sense of unity and identity.

The language of the first peoples was grounded in the earliest circumstances of life, and these became the first elements of their literature. Lacking a vocabulary that would enable them to make sophisticated abstractions, the first Greeks used a single name or word to refer to several things at once. For example, Jove (Heyne used the Latin name) originated among the Pelasgoi as a fertility fetish, but the idea of Jove could refer to many different things depending on the context.[43] 'Jove' meant the force of life, the annual cycle of seasons, any weather phenomenon, the sky, or any of a number of other effects of nature. Aeschylus defined Jove/Zeus: 'Zeus is the air, Zeus earth, and Zeus the sky, / Zeus everything, and all that's more than these.'[44] That is, language – abstraction in primitive language – was built not by forming new words, at least not initially, but by applying existing words (in this case a name, Jove) to various natural phenomena. Zeus/Jove therefore was much more than a character in the mythological cycles as described by the poets – the slinger of thunderbolts, philandering spouse of Hera, and victor over titans. These tales were relatively late developments. Zeus/Jove earlier had been the explanation and description of the sky and of natural phenomena coming from the sky at a time when the Pelasgoi language lacked other terms for meteorological effects. In this plurality of meanings, Heyne found, Zeus was comparable to the deities of other peoples, such as the Libyan Amon and the Egyptian Serapis. Other peoples adopted the idea of Jove, most notably the Cretans. Poets eventually turned the popular idea of Jove into the god Jupiter. Thus a spiritual idea could alternately refer to a fetish, an object, a force of nature, and a personality in the classical pantheon. Heyne's goal was to take what had been written down by Homer, Hesiod, pseudo-Apollodorus, Pindar, and other poets and decipher what ideas, like 'Jove,' ultimately lay behind the stories that became the poetic mythology of the ancient Greeks.

Mythical ideas emerged long before writing, and the most effective way for a nation to remember its sayings was through song. Songs acted as the nation's first literature, which was composed in a 'mythic style.'[45] Lacking the vocabulary to speak abstractly, people in a mythic stage compensated by using allegories and imagery in their songs. Hence many stories were filled with references to physical and natural events:[46] 'From these very principles and elements, as the life of men was cultivated, speech became more polished. They became accustomed to allegory, tropes, the first metaphors, and figures of speech. Stories (apologi), the Aesop's fables, and parables had their place here. Other kinds of simile and comparison were invented as well.'[47]

Myths were tied to the land, and reflected the collective experience of the tribe or nation in that land. How nature manifested itself to the nation – through fire, famine, floods or consistently bountiful soil and mild climate – played a large role in determining the national mindset and, as a result, the national memory preserved in the mythology. The Greeks, for example, had joyous festivals, whereas the Phoenicians and Syrians developed religions of fear and severity, with evil demons predominating in their public cults.[48] The sources of a people's mythology, which preserved its collective experience and mindset, were bound up with the physical place occupied by the people in its earliest days. From these myths derived a people's national identity, sense of patriotism, and understanding of who they had been and where they had come from.

The mythological origins of ancient religion were not the work of God or of any specific human genius. Human genius was a result, not a cause, of mythology and early religion. The structures of and influences on human life shaped religion, but the initial shaping was not the result of any conscious human activity. To find the unconscious, yet human, forces that produced first myth, then religion, then the national genius was the goal of Heyne's philology. In finding those forces, he believed, one could not limit one's philological study to the Homers, Hesiods, and Pindars of antiquity, that is, to the best of the poets. Instead, one had to understand the common mindset, the audience to whom the poets addressed themselves. One had to know the body of fables possessed by the common memory and the common, non-poetic speech, to which the poets constantly alluded in their metaphors and other figures of speech.

One could not see clearly without grasping the manner of ancient common speech and of making fables. It was not easy to understand *Oedipus*, for example, unless one knew the other poets in Sophocles's age and the body of fables they had to draw upon. 'If we hold that fables are merely mind games,' Heyne taught, 'then ours is a wretched lot, having lost a good part of that age by fleeing "trifles."'[49] The stories told by Homer and Hesiod were not simply fictitious fables invented by those poets for the amusement or edification of their audiences. Rather, myths were the archives of national memory, the vehicle by which historical events and philosophic truths were handed down from one generation to the next. Myths were the necessary vehicle of expression for the first efforts of the human mind.

In the modern age, historia literaria served the same function as ancient myth: the archive of memory and knowledge, preserved now in scientific books rather than in song. Both projects, historia literaria and mythology, quickly became aligned with cultural history once this latter field became a coherent enterprise after about 1780.[50] That is, both historia literaria and mythology were directed towards reconstructing the culture of past ages – historia literaria for the more recent ones, on the basis of written sources, and mythology for the more distant ones, on the basis of oral sources. For both, the goal was to recover whatever fragments of knowledge could be salvaged from the wreckage of human history. In the case of mythology, the myths were relatively few, and the primitive ideas concealed in the stories and songs could be extracted only with great patience and learning. In the case of historia literaria, the opposite problem confronted the scholar: how to organize the tremendous volume of existing knowledge into a coherent narrative that told the whole story of human cultural development.

The clearest example of the parallel goals of historia literaria and mythology and their convergence in the cultural history of the late eighteenth and early nineteenth centuries is presented by the work of Johann Gottfried Eichhorn.[51] Trained in the mythology of Heyne and the oriental languages of J.D. Michaelis, inventor of the 'higher criticism' of the Bible, Eichhorn set aside his Old Testament scholarship at the height of his career in order to pursue historia literaria. Why would he do that? Historia literaria had supposedly been dead for two generations, and Eichhorn struggled mightily to grasp the subject in the 1790s, only to produce an embarrassingly incompetent history of medieval literature.[52] After nearly a decade of work, he did succeed in developing a four-part scheme encompassing the history of Western civilization and the history of science, but the result does not seem worth the effort.

In fact, Eichhorn's Old Testament scholarship had always been about human cultural development. Hebrew literature was the oldest extant body of literature then known, reaching far deeper into human history than any other. Certainly it was older than Heyne's Greek sources, most of which were compiled in the third century BCE from literary fragments that certainly were no older than about 750 BCE. The methods Heyne applied to get behind the Homeric texts and back to the mind and culture of the Greeks in their Dark Age and beyond, Eichhorn applied to the Hebrews, reaching back to Moses, the Patriarchs, and even further. Both Heyne and Eichhorn hoped to observe the spirit of the nation as close to its origin as possible. Eichhorn's chief interest was not the Bible. He was not interested in God but in humanity, and the sacred texts were a means to an understanding of human cultural development. That was why he developed methods for dating Hebrew literature: identifying the time and place in which the texts in their present form were redacted; identifying the fragments from which they were composed and dating those fragments (e.g., the J and E sources of Genesis); and attempting to glean from the text's vocabulary something about the author. Using the information gathered by means of these methods, Eichhorn could chart the development of the collective mind of the Hebrew nation. Through historia literaria he could do the same for modern Europe, by charting the history of the disciplines organized variously in the volumes of the *Weltgeschichte* and *Litteraturgeschichte*.

In both stages of his career, as biblical scholar and as *Literaturhistoriker*, Eichhorn operated as a humanist, and here is perhaps the real significance of the persistence of sixteenth-century encyclopaedism into the nineteenth century. The point is less that sixteenth-century historia literaria was a form of cultural history *ante litteram* than that the later historia literaria remained a humanist project. Eichhorn himself acknowledged his debt to his seventeenth- and sixteenth-century predecessors when he described his Old Testament higher criticism as 'a new name to no humanist.'[53] In both projects Eichhorn collected fragments of knowledge, organized them as comprehensibly as he could, and attempted to reconstruct an entire cultural system as it developed over time. Whether successful or not, Eichhorn attempted what Vives, Mylaeus, Bacon, and Morhof had attempted, that is, to write an all-inclusive history of the circle of learning.

Notes

1 Michael Denis, *Einleitung in die Bücherkunde*, 2 vols (Vienna, 1777–8).

2 Christoph Meiners, *Revision der Philosophie* (Göttingen and Gotha, 1772), 184; Hieronymus Andreas Mertens, *Hodegetischer Entwurf einer vollständigen Geschichte cer Gelehrsamkeit*, 2 vols (Augsburg: 1779–80), vol. 1, 'Vorrede.'

3 Johann Christoph Adelung, *Kurzer Begriff menschlicher Fertigkeiten und Kenntnisse*, 4 vols (Leipzig, 1778).

4 'Die Literaturgeschicht ist zugleich die Geschichte des menschlichen Geistes, die Schilderung des Ursprunges der menschlichen Kenntnisse' (Denis, *Einleitung in die Bücherkunde*, vol. 2, p. 1).

5 Historia literaria drew on the tradition of medieval encyclopaedias such as those of Vincent of Beauvais, Matthew of Paris, and, much earlier, Isidore of Seville. Hugh of St Victor's guide to the disciplines, the *Didascalicon* (1130s), an important predecessor of historia literaria, was recopied and then re-printed until the mid-seventeenth century. For the circulation history see the preface to Charles Henry Buttimer's critical edition of the text (Washington, 1939).

6 Rudolf Blum, 'Die Literaturverzeichnung im Altertum und Mittelalter: Versuch einer Geschichte der Bibliographie von den Anfängen bis zum Beginn der Neuzeit,' *Archiv für Geschichte des Buchwesens* 24 (1983): 1–256; also R.H. and M.A. Rouse, 'Bibliography before Print: The Medieval *De viris illustribus*,' in *The Role of the Book in Medieval Culture: Proceedings of the Oxford International Symposium 26 Sept. – 1 Oct. 1982*, vol. 1, ed. Peter Ganz (Turnhout, 1986), 133–53.

7 Lipsius, edition and commentary of Tacitus, cited after Wilhelm Kühlmann, *Gelehrtenrepublik und Fürstenstaat: Entwicklung und Kritik des deutschen Späthumanismus in der Literatur des Barockzeitalters* (Tübingen, 1982), 55 n12. For the perception of cultural decline in the sixteenth century, see pp. 22–55. See also Arnaldo Momigliano, 'The First Political Commentary on Tacitus,' *Journal of Roman Studies* 37(1947): 91–100.

8 Kühlmann, *Gelehrtenrepublik*, 93.

9 Erasmus, *Adages*, II.1.1, cited after Kühlmann, *Gelehrtenrepublik*, 21 n11.

10 Melanchthon, *In laudem navae scholae* (1526) = *Werke in Auswahl*, ed. Robert Stupperich (Gütersloh, 1951), III.69, cited after Kühlmann, *Gelehrtenrepublik*, 21 n11.

11 P. Valleius Paterculus, *Historiae Romanae*, ed. Beatus Rhenanus (Basel, 1520). Beatus Rhenanus sent the manuscript to the publisher, along with a hand-written transcription made by 'a certain friend.' In 1786 a manuscript of Valleius Paterculus, probably the same one, was reported to have been sold.

See *Texts and Transmissions: A Survey of the Latin Classics*, ed. L.D. Reynolds (Oxford, 1983), 432 n2.

12 *T. Livii Patavini Quintae decadis libri quinque ... ex vetustissimo codice cuius copiam nobis fecit celebre Monasterium Loresense*, ed. Simon Grynaeus and Desiderius Erasmus (Basel, 1531). Sometime between then and 1665 a quaternion – containing 41.1.1–41.9.10 – went missing. Grynaeus's edition is the only surviving exemplar of that section. What remains of the manuscript has been preserved as *Codex Vindobonensis Lat. 15 phototypice editus*, ed. Carl Wessely (Leiden, 1907).

13 *T. Livii Patavini Latinae Historiae principis decades tres*, ed. Beatus Rhenanus and Sigismund Gelenius (Basel, 1535). Codex Vormatiensis contained books 1–10, and Codex Spirensis contained books 26–40. A single surviving leaf containing a fragment of book 28 might be from the lost Speyer manuscript. See G. Billanovich, 'Petrarch and the Textual Tradition of Livy,' *Journal of the Warburg and Courtauld Institutes* 14 (1951): 137–208; also *Titi Livi Ab urbe condita*, books 31–5, ed. A.H. McDonald (Oxford, 1865), xxxvii. In general, see *Texts and Transmissions: A Survey of the Latin Classics*, ed. Reynolds (n11 above), 205–14; G. Billanovich, *La tradizione del testo di Livio e le origini dell'umanesimo*, 2 vols (Padua, 1981); and Rudolph Pfeiffer, *History of Classical Scholarship, 1300–1850* (Oxford, 1976), 85.

14 Ernst Cassirer, *Das Erkenntnisproblem in der Philosophie und Wissenschaft der neueren Zeit*, vol. 1 (Berlin, 1922), 127.

15 Rita Guerlac, introduction to Juan Luis Vives, *Against the Pseudodialecticians: A Humanist Attack on Medieval Logic* (Dordrecht, 1979), 29; Juan Luis Vives, *De disciplinis libri XX* (Cologne, 1536), republished as vol. 6 of Vives, *Opera omnia*, 8 vols (Valencia, 1782–90; repr. London, 1964).

16 Christophorus Mylaeus, *De scribenda universitatis rerum historia libri quinque* (Basel, 1551). See Donald R. Kelley, 'Writing Cultural History in Early Modern Europe: The Case of Christophe Milieu and His Project,' *Renaissance Quarterly* 52 (1999): 342–65. See also idem, 'The Development and Context of Bodin's Method,' in *Jean Bodin: Verhandlungen der internationalen Bodin-Tagung in München*, ed. Horst Denzer (Munich, 1973), 129–50; Arno Seifert, *Cognitio historica: Die Geschichte als Namengeberin der frühneuzeitlichen Empirie* (Berlin, 1976); and Wilhelm Schmidt-Biggemann, *Topica universalis: Eine Modellgeschichte humanistischer und barocker Wissenschaft* (Hamburg, 1983), 23–31.

17 Johann Alsted, *Scientiarum omnium encyclopedia* (Lyon, 1649); idem, *Thesaurus chronologiae*, 4th ed. (Herborn, 1650); G.J. Vossius, *De philosophia et philosophorum secta* (The Hague, 1658); idem, *De artium et scientiarum natura ac constitutione libri 5* = supplem. 3 of *Tractatus philologici de rhetorica, de poetica,*

de artium et scientiarum natura ac constitutione (Amsterdam, 1697); Petrus
Lambecius, *Liber primus prodromi historiae literariae* (Hamburg, 1659); Johann
Jonius, *Descriptoribus historiae philosophiae libri I* [1659] (Jena, 1716). See
Howard Hotson, *Johann Heinrich Alsted: Between Renaissance, Reformation, and
Universal Reform* (Oxford, 2000); Helmut Zedelmaier, *Bibliotheca universalis
und Bibliotheca selecta* (Cologne, 1992); Schmidt-Biggemann, *Topica universalis*
(n16 above).

18 D.G. Morhof, *Polyhistor, sive de notitia auctorum et rerum commentarii. Quibus
praeterea varia ad omnes disciplinas consilia et subsidia proponuntur* (Lübeck,
1688). Later editions were entitled *Polyhistor literarius, philosophicus, et
practicus.* I have used the third edition, 3 vols in 1 (Lübeck, 1732). For a
detailed publication history of the *Polyhistor* documenting the contributions
of many scholars and the existing compendiums used in compiling the work
by Morhof and his posthumous editors, see Johannes Möller's preface to
volume 2. There is no modern biography of Morhof. But see *Mapping the
World of Learning: The Polyhistor of Daniel Georg Morhof,* ed. Françoise Waquet
(Wiesbaden, 2000). See also Waquet, 'Le *Polyhistor* de Daniel Georg Morhof,
lieu de mémoire de la République des Lettres,' in *Les lieux de mémoire et la
fabrique de l'oeuvre: Actes du 1er colloque du Centre International de Recontres sur
le XVIIe siècle (Kiel, 29 juin–1er juillet 1993),* ed. Volker Kapp (Paris, 1993),
47–60; Martin Gierl, 'Bestandsaufnahme im gelehrten Bereich: Zur Entwicklung der "Historia literaria" im 18. Jahrhundert,' in *Denkhorizonte und
Handlungsgeschichte: Historische Studien für Rudolf Vierhaus zum 70. Geburtstag*
(Göttingen, 1992), 53–80; idem, *Pietismus und Aufklärung: Theologische
Polemik und die Kommunikationsreform der Wissenschaft am Ende des 17.
Jahrhundert* (Göttingen, 1997), 516–42; and Schmidt-Biggemann, *Topica
universalis* (n16 above), 265–72.

19 Nicolaus Hieronymus Gundling, *Historia philosophiae moralis,* pars prima, in
qua de opinionibus variarum sectarum de scriptis libris et auctoribus eo
pertinentibus ea qua par est libertate disseritur, etc. (Halle, 1706). See
Martin Mulsow, 'Gundling vs. Buddeus: Competing Models of the History of
Philosophy' in *History and the Disciplines,* ed. D.R. Kelley (Rochester, NY,
1997), 103–25.

20 For example, on Egypt, he pointed to John Marsham, John Spencer,
Athanasius Kircher's editions of Coptic texts, and the work on Egypt by
Hermann Witsius and Isaac Casaubon. See Jan Assmann, *Moses the Egyptian:
The Memory of Egypt in Western Monotheism* (Cambridge, MA, 1997), especially
55–79 and 91–3.

21 C.A. Heumann, *Acta philosophorum,* vol. 1 (Halle, 1715), 1032–9, for example, wished that Gundling had published more of the projected work.

22 N.H. Gundling, *Sciagraphia historiae literariae* (Halle, 1703).

23 Reviewing the state of the art of historia literaria fifteen years later, Heumann warned the reader to use caution when consulting the early works in the genre, including Gundling's *Sciagraphia* and B.G. Struve's *Introductio in notitiam rei litterariae et usum bibliothecarum* (Jena, 1704) (C.A. Heumann, *Conspectus Reipublicae Literariae*, vol. 2 [Hanover, 1718], 11–12).

24 C.A. Heumann, *Acta philosophorum, das ist: Grundl. Nachrichten aus der Historia philosophica, nebst beygefügten Urtheilen von denen dahin gehörigen alten und neuen Büchern* (Halle, 1715–26; repr. Bristol, 1997).

25 Thomas Stanley, *History of Philosophy* (London, 1655, 1687, and 1701); also reviewed in *Acta eruditorum* (Leipzig, 1702), 45, and Supplem., vol. 2, p. 356. At the suggestion of Clericus, *Bibliotheque universelle* (1687), Gottfried Olearus translated Stanley's work into Latin (Leipzig, 1711). Heumann reviewed Stanley's life and work, *Acta philosophorum*, vol. 1, pp. 523–45. One need look no further to see where Gundling derived his information.

26 The review of Georg Horn, *Historiae philosophicae libri septem, quibus origine, successione, sectis et vita philosophorum ab orbe condita ad nostram aetatem agitur* (Leiden, 1655), is in Heumann, *Acta philosophorum*, vol. 1, pp. 1039–61.

27 Heumann, *Acta Philosophorum*, vol. 1, pp. 1032–9.

28 *Conspectus Reipublicae Literariae sive via ad historiam literariam iuventuti studiosae aperta a Christophoro Augusto Heumanno, D.* (Hanover, 1718, 1726, 1733, ... 1791).

29 Morhof, *Polyhistor* (n18 above), I.1.2.4.

30 Heumann, *Conspectus Reipublicae Literariae*, chap. 2, paragraphs 1–3 for the synthetic method; chap. 2, paragraphs 4–11 for the analytic method. Page numbers vary in the eight editions, but the organization is constant.

31 Conrad Wiedemann, 'Polyhistors Glück und Ende. Von Daniel Georg Morhof zum jungen Lessing,' in *Festschrift Gottfried Weber zu seinem 70. Geburtstag*, ed. H.O. Burger and K. v. See (Bad Homburg, 1967), 215–35. For this periodization, see Gunter E. Grimm, 'Vom Schulfuchs zum Menschheitslehrer. Zum Wandel des Gelehrtentums zwischen Barock und Aufklärung,' in *Über den Prozeß der Aufklärung in Deutschland im 18. Jahrhundert. Personen, Institutionen und Medien*, ed. H.E. Bödeker and U. Hermann (Göttingen, 1987), 14–38; G.E. Grimm, *Literatur und Gelehrtentum in Deutschland: Untersuchungen zum Wandel ihres Verhältnisses zum humanismus bis zur Frühaufklärung* (Tübingen, 1983), especially 225ff and 426ff; Herbert Jaumann, 'Ratio clausa. Die Trennung von Erkenntnis und Kommunikation in gelehrten Abhandlungen zur Respublica literaria um 1700 und der europäische Kontext,' in *Res Publica Litteraria: Die institutionen der Gelehrsamkeit in der frühen Neuzeit*, ed. S. Neumeister and C. Wiedemann (Wiesbaden, 1987),

409–29, especially 414; and Gierl, *Pietismus und Aufklärung* (n18 above), 516.

32 Parodies of polymathia like Lessing's *Der junge Gelehrte* (1748) are evidence not of the irrelevance but of the relevance of encyclopaedic learning. See Anthony Grafton, 'The World of the Polyhistors: Humanism and Encyclopedism,' *Central European History* 18 (1985): 31–47; and the beginning of the chapter 'Prolegomena to Friedrich August Wolf' in idem, *Defenders of the Text: The Traditions of Scholarship in an Age of Science, 1450–1800* (Cambridge, MA, 1991).

33 Nikolaus Hieronymus Gundling, *Vollständige Historie der Gelahrheit, oder ausführliche Discourse, so er in verschiedenen Collegiis Literariis, so wohl über seine eigenen Positiones, als auch vornehmlich über Tit. Herrn Inspectoris D. Christophori Augusti Heumanni Conspectum Reipublicae Literariae gehalten ...*, 5 vols (Frankfurt and Leipzig, 1734–6).

34 Those chapters were on 1) the nature and parts of historia literaria; 2) all the works of historia literaria; 3) the art of writing (mss and palaeography); 4) the origin and progress of the study of literature to our age (synthetic); 5) the fates of the disciplines, or their origin and progress (analytic); 6) how to find the best books; and 7) how to find the best authors. Gundling's method was uniform through the work: he gave an author's name, when he lived, where he was born and worked, where he was educated; he then briefly described the contents of the author's works and their value. The editor, C.F. Hempel, annotated Gundling's text with footnoted observations, many of them taken from Gundling's earlier writings. There is far more material by the editor than from Gundling's text itself. Many pages had a single line of text and were filled with two-column, small-font notes, many of which were essays in their own right.

35 Johann Brucker, *Historia philosophiae critica*, 4 vols in 5 (Leipzig, 1736–40). See Constance Blackwell, 'Thales Philosophus' in *History and the Disciplines*, ed. Kelly (n19 above); and *From the Cartesian Age to Brucker*, vol. 2 of *Models of the History of Philosophy*, ed. C.W.T. Blackwell and Philip Weller (Dordrecht, 1993–), English ed. of *Storia delle storie generali della filosofia*, ed. Giovanni Santinello (Brescia, 1981–).

36 Johann Heinrich Zedler, *Grosses vollständiges Universal-Lexicon ...*, 64 vols (Halle and Leipzig, 1732–50).

37 Johann Friedrich Bertram, *Anfangs-Lehren der Historie der Gelehrsamkeit, zum Gebrauch der auf Schulen studirenden Jugend abgefast: Sammt e. Discurs über d. Frage ob, u. wie ferne es rathsam sey, Historiam literariam auf Schulen u. Gymnasiis zu tractiren* (Braunschweig, 1730); Philipp Ernst Bertram, *Entwurff einer Geschichte der Gelahrheit* (Halle, 1764); Mertens, *Hodegetischer Entwurf einer vollständi-*

gen Geschichte der Gelehrsamkeit (n2 above); S.F.G. Wahl, *Versuch einer Allgemeinen Geschichte der Litteratur,* 2 vols (Erfurt, 1787–88).

38 Adelung, *Kurzer Begriff menschlicher Fertigkeiten und Kenntnisse* (n3 above); idem, *Versuch einer Geschichte der Cultur des menschlichen Geschlechts* (Leipzig, 1782).

39 *Conspectus reipublicae literariae siue via ad historiam literariam iuuentuti studiosae,* aperta a Christoph. Aug. Heumanno D. Editio octaua quae ipsa est nouae recognitiones prima, procurata a Ieremia Nicolau Eyring (Hannover, 1791, 1797). Previously Eyring had written a *Synopsis historiae literariae, qua Orientis, Graeca, Romana item aliarum linguarum scriptis cultarum literatura tabulis synchronisticis exhibetur,* 3 parts (Göttingen, 1783–84).

40 J.G. Eichhorn, *Allgemeine Geschichte der Cultur und Litteratur des neuern Europa,* vol. 1 (Göttingen, 1796), lxxvi.

41 *The Works of Francis Bacon,* vol. 1 (London, 1858), 'De augmentis scientiarum,' II.4, p. 503. See the parallel in John Barclaius, *Icon Animorum,* (London, 1614; repr. as late as Leipzig, 1733), chap. 2: 'Each age has its own genius, completely different from the others. Moreover each region has its own spirit, which drives men's minds toward certain inclinations and mores. The goal of this work is to investigate those spirits' (cited after Erich Hassinger, *Empirisch-Rationaler Historismus: Seine Ausbildung in der Literatur Westeuropas von Guiccardini bis Saint-Evremond* [Bern, 1978], 143 [my translation]. See also D.T. Starnes, 'The Figure Genius in the Renaissance,' *Studies in the Renaissance* 11 (1964): 234–44.

42 Christian Gottlob Heyne, ed., *Apollodori Atheniensis bibliothecae libri tres et fragmenta,* 2nd ed., 3 vols (Göttingen, 1803), vol. 2, p. xvi. Cf. Heyne's preface to Martin Gottfried Hermann, *Handbuch der Mythologie aus Homer und Hesiod* [Berlin and Stettin, 1787], ii.

43 Heyne, 'Vita antiquissimorum hominum Graeciae ex ferorum et barbarorum populorum comparatione illustrata. Commentatio I. Ad commendandum nouum Prorectorem Godofr. Less d. 2. Julii 1779,' in *Opuscula academica collecta et animadversionibus locupletata,* vol. 3 (Göttingen, 1788), 14.

44 Aeschylus, Fragment 30 (Heliades), in *Die Tragödien und Fragmente,* ed. F. Stoessl (Zürich, 1952), 423; trans. Michael Grant, *Myths of the Greeks and Romans* (New York, 1962), 104.

45 Heyne, 'Sermonis mythici seu symbolici interpretatio ad caussas et rationes ductasque inde regulas revocata' (1807), *Commentationes Societatis Regiae Scientiarum Gottingensis* 16 (1808): 285–323.

46 Heyne, 'Proludunter nonnulla ad quaestionem caussis fabularum seu mytharum veterum physicis,' in Heyne, *Opuscula academica collecta et animadversionibus locupletata,* vol. 1 (Göttingen, 1785), 187.

47 Ibid., 192.

48 Ibid., 204.

49 Heyne, *Apollodori* (n42 above), vol. 2, p. xviii.

50 Adelung, *Versuch einer Geschichte der Cultur des menschlichen Geschlechts* (n38 above); D.H. Hegewisch, *Allgemeine Ueberblick der deutschen Kulturgeschichte bis zu Maximilan I* (Hamburg, 1788); Johann David Hartmann, *Versuch einer Kulturgeschichte der vornehmsten Völkerschaften Griechenlands,* 2 vols (Lemgo, 1796–1800); Friedrich Majer, *Zur Kulturgeschichte der Völker,* 2 vols (Leipzig, 1798); Daniel Jenisch, *Geist und Charakter des 18. Jahrhunderts,* 3 vols (Berlin, 1800–1); idem, *Universalhistorischer Ueberblick der Entwicklung des Menschengeschlechts ...: Eine Philosophie der Culturgeschichte,* 2 vols (Berlin, 1801). See Jörn Garber, 'Von der Menschheitsgeschichte zur Kulturgeschichte. Zum geschichtstheoretischen Kulturbegriff der deutschen Spätaufklärung,' in Garber, *Spätabsolutismus und bürgerliche Gesellschaft* (Frankfurt am Main, 1992), 409–33; Volker Hartmann, 'Die deutsche Kulturgeschichtsschreibung von ihren Anfängen bis Wilhelm Heinrich Riehl,' dissertation, University of Marburg, 1971.

51 Giuseppe D'Alessandro, *L'Illuminismo dimenticato: Johann Gottfried Eichhorn (1752–1827) e il suo tempo* (Naples, 2000).

52 J.G. Eichhorn, *Allgemeine Geschichte der Cultur und Litteratur des neuern Europa,* 2 vols (Göttingen, 1796–9).

53 J.G. Eichhorn, *Einleitung ins Alte Testament,* 2nd ed. (Leipzig, 1787), introduction (unpaginated).

chapter seven

New Paths of Antiquarianism in the Nineteenth and Early Twentieth Centuries: Theodor Mommsen and Max Weber

WILFRIED NIPPEL

Obviously, the title of my paper echoes Momigliano's *New Paths of Classicism in the Nineteenth Century*.[1] In these 1982 lectures Momigliano dealt at large with the nineteenth-century discussion on the origins and development of landed property in ancient Rome from Niebuhr through Mommsen to Weber. He pointed out that Weber's work represented a virtually new approach to this subject but was nevertheless indebted to Mommsen.[2] In an aside in a 1958 review, Momigliano had already made the more general point that Max Weber could be seen as a pupil of Mommsen. 'Pupil' here implies not only a personal relationship but also that the systematic structure of antiquarian research was continued in the systematic structure of sociological research.[3]

In the following I should like to treat again the path from Niebuhr to Mommsen and Weber with respect to this more general perspective. This means following Momigliano's famous dichotomy between the historian and the antiquarian.[4] The distinction between a chronological and a systematic approach to history, which had originated in antiquity and was kept up until the nineteenth century, led to a new and complicated relationship during that century. Historiography came to be seen as a discipline that should be based on original research but still meet literary standards; antiquarian works should no longer simply serve as explications of ancient literary texts or as random collections of monumental sources, but contribute to a comprehensive and systematic account of ancient culture.

Momigliano also emphasized that protagonists of the new German nineteenth-century *Altertumswissenschaft* were inclined to ignore or underrate the achievements of the older antiquarian tradition.[5] In 1810 and 1811 Barthold Georg Niebuhr, who had asked for leave from his post in the Prussian government, lectured on Roman history at the newly founded Berlin University. His lectures had a tremendous impact on the audience, which included scholars and government officials of high rank. One of them, Friedrich Karl von Savigny, stated that the auditors had witnessed to the beginning of a new epoch in the treatment of Roman history.[6] That assessment was commensurate with Niebuhr's self-confidence, which had him led to declare proudly that he had not made use of any scholarly literature; he assumed there had been no considerable scholarly progress since the sixteenth-century works of Sigonio.[7] Later, Niebuhr had to learn that the fundamental doubts about the reliability of the early Roman tradition had been developed since the late seventeenth century by scholars like Perizonius,[8] members of the French 'Académie des Inscriptions,' and Louis de Beaufort.[9] Nevertheless, he commented that those predecessors had been interested in raising doubts about the trustworthiness of the sources but had been unable to discern the true kernels of the tradition and then use them to present a historiographical work on Rome. 'To destroy the falsification may be sufficient for the critic ... yet the historian has to offer something positive'.[10]

Struggling with this task, Niebuhr became entangled in lengthy and badly arranged discussions of the regal period and the early Republic. Contemporary readers – including Goethe and Hegel – attested that he had not succeeded in incorporating his inquiries of the sources into a work of narrative history,[11] and August Wilhelm Schlegel predicted that in the long run Niebuhr's work would fundamentally alter the treatment of Roman antiquities.[12] Niebuhr's intention, however, had been to write a history from the viewpoint of the active politician ('Geschäftsmann') and not the antiquarian; Roman history was to contribute to the proper understanding of the problems of his own time.[13] That is why Niebuhr thought that in the future the genres of history and antiquities should once again be separated. He was sure that his 'system' of the Roman constitution would iron out the chaotic misunderstandings on this field[14] and dreamed of solving the problems of Roman constitutional law once and for all.[15] Such a definitive account would serve as an introduction to a new Roman history that would be narrated without scholarly digressions – just as it was by the ancient Romans.[16] In the third volume of his history (published posthumously in 1832), he even inserted fictitious speeches.

Theodor Mommsen could have practised this same differentiation of genres, but he set quite different priorities. In his curriculum vitae on the occasion of obtaining his doctorate (Kiel, 1843), Mommsen wrote that he had become fascinated by antiquarian studies on the Roman popular assemblies and the criminal courts, as well as on inscriptions. Accordingly, he distanced himself from 'proper jurisprudence' and 'only the conviction that the Roman State should be seen in the light of Roman jurisprudence' had prevented him from changing faculties.[17]

From the very beginning of his own scholarly work, the jurist Mommsen had been convinced that Niebuhr's method did not meet appropriate scholarly standards. In the preface to his book on the Roman *tribus* system, published in 1844, the young Mommsen had mocked Niebuhr's 'splendid fantasies' which, he said, had been the starting point of his own considerations. 'Who would wish never to have been mistaken in company with Niebuhr?'[18] But now he was sure that he had succeeded in getting rid of the 'fog of false hypotheses' and in reconstructing the complete picture of the institution out of the 'shambles of Roman antiquities.'[19] And that required the systematic examination of the epigraphic evidence that should serve as the touchstone for the literary tradition.

The young Mommsen had made up his mind that the complete collection of the Latin inscriptions was the main task of his future scholarly work. He started this project with a study tour to Italy in the years 1844–7. In a letter to his friend Otto Jahn written in May 1845, Mommsen expressed his confidence that with his epigraphic studies he would start a 'revolution in antiquarian and historical literature'; Germany just needed a proper impulse in order to carry on from the point where Scaliger had left off.[20] Two years later, in his memorandum to the Berlin Academy,[21] Mommsen claimed that the time had come to replace the older collections of the sixteenth to eighteenth centuries (Gruter, Scaliger, and Muratori), which, owing to their incompleteness and lack of textual criticism, were totally outdated.

It is well known that Mommsen's project for a *Corpus inscriptionum Latinarum* to be undertaken by the Prussian Academy met with considerable opposition despite Savigny's support.[22] The Academy's secretary, August Boeckh, especially did not accept Mommsen's premises, that first, such a corpus had to be based on autopsy of the inscriptions, and second, that a systematic search would lead to a multiplication of the evidence. Mommsen's approach was a slap in the face of Boeckh, whose *Inscriptiones Graecae* had been based on the collation of older editions. Not until 1853 did the Prussian Academy accept Mommsen's proposal in principle, and only in 1858 did he obtain a full-time appointment at the Academy as organizer of the project.

In his Prussian Academy address in the same year, Mommsen declared that epigraphy had to get rid of the 'mess of falsifications and four centuries of the works of dilettanti' (there is no word of respect here for the merits of learned predecessors since the Renaissance).[23] The complete collection of all evidence, the 'organization of the archives of the past,' should be the basis of historical scholarship. This ideal of completeness implied agnosticism with respect to historical and systematic questions: 'The archivist does not ask whether every piece he keeps and has to keep is really worth keeping.'[24]

To this task Mommsen devoted most of his time in the ensuing decades. The importance of the *Corpus inscriptionum Latinarum* lay also in the fact that Mommsen established a new organization of scholarship, a scholarly mass production based on division of labour ('Großbetrieb der Wissenschaft').[25] It was no longer a matter for a few outstanding erudites, as it had been in former centuries.

The evidence of inscriptions, however, was of only limited importance for the history of the Roman Republic, which still had to be based chiefly on literary sources. Mommsen had already revolutionized historical literature on this subject with his *Römische Geschichte*, published between 1854 and 1856. But this revolution was, in a sense, an accident. In 1851, Mommsen had accepted the offer of a publishing house to write a work on Roman history for the educated public. At that time the Prussian Academy had not yet decided on the *Corpus inscriptionum Latinarum*, and Mommsen had just been dismissed from his professorship at Leipzig by the Saxon government because of his involvement in the revolutionary events of 1849. He was therefore in a precarious situation and was attracted by the prospect of earning money. That Mommsen was able to write, within a scant few years, three volumes covering Roman history from the beginnings until Caesar seems astonishing – not only because he simultaneously carried on a number of other works but also because he could not draw on manuscripts prepared for university lectures. In Leipzig, Zürich (since 1852), and Breslau (since 1854), he had occupied professorships of Roman law with a heavy teaching load on Roman private law.

The tremendous success of Mommsen's *Römische Geschichte* with the general public was especially due to his inserting of drama into the narrative and his constant use of a modernizing terminology that evoked associations with the political and social struggles of his own times.[26] Mommsen wrote from the point of view of historical necessity, which included the national unification of Italy and the transformation of the

Republic into a democratic monarchy, as allegedly achieved by Caesar.[27] All political actors were judged according to whether or not they had fostered the necessary progress. Karl Wilhelm Nitzsch wrote in a review that Mommsen's work gave 'the impression of an unreflected outpouring and yet claimed for itself the authority of a definitive and well-founded judgment.'[28]

The basis of Mommsen's judgments is not always easily to discern. This holds especially true for his treatment of the earliest epochs, which consisted only of outlines of the main structures. For example, Mommsen reconstructed the pre-Roman development from linguistic evidence and dealt with the regal period without giving the traditional names of the (allegedly only seven) kings. He did not explain by which criteria he felt able to extract the primordial governmental, legal, social, economic, and religious structures from a literary tradition that in all other respects was so unreliable that a narrative history could start only with the middle republic.[29] There was no discussion of earlier works on Roman history – especially Niebuhr's, from which Mommsen's approach differed fundamentally. Mommsen thought it inappropriate to discuss his methodological premises and the results of his research in a work of historiography that, in his view, should serve 'political education'[30] and needed more the gifts of an artist than of a scholar.[31] His fundamental assumption that the key to early Roman history was the reconstruction of its legal institutions was developed only in later articles, especially those collected in the two volumes of *Römische Forschungen*, which appeared in 1864 and 1879. Mommsen's treatment of the history from the middle republic onwards presented a combination of narrative political history with structural accounts of religion, economy, and culture. His *Römische Geschichte* therefore represented a new genre of historiography, since it treated both events in their succession and conditions and structures, which, according to Friedrich August Wolf, belonged to the separate disciplines of historiography and antiquities.[32]

Whereas the 'Römische Geschichte' offered a new blend of historiographical and antiquarian presentation, Mommsen's monumental *Römisches Staatsrecht*, published between 1871 and 1888, presented a new type of antiquarian work, which Mommsen himself later considered his most important scholarly achievement. This work stood in the tradition of *antiquitates publicae*, the collection of evidence with respect to political institutions. According to Mommsen, however, this evidence had to be used to build up a system of Roman public law emphasizing the fundamental institutions and legal conceptions that for a thousand years underlay Roman statehood despite all changes in the constitution. Formally, Mommsen's work was a revised edition of a part of Wilhelm Adolph Becker's *Handbuch der Römischen Alterthümer, nach den Quellen bearbeitet*. It had been continued by Joachim Marquardt and appeared between 1843 and 1856. Mommsen took over those parts that Becker and Marquardt had called 'Staatsalterthümer' and 'Staatsverfassung.' There is a certain irony that the parts called 'römische Staatsverwaltung' – on the provinces, the cities, the financial and military system, the priesthoods – which depended to a far higher degree on the use of the inscriptions, remained with Marquardt, who published the revised edition.[33]

The new title of Mommsen's manual is programmatic. According to Mommsen, 'Staatsrecht' meant that every institution had to be depicted in its peculiarity as well as in its relation to the entire system and this demanded a comprehensive understanding ('vollständige Einsicht in das Wesen des römischen Organismus überhaupt').[34] In his preface, Mommsen also stated unmistakably that he followed Becker only with respect to the materials to be treated and that otherwise his was a totally new work. He surely did not believe his own assertion that manuals would become outdated sooner than other scholarly productions – at least not with respect to his own work.

In contrast to Becker and the authors of other traditional handbooks on Roman public antiquities, Mommsen did not start with a survey of sources and learned literature. He said that he would neither discuss alternative conceptualizations of Roman constitutional law nor take issue with the mass of specialized dissertations on technical details since the majority of them were simply not worth it. There was a 'hustle and bustle on the antiquarian building site where many busy people just throw the beams and bricks into disorder without being able to increase the building materials or to build themselves.'[35] Mommsen presented himself as the only architect of an edifice that could properly be called *Römisches Staatsrecht* since it was based on firm pillars. And those pillars were the conceptually self-referential, but fundamental, ideas of Roman public law.[36]

Mommsen also made perfectly clear that he was following the model of modern manuals on Roman private law. For him, the scholarly progress ('rationeller Fortschritt') achieved by nineteenth-century pandectists consisted in the reconstruction of the invariant kernels of legal institutions and of a hierarchy of clear-cut legal categories.[37] To construct an equivalent system with respect to Roman constitutional law meant skipping consideration of the historical development of the peculiar institutions and also giving up the traditional periodization (Kingdom, Republic, Empire). And all phenomena that could not be grasped in legal terms were relegated from the 'Staatsrecht' as belonging only to historical accounts.

Remarks of this kind indicate that Mommsen was always aware that constitutional law was embedded in social structures but that a reconstruction of the system had to radically abstract from them. It would be worth analysing all those passages in which Mommsen played with the distinction between 'staatsrechtlich' and 'historisch' or with the opposition between 'rechtlich' and 'faktisch.'[38]

The consequences are clear: institutions were each to be treated systematically through a stretch of a thousand years from the primordial monarchy to the establishment of a new order by Diocletian and Constantine. The early kingdom, the Republican magistracy and the principate were presented as different emanations of the system of the magistracy.[39] That is why Mommsen devoted the entire first volume to 'general foundations' of the magistracy before treating the particular offices. All in all, three of five volumes dealt with the magistracy, whereas the citizenry and senate were treated at considerably shorter length. That was, of course, not by accident; categories like *imperium, auspicium,* and *potestas* could be understood as signifying the legal continuity of the magistracy, and in contrast to the senate and the popular assemblies the magistracy had been subject to a great number of regulations by particular legislation. Since senate and popular assemblies could function only in cooperation with office-holders, the magistracy was the institutional kernel from which the system of constitutional law could be developed.

The crucial problem for Mommsen was, of course, that constitutional law could not be reconstructed from the Roman literature in the same way the pandectists could use the writings of the Roman jurists that were collected in the *Corpus iuris civilis.* Roman jurisprudence was not much interested in public law; in the late Republic, some antiquarian literature was produced on certain questions of constitutional and sacral law, but it has survived only in fragments and indirect quotations.[40] Mommsen had to extract his categories from all kinds of literary sources and give them a juridical precision that the sources themselves did not provide.[41] The jurist Otto Gradenwitz commented in an obituary that Mommsen had better solved the task of elevating Roman public law to the level of private law than the Roman jurists themselves would have been able to do.[42]

For all periods of Roman history for which no contemporary evidence was available, one had basically to draw on the annalistic tradition. The crucial question was whether the late Republican annalists indeed possessed any reliable information about the times before the fourth century BCE. Some of Mommsen's nineteenth-century critics pointed out that the same author who did not trust these sources with respect to historical events was convinced that they were basically right with regard to public law. Benedictus Niese commented on the *Staatsrecht* that Mommsen seemed to overestimate considerably the value of the annalistic tradition, since he used it for the reconstruction of the earlier period's public law whereas the results of source criticism suggested that they could serve as evidence only for the system of later times.[43]

Of course, Mommsen was well aware of the problem. In an 1864 article on the legal status of patricians, and plebeians, he declared that he would concentrate on historically documented periods ('historisch beglaubigte Zeiten') and use legends from earlier periods only as evidence for the times in which they had been fixed. It was a further step to try to develop hypotheses about origins; in general, one had always to differentiate between a historical and a hypothetical field of research.[44]

In the *Staatsrecht*, however, Mommsen gave up this reservation. In a number of cases, he based a constitutional rule on pieces from the literary tradition that at the same time he characterized in the footnotes as historically worthless. If there were divergent traditions, Mommsen made a choice between them not according to their relative source value but according to which one better fit into his system. For example, the annalistic tradition had divergent versions on the origin of the Tribunate of the Plebs – two, four, or five tribunes from the beginning – which were treated again and again in nineteenth-century scholarship from the point of view of source criticism. Mommsen declared that the tribunate was created by analogy with the consulate; therefore, it must have started with two tribunes.[45] Mommsen is aware that his assumption of the tribunes' *maior potestas* is in contradiction to Cicero's understanding in the third book of *De legibus*. But, he says, Cicero's account is not systematically construed ('nicht streng disponirt')[46] – leaving Ludwig Lange to wonder if Cicero would have altered his account if he had had access to Mommsen's *Staatsrecht*.[47] Or, Mommsen could comment that a historically absurd story could still be adequately invented ('correct erfunden') with respect to a certain rule of the constitution.[48] In a number of cases he postulated that a new institution or a new practice had been introduced by legislation even when such a law was never

mentioned in the ancient evidence.[49] That corresponded with his fundamental assumption that modifications of the constitutional system had
to be based on popular legislation.[50]

In a review of 1845, Mommsen had already formulated the motto:
'The system implies a truth of its own' ('Das System ist seine eigene
Wahrheit').[51] In an address to the Berlin Academy in 1879, he said that
sources had to be tested by the logic of facts, so that the impossible
elements could be eliminated from the mess of undigested traditions
and the consequences of the laws of development be postulated even
when they were not recognized in the evidence.[52] In a later statement,
he proclaimed that only the jurists – and not the historians – could
reconstruct those periods for which reliable sources were lacking.[53]

This implied a complete about-face from an approach to source criticism that searched for the traditions behind the surviving sources. This
kind of analysis had originated within the antiquarian research of the
Renaissance and had revolutionized historiography since Niebuhr, but
now it had been declared irrelevant for the new type of antiquarianism
presented by Mommsen's work.[54] That is why Mommsen, if with a degree
of lip service, on certain occasions could still praise Niebuhr as a pioneer
who had introduced a genuine juristic approach into Roman history.[55]

Ever since its publication, Mommsen's *Staatsrecht* has been forcefully
criticized in a number of respects. Ludwig Lange protested that Mommsen
would present his hypotheses as dogma for which he claimed scholarly
infallibility.[56] Again and again the *Staatsrecht* has been considered a
stumbling block to a proper historical analysis. However, the work is still
used by all scholars working in the field of Roman constitutional history
and law, not only because of Mommsen's unsurpassed command of the
material, but also because he offered solutions to so many inescapable –
still – scholarly problems. An admission that he could not offer a sufficient explanation is highly unusual in the *Staatsrecht*.[57] Even today there
is no manual that can substitute for Mommsen's *Staatsrecht*.[58] As
Momigliano explained in a review of 1949, 'Mommsen cannot be replaced by people who are smaller than Mommsen.'[59]

Most of the twentieth-century commentaries on the *Staatsrecht* either
have been part of overall assessments of Mommsen's life and work or
were articulated in connection with the discussion of peculiar points of
Roman constitutional law and history. We badly need comprehensive
studies of the work in order to show how Mommsen extracted his
categories from the ancient evidence and thereafter applied them once
again to the sources.

Furthermore, it remains to be examined whether Mommsen was really the lonely figure without predecessors worth mentioning, as he liked to style himself. On some occasions, especially in the review just mentioned, Momigliano pleaded for research on this subject,[60] but his suggestions for necessary studies have been taken up only partially.

It now seems clear that Mommsen had followed Joseph Rubino's *Untersuchungen über römische Verfassung und Geschichte*, published in 1839, not only with respect to the general theory of the invariance of the constitution's main features (and the reliability of the sources in so far as they give the adequate terminology),[61] but also with regard to the particular point that the *imperium* of the kings, which was later conferred on the consuls, did not derive from the people.[62] But Mommsen also drew on the opposite theory of Becker that the sovereign people had created the kingdom and elected its incumbents.[63] That explains some of the contradictions manifest in the *Staatsrecht*.[64] We need more comprehensive comparisons of this sort with his immediate predecessors in order to understand fully the basic premises of Mommsen's approach.

And Mommsen's *Staatsrecht* has to be compared also with outstanding works of the older tradition that he himself did not refer to. His first book on the *tribus* contained a number of references to nineteenth-century work but only a few hints that the subject had been treated by great Renaissance scholars like Sigonio (though Lipsius is quoted on some matters). Mommsen's silence apparently implied a judgment and was not due just to ignorance. In a review of the same year (1844), Mommsen mentioned Sigonio as one of those sixteenth-century scholars who did no more than collect the evidence.[65]

In 1875, Mommsen's friend Jacob Bernays[66] published a review article on the *Römisches Staatsrecht*.[67] Bernays praised it as the culmination of four centuries of scholarship. Though full of admiration for Mommsen's work, he did not, however, accept Mommsen's position that the older works on *Staatsaltertümer* were not worth remembering. Bernays pointed out that there were at least two scholars who had achieved a scholarly level far higher than that of the usual compilers of antiquities and who therefore should be considered predecessors of Mommsen in a certain sense – Carlo Sigonio with his *De antiquo iure civium Romanorum* of 1560 and Louis de Beaufort with his *La République romaine ou plan général de l'ancien gouvernement de Rome* of 1766.[68] In the past decades some important studies have been published on both authors, fully justifying Bernays's estimation; yet Momigliano's suggestion that recourse to these works might help to conceptualize an alternative approach to Mommsen's *Staatsrecht* has not been taken up, as far as I can see.[69]

In the late nineteenth century, Mommsen's *Staatsrecht* had a revolutionary impact on the traditional genre of antiquities, which had long been criticized as presenting 'a mishmash of trifles making up a lumber room for all sorts of materials that could not be disposed of elsewhere.'[70] The use of 'Altertümer' in the title of manuals disappeared within a generation. In Greek history, the *Staatsaltertümer* were replaced by *Staatskunde*; for other subjects, systematic works were presented as histories of a new kind, like *Kulturgeschichte* (Jacob Burckhardt), *Sittengeschichte* (Ludwig Friedländer), *Rechtsgeschichte* (Otto Karlowa), *Verwaltungsgeschichte* (Otto Hirschfeld), and *Agrargeschichte* (Max Weber).

With respect to this systematic approach, the work of Max Weber can be seen as inspired by Mommsen's lead. Weber was not a pupil of Mommsen in a formal sense; only once did he attend a university lecture by Mommsen. Momigliano's remark, quoted above, referred to a famous episode of 1889. To obtain his doctorate in jurisprudence at Berlin University, Weber had not only to submit a dissertation – on the medieval trading companies in his case – but also to undergo a disputation in which he was required to propose and defend theses on other subjects. One thesis concerned his idea of a connection between the legal status of land and the methods used by Roman land surveyors. Seventy-one-year-old Theodor Mommsen, an acquaintance of the Weber family, took part in the disputation, and commented – with conviction – that although he was not really convinced by this particular assertion he could not think of a better successor than Max Weber.[71]

Weber developed the thesis in his 'Habilitationsschrift' of 1891, *Die Römische Agrargeschichte in ihrer Bedeutung für das Staats- und Privatrecht.* Jürgen Deininger, the editor of the *Römische Agrargeschichte* in the new *Max Weber Gesamtausgabe*, has shown how heavily Weber drew on Mommsen's *Römische Geschichte* for his general account of Roman agrarian history beyond, simply using a great number of Mommsen's scholarly articles and the *Corpus inscriptionum Latinarum.*[72] Weber himself stated in the preface that his method was indebted to Mommsen, who had laid the foundations for any study of Roman constitutional and administrative law.[73] But his peculiar idea that survey techniques corresponded with the legal status of land had been taken over, rather, from August Meitzen's work on Germanic agrarian history. Max Weber considered himself a pupil of Meitzen.[74]

Mommsen was still not convinced that Meitzen's approach could be transferred to Roman history. But he took Weber's theory seriously enough to reply with a long article in which he pointed out that in the Roman case such a congruence could not be stated.[75] At the same time, Mommsen praised, on principle, Weber's effort to analyse the works of the Roman *agrimensores* from a legal and economic, and not a philological, point of view.[76] Weber's methodological approach, of drawing conclusions from later to earlier periods and interpreting the evidence according to the nature of things ('Natur der Sache'),[77] clearly resembled Mommsen's.

One substantial idea that Weber did take over from Mommsen was that the territorial expansion of the Roman Republic fostered the development of agrarian capitalism on an unprecedented scale. This ancient capitalism's capacity for development, or, rather, the limits of this capacity, became a major subject of Weber's later work, such as the 1896 article on the social causes for the decline of ancient culture ('Die sozialen Gründe des Untergangs der antiken Kultur') and, especially, the surveys of the agrarian history of ancient civilizations ('Agrarverhältnisse im Altertum') in three successive editions of the *Handwörterbuch der Staatswissenschaften,* which in the final version of 1909 became a book-length text. Weber now joined a debate on the general character of the ancient economy that had been started by economic historians such as Karl Rodbertus and Karl Bücher, whose allegedly primitivist interpretation was challenged by ancient historians such as Karl Julius Beloch and Eduard Meyer. Weber accepted Bücher's position in so far as it was considered an ideal type.[78] It was at least partly within the context of his work on ancient history that Weber developed his methodological concepts.[79] Weber digested an astonishing amount of specialized literature on ancient civilizations; that he finally decided to treat not only Greece and Rome but also ancient Egypt, Mesopotamia, and Israel was, however, due to the impact of Eduard Meyer's monumental *Geschichte des Altertums,* as once again Momigliano has pointed out.[80]

Weber was bedevilled by the question of why the ancient world had produced a capitalism based on war and booty, state monopolies, tax farming, and trade but had not been able to develop the peculiar 'rational' capitalism that had taken off only in the later Middle Ages. In his later work on the sociology of world religions, he tried to broaden his perspective not only by trying to establish the interplay of environmental, economic, legal, and political structures but by taking into account the religious factor as well.[81]

All in all, the development of Weber's work towards cross-cultural comparisons and universally applicable ideal types, as manifest in *Wirtschaft und Gesellschaft,* marks the long distance he had travelled away from Mommsen, though he came back to Mommsen – be it approvingly or critically – whenever he discussed features of ancient Rome. Weber's work is a peculiar synthesis of materials and approaches taken from a number of disciplines, like classics, history, economics, law, and religious studies. It followed Mommsen's lead in the sense that historical materials were organized with respect to systematic points of view.[82] The construction of ideal types implied a rigorous selection of materials from the contingency of historical survival. Whereas Mommsen had used categories from the sources to build a coherent system that allegedly corresponded to the structures of one historical society, Weber felt free to use historical categories as well as artificially coined terms (or a mixture of the two) to interpret and compare structures of a great number of societies from an external vantage point, namely, the uniqueness of modern Western civilization. The work of the mature Max Weber therefore cannot properly be considered a new kind of antiquarianism, though the development of his methodology was indebted to the kind of ideal types 'avant la lettre' that Mommsen (but also the historical school of national economy) had constructed before.

Thanks to Momigliano, we learned not to treat Mommsen and Weber as demigods creating new disciplines out of nothing, and also that there was more than a biographical connection between the two scholars. To demonstrate that they themselves belonged to an intellectual tradition is not to doubt or diminish their ingenuity, but to help illuminate their achievement – the establishment of fundamental assumptions that continue to direct research in a number of disciplines to this very day.

Notes

1 Middletown, CT, 1982 (*History and Theory* Beiheft 21); compare also Momigliano, 'Dopo Max Weber?' (1978), in Momigliano, *Sesto contributo alla storia degli studi classici e del mondo antico* (Rome, 1980), 295–312. Various volumes of Momigliano's *Contributi* are referred to in short-title form hereafter.

2 Momigliano, *New Paths*, 29ff.

3 *Gnomon* 30 (1958): 3.

4 'Ancient History and the Antiquarian' (1950), in Momigliano, *Contributo* (Rome, 1955), 67–106.

5 Compare also Anthony Grafton, 'Prolegomena to Friedrich August Wolf,' *Journal of the Warburg and Courtauld Institutes* 44 (1981): 101–29; idem, 'Polyhistor into "Philolog": Notes on the Transformation of German Classical Scholarship, 1780–1850,' *History of Universities* 3 (1983): 159–92.

6 See Niebuhr's letter to Dore Hensler of 10 November 1810, in *Die Briefe Barthold Georg Niebuhrs*, ed. Dietrich Gerhard and William Norvin, vol. 2 (Berlin, 1929), 165; and 'Erinnerungen an Niebuhr's Wesen und Wirken, durch seine Briefe veranlaßt,' in Friedrich Karl von Savigny, *Vermischte Schriften*, vol. 4 (Berlin, 1850; repr. Aalen, 1968), 216.

7 Niebuhr, *Römische Geschichte*, vol. 1 (Berlin, 1811), xii, 7.

8 Compare Arnaldo Momigliano, 'Perizonius, Niebuhr, and the Character of Early Roman Tradition' (1957), in *Secondo contributo* (Rome, 1960), 69–87; Hendrik J. Erasmus, *The Origins of Rome in Historiography from Petrarch to Perizonius* (Assen, 1962); Ronald T. Ridley, 'The Historical Observations of Jacob Perizonius,' *Atti della Accademia Nazionale dei Lincei*, ser. 8, vol. 32, fasc. 3 (1989).

9 See n69 below. Though Niebuhr later took notice of Beaufort's work on the political system of the Roman Republic, his judgment is generally based on Beaufort's earlier work *Dissertation sur l'incertitude des cinq premiers siècles de l'histoire* (1738), which was seen as a piece of historical Pyrrhonism; see Niebuhr's preface to the second edition, in *Römische Geschichte: Neue Ausgabe*, ed. M. Isler, vol. 1 (Berlin, 1873), xxvii; idem, *Vorträge über römische Alterthümer*, ed. M. Isler (Berlin, 1858), 17; and *Vorträge über römische Geschichte*, ed. M. Isler, vol. 1 (Berlin, 1846), 72.

10 'Die Zerstörung des Betrugs mag dem Kritiker genügen, ... der Historiker aber bedarf Positives' (Niebuhr, *Römische Geschichte*, vol. 1, p. x).

11 Ernst Grumach, *Goethe und die Antike*, vol. 1 (Berlin, 1949), 48; Georg W.F. Hegel, *Vorlesungen über die Philosophie der Geschichte: Werke 12* (Frankfurt am Main, 1986), 342; and anonymous review, in *Jenaische Allgemeine Literatur-Zeitung* 13 (1816): 57–75. Later, Hippolyte Taine would moan, 'Quelle horrible lecture!' (*Essai sur Tite – Live* [Paris, 1882], 108).

12 'Muß dieses Buch, gehörig benutzt, mit der Zeit die ganze Lehre von den römischen Alterthümern umgestalten' (A.W. von Schlegel, *Sämmtliche Werke*, ed. Eduard Böcking, vol. 12 [Leipzig, 1847], 512). The review had first appeared in *Heidelberger Jahrbücher* in 1816. For the impact of Niebuhr's work in this sense, compare Albert Schwegler, *Römische Geschichte*, vol. 1 (Tübingen, 1867), 152f.

13 Niebuhr's research in Roman history had started with investigations into the *leges agrariae* and was motivated by the contemporary issue of 'Bauern-befreiung'; compare Arnaldo Momigliano, 'Alle origini delle interese su Roma arcaica: Niebuhr e India' (1980), in *Settimo contributo* (Rome, 1984),

155–67; Alfred Heuß, *Barthold Georg Niebuhrs wissenschaftliche Anfänge*
(Göttingen, 1981); and Gerrit Walther, *Niebuhrs Forschung* (Stuttgart, 1993).

14 'Ich bin vollkommen gewiß daß mein, fast ganz neu entdecktes, System
der Grundbeschaffenheit und allmählichen Ausbildung der römischen
Verfassung das Chaos welches bisher waltete in kurzem ganz verdrängen
muß' (letter to Perthes of 11 April 1812, in *Die Briefe Barthold Georg Niebuhrs*,
vol. 2, p. 26); and see the letter to D. Hensler of 7 December 1810, ibid.,
177. Compare Niebuhr's remark that the great seventeenth-century scholar
Johann Friedrich Gronovius had not understood the Roman constitution at
all (*Römische Geschichte*, vol. 2 [Berlin, 1812], 8 n3).

15 Letter to D. Hensler of 19 March 1811, in *Die Briefe Barthold Georg Niebuhrs*,
vol. 2, p. 193f; Niebuhr, *Vorträge über römische Alterthümer*, 20f, 24f; idem,
Vorträge über römische Geschichte, 75.

16 Letter to the Prussian crown prince of 17 November 1830, in *Barthold Georg
Niebuhr. Briefe: Neue Folge 1816–1830*, vol. 4, ed. Eduard Vischer (Bern, 1984),
117.

17 Quoted in Lothar Wickert, *Theodor Mommsen: Eine Biographie*, vol. 1 (Frankfurt am Main, 1959), 165f.

18 Later, Fustel de Coulanges expressed his distance from German scholarship
with the remark that he would prefer to be in error with Livy instead of with
Niebuhr; see Numa Denis Fustel de Coulanges, 'Une leçon d'ouverture et
quelques fragments inédits de Fustel de Coulanges,' *Revue de synthèse historique* 2 (1901): 258. For the same attitude on the part of Johann Jakob Bachofen, compare Wilfried Nippel, *Griechen, Barbaren und 'Wilde'* (Frankfurt am
Main, 1990), 102f.

19 Mommsen, *Die römischen Tribus in administrativer Beziehung* (Altona, 1844),
vi f. On Mommsen's dissociation from Niebuhr, compare Alfred Heuß,
'Niebuhr und Mommsen. Zur wissenschaftsgeschichtlichen Stellung Theodor Mommsens' (1968), in Heuß, *Gesammelte Schriften*, vol. 3 (Stuttgart,
1995), 1699–1716.

20 *Theodor Mommsen – Otto Jahn: Briefwechsel, 1842–1868*, ed. Lothar Wickert
(Frankfurt am Main, 1962), 20f.

21 Text in Theodor Mommsen, *Tagebuch der französisch-italienischen Reise 1844/
45. Mit einem Anhang: Mommsens Denkschrift über das Corpus inscriptionum
Latinarum 1847*, ed. Gerold Walser (Bern, 1976).

22 See Adolf Harnack, *Geschichte der Königlich Preußischen Akademie der Wissenschaften zu Berlin*, vol. 1.2 (Berlin, 1900), 898ff; Otto Hirschfeld, 'Gedächtnisrede auf Theodor Mommsen' (1904), in Hirschfeld, *Kleine Schriften* (Berlin,
1913), 931–65; Lothar Wickert, *Theodor Mommsen*, vols 2 and 3 (Frankfurt am
Main, 1964–9); and Stefan Rebenich, *Theodor Mommsen: Eine Biographie*
(Munich, 2002), 43–52, 80–5.

23 The only authority he acknowledged in this field was the San Marino scholar
Bartolomeo Borghesi (1781–1860). Mommsen visited Borghesi in 1845 and
1847. Borghesi encouraged Mommsen to take up his epigraphical project
and recommended it to the Berlin Academy. After Borghesi's death,
Mommsen declared Borghesi the only teacher he had ever had; quoted
by Wickert, *Theodor Mommsen*, vol. 1, 163. On Borghesi's importance for
Mommsen's work on Roman coinage, see Michael H. Crawford, 'From
Borghesi to Mommsen: The Creation of an Exact Science,' in *Medals and
Coins from Budé to Mommsen*, ed. Crawford (London, 1990), 125–32.

24 'Antrittsrede 8. Juli 1858,' in Mommsen, *Reden und Aufsätze* (Berlin, 1905), 36.

25 Mommsen's address to Harnack of 1890, in *Reden und Aufsätze*, p. 209; Adolf
Harnack, 'Vom Großbetrieb der Wissenschaft,' in Harnack, *Aus Wissenschaft
und Leben*, 2 vols (Gießen, 1911), vol. 1, pp. 10–20; 'Theodor Mommsen,'
ibid., vol. 2, pp. 323–32; Ulrich von Wilamowitz-Moellendorff, *Geschichte der
Philologie* (Leipzig, 1921; repr. Stuttgart, 1998), 71. On the collaboration of
Mommsen and Harnack beginning in the late 1880s, see Stefan Rebenich,
*Theodor Mommsen und Adolf Harnack: Wissenschaft und Politik im Berlin des
ausgehenden 19. Jahrhunderts* (Berlin, 1997).

26 On Mommsen's alleged promotion of Caesarism or Bonapartism, compare
Wilfried Nippel, 'Charisma und Herrschaft,' in *Virtuosen der Macht*, ed.
Nippel (Munich, 2000), 14f.

27 Compare Christian Meier, 'Das Begreifen des Notwendigen. Zu Theodor
Mommsens *Römischer Geschichte*,' in *Formen der Geschichtsschreibung*, ed.
Reinhart Koselleck et al. (Munich, 1982), 201–44.

28 Nitzsch, *Neue Jahrbücher für Philologie und Pädagogik* 73 (1856): 717.

29 Compare the criticism by Ludwig Lange, 'Die neuesten Darstellungen der
ältesten Zeiten der römischen Geschichte,' *Allgemeine Monatsschrift für
Wissenschaft und Literatur* (1854): 848, 859.

30 This is, however, a late formulation, in a letter to Heinrich Sybel of 1895;
quoted by Lothar Wickert, *Theodor Mommsen*, vol. 4 (Frankfurt am Main,
1980), 239.

31 'Rektoratsrede 1874,' in Mommsen, *Reden und Aufsätze*, 14f. Compare Albert
Wucher, *Theodor Mommsen. Geschichtsschreibung und Politik* (Göttingen, 1956);
Alfred Heuß, 'Theodor Mommsen als Geschichtsschreiber' (1988), in Heuß,
Gesammelte Schriften, vol. 3, pp. 1744–1802.

32 Wolf, *Darstellung der Altertumswissenschaft nach Begriff, Umfang, Zweck und Wert*
(1807; repr. Berlin, 1986), 55: '"Begebenheiten und Ereignisse in ihrer
Aufeinanderfolge" versus "Zustände und Verfassungen."'

33 Marquardt, *Römische Staatsverwaltung*, 3 vols (Leipzig, 1873–8).

34 This and the following quotations are taken from the introductions to the

three editions (1871, 1876, 1887) of the first volume, all in *Römisches Staatsrecht*, 3rd ed. (Leipzig, 1887; repr. Graz, 1952).

35 'Ein Getümmel auf dem antiquarischen Bauplatz, [wo] viele geschäftige Leute bloss die Balken und Ziegel durcheinander werfen, aber weder das Baumaterial zu vermehren noch zu bauen verstehen.' Mommsen had already used this metaphor, in a letter to Wilhelm Henzen in 1845, when he complained that his future engagement with the inscription corpus would imply that he had to produce the bricks for other people instead of building a house himself; quoted by Wickert, *Theodor Mommsen*, vol. 2, p. 106. Later, in a letter of 1870, Jacob Bernays attested to Mommsen that he was architect and construction worker ('Baumeister und Kärrner') in one and the same person; quoted ibid., vol. 3, p. 338.

36 '[Eine] begrifflich geschlossene und auf consequent durchgeführten Grundgedanken wie auf festen Pfeilern ruhende Darstellung.'

37 Compare Alfred Heuß, *Theodor Mommsen und das 19. Jahrhundert* (Kiel, 1956; repr. Stuttgart 1996); Jochen Bleicken, *Lex publica: Gesetz und Recht in der römischen Republik* (Berlin, 1975), 16ff; and Yan Thomas, *Mommsen et l''Isolierung' du droit* (Paris, 1984).

38 Compare Karl Joachim Hölkeskamp, 'Zwischen "System" und "Geschichte". Theodor Mommsens *Staatsrecht* und die römische "Verfassung" in Frankreich und Deutschland,' in *Die späte römische Republik: Un débat franco-allemand d'histoire et d'historiographie*, ed. Hinnerk Bruhns et al. (Rome, 1997), 93–111.

39 For the background of nineteenth-century constitutional thought, compare Hans Kloft, 'Verantwortung und Rechenschaftspflicht. Überlegungen zu Mommsens Staatsrecht,' in *Imperium Romanum: Studien zu Geschichte und Rezeption. Festschrift für Karl Christ zum 75. Geburtstag* (Stuttgart, 1998), 410–30. The fiction of the ruler as a magistrate Mommsen could apply (though with considerable difficulties) to the principate yet not to the emperor in late antiquity; this explains the chronological limit of his account.

40 Compare Alfred Heuß, 'Zur Thematik republikanischer "Staatsrechtslehre"' (1978), in Heuß, *Gesammelte Schriften*, vol. 2 (Stuttgart, 1995), 1300–18; Elizabeth Rawson, *Intellectual Life in the Late Roman Republic* (London, 1985), chap. 16; and Manfred Fuhrmann, 'Erneuerung als Wiederherstellung des Alten. Zur Funktion antiquarischer Forschung im pätrepublikanischen Rom,' in *Epochenschwelle und Epochenbewußtsein*, ed. Reinhart Herzog and Reinhart Koselleck (Munich, 1987), 131–51.

41 This holds true also for Roman criminal law; see Mommsen, *Römisches Strafrecht* (Leipzig, 1899), vii f, 4, 126f, 525.

42 Gradenwitz, 'Theodor Mommsen,' *Zeitschrift für Rechtsgeschichte: Romanistische*

Abteilung 25 (1904): 11; compare Karl Johannes Neumann, *Entwicklung und Aufgaben der Alten Geschichte* (Straßburg, 1910), 15. See also the older Mommsen's statement that thinking like a lawyer was the basis of his scholarship though he had not achieved his results on the territory of Gaius and Ulpian; letter to L. Goldschmidt of 1891, quoted by Wickert, *Theodor Mommsen*, vol. 1, p. 456.

43 Niese, review of *Römisches Staatsrecht*, vol. III, *Göttingische Gelehrte Anzeigen* (1888): 954f; compare idem, *Grundriss der Römischen Geschichte nebst Quellenkunde*, 3rd ed. (Munich, 1906), 15; Julius Kaerst, 'Theodor Mommsen,' *Historische Vierteljahrschrift* 7 (1904): 336; and Karl Johannes Neumann, 'Römische Staatsaltertümer,' in *Einleitung in die Altertumswissenschaft*, vol. 3, ed. Alfred Gercke and Eduard Norden (Leipzig, 1912), 420f.

44 'Die patricischen und die plebejischen Sonderrechte in den Bürger- und den Rathsversammlungen,' in Mommsen, *Römische Forschungen*, vol. 1 (Berlin, 1864), 132.

45 *Römisches Staatsrecht*, vol. II, 1, p. 274 n1. On Mommsen's treatment of the tribunate, compare Ernst Badian, 'Tribuni Plebis and Res Publica,' in *Imperium sine fine: T. Robert S. Broughton and the Roman Republic*, ed. Jerzy Linderski (Stuttgart, 1996), 187–225.

46 *Römisches Staatsrecht*, vol. I, p. 26 n1.

47 Review of Mommsen, *Römisches Staatsrecht*, vol. I, in Ludwig Lange, *Kleine Schriften aus dem Gebiete der classischen Alterthumswissenschaft*, vol. 2 (Göttingen, 1887), 159.

48 *Römisches Staatsrecht*, vol. II, 1, p. 279 n1.

49 Compare Donald McFayden, 'A Constitutional Doctrine Re-Examined,' in *Studies in Honor of Frederick W. Shipley* (St Louis, 1942), 1–15.

50 *Römisches Staatsrecht*, vol. III, 1, p. 313. Compare Frank Behne, 'Volkssouveränität und verfassungsrechtliche Systematik. Beobachtungen zur Struktur des Römischen Staatsrechtes von Theodor Mommsen,' in *Res Publica Reperta. Zur Verfassung und Gesellschaft der römischen Republik und des frühen Prinzipats. Festschrift für Jochen Bleicken zum 75. Geburtstag* (Stuttgart, 2002), 124–36.

51 Mommsen, *Gesammelte Schriften*, vol. 3 (repr. Berlin, 1965), 546.

52 'An der Logik der Tatsachen zu prüfen, aus dem trüben Wust unverstandener und unverständlicher Tradition das innerlich Unmögliche auszuscheiden, das durch die notwendigen Gesetze der Entwickelung Geforderte auch da zu postulieren, wo es in der Überlieferung verwirrt oder aus ihr verschollen ist' (Mommsen, *Reden und Aufsätze*, 199).

53 'Vor der Plattheit derjenigen historischen Forschung, welche das was sich nie und nirgend begeben hat, bei Seite lassen zu dürfen meint, schützt den

Juristen seine genetisches Verständniss fordernde Wissenschaft' (Mommsen, *Abriß des römischen Staatsrechts* [1893; repr. Darmstadt, 1974], xvii. On Mommsen's understanding of a juridical approach, compare also Gerrit Walther, 'Theodor Mommsen und die Erforschung der römischen Geschichte,' in *Historicization – Historisierung*, ed. Glenn W. Most (Göttingen, 2001), 249ff.

54 This point is made with respect to Rubino, whose conception became fundamental for Mommsen (see below), by Karl Wilhelm Nitzsch, *Die römische Annalistik von ihren ersten Anfängen bis auf Valerius Antias* (Berlin, 1873), 5.

55 'Die Aufgaben der historischen Rechtswissenschaft' (1848), in Mommsen, *Gesammelte Schriften*, vol. 3, p. 587; academy adresses of 1858 and 1879, in idem, *Reden und Aufsätze*, 36, 199.

56 Lange, *Kleine Schriften*, vol. 2, p. 163. Written in 1872, just after the declaration of the pope's infallibility, it was a particularly malicious remark given Mommsen's strong anti-Catholic position. As the author of *Römische Alterthümer* (1856–71), Lange was indignant at being included in the number of authors Mommsen had not considered worth discussing. He praised the greater objectivity of Marquardt, who did not follow Mommsen's example; see Lange, 'Jahresbericht über die römischen Alterthümer,' *Bursians Jahresberichte über die Fortschritte der classischen Alterthumswissenschaft* 2 (1873): 841f. For a later attack on Mommsen's 'dogmatism' compare, e.g., J.S. Reid, 'On Some Questions of Roman Criminal Law,' *Journal of Roman Studies* 1 (1911): 68–99.

57 *Römisches Staatsrecht*, vol. II, 1, p. 292 n4.

58 The legal historian Wolfgang Kunkel had massively attacked Mommsen's dogmatic approach; see 'Magistratische Gewalt und Senatsherrschaft,' in *Aufstieg und Niedergang der Römischen Welt*, vol. 1.2 (Berlin, 1972), 3–22; and 'Theodor Mommsen als Jurist,' *Chiron* 14 (1984): 369–80. However, when his long-expected work on the Roman constitution was published posthumously, it turned out that Kunkel, who had declared that the senate was the heart of the system, had only (almost) completed the volume on the magistracy, *Staatsordnung und Staatspraxis der römischen Republik. Zweiter Abschnitt: Die Magistratur* (Munich, 1995); see the reviews by Wilfried Nippel, *Zeitschrift für Geschichtswissenschaft* 45 (1997): 548–50; and Jochen Bleicken, 'Im Schatten Mommsens,' *Rechtshistorisches Journal* 15 (1996): 3–28.

59 Momigliano, review of Ernst Meyer, *Römischer Staat und Staatsgedanke, Journal of Roman Studies* 39 (1949): 156.

60 One way to 'prepare the future *Staatsrecht* ... is by saving what is worth saving in the earlier interpreters of Roman Law and Constitution. There is no

excuse for allowing them to remain "lacrimabiles" and "ignoti" under the dust of our libraries' (ibid.).

61 Joseph Rubino, *Untersuchungen über römische Verfassung und Geschichte* (Cassel, 1839), vi ff, xv, 4, 107f.

62 Rubino, *Untersuchungen*, especially 110. Compare Alfred Heuß, 'Gedanken und Vermutungen zur frühen römischen Regierungsgewalt' (1982), in Heuß, *Gesammelte Schriften*, vol. 2, p. 908–85. Mommsen acknowledged the importance of Rubino's book by giving him the extraordinary honour of a verbatim quotation; see *Römisches Staatsrecht*, vol. I, p. 90. However, he did not accept Rubino's assumption of a hereditary monarchy; see *Römisches Staatsrecht*, vol. II, 1, p. 8.

63 Wilhelm Adolph Becker, *Handbuch der römischen Alterthümer*, vol. 2.1 (Leipzig, 1844), 294ff.

64 Compare Adalberto Giovannini, 'Magistratur und Volk. Ein Beitrag zur Entstehungsgeschichte des Staatsrechts,' in *Staat und Staatlichkeit in der frühen römischen Republik*, ed. Walter Eder (Stuttgart, 1990), 406–36; idem, 'De Niebuhr à Mommsen: remarques sur la genèse du "Droit public,"' *Cahiers du Centre Glotz* 3 (1992): 167–76.

65 Review of Geib, *Geschichte des römischen Criminalprocesses*, in Mommsen, *Gesammelte Schriften*, vol. 3, p. 469f. For a more positive though not unequivocal assessment of Sigonio's work on the Roman criminal courts, see August Wilhelm Zumpt, *Das Criminalrecht der Römischen Republik*, vol. 1.1 (Berlin, 1865), vi f. That a traditional definition of the Roman *nobilitas* in terms of its *ius imaginum*, which was taken for granted by scholars (including Mommsen) up to the nineteenth century, in fact goes back to Sigonio is shown by Annie N. Zadoks-Josephus Jitta, *Ancestral Portraiture in Rome and the Art of the Last Century of the Republic* (Amsterdam, 1932), 97–110; compare also Adam Afzelius, 'Zur Definition der römischen Nobilität in der Zeit Ciceros,' *Classica et mediaevalia* 1 (1938): 41f.

66 On Bernays, compare Arnaldo Momigliano, 'Jacob Bernays,' in *Quinto contributo* (Rome, 1975), 127–58; Hans Bach, *Jacob Bernays: Ein Beitrag zur Emanzipationsgeschichte der Juden und zur Geschichte des deutschen Geistes im neunzehnten Jahrhundert* (Tübingen, 1974); and Lothar Wickert, 'Theodor Mommsen und Jacob Bernays,' *Historische Zeitschrift* 205 (1967): 265–94.

67 'Die Behandlung des Römischen Staatsrechtes bis auf Theodor Mommsen,' repr. in Jacob Bernays, *Gesammelte Abhandlungen*, vol. 2, ed. Hermann Usener (Berlin, 1885), p. 256–75.

68 'Welche sich über den Tross der Antiquitätenschreiber weit erhoben und die Richtung einschlugen, in welcher Mommsen uns jetzt zum Ziele führt' (ibid., p. 259).

69 Giovanni Forni, 'Tribu' romane e problemi conessi dal Biondo Flavio al
    Mommsen,' in *Studi di storia antica in memoria di Luca de Regibus* (Genoa,
    1969), 17–90; William McCuaig, *Carlo Sigonio: The Changing World of the Late
    Renaissance* (Princeton, 1989); idem, 'The Fasti Capitolini and the Study of
    Roman Chronology in the Sixteenth Century,' *Athenaeum* 79 (1991): 141–59;
    idem, 'Antonio Agustin and the Reform of the Centuriate Assembly,' in
    Antonio Agustin between Renaissance and Counter-Reform, ed. Michael H. Craw-
    ford (London, 1993), 61–80; Ronald T. Ridley, 'Gibbon's Complement:
    Louis de Beaufort,' *Memorie: Istituto Veneto di scienze, lettere ed arti* 40: 3 (1986);
    and Mouza Raskolnikoff, *Histoire romaine et critique historique dans l'Europe des
    Lumières* (Paris, 1992).

70 'Ein Mischmasch von verschiedenen Dingen, zum Theil auch von unbedeu-
    tenden Kleinigkeiten, ja eine Rumpelkammer, in welche man hineinwarf,
    was man anderwärts nicht brauchte' (Karl Otfried Müller, review of Wachs-
    muth, *Hellenische Alterthumskunde*, *Göttingische Gelehrte Anzeigen* 184 [1831]:
    1827). For several other statements of this sort, compare Wilfried Nippel,
    'Von den "Altertümern" zur Kulturgeschichte,' *Ktèma* 23 (1998): 17–24.

71 See Jürgen Deininger, 'Editorischer Bericht,' in Max Weber, *Die Römische
    Agrargeschichte in ihrer Bedeutung für das Staats- und Privatrecht*, ed. Deininger,
    (*Max Weber Gesamtausgabe*, vol. I/2, Tübingen, 1986), 55ff. The discussion
    seems to have been continued privately; see ibid., 197 n102. According to
    Paul Honigsheim, a pupil of Weber, Mommsen (after Weber's *Habilitation* in
    1891) thought of promoting Weber to a chair of either ancient history or
    Roman law; see Honigsheim, 'Max Weber in Heidelberg,' in *Max Weber zum
    Gedächtnis*, ed. René König and Johannes Winckelmann (Cologne, 1963),
    205.

72 Deininger, 'Einleitung,' in Weber, *Römische Agrargeschichte*, especially 23f. See
    the list of Mommsen's articles used by Weber, ibid., 376–8.

73 Weber, *Römische Agrargeschichte*, 100. Weber does not mention Niebuhr's
    chapter on the Roman *agrimensores* (*Römische Geschichte*, vol. 2, p. 532ff),
    which goes back to Niebuhr's earlier studies on Roman agrarian law.

74 Weber, *Römische Agrargeschichte*, 100; and his letter of 1910 after Meitzen's
    death, in Max Weber, *Briefe 1909–1910*, ed. M. Rainer Lepsius and Wolfgang
    J. Mommsen (*Max Weber Gesamtausgabe*, vol. II/6, Tübingen, 1994), 382. On
    the intellectual background of the young Weber, including his relationship
    to Meitzen and Mommsen, compare also Luigi Capogrossi Colognesi,
    Max Weber e le società antiche, 2nd ed. (Rome, 1990); and Realino Marra,
    Capitalismo e anticapitalismo in Max Weber (Bologna, 2002).

75 Mommsen, 'Zum römischen Bodenrecht' (1892), repr. in Mommsen,
    Gesammelte Schriften, vol. 5 (repr. Berlin, 1965), 117. Weber accepted

Mommsen's criticism only partly; see 'Agrarverhältnisse im Altertum,' in Weber, *Gesammelte Aufsätze zur Sozial- und Wirtschaftsgeschichte* (Tübingen, 1924; repr. 1988), 222ff, 287.

76 In a review of 1845, Mommsen had noted that the works of the *agrimensores* were the domain of the philologists and not the jurists; see *Gesammelte Schriften*, vol. 3, p. 547.

77 Weber, *Römische Agrargeschichte*, 97.

78 Weber, *Gesammelte Aufsätze zur Sozial- und Wirtschaftsgeschichte*, 7.

79 Compare Wilfried Nippel, 'Methodenentwicklung und Zeitbezüge im althistorischen Werk Max Webers,' *Geschichte und Gesellschaft* 16 (1990): 355–74.

80 'Max Weber di fronte agli storici dell'antichità,' in Momigliano, *Settimo contributo* (Rome, 1984), 245–51.

81 Compare Wilfried Nippel, 'Einleitung,' in Max Weber, *Wirtschaft und Gesellschaft. Teilband 5: Die Stadt*, ed. Nippel (*Max Weber Gesamtausgabe*, vol. I/22-5, Tübingen, 1999); idem, 'From Agrarian History to Cross-Cultural Comparisons: Weber on Greco-Roman Antiquity,' in *The Cambridge Companion to Weber*, ed. Stephen Turner (Cambridge, 2000), 240–55.

82 That Weber's sociology of law is methodologically indebted to Mommsen's *Staatsrecht* is suggested by Bernhard K. Quensel and Hubert Treiber, 'Das "Ideal" konstruktiver Jurisprudenz als Methode. Zur "logischen Struktur" von Max Webers Idealtypik,' *Rechtstheorie* 33 (2002): 118.

chapter eight

From Antiquarianism to Anthropology

PETER BURKE

The aim of this chapter is to discuss some of the continuities, or at least the intellectual relations, between the antiquarianism of the Renaissance and the later practices of social or cultural anthropology. It is inspired by the work of Arnaldo Momigliano and reflects some of his many interests, ranging from Herodotus to Durkheim, with ample space in between them for thoughts on early modern scholars such as Justus Lipsius, Isaac Casaubon, and a host of lesser figures.

Histories of anthropology tend to begin with the formal establishment of the discipline in the nineteenth century or, at earliest, with the intellectual heritage of the Enlightenment.[1] Momigliano, on the other hand, was well aware of connections between the antiquarian movement of the sixteenth and seventeenth centuries (inspired by the ancient Roman scholar Varro) and what we now call 'ethnography' or 'anthropology,' just as he was aware of the contributions of that movement to social and cultural history.[2]

On one side, Momigliano famously stressed the antiquaries' 'revolution in historical method' and their interest in 'non-literary evidence.'[3] On the other, he presented Herodotus as an ethno-historian, working 'on the basis of sightseeing and oral tradition.' Herodotus, who regularly described the food, clothes, and housing of different peoples and their marriage and funeral rituals, was condemned by Thucydides, who had a very different view of the nature of history. It was 'the new ethnographic research' of the Renaissance, stimulated by the discovery of America and the rise of the Ottoman Empire, that was 'the main factor in the revaluation of Herodotus.'[4] An interest in ethnography also informs Momigliano's book on *Alien Wisdom*, concerned with encounters between cultures in the ancient world, in which he praises 'what Polybius makes of that anthropologist's delight, the funeral processions in which the Roman aristocrats paraded hirelings dressed as their own ancestors.'[5]

All the same, Momigliano never commented at length on the contribution of the antiquarians to anthropology, and discussions of the subject are rare. Curiously enough, two of these discussions appeared a year apart in the mid-1960s, an article by John H. Rowe and a book by Margaret Hodgen. Rowe argued that 'the anthropological tradition of interest in differences between men had its beginning in the Italian Renaissance ... and specifically in Renaissance archaeology,' by which he means the work of humanists such as Lorenzo Valla, Flavio Biondo, and Pietro Martire d'Anghiera.[6] As for Hodgen's book, it claims to be no more than a provisional 'exploration' of an intellectual 'inheritance' from scholars of the sixteenth and seventeenth centuries who 'laid the foundations of modern anthropology.'[7] The book does not discuss the antiquarian movement, although it does describe some of the scholars mentioned in the text as 'antiquaries,' from Guillaume Du Choul to William Brerewood.[8]

These studies made valuable contributions to the subject, but they do not tell the whole story. They omit a number of important figures, such as Onofrio Panvinio and Lorenzo Pignoria in Italy, Etienne Pasquier and Claude Fauchet in France, and Johannes Bureus and Thomas Bartolin in Scandinavia. Another problem is the fact that the two authors' concern with what they call 'foundations' may give a false impression of a smooth transition from antiquarianism to anthropology, an impression that I shall try to correct in the pages that follow.

Antiquarianism, Anthropology, Archaeology

A short essay on a large subject needs a sharp focus, including a precise definition of both antiquarianism and anthropology. As a cultural practice, antiquarianism may be defined by its concern for the material remains of the past, together with a wide conception of that past, including everyday life, since the evidence of artefacts, combined with that of texts, allowed a more detailed and accurate reconstruction of 'customs' (modes of eating and drinking, marriage and burial, etc.) than was possible from texts alone. For the most part amateurs working in their spare time, humanist antiquarians were not confined to a single discipline but could move back and forth as they wished between literary and non-literary evidence, Romans and barbarians.

In the case of anthropology, I shall privilege ethnography, in other words the description and interpretation of manners and customs, at the expense of ethnology, an approach concerned with comparison and generalization. I shall also stress the intellectual egalitarianism that is built into the discipline and takes three main forms. In the first place, a concern with every kind of society on equal terms. In the second place, an interest in every kind of person in a given society, young and old, male and female, and so on. In the third place, a concern with every aspect of everyday life, however trivial it may seem. As the German-American anthropologist Franz Boas wrote, 'To the ethnologist, the most trifling details of social life are important.'[9]

Antiquarianism was an informal practice, movement, or tradition, usually institutionalized, if at all, in voluntary associations, such as the English College of Antiquaries, founded around the year 1586 and re-founded as the Society of Antiquaries in 1707.[10] Sweden was a rare exception to this rule, since a *Riksantikvariat*, or 'State Office of Antiquities,' was founded in 1630, a chair in antiquities at Uppsala University in 1662, and a College of Antiquities in 1666. The government supported antiquaries because the idea that the Swedes were the descendants of the ancient Goths was considered to be of political use in the seventeenth century.[11]

Anthropology, on the other hand, was recognized as a profession and as a university department soon after the term (like 'ethnography,' 'ethnology,' and their equivalents in other languages) came into general use in the middle of the nineteenth century.

It is difficult to write about the history of these two practices without mentioning a third, archaeology, which emerged from antiquarianism and became a profession a generation or two before anthropology.[12] To this day, there is a Faculty of Archaeology and Anthropology at Cambridge University, joining the study of the world before writing and of peoples without writing in a single department, deriving from the University Museum of Archaeology and Ethnology founded in 1883. At Harvard, the Peabody Museum of American Archaeology and Ethnology had already made the same link. In Paris, archaeology and anthropology were once joined at the Musée de St-Germain, organized by Henri Hubert, a follower of Emile Durkheim.

It will also be necessary to say something, however briefly, about the rise of another form of study that attracted amateur scholars before it became an academic discipline: folklore. In Britain, for example, the Folklore Society was founded in 1878, soon after the Anthropological

Society. The subject has always been a marginal one in English universities, perhaps because anthropology occupied the space in which it might have flourished. On the other hand, it was national folklore rather than the anthropology of exotic peoples that became a focus of interest in Scandinavia and Central Europe, where the continuity between the antiquarian tradition and later ethnography remains clearer than in Britain.[13]

There are two obvious but opposite dangers that an essay of this kind must try to escape. On the one hand, there is the danger of offering a Whig interpretation of historiography, overemphasizing continuity, making the rise of anthropology appear inevitable, or even presenting Herodotus, say, as a Greek Evans-Pritchard or Lévi-Strauss. On the other hand, there is the peril of a Foucauldian interpretation of the 'invention' of anthropology that overemphasizes social and cultural ruptures. In what follows I shall try to avoid these extremes and discuss the relation between the two practices in terms of traditions that are constantly being reinterpreted and reconstructed, sometimes radically, according to the changing needs of different generations of inheritors.

The Humanist Tradition

Any argument for continuity between the practices of Renaissance scholars and those of later anthropologists must confront the problem of what was described above as 'intellectual egalitarianism.' Like the ancient scholars on whom they modelled themselves, the humanists prized the idea of the 'dignity of history.' This idea was an obstacle to the study of the less dignified parts of the past, such as everyday life or the deeds of ordinary people, rejected on the grounds that such activities were not 'worthy of being remembered.'[14]

However, in attempting to resurrect the culture of ancient Rome, the humanist scholars were compelled to take the history of antiquities very seriously – more seriously than the ancient Romans themselves had done. They became, for example, more concerned than before with images as evidence.[15] Italian, German, and English chorographies, that is, regional histories, all reveal a concern with material culture and everyday life. The objects sought and cherished by the antiquarians – clothes, rings, bracelets, shoes, vehicles, beards, lamps, and so on – were often dug out of the ground.[16] In that sense the antiquarians might be described as practising 'archaeology,' a term that came into use at this time to describe the study of antiquities, although it included language as well as material culture. Humanist lawyers and others studied the history of practices such as burying the dead, reclining at table, feasting, and crucifying criminals. The concept of a 'way of life' (*manière de vivre*) that appears in some antiquarian studies, especially in France, expresses this interest in customs as well as the desire to integrate the surviving fragments of antiquity into a general picture of the past.

The past studied by the antiquarians was not confined to Greece and Rome. It included other parts of the ancient world, notably Egypt, and also what might be called 'barbarian antiquities.' Swedish antiquaries played a particularly important part in the study of the barbarians, thanks to the cult of the Goths, which was supported by the government in the seventeenth century. A major study of this kind was a chorography of the Sami (then known as Lapps), describing their language, religion, magic, food, clothes, housing, weddings, and so on. Written by a German antiquary resident in Sweden, Johann Scheffer, who also made studies of the ships and the rings of the ancients, this work has been described as 'proto-ethnographic.'[17]

Eighteenth-Century Antiquarianism

A general history of the antiquarian movement remains to be written. A major problem its author will have to face is that of the chronology of the movement. Did it go into decline in the seventeenth century, or did it continue to flourish in the eighteenth century or even later? My own impression is that eighteenth-century antiquarians continued to produce an impressive body of work and that such work was becoming increasingly ethnographic.

In France, for example, Jean-Baptiste de la Curne de Saint-Palaye studied the history of medieval noble customs in his *Mémoires sur l'ancien chevalerie* (1746–50). His work was used to good effect by Voltaire in his famous essay on the history of manners.[18] In the Netherlands, Cornelis van Alkemade, a patrician from Rotterdam and a collector of antiquities, published *Nederlands Displegtigheden* (1732), discussing the food and drink, the rituals, the feasts, and the propensity to drunkenness of the ancient Batavians, supposedly the ancestors of the Dutch, and illustrating their drinking horns and goblets.

In Italy, the librarian Ludovico Antonio Muratori discussed medieval customs such as games, festivals, chivalry, and ordeals in his *Antiquitates*, a book that renders homage in its title to the antiquarian tradition.[19] Michelangelo Carmeli, professor of oriental languages at the University of Padua, published a collection of essays on the history of festivals, the use of water and fire in ritual, the practice of flagellation, and the meanings ascribed to the right hand (a century and a half before the classic study of that topic by the anthropologist Robert Hertz).[20]

In contrast to Scheffer's *Lapponia,* which was based on texts and artefacts preserved in collections, Knud Leem's study of the Sami was the work of a Norwegian pastor who lived among them and described their way of life, their *Levemaade* as he called it, at first hand.[21] The same interest in *Lebensart* – religion, clothing, food, customs (*Sitten*), festivals, language, and so on – can be found in Georg Steller's description of a similar culture, that of the Siberians. Steller was an expatriate German who joined Vitus Bering's official scientific expedition to Kamchatka, which lasted from 1732 to 1743.[22] Both Leem and Steller based their ethnographies on direct and systematic observation, on what would later be known as 'fieldwork.' All the same, there are striking similarities between their accounts and the chorography written by Scheffer the antiquarian.

These monographs, despite their high standards of scholarship, probably had less intellectual importance in their own time than their equivalents in the sixteenth and seventeenth centuries. They were challenged by the rise of comparative studies.

Comparative Studies

Awareness of the diversity of customs over the globe encouraged comparative studies, especially in the field of religion and mythology. The images of the barbarians of antiquity and the savages of the New World influenced each other, as in the famous case of the drawings of North American Indians by John White, made in Virginia in 1585, drawings that were used as a basis for illustrations of the ancient Britons.[23]

A French bishop, Pierre-Daniel Huet, and a French Calvinist pastor, Samuel Bochart, published ambitious studies of comparative mythology. Bochart argued, for instance, that the story of Noah was a prototype for classical and other myths.[24] The Jesuit Joseph-François Lafitau, a missionary in Canada, published in 1724 a description of 'the manners of the American savages compared with the manners of early times,' essentially a comparison between the ancient Greeks and the Iroquois.[25] The Dane Jens Krafft, professor of mathematics at the college for nobles at Sorø, went further in the same direction in a general study of 'Savage People,' comparing their customs and 'mode of thought' (*Taenke-Maade*) with those of peoples that had been described by classical writers.

The Sense of System

Where Krafft was mainly descriptive, Vico and Montesquieu had a sharper sense of the systems underlying cultural variety and change. Vico distinguished three kinds of 'custom,' in three types of society, whereas Montesquieu discussed the relation between laws and 'manners' in three kinds of political regime. Both of them drew heavily on information derived from travellers to other continents, but they also made use of the work of antiquarians. Thus Montesquieu quotes Budé, Cujas, and Bartholin, and Vico used the work of Bochart, John Selden, and probably the *Antiquitates Homericae*, published in 1677 by the Dutch scholar Everard Feith.[26]

'System' was a new term in the early modern period, associated with the idea of 'method.'[27] Accordingly, the textbook writer Bartholomaeus Keckermann produced a *Systema logicae* (1600), a *Systema ethicae* (1607), and a *Systema disciplinae politicae* (1608). Ralph Cudworth described what he called the *True Intellectual System of the Universe* (1678). An alternative term was 'syntagma,' as in the cases of G.A. Struve, *Syntagma juris feudalis* (1653), and Pierre Gassendi, *Syntagma philosophiae Epicuri* (1659). These terms were ambiguous in the sense that they sometimes referred to intellectual systems devised by individuals or embodied in academic disciplines, and sometimes to what might be called objective systems, from the solar system or the 'system of nature' to the laws of a particular society.

The antiquarian John Selden made an important point of a 'structuralist' kind when he compared the English state to a ship 'that by often mending had not piece of the first materials, yet was the same.' In other words, the system outlived its elements. Using the same metaphor as Selden, Sir Matthew Hale (1609–76) in his *History of the Common Law of England*, declared: 'They are the same English laws now, that they were 600 years since in the general. As the Argonauts Ship was the same when it returned home, as it was when it went out, tho' in that long voyage it had successive Amendments, and scarce came back with any of its former Materials.'[28] Between Selden and Hale, Nathaniel Bacon (1593–1660) had described the Saxon commonwealth as 'a beautiful composure, mutually dependent in every part from the Crown to the clown.'[29] The idea of mutual dependence would frequently recur in the eighteenth and nineteenth centuries, before it became a cornerstone of functionalist anthropology in the first half of the twentieth century.

Gradually the idea of a system of laws developed into the idea of society as a system. Vico sometimes used the term *sistema*, and Montesquieu argued that the three forms of government he distinguished each had its *structure particulière*. Adam Ferguson wrote of a 'system of manners,' and Adam Smith of 'systems of political economy.' The idea of a given society having its own system or structure, different from others, had important political implications. It suggested the possibility that its present structure could be changed. Accordingly, the French revolutionaries consciously tried to sweep away the social order of what they called the 'old regime.'

The Feudal System

One element of the old regime that the revolutionaries tried to abolish was of course feudalism, *féodalité*, viewed by a number of late eighteenth-century French writers as an institution that was at once useless and inhumane.[30] In English, the phrase 'feudal system' is recorded in the middle of the eighteenth century especially in the work of Scotsmen such as John Dalrymple (who first used the term in print in 1757 in his *Essay towards a General History of Feudal Property in Great Britain*), Adam Smith, William Robertson, David Hume, John Millar, and Gilbert Stuart.[31]

These writers built on the work of the humanist lawyers. If, following John Pocock, we describe the work of Jacques Cujas, François Hotman, Henry Spelman, and other legal antiquaries as 'the discovery of feudalism,' it does not seem too far-fetched to describe the work of the eighteenth-century Scots as a second discovery.[32] The rediscoverers believed that different types of society existed. The feudal system was 'a species of government,' as Robertson called it, or 'a species of civil polity,' to use the words of Hume. Parallels were drawn between the social microcosm and the macrocosm: 'the territory of a baron was in miniature the model of a kingdom,' as Robertson put it. Robertson also noted similarities or connections between different parts of Europe, a 'general system, of which every kingdom forms a part.'

The phrase 'feudal system' also expressed a sense of what might be called the 'lateral' connections among laws, manners, and so on. There was a great increase in the number of nouns to which the adjective 'feudal' was applied. In his *Treatise on Feuds and Tenures* (written 1639), the antiquarian Sir Henry Spelman had discussed feudal customs, earldoms, escheats, homage, lands, law, lords, rights, rites, service, servitudes, tenures, and vassals. In the eighteenth century, however, this list of nouns expanded to include anarchy, chivalry, manners, principles, and times, as historians in Scotland and elsewhere paid increasing attention to what they were coming to call 'the history of society.' Gilbert

Stuart, for instance, argued that 'fiefs and chivalry were mutually to act upon one another.'

The Discovery of the People

Most studies of antiquities were more concerned with their geography and their chronology than what we might call their sociology. However, the English antiquarian John Aubrey declared an interest in 'old wive's fables,' rather than dismissing them like the majority of his learned contemporaries. Again, in their *Acta sanctorum*, the Jesuit scholars known as the 'Bollandists' discussed what they called 'little traditions' (*tradi-tiunculae*) centuries before the anthropologist Robert Redfield did the same thing.[33] From the eighteenth century onwards, there is evidence of increasing interest in the kind of people whose customs and artefacts were being studied.

Two examples from the same English city, Newcastle, testify to this increasing interest. In 1725 the Newcastle clergyman Henry Bourne (1694–1733) published a study of local customs and festivals under the title *Antiquitates vulgares*. Bourne's own origins were humble, which helps explain his interest in his subject, although he attempted to distance himself from it. He was a moralist who not only described popular culture but also offered a critique, distinguishing the customs that 'may be retained' from those 'which ought to be laid aside.' He frequently criticized the irreverence and indecency of the behaviour of ordinary people, and as Protestants often did, he viewed the customs he disliked as survivals of both popery and paganism. His work was not purely antiquarian but a contribution to a movement that has been described as the 'reform of popular culture.' Conversely, some of the reformers of the sixteenth and seventeenth centuries had already included historical reflections in their critiques, comparing Carnival to the ancient Bacchanalia and the May Games to the Feast of Flora.[34]

Some fifty years later, in 1777, another Newcastle clergyman, John Brand (1744–1806) published his *Observations on Popular Antiquities: Including the Whole of Mr. Bourne's 'Antiquitates vulgares,' with Addenda to Every Chapter of That Work*. Brand too made some criticisms of popular customs. However, there was an important difference of emphasis between the two books. Bourne was more of a moralist than a scholar, whereas Brand, a Fellow of the Society of Antiquaries, was more of a scholar than a moralist.[35]

A concern with popular antiquities became still more important in the early nineteenth century, the age of what has been called the 'discovery of the people' and their culture. In Britain, for example, Henry Ellis (1777–1869), secretary to the Society of Antiquaries, produced a new edition of Bourne and Brand in 1813. The engraver Joseph Strutt (1749–1802) published a study *Sports and Pastimes of the People of England* (1801), and the bookseller William Hone (1780–1842) discussed the same topics in his *Everyday Book*, a weekly published from 1826 onwards. The link between scholars of humble origin and the study of popular antiquities will be obvious enough.

In the first half of the nineteenth century, the study of popular culture focused on immaterial culture – on 'folklore,' folk songs, and folk tales. After 1850, on the other hand, an increasing interest in the material culture of the people is revealed by the rise of the folk museum. In the case of these open-air museums of peasant culture, the Scandinavians were the pioneers. In Sweden, the display of folk arts at the Paris Exhibition of 1867 inspired Artur Hazelius to found the 'Nordic Museum' in 1880. This example was followed by the creation of museums at Bygdøj in Oslo and Lyngby in Copenhagen and, later, in many other parts of Europe.

It is unlikely that so much effort would have been expended on the study of popular culture in the nineteenth century had it not been for the rise of nationalism. Strutt, for example, presented his work on sports as a contribution to the study of 'national antiquities.' Published collections of popular ballads or folk tales tended to be national collections, German, Russian, Danish, and so on. Conversely, national histories of the Czechs, Swedes, Greeks, and others included the word 'people' in their title. It was often argued that the peasants had preserved national traditions in the purest form because they had had less contact with foreigners, so the peasants represented the people as a whole. Peasant costume came to be viewed as national costume, and the rural artefacts displayed in 'folk museums' as national artefacts. Popular culture, despite its regional base, had been nationalized.[36]

The Idea of Evolution and the Discovery of the Primitive

From the middle of the eighteenth century, the framework into which studies of antiquities could be fitted came to include the theory of the four stages of society, the hunting, pastoral, agricultural, and commercial stages discussed at length by Smith, Robertson, and Hume in Scotland and by Turgot and others in France.[37] In the nineteenth century, theorists such as Auguste Comte and Herbert Spencer wrote about social and cultural evolution from savagery to civilization via a succession of stages of development, to be seen in religion as well as in material culture.[38]

This schema was often used for the organization of exhibits in museums, with successive rooms displaying the artefacts of more or less 'primitive' peoples. The idea of the primitive came into general use in the 1860s and 1870s, the age of what has been called 'the invention of primitive society.'[39] One of the texts that launched the term was *Primitive Culture* (1871) by Edward Tylor (1832–1917), describing the everyday practices of a wide range of societies in order to establish cultural 'laws,' of which the most famous was the doctrine of 'survivals' from an earlier age into a later one, including survivals of animistic beliefs in the modern world.[40] Sociologists and psychologists were among the scholars most interested in the idea of the primitive, but anthropologists gradually emerged as the specialists in the subject.

The Specialization of Disciplines

Specialization and professionalization was a major feature of the social history of nineteenth-century Europe. Architecture, accountancy, engineering, and other occupations achieved autonomy at this time, and associations were founded to maintain standards and control entry into these professions. History too became professional in Germany and France in the first half of the nineteenth century.[41] Sociology followed in the second half of the century, in France with Emile Durkheim and his followers, and in the United States with Franklin Giddings at Columbia University and Albion Small at Chicago, both of them appointed to chairs in the new discipline in the 1890s.

In similar fashion, archaeologists were coming to distinguish themselves by their emphasis on systematic excavation (as opposed to ordinary digging) and also by a special emphasis on stratigraphy, that is, a concern for the physical context in which objects were found.[42] Beginning in early nineteenth-century Denmark with Christian Thomsen and Jens Worsaae, they offered a new periodization of human history, based on material culture: the stone, bronze, and iron ages. The frontier between anthropology, the study of peoples without writing, and archaeology, the study of history before writing was invented, remained open until the early twentieth century, and leading anthropologists such as Franz Boas (1858–1942) and Robert Marett (1866–1943) conducted excavations (in Mexico and Jersey respectively). After that time the two disciplines diverged, so much so that archaeologists of the 1960s and 1970s such as Lewis Binford and Colin Renfrew, who drew on anthropology for ideas, were treated as heretics by their colleagues.

Folklore

Another discipline to emerge, or, more exactly, to become separate from its neighbours, at this time was folklore, or *Volkskunde*. One of its founders was Jakob Grimm (1785–1865), although he would have described himself as a philologist interested in mythology rather than a professional student of 'folklore.' The English translation of *Volkskunde* was launched in 1846 by an admirer of Grimm, William Thoms (1803–85), and taken up in France and Italy as well as in the English-speaking world. Societies for the study of folklore were founded in a number of countries, and specialized journals were published. In 1898 the first chair in folklore was established, at the University of Helsinki. The location is revealing. The study of folklore, or 'folk-life' as it is sometimes called, has been taken more seriously, especially in the academic world, in Scandinavia and in East-Central Europe than elsewhere. In France, by contrast, leading folklorists such as Paul Sébillot (1843–1918) and Arnold van Gennep (1873–1957) worked outside the university. In the British Isles, the folklore movement has been stronger in Wales, Ireland, and Scotland than in England. There are no departments of folklore, far as I know, in English universities. There is no English equivalent to the Irish Folklore Commission, founded in 1935 to collect popular oral traditions. The support of the British government went not to folklore but to anthropology.

The Rise of Anthropology

In this context of professionalization, anthropology too was gradually turned into an autonomous discipline, which went by a variety of names. In German it was sometimes known as *Völkerkunde*, the comparative study of peoples worldwide, as opposed to *Volkskunde*, the study of one's own people. In both the Germanic and the Romance languages, the new discipline was also known as 'ethnography' or 'ethnology.'

The practitioners of the new discipline, distinguishing themselves from their colleagues in archaeology, folklore, geography, sociology, and psychology, tried to become and also to be seen as professionals. Following a brief period in which the new subject was organized in voluntary associations, such as the Société Ethnologique (1839), the Société d'Anthropologie de Paris (1859), the Anthropological Society of London (1863), the Anthropologischer Gesellschaft of Berlin, and so on, anthropology took on an institutional form, often with the support of governments. The Smithsonian Institution at Washington, for instance, goes back to 1846, its Bureau of Ethnology (concerned with the North American Indians) to 1879.

Museums played an important role in the rise of the new discipline. An ethnographic museum was founded in St Petersburg as early as 1837, and another in Copenhagen in 1848. In 1873, Adolf Bastian (1826–1905) founded an anthropological museum in Berlin, the Königliche Museum für Völkerkunde. The first anthropological museum in Spain dates from 1875. The Cambridge University Museum of Archaeology and Ethnology was established in 1883, the Pitt-Rivers Museum at Oxford in 1884 (its first keeper was Edward Tylor).

The professionalization of anthropology was both marked and assisted by the foundation of specialized journals, such as Bastian's *Zeitschrift für Ethnologie* (1869), the Spanish *Revista de antropología* (1874), and the *American Anthropologist* (1888). Courses in the new discipline were established at Clark University in 1888 and soon afterwards at Columbia (1896) and California (1901).[43] The first chair in anthropology in Spain was founded in Madrid in 1892.[44] The first post in anthropology at Oxford was created in 1884, when Tylor was made a Reader in the subject (he became a professor in 1896). Tylor, who was not an academic but a scholar of private means, had no students. However, a diploma in anthropology was founded in Oxford in 1905. It owed a good deal to the efforts of Robert Marett, Reader in Anthropology at Oxford from 1910 to 1936. In Cambridge, Alfred Haddon (1855–1940) became lecturer in Ethnology in 1900 and Reader in 1909. Practitioners would henceforth be trained in the discipline. Marett's pupils included Edward Evans-Pritchard, and Marett was succeeded on his retirement by Alfred Radcliffe-Brown.

The rise of anthropology as a profession led to an emphasis on the method of 'fieldwork' (as practised by Bronislaw Malinowski, for instance, in the Trobriand Islands) as a training for new recruits. If an anthropology of anthropologists were to be written, its author would doubtless describe fieldwork as an initiation ritual and the story of Malinowski in the Trobriands as a myth of origin. The increasing emphasis on fieldwork in the 1920s and 1930s was linked to a break with the discipline of history. Like sociologists, anthropologists turned to the study of society by means of direct observation, abandoning their earlier interest in social and cultural evolution.

A third major development, linked to Franz Boas in particular, affected the concept of culture. Tylor had already defined culture more broadly than his contemporaries Matthew Arnold and Jacob Burckhardt in the very first sentence of *Primitive Culture*, where he wrote of culture 'in its wide ethnographic sense' as 'that complex whole which includes knowledge, belief, art, morals, law, custom, and any other capabilities and habits acquired by man as a member of society.' Boas and his followers Ruth Benedict, Ralph Linton, and Margaret Mead went further by using the term 'culture' in the plural, implicitly placing the Trobrianders (say) and the Germans on an equal footing. This is the 'egalitarianism' mentioned in the opening paragraphs of this essay.[45]

Anthropology and Empire

The rise of anthropology as an academic discipline owes a good deal to the rise of empire, as the British example suggests with exemplary clarity.[46] In 1900 the president of the Folklore Society and the president of the Anthropological Institute attempted to persuade the government to fund the study of anthropology, arguing that a knowledge of the subject was useful to colonial administrators. In 1904–5, Haddon was invited to give a course on anthropology at the London School of Economics – soon to be a centre for the new discipline – because it was considered likely to interest civil servants and missionaries. The Oxford diploma discussed above was created in order to train colonial officials. British anthropologists worked mainly in the territories of the British Empire in Africa and elsewhere. The British in India – clergy, district magistrates, and their wives – collected and published local folk tales. This involvement with empire, and so with peoples remote from Europe, encouraged the separation of anthropology from folklore.

Ruptures and Continuities

It is time to sum up and to return to the problem from which this essay began, the dangers of both the Whig and the Foucauldian approaches. It is clear enough what is wrong with the Whig approach. It eliminates the cultural distance between the leading antiquarians of early modern Europe and the anthropologists of the twentieth century, and it makes the rise of anthropology appear the result of planning rather than a reaction to changing circumstances.

As for the opposite, Foucauldian approach, which emphasizes rupture with the past and what might be called the 'invention' of anthropology (along with the idea of the 'primitive'), it has both strengths and weaknesses. As a discipline or an institution, anthropology was indeed invented at a particular period, and the rise of the profession led, by the 1930s if not before, to the creation of a distinctive method as well as to a sense of collective identity and a desire to distinguish anthropologists from their neighbours (sociologists, geographers, historians, psychologists, archaeologists, and folklorists). In the course of debating with one another, anthropologists developed a technical language of their own that cut them off from the past as it did from the general public, though they rediscovered both the past and the public a generation later, in the age of Clifford Geertz and Marshall Sahlins.

On the other hand, turning from institutions and identity to ideas and interests, common elements between the disciplines are not difficult to discern. It is important not to date professionalization too early. Continuities among folklore, archaeology, anthropology, and the antiquarian movement are not difficult to discern. For example, Worsaae's book was translated into English as *The Primeval Antiquities of Denmark* and dedicated to the Fellows of the Society of Antiquaries. Jakob Grimm published a book on German legal antiquities (*Deutsche Rechtsaltertümer*, 1828). Thoms explained his new term 'folklore' as referring to 'what we in England designate as Popular Antiquities.' The link to the tradition of Bourne, Brand, Strutt, and Hone is clear enough.

A few more British examples may suggest the importance of continuities. The antiquary John Aubrey's *Remains of Gentilism and Judaism* (ca. 1686–9) was first published in 1881, by the Folklore Society. George L. Gomme (1853–1924) combined interests in history, archaeology, anthropology, and folklore. He edited the *Antiquary*, the *Archaeological Review*, and the *Folklore Journal*. He was a Fellow of the Society of Antiquaries, a Fellow of the Anthropological Institute, and President of the Folklore Society. Robert Marett was not only Reader in Social Anthropology at Oxford but also an archaeologist and, like Gomme, President of the Folklore Society. He described folklore and prehistoric archaeology as ingredients in his 'anthropological salad.'[47] Among Marett's pupils, besides anthropologists such as Edward Evans-Pritchard and John Peristiany, was the archaeologist O.G. Crawford and also Thomas Kendrick (1895–1979), who began his career as a prehistoric archaeologist but went on to be Keeper of British and Medieval Antiquities at the British Museum, secretary of the Society of Antiquaries, and the author of *British Antiquity* (1950) – and, as Anthony Grafton has suggested, the straw man in Momigliano's 'Ancient History and the Antiquarian.'

It is also clear that a cultural inheritance was passed on by the antiquaries to the anthropologists, especially to the generation before Malinowski, even if the antiquarian tradition was first reconstructed and then forgotten. For example, the interest taken by Tylor and others in 'survivals' of the past in the present linked anthropology with the antiquaries concerned with the 'remains' or 'vestiges' of former times to be found in remote parts.[48] Indeed, Tylor regularly cited antiquarians, among them Brand and Strutt. His disciple Andrew Lang did the same, so that a historian of folklore has suggested that 'a firm thread runs from Camden to Lang.'[49] To this day, the organization of ethnographies is not unlike that used by the early modern chorographers, with sections on food, clothes, housing, festivals, religion, and so on. Franz Boas's famous definition of ethnology applies equally well to antiquities: 'the study of the total range of phenomena of social life.'

The study of the classics was another bridge between humanism and anthropology. Sir James Frazer was a professional classicist before he turned to comparative studies, and his anthropological notebooks reveal his debt to a number of humanists and antiquarians from the fifteenth-century pope Pius II (who wrote about the customs of the Ruthenians) on.[50] In Oxford, one of the founders of the diploma in social anthropology was a classical archaeologist, J.L. Myres. Robert Marett also came to anthropology from classics and encouraged an anthropological interpretation of the classics, an approach that was also followed by Jane Harrison in Cambridge. The idea that the ancient Greeks were in a sense 'primitive' may have been shocking when Nietzsche put it forward in 1872. However, it was an idea that gained considerable acceptance a generation later, when Aby Warburg, for example, compared the serpent rituals of ancient Greece with those of the Indians of New Mexico.[51] The classicist Momigliano's interest in anthropology can itself be placed in a cultural tradition.

Notes

1 For example, Marvin Harris, *The Rise of Anthropological Theory* (New York, 1968), 10–15.

2 Arnaldo Momigliano, *The Classical Foundations of Modern Historiography* (Berkeley and Los Angeles, 1990), 1, 68–70.

3 Arnaldo Momigliano, 'Ancient History and the Antiquarian' (1950; repr. in his *Studies in Historiography* [London, 1966], 1–39); cf. *The Classical Foundations*, 54–79.

4 Arnaldo Momigliano, 'The Place of Herodotus in the History of Historiography' (1958; repr. in *Studies in Historiography*, 127–42), 140; cf. *The Classical Foundations*, 29–53.

5 Arnaldo Momigliano, *Alien Wisdom* (Cambridge, 1975), 27.

6 John H. Rowe, 'The Renaissance Foundations of Anthropology,' *American Anthropologist* (1965): 1–14.

7 Margaret T. Hodgen, *Early Anthropology in the Sixteenth and Seventeenth Centuries* (Philadelphia, 1964), 7–8.

8 Hodgen, *Early Anthropology*, 133, 327.

9 Franz Boas, *Race, Language, and Culture* (New York, 1948), 632.

10 Joan Evans, *A History of the Society of Antiquaries* (London, 1956).

11 Johan Nordström, *De Yverborenes Ö* (Stockholm, 1934).

12 Bruce Trigger, *A History of Archaeological Thought* (Cambridge, 1989); Alain Schnapp, *La conquête du passé: aux origines de l'archéologie* (Paris, 1993).

13 Tamás Hofer, 'Anthropologists and Native Ethnographers at Work in Central European Villages,' *Anthropologica* 12 (1970): 5–19.

14 Details in Peter Burke, 'The Rhetoric and Anti-Rhetoric of History in the Early Seventeenth Century,' in *Anamorphosen der Rhetorik: Die Wahrheitspiel der Renaissance*, ed. Gerhard Schröder et al. (Munich, 1997), 71–9.

15 Peter Burke, 'Images as Evidence in Seventeenth-Century Europe,' *Journal of the History of Ideas* 64 (2003): 273–96.

16 Trigger, *A History of Archaeological Thought*; Schnapp, *La conquête du passé*.

17 Johannes Scheffer, *Lapponia* (Frankfurt, 1673); Gloria Flaherty, *Shamanism in the Eighteenth Century* (Princeton, 1992), 36–40.

18 Lionel Gossman, *Medievalism and the Ideologies of the Enlightenment* (Baltimore, 1968).

19 Sergio Bertelli, *Erudizione e storia in Ludovico Antonio Muratori* (Naples, 1960), 395–419.

20 Michelangelo Carmeli, *Storia di vari costume sacri e profane*, 2 vols (Padua, 1750); cf. Robert Hertz, 'La pre-eminence de la main droite,' *Revue philosophique* (1909).

21 Knud Leem, *Finmarkens Lappen* (Copenhagen, 1767).

22 Georg W. Steller, *Beschreibung von dem Lande Kamtschatka* (1774; repr. Stuttgart, 1974).

23 Thomas Kendrick, *British Antiquity* (London, 1950), 121ff.

24 Samuel Bochart, *Geographia Sacra* (Caen, 1646).

25 Joseph-François Lafitau, *Moeurs des sauvages ameriquains compares aux moeurs des premiers temps* (Paris, 1724).

26 On Montesquieu, Raymond Aron, *Main Currents in Sociological Thought*, 2 vols (Harmondsworth, 1965), vol. 1, pp. 17–62; on Vico, Peter Burke, *Vico* (Oxford, 1985).

27 Neal W. Gilbert, *Renaissance Concepts of Method* (New York, 1960); Wilhelm Schmidt-Biggemann, *Topica universalis* (Hamburg, 1983), 82ff.

28 John Fortescue, *De laudibus legum Angliae*, ed. John Selden (1616; 2nd ed. London, 1660), 18; Matthew Hale, *The History of the Common Laws of England* (posthumously published, 1713); ed. Charles M. Gray (Chicago 1971), 40.

29 Nathaniel Bacon, *An Historical Discourse of the Uniformity of the Government of England* (London, 1647), 112.

30 J.Q.C. Mackrell, *The Attack on Feudalism in Eighteenth-Century France* (London, 1973).

31 Peter Burke, 'Scottish Historians and the Feudal System: The Conceptualisation of Social Change,' *Transactions of the 5th International Congress on the Enlightenment*, vol. 2 (Oxford, 1980), 537–9.

32 John Pocock, *The Ancient Constitution and the Feudal Law* (1957; 2nd ed. Cambridge, 1987), 70–123.

33 Robert Redfield, *Peasant Society and Culture* (Chicago, 1956).

34 Peter Burke, *Popular Culture in Early Modern Europe* (1987; 2nd ed. Aldershot, 1994), 207–43.

35 Richard Dorson, *The English Folklorists* (London, 1968), 10–25.

36 Peter Burke, *Popular Culture in Early Modern Europe* (London, 1978; rev. ed. Aldershot, 1994), 3–22; Anne-Marie Thiesse, *La création des identités nationales: Europe xviii–xxe siècle* (Paris, 1999), 161–231.

37 Ronald Meek, *Social Science and the Ignoble Savage* (Cambridge, 1976).

38 John Burrow, *Evolution and Society* (Cambridge, 1966).

39 Adam Kuper, *The Invention of Primitive Society* (London, 1988).

40 On Tylor, Dorson, *The English Folklorists*, 187–97; Adam Kuper, *Culture: The Anthropologist's Account* (Cambridge, MA, 1999), 56–60.

41 Wolfgang Weber, *Priester der Klio* (Frankfurt, 1984); Pim Den Boer, *History as a Profession: The Study of History in France, 1818–1914* (1987; English trans. Princeton, 1998).

42 Harris, *The Rise of Anthropological Theory*; George W. Stocking, Jr, *Race, Culture, and Evolution* (New York, 1968).

43 Regina D. Darnell, 'The Development of American Anthropology, 1879–1920,' Ph.D. thesis, University of Pennsylvania, 1969.

44 M.A. Puig-Samper, *La antropologia española del siglo xix* (Madrid, 1983).

45 Stocking, *Race, Culture, and Evolution*; Kuper, *Culture*, 59–68.
46 Henrika Kuklick, *The Savage Within: The Social History of British Anthropology, 1885–1945* (Cambridge, 1991); Jack Goody, *The Expansive Moment: Anthropology in Britain and Africa, 1918–1970* (Cambridge, 1995).
47 Robert R. Marett, *A Jerseyman at Oxford* (London, 1941), 216.
48 Edward Tylor, *Primitive Culture*, 2 vols (London, 1871), vol. 1, pp. 63–144; Hodgen, *Early Anthropology*, 441–6.
49 Dorson, *The English Folklorists*, 441.
50 James Frazer, *The Native Races of Asia and Europe* (London, 1939); Robert A. Ackerman, *J.G. Frazer* (Cambridge, 1987).
51 Sally C. Humphreys, *Anthropology and the Greeks* (London, 1978), 17–30; Peter Burke, 'Aby Warburg as Historical Anthropologist,' in *Warburg*, ed. Horst Bredekamp (Weinheim, 1991), 17–21.

chapter nine

From Antiquarian to Archaeologist? Adolf Furtwängler and the Problem of 'Modern' Classical Archaeology

SUZANNE MARCHAND

One striking feature of Arnaldo Momigliano's fascinating Sather Lecture 'The Rise of Antiquarian Research' is that by and large he collapses a distinction cherished by many of his nineteenth-century classicist forebears, namely, that between antiquarian and archaeologist. For Momigliano, both types were defined by an attachment to 'systematic descriptions of ancient institutions, religion, law, finances,' a usually a- or anti-political rejection of grand narratives, and a wonderfully strange attraction to unconventional bits of data.[1] Although this interchangeable use of the terms surely reflected early modern practice, scholars working in Winckelmann's wake would have found Momigliano's failure to list among archaeology's tasks the study of works of art to be a critical one. His essay, indeed, quite curiously omits a direct discussion of the afterlife of the antiquarian tradition in the history of classical archaeology. Perhaps Momigliano believed this trajectory was too obvious to warrant tracing; or perhaps, as a historian rather than an archaeologist, he felt that the history of archaeology was not his business. Or, perhaps, there is something more – for the history of classical archaeology resists, in many respects, the still partly Whiggish sort of history of science Momigliano was writing, in which antiquarianism and aestheticism dissolve in favour of the emergence of modern historical writing and documentation, something Momigliano dates to the generation of Edward Gibbon and B.G. Niebuhr. It is certainly the case that classical archaeology had not, by this time, completed its transition to 'modernity' – it had developed few of the techniques and approaches specialists now employ, and had barely established a toehold in the universities. But when, then, did archaeology break from the antiquarian tradition and become 'modern'? This is not a question Momigliano wished to answer, but in the light of his work, and the rich recent literature it has spawned, it might be a reasonable one to ask now.

Until rather recently, defining the 'modern' in 'modern archaeology' was not so difficult; drawing sharp distinctions between the dilettantish antiquarians of the pre-modern era and the scientific excavators of the later nineteenth century, standard histories of the field presumed that the development of on-site, grand-scale excavations marked the moment at which archaeology shrugged off its amateur coils and became 'modern' and 'scientific.' But a virtual explosion of excellent work on early modern antiquarian knowledge, on the one hand, and critiques of 'scientific' archaeology, on the other, have rendered this heroic narrative deeply problematical.[2] Recent work by scholars such as Anthony Grafton, Alain Schnapp, Paula Findlen, Joseph Levine, and Grazia Lolla, to cite just a few of the best,[3] clearly shows that pre-professional, 'armchair' scholarship was often very detailed, insightful, critical, and 'cutting edge'; if collections were small and private, and travel limited, still there were many scholars before the 'modern' age who knew artefacts well, and exchanged information and ideas about them through the mails, or by circulating through each other's libraries and collections. This literature – soon to be supplemented by the work of Tamara Griggs on the culture of early modern antiquarianism in Rome and of Giovanna Ceserani on the study of Magna Graecia[4] – has helped us understand much better the chronology here, the transformations of Renaissance learning into Baroque erudition, and the challenge posed to the latter by the Enlightenment's emphasis on taste and utility. With respect to the history of the collection and investigation of objects, we now know that the modern (public) museum is intimately related to the older cabinets of curiosity, private galleries, and salon exhibitions, and that our notions of historical 'style' have deep roots in early modern studies of numismatics, philology, palaeontology, and what one might call folklore.

Meanwhile, scholars working from the other end have shown that there is much overlap between the era of antiquarian travel and trade, of the circulation of sketches and the visiting of private collections, and the era of public museums, state-funded excavations, and professional journals. Dilettantes and grave robbers certainly survived the transition to 'big archaeology,' as did the tradition of local archaeological work. Moreover, as recent studies of individual archaeologists have shown, even the 'big' digs often re-confirm the preconceptions of the diggers: Schliemann went looking for Troy, and found it; Arthur Evans went looking for King Minos's palace, and found that too.[5] Nationalist and racist ideologies, it is now clear, often shaped the practices of nineteenth- and twentieth-century archaeologists.[6] Prepared by recent work in the history of science, we should by now realize that just because a project is big, or publicly funded, or technology-intensive, it is not necessarily 'objective.' We can now clearly see the mid-eighteenth-century rise of Winckelmannian neoclassical aestheticism and the equally powerful evolution of non-classical antiquarian studies as points of departure for a nineteenth century that neither leaves the ancients behind nor 'invents' modern history, two old canards that can now be safely dispensed with. But what, then, did the nineteenth century contribute? When, as concerns the study of artistic monuments, did the age of the archaeologist-antiquaries really end? That is a question that can now be more accurately and critically posed, as I seek to do in this essay.

That the great historian of archaeology Alain Schnapp has recently posed precisely this question suggests that it is indeed a timely one. In an essay entitled 'Between Antiquarians and Archaeologists – Continuities and Ruptures' (2002), Schnapp argues that the early modern period saw the social transformation of the antiquarian, whereby was created a community of scholars who shared the same rules of classification and means of sharing information. By the mid-eighteenth century, antiquarians had begun to develop historical typologies for mundane objects, stratigraphic conceptions, and an interest in the social function (rather than simply the aesthetic appearance) of objects. Once what Schnapp calls the 'veil of theological suspicion' – which hung over early modern studies of the remote past – was removed by nineteenth-century natural science and secularization, and once broad, international frameworks were adopted for the comparison of objects, then archaeology proper could emerge: 'Archaeology can be said to emancipate itself from the antiquarian tradition when it asserts, more or less vocally, its specific identity: the identity of humankind in nature, which effectively abolished the barrier which so frightened Cuvier between human and divine history, and the identity of humankind in culture, which renders the diversity of populations and traditions all amenable to an archaeological approach.'[7] This is a very useful argument, and one that squares well with other important histories of the discipline, Bruce Trigger's *History of Archaeological Thought* (1989) and Eve Gran-Aymerich's *Naissance de l'archéologie moderne, 1789–1945* (1998); but does it work for *classical* archaeology? Taking a closer look at nineteenth-century developments may help to refine this set of claims.

One of the features the volumes by Schnapp, Trigger, and Gran-Aymerich share is the tendency to lump classical archaeology together with the prehistorical kind, and treat modernization as essentially the process of accepting an anthropological understanding of culture (which entails giving up aesthetic judgments). As all three scholars know very well, however, there were self-interested, ideological, and pragmatic reasons why classicists resisted embracing this approach; first of all, a relativistic understanding of culture flew in the face of – in fact was concocted precisely to destroy – the neohumanist presumption that classical antiquity was not only special but even exemplary. Classical archaeologists, usually great lovers of Greek statuary, could not easily be convinced of 'the identity of humankind in culture.' Second, adopting such a view, for classical archaeologists, meant accepting a kind of institutional 'normalization' that would have made their special power to shape European culture – and many of their jobs – obsolete. Third, by the nineteenth century there was already a long tradition of antiquarian excavation and categorization of objects, and by the century's end, plenty of objects to examine and catalogue. In an era of positivist principles and increasing specialized pursuits, classicists were easily convinced that they could continue this work without introducing cultural comparisons (or equalizations) or trying to write a cultural history based primarily on artefacts not texts (a risky business at any time). Classical archaeology may well have developed identifiably modern practices and features – such as stratigraphic excavation, or the preferring of modern to ancient judgments – by the end of the nineteenth century, but it did not travel the same paths into the twentieth century as did its prehistorical sister. It did not want, and it did not need, to do so. It accommodated itself to new scholarly demands less by adopting a new natural scientific and anthropological worldview than by adapting existing antiquarian practices.

The transformation of the antiquarian tradition lies at the centre of the following essay, which treats in detail the career of one German 'Archäolog,' Adolf Furtwängler (1853–1907). The career of Furtwängler, who has recently been both called 'the greatest representative of 19th-century positivism'[8] and characterized as a philhellene cut entirely from Winckelmannian cloth,[9] beautifully illustrates the struggles classical archaeology experienced in making the transition from normative to non-normative cultural history, and, it is hoped, the ways in which here, too, antiquarian erudition continued to matter long after the antiquaries had gone. Furtwängler was not really a fieldwork specialist; he belongs to a type of non-excavators who, in German at least, are still often called 'Archäolog,' namely, university and museum scholars who traffic heavily in the material culture of the ancient world. Indeed, now that excavation permits and funding are rather hard to come by, this type of 'archaeologist' is somewhat more common than the field excavator, in the heroic manner of Schliemann or Flinders Petrie. Furtwängler, in any event, was an Archäolog of consequence, one who came to trust his own eye in preference to the statements of classical authors, to adopt evolutionary models to understand the development of Greek ornament, and to use (at least in some of his projects) a broad comparative framework. But classical artefacts remained for him more or less sophisticated works of art, not pieces of a socio-cultural puzzle; nor would he have accepted the equality of cultures. In this, I believe, he was very much like his exact contemporary Wilhelm Dörpfeld, and other members of this first generation to experience the benefits and disappointments of grand-scale fieldwork. In putting this largely forgotten figure in the context of his time, and in the company of his contemporaries, I hope to demonstrate the multiple ways in which German classical archaeology, by the fin de siècle, was and was not 'modern.'

To take the full measure of Furtwängler, and of the German classicists of the generation of the 1870s (which included, after all, not only Furtwängler but also Wilhelm Dörpfeld, Friedrich Nietzsche, and Ulrich von Wilamowitz-Moellendorff), we must first do a little excavation ourselves, noting some important changes in antiquarian archaeology between the world of Peiresc and that of Furtwängler's mentor, Heinrich Brunn (1822–94). The focus on Germans here is of course the result of my own proclivities, but there are numerous other reasons to put the Germans at the centre of the nineteenth-century history of archaeology. Though the 'belated' nation at first lagged behind the collectors and scholars associated with the Louvre and the British Museum, by century's end the Germans were recognized as the field's pace-setters. Certainly, the Reich was much more heavily invested than other European states in the securing and exploiting of new excavation sites after 1871, and archaeological publications there, popular and professional, were probably much more numerous than was the case elsewhere. Quite obviously, this geographical shift alone (from Rome and, to a lesser extent, Paris, to Berlin, Bonn, and Munich) made for a new set of constraints and opportunities, and brought into play new social, economic, and political forces; however, it remains to be seen how exactly this change in the centre of intellectual gravity transformed the study of ancient artefacts.

If, in the seventeenth century, Peiresc and his fellow antiquarians had amassed enormous private collections of objects, these were still small and highly inaccessible compared to the huge new public museums opening their doors in mid-nineteenth-century Europe. The rate at which collections swelled over the course of the century was prodigious: K.F. Schinkel's royal museum, too large for the Prussian collection when it opened in 1830, soon had to be supplemented – in Berlin alone! – with a 'Neues Museum,' a Nationalgalerie, an ethnographic museum, a Museum für Kunst und Gewerbe, a Museum für Vaterländische Altertümer, a Hohenzollern Museum, a Kaiser Friedrich Museum, and numerous sub-museums created to house and organize the state's collections. The same could be said of 'archaeological' publications: elegant, expensive volumes of engravings had become increasingly commonplace since the days of Bernard de Montfaucon's five-volume *Antiquité expliquée* (1719) and the Comte de Caylus's *Recueil d'antiquités égyptiennes, étrusques, et romanes* (1752), but in succeeding decades the volumes continued to swell, and prices continued to fall (fig. 1). By 1857–8, with the publication of Johannes Overbeck's *Geschichte der griechischen Plastik für Künstler und Kunstfreunde*, it was at least possible for a middle-class consumer to have 160 engravings of Greek pieces immediately at hand (fig. 2). By mid-century, one could order engravings of famous monuments; a few years later, mass-produced casts and photographs were also available for purchase. In no way, however, was this expansion limited to Greek artefacts; the enormously increased rate of publishing of local (usually prehistorical or medieval) materials is one testimony to this, as is, on the other hand, the lavish travel reports issued upon Richard Lepsius's return from a three-year sojourn in Egypt (1842–5), which ran to twelve volumes, so luxuriantly heavy as to be almost impossible to lift off library shelves. Thanks to the development of museums and the expansion of antiquarian publishing, by 1870 – before, that is, the beginning of real fieldwork – the possibilities for visual analysis and comparison were already expanding at a rate so rapid that no one could imagine the acceleration that would occur in the half-century to follow.

This does not mean, however, that artefacts and their interpreters were held in particularly high scholarly esteem. If some seventeenth-century antiquarians, living in an age of highly polemical history-writing, had trusted the evidence of artefacts and especially coins (of which there might be many copies) over a literary tradition seen to be biased and untrustworthy, by the later eighteenth century this direction had reversed itself; even Winckelmann, so absorbed in the contemplation of artefacts and dismissive of library-bound 'scribblers,' relied heavily on literary sources for his periodizations and interpretations. His effusive praise of the Laocoön, Luca Giuliani has recently shown, was shaped initially by other travellers' texts, and he had great difficulty rethinking his claims after actually seeing the sculpture he had described.[10] Neoclassical aesthetics were built on encounters with texts, not with artefacts; Lessing's influential *Laokoon* (1766), indeed, set up a hierarchy of the arts that clearly demoted sculpture and painting to the second tier.[11] The new philology, institutionalized by F.A. Wolf and Wilhelm von Humboldt, did not make travel a necessity and treated material evidence as a distinctly lesser form of historical knowledge. Most early nineteenth-century 'archaeologists'[12] (to say nothing of philologists) never visited Greece, and their use of monuments was chiefly iconographic, that is, they used artefacts to illustrate the ways in which 'the' Greek gods had been depicted (and to identify who was who in important pieces), not to characterize the 'mind' of, say, mid-fifth-century Attica, or to create stylistic sequences.[13] Even those who did lean in the direction of *Sachphilologie* were not particularly interested in obtaining and viewing authentic artefacts; August Boeckh, for example, maintained that he knew what Greece and Rome had looked like in antiquity, and that was enough for him.[14] K.O. Müller, who found iconography a useful means for understanding the Greek gods, did go to Greece, ten years after the publication of his *Handbuch der Archäologie der Kunst* (1830). But, unfamiliar with the physical strains of fieldwork, he suffered a sunstroke at Delphi while copying an inscription. Müller's death was tragic proof that the textual, in this period, unquestionably still trumped the material.

Outside the universities, and particularly outside classics, however, the situation was rather different. Of course, some early excavations by this time had already taken place: the mid-eighteenth-century excavations at Pompeii, famously, had yielded wonderful material, and many aristocratic connoisseurs went to visit the site. Preliminary digs had been held at Aegina, and the excavators – most of them German – had auctioned off the finds to European buyers, including Ludwig I of Bavaria, who bought the archaic period sculptures for his Glyptothek despite their failure to live up to neoclassical standards of serenity and grandeur. Architects, in particular, often insisted upon seeing sites and objects for themselves. Following in the tradition of Stuart and Revett, Carl Haller von Hallerstein, in the company of the English architects J. Foster and C.R. Cockrell, visited Athens as early as 1810 and assisted in the excavations at Aegina in 1811; he continued to work at various sites in Greece until his death in 1817.[15] Gottfried Semper, to whom we will return in a moment, spent three years in Greece in the early 1830s, and his colleagues, Friedrich Adler and Wilhelm Dörpfeld, to name just two slightly younger architects, would be highly influential in the development of archaeology as a field science. But academic classicists, until the 1870s, paid relatively little attention to architects, to museum curators (who remained chiefly courtiers), and to travellers; even scholars devoted to the study of ancient architecture, like Alois Hirt (who taught architectural history at the Berlin Bauakademie after 1799, and archaeology at Berlin University after 1810), were not particularly interested in seeing, much less conserving or excavating, real classical structures.[16] As the university system increasingly monopolized the study of the classical world, aristocrats, museum curators, and travellers found their sort of knowledge devalued and/or treated as data to be processed by an increasingly hierarchical republic of letters, one in which library-oriented philologists sat at the peak, and 'field'-oriented antiquarians at the foot, of the intellectual pyramid.

Even more notably, university classicists in the early nineteenth century, with a few exceptions such as F.G. Welcker, cut themselves off from what became a more and more popular pursuit – the study of local, Germanic and medieval, antiquities. As Alain Schnapp has shown in wonderful detail, northern Europeans, by the seventeenth century, were well aware that their own local histories, many parts of which were not described in texts, could be fleshed out by the use of artefacts.[17] Brent Maner, too, notes the persistence of this tradition throughout the eighteenth century, much of it inspired and shaped by Tacitus's *Germania*.[18] Again by the 1830s, and outside the universities, we begin to see an enormous increase in the scale of this sort of inquiry, as both provincial patriotism and liberal nationalism sparked new interest in European origins, and as geology and evolutionary thought provoked new debates on speciation and human development. Now a new, increasingly leisured middle class participated aggressively in the founding of local antiquities societies, museums, and journals. In the new local museums, a wider audience was treated to increasingly crowded cases displaying vases, coins, weapons, tools, jewellery, and figurines (to give just a few examples of available genres); anyone with deeper scholarly interests or keener collecting passions could page through the growing journal literature, produced by the hundreds of local antiquities societies. As excavation and monument conservation became increasingly widely practised, the number of knowledgable local antiquarians grew, especially in the non-professionalized study of Germanic and Christian artefacts; in search of both models and erudition, many of them turned back to the local, empiricist traditions of the past in conscious or unconscious resistance to the aestheticized, increasingly professionalized realm of ancient history.[19] But even such positivistic moves did not earn these fields university standing, a phenomen on that would spawn among prehistorians increasingly bitter resentment towards classicists.

The institution that would ultimately make antiquarian knowledge fashionable again in academic circles was one established neither in Germany nor in Greece, but in the city that deserves to be called antiquarianism's *Heimat*, Rome.[20] There, in 1829, an international group of connoisseurs had founded the Institut für Archäologische Korrespondenz (IfAK); the core members were young German aesthetes fascinated by ancient architecture and mythology, on the one hand, and a handful of French and Italian aristocratic erudites, on the other. One of the founding members, Eduard Gerhard (1795–1867), was particularly influential; possessing university (philological) credentials but an antiquarian's devotion to eclectic collecting, Gerhard devoted himself to seeing and publishing as many monuments as possible – and to promulgating the positivist notion that one must see a thousand monuments in order actually to understand a single artefact.[21] By making the IfAK a respectable scholarly institution, and then converting it into an exclusively German 'school,' Gerhard also made spending time among the ruins and artefacts desirable, and realizable, for a few young German scholars, often poorer than their French and English counterparts. His close connections to the Prussian court (not academic regard for his work) accounted for his appointment to a professorship at the University of Berlin in 1843 and to the curatorship of the sculpture department of the Royal Museum in 1854. By 1871, under Gerhard's guidance, the German school had established a scholarly journal, a more popular *Archäologische Zeitung*, a celebratory 'Winckelmannstag,' and, finally, a branch 'institute' in Athens; his organizational efforts, along with the excavations at Olympia and Pergamon, would give the study of material culture new clout.

Gerhard and the IfAK (renamed the Deutsches Archäologisches Institut, in 1871) gave the study and collection of authentic objects new cultural prominence and respectability. But there remained a hierarchy – philologists and historians were still more respectable than archaeologists, and students of classical archaeology much more respected than scholars who specialized in prehistorical or 'oriental' artefacts. Even the eclectic Gerhard had opposed reducing the IfAK's intense pursuit of classical scholarship by devoting serious study to a 'colorful crowd of far-flung objects,' which included Celtic and American graves, Byzantine diptychs, and modern 'Oriental' art.[22] If archaeology – classical, Germanic, and oriental – was becoming increasingly popular with the wider public, in academia its practitioners, by the 1870s, were still considered little better than dilettantish treasure-hunters or collectors of useful data – perhaps one reason the German archaeological community reacted so negatively to the appearance of that most authentic of treasure-hunting dilettantes, Heinrich Schliemann.

Schliemann's Trojan and Mycenaean digs were, to be sure, important lessons in the irrelevance of neohumanist paradigms for the understanding of the wider cultural history of the Greeks; his use of natural scientific models (he developed a close and useful friendship with the prehistorian-cum-pathologist Rudolf Virchow), his increasing dependence on Dörpfeld's technical expertise, and his rising appreciation for mundane pottery are all testimony to the ways in which excavation drew the inquirer further and further from texts and aesthetic norms. But Schliemann's challenge was particularly worrisome because it reflected the fact that in the wider culture as well, neohumanist models were under fire; the natural sciences, most obviously, had begun to emphasize their superior *Wissenschaftlichkeit*, and their greater national utility. In the 1860s the school reform movement began to agitate for the creation of new, more 'modern' and utilitarian secondary schools – in which the sciences and modern languages would receive more emphasis – and for the opening of the universities (and through them, civil service posts and the free professions) to graduates of these schools. Though classicists managed to retain their roles as cultural gatekeepers even after the 1890 school conference broke the Gymnasium's formal monopoly, the school reform movement galvanized a second sort of *Kulturkampf* in the new Reich, in which the antagonists were not Catholics and Protestants, but proponents of 'modern,' 'useful' education against defenders of traditional humanistic *Bildung*. Complicating this struggle, after about 1900, would be a vitalistic generational revolt within the Gymnasien themselves, spearheaded by Nietzsche-readers and devotees of Stefan George.[23]

In light of all these changes, within and around archaeology, what happened in the 1870s and 1880s can be seen partly as 'modernization,' partly as nationalization, and partly as a defensive strategy against the likelihood of classicism's demise. That things changed so speedily was in part due to the rapid nationalization of classical archaeology, as excavations ceased (for the most part) to be private endeavours and state-credentialled experts took over the direction both of excavations and of the museums. The museums were perhaps the first place in which specialization, professionalization, and the adoption of natural scientific models occurred. This happened in part simply because of the enormous increase in the volume of artefacts museum assistants had to process, as enormous collections, like Richard Lepsius's cache of 15,000 Egyptian objects, overwhelmed their work spaces. As Luca Giuliani writes of the phenomenal expansion in public collections taking place across Europe in the later nineteenth century, 'The increasing amount of material made the specialization of the classificatory system essential; in an immediate reaction to this [specialization], classification in the later nineteenth century became a central area of concentration in archaeological scholarship: the function of the natural sciences as a model was obvious.'[24] What was perhaps less obvious, but also consequential, was the calling back into play of antiquarian knowledge and techniques of sorting and depicting artefacts that had no obvious relationship to texts. Texts like Gottfried Semper's *Der Stil* (see below) and, even more important, the journal literature produced by local antiquarians offered assistance to those struggling to make sense of undocumented finds; in the 1860s, for example, Alexander Conze, destined to be a pivotal archaeological organizer, used this antiquarian literature to lay the basis for understanding Greek Geometric art, and Semper, as we will see, was essential in Furtwängler's attempts to trace the development of Mycenaean pottery.[25] As museum budgets and collections increased, so too did the need to historicize displays more fully, and to fill in gaps in the collection with authentic, if not especially beautiful, objects. But the beautiful objects (especially Greek sculptures) – often in the form of plaster casts – were still the most prominently displayed, the most written about, and the most coveted artefacts. It is into this world, uneasily balanced between historicism and aestheticism, that Adolf Furtwängler must now be placed, and his earning of the title 'the Linneaus of archaeology'[26] further explained.

In introducing our man Furtwängler, it is perhaps sufficient to note his birth date, 1853, and birthplace, Freiburg im Breisgau, a deeply Catholic part of what was then, still, the independent state of Baden. Furtwängler's father had aspired to be an archaeologist and had, quite unusually for his generation, actually visited Greece, but being an 'enthusiastic, and scientifically active, but unworldly [*weltfremd*] Humanist,' he selected teaching instead, and became the director of the local Gymnasium.[27] Papa saw to it that the young Adolf followed the usual academic path for aspiring civil servants, pastors, doctors, lawyers, *and* professors – that is, he was trained at the Gymnasium, chiefly in classical languages. Continuing along this path, Furtwängler, in 1870, embarked upon the study of philosophy and classical philology at the University of Freiburg. Looking back on this experience in 1874, the young Adolf remembered his longing for beauty – and his disappointment with philological drudgery;[28] indeed, the problem of the relationship between beauty and scientific drudgery would dog him throughout his life. In 1871 the south-German student heard his first lectures in 'archaeology,' 'Architectural Antiquities in Conjunction with the Explanation of Relevant Sections from Vitruvius.'[29] The fledgling discipline apparently thrilled him, but he felt he could not aspire to its study, perhaps because he could not afford the books, travel, and artefacts necessary for specialists.[30] After moving to the University of Leipzig, he despaired of his talent for scholarship, but his confidence began to return when he took up the study of archaeology again in his second semester. He then transferred to the University of Munich, where, as a devoted student of Heinrich Brunn, he threw himself passionately into archaeological researches.

Furtwängler's teacher, Heinrich Brunn (1822–94), was a product of the mid-century archaeological ferment, and it is critical here to devote a few words to this scholar in order to suggest the continuities that link his generation backward to Winckelmann's world as well as forward to Furtwängler's post-1875 milieu. In many ways, Brunn was not a typical mid-century classicist; though trained primarily in textual interpretation and dependent upon it for his iconographic interpretation of individual monuments as well as his history of art, he also spent almost twenty years (1843–53; 1856–65) living in Rome. There he gained a wide knowledge of ancient material culture, which he put to good use when appointed to the Munich chair of archaeology and numismatics in 1865, a post that brought with it the curatorship of the Bavarian imperial coin collection and, later, the vase collection and the sculpture museum (Glyptothek). He is said to have been artistically talented,[31] and he certainly used his 'eye' more extensively than did his classicist contemporaries. If his *Geschichte der griechischen Künstler* (2 vols, 1853–9) had no illustrations and used literary evidence to divide artists into schools, already here he was describing nationally defined formal conventions that constrained the artistic production of each age. By the 1870s he was using his eye for anatomical details to place unlabelled sculptural fragments into chronological sequence, to determine their place of origin, and even to guess at their authorship.[32] Instrumental in his evolution towards 'Anschauung' was not only his long commerce with ancient objects during his stays in Rome, but also his reading of Gottfried Semper's *Der Stil in den technischen und tektonischen Künsten oder praktische Ästhetik* (2 vols, 1860, 1863), a study of the evolution of designs in the minor arts that may well have been inspired by Georges Cuvier's exhibit of animal skeletons at the Jardin des Plantes.[33] More than any member of his generation (with the possible exception of Gerhard), Brunn took advantage of the technological revolution occurring around him and developed a deep commitment to the study of forms. By the 1880s Brunn had become an ardent proponent of archaeology as a science of the eye, one that should depend on 'Anschauung' and thus win its autonomy from philology.[34]

Brunn undoubtedly shared with his student his rich knowledge of artefacts, as well as opened to him the collections under his supervision; he also lent Furtwängler his copy of Semper in 1874.[35] Furtwängler read this study of design dynamics, which was at once graecophile and historicizing, with great interest; it is possible that his interest in Darwinism also dates to this era.[36] From Semper he could have learned a great deal about different types of vessels and architectural elements, about their utilitarian functions and the enormous diversity of forms. He could certainly have learned a pseudo-evolutionary logic, the development of abstract from more natural forms, as well as the delight in the diversity of rather humble, useful human creations that Semper openly exhibited. He could not, however, have learned either iconographic interpretation or chronological sequencing from Semper, who cared rather little about iconography and whose typologies are defined by structure, materials, and use first, and by very loose chronological and national categorizations afterwards (fig. 3). Semper was no cultural relativist; *Der Stil* repeatedly emphasized the superior combination of natural and ideal, utility and freedom exhibited in Greek art alone.[37] But through the polymath architect, Furtwängler was introduced to a huge and diverse collection of forms, many of them of purely ornamental or structural value, and thus unlikely to be explicable (or datable) by recourse to ancient texts.

In any event, reading Semper and visiting museums engendered a kind of positivist frustration at the limited resources he had at his command. In September 1874 he wrote to Brunn from Freiburg, 'Above all I have to complain that there is so little visual experience available here, and that means that I am unable to follow or judge many observations, especially those that treat technical-historical matters.' Indeed, he was grateful later that year to discover a cast collection in town that boasted, as one of its eight statues, a copy of the 'Boy Removing a Thorn.'[38] Chiefly, however, it seems that he laid the basis for what Ludwig Curtius called his 'enormous knowledge of monuments' by working through the Russian Academy of Sciences' *Compte-rendus de la Commission Impériale Archéologique* (volume 1 appeared in 1859–60) in the Munich Staatsbibliothek, looking up every monument cited in the work of earlier authors. This work apparently laid the basis for his doctoral dissertation, 'Eros in Vase Painting,' and several other essays, which, as Curtius claimed, combined the older tradition of (iconographic) archaeology with a special sort of 'command of the materials and creation of lucid linkages.'[39]

Furtwängler followed Brunn in believing that there was a sort of instinctive understanding that good archaeologists brought to their judgments, one that filled in for gaps in their knowledge.[40] But he also lamented the *unwissenschaftlich* nature of archaeological argument, observing in a letter of November 1874: 'Our art historical judgments are often still so arbitrary!'[41] And he would not have philosophy fill in those gaps – the aesthetic philosophies of Schiller and Kant, he argued, dealt too much in concepts and words, and deviated too much from historical facts.[42] Nor would the *Compte-rendus* and the antiquarians long suffice to quench his thirst for more 'Anschauung' – and more stuff. Furtwängler had already been bitten by what one might call the positivist bug, and at this stage of the game, the cure to be prescribed was obvious. It was time to go to Rome.

A reliable mentor, Brunn arranged the funding, and by the fall of 1876, Furtwängler was ensconced in the Holy City. Here the young man diligently set about writing a study of Pliny's art historical sources, a subject Brunn had recently opened up for new scrutiny.[43] This defence of Brunn's iconoclastic position (that Pliny's sources went far beyond a lost art history of Varro) presented the claim that Pliny must have used the insights of a Greek artist, Pasiteles, in assessing the beauties of particular works of art.[44] Furtwängler's work here was by no means a signal departure, nor was it a study that had to be pursued 'on site'; it did not involve in any form new technologies, travel, or 'Anschauung.' Thus it did not prepare Furtwängler for the two tasks he would soon be asked to take up: the cataloguing of Schliemann's Mycenaean vases and of the Olympia bronzes. The result of these two projects was, according to Ludwig Curtius, epoch-making for classical archaeology: 'For in these works large classes of monuments were used, not, as earlier, to explicate ancient texts, but as a source for the understanding of great historical developments, about which the literary tradition was silent.'[45] Clearly, Curtius gave his mentor and friend too much, and the antiquarian tradition (and Semper) too little, credit, but it is certainly the case that Furtwängler was the archaeologist (rather like Pitt Rivers in prehistory or Flinders Petrie in Egyptology) who managed to bring to antiquarian practices new breadth, new functions, and new respect without anything much in the way of practical or intellectual preparation.

Chronologically, Furtwängler's involvement with the Mycenaean vases began first, though his innovative work on them post-dates his Olympia experience.[46] Together with Georg Loeschcke, Furtwängler was commissioned by the newly-founded Deutsches Archäologisches Institut, Athens (one of the descendants of the IfAK), to study the pottery turned up in Heinrich Schliemann's widely criticized, but hugely publicized, excavation at Mycenae (fig. 4). This was a task delegated to men low on the professional totem pole, one Schliemann had rejected, both because of its lack of glamour and because of its difficulty: owing to the antiquity of the potsherds, there were no parallel objects with which to compare them (a phenomenon that initially led some critics to date them to the early Middle Ages).[47] In early 1878, Furtwängler and Loeschcke began the sorting of what they described as 'whole mountains of sherds,' which had been piled up in an empty room in the Athens Polytechnion; lacking iconographical markings or contemporary parallels, at first they used colour, shape, and firing techniques to classify the fragments; by 1886 they had adopted a Semperian categorization, and made a first pass at determining the 'evolutionary stages of ornamentation' by moving from clear and functional representations of natural objects (like polyps and shells) to elaborate and 'misunderstood' pure designs[48] (fig. 5). Furtwängler had not yet arrived 'on site,' but he was now in Greece, and most important, he was confronting antiquarian problems hugely exacerbated by the new scale of excavations: not only how to understand and explain artefacts that lacked aesthetic appeal and textual referents, but also how to establish some sort of personal affinity with 'the stuff.' Already by February, Brunn was warning him not to lose sight of the *artistic* side of artefacts and to keep the 'connectedness of the whole' in view.[49]

By this time, others too were facing the same sort of challenges, most notably the historian-turned-archaeologist Ernst Curtius, who had finally managed (after twenty years' effort) to get the German government to fund excavations at Olympia. Olympia, like most other objects of grand-scale excavation, did not need to be 'found'; its location had been re-established by an English traveller, Richard Chandler, in 1766, and a French expedition had even begun 'excavations' in 1829, which brought a number of promising metopes back to Paris. The German dig began in the fall of 1875, and the expectations were enormous. The excavation treaty itself, negotiated between the (Danish) king of Greece and the German crown prince, was an important cultural and political act; conferring on the Germans the right to excavate in exchange for the assurance that all finds would remain in Greece, it was seen as an act of aggression by many in the Greek parliament, and as one of absurd beneficence by Germans like Bismarck.[50] Given literary testimony to Phidias's presence at Olympia, it was hoped that the Temple of Zeus, at least, would yield large amounts of 'golden age' sculpture. Discussion of the results was not limited to the experts; it seems that the German public as a whole was extremely well informed and was interested in the progress of the digs, which were very much regarded as a 'national' endeavour, an act of cultural philanthropy on the part of a nation that had just reconfigured modern Europe through war.[51] From the first, the excavators were under pressure to produce Winckelmannian results; when, after three months of finding nothing of the sort, they began to uncover large sculptural fragments from the temple pediments, every-one breathed a sigh of relief.

The excavators soon discovered a lovely (but headless!) Nike, attrib-uted to Paionios, and during the autumn 1877 season, the team exca-vated a beautiful male nude, later determined to be the Hermes of Praxiteles (and recently shown to be a Roman copy of a lost Greek original). But the Hermes was to be the last aesthetically satisfying find, and the Olympia excavators now had to justify, to themselves, to the German public, and, worst of all, to Bismarck and the Reichstag, the continuation of the dig. It certainly was not as if they found 'nothing' – they found huge quantities of *Kleinkunst*, in addition to many sculptural fragments (fig. 6). In early 1880, Ernst Curtius reflected on the dig's mixed blessings in a letter to his brother: 'Now we are hacking our way through the centre of the Altis and finding wonderful ancient clay images of Hera and the like,' he wrote, 'but that doesn't help us with the general public.'[52] Furtwängler himself described the excavated bronze objects in the following, less than promising way: 'In total opposition to the finds of complete, carefully assembled objects in ancient graves, the mass of Olympia bronzes consists really only of the rubbish of the ancient times, in small worthless things or in single fragments of larger ones.'[53] By 1880, Furtwängler, now lecturing at the University of Bonn, had only ten students in his course, though it dealt with Olympia in detail.[54] Still, Curtius's clout and the excavators' insistence on the *historical* importance of their work sufficed to persuade the Kaiser to fund the dig until 1881 – after which time museological and popular interest shifted to new sites on the coast of Asia Minor.

An equally informative and productive dig today would be nothing less than an international sensation. But aesthetic expectations in 1875 were much higher, and consequently the scale of the finds was little substitute for their less-than-Winckelmannian nature. The Zeus temple pediments in particular were a terrible disappointment (fig. 7). Not only were they in bad condition, they seemed rather crudely formed and hard to square with the literary tradition. Misreading Pausanias, the ancient traveller who described the temple complex in the greatest detail, contemporaries had assumed that the Olympia temple *post-dated* the Acropolis sculptures, and that the pediments had been sculpted by Paionios, a northern Greek artist, and by Alkamenes, an Athenian and student of Phidias. Why, then, did they not live up to the aesthetic standards of the Elgin marbles?[55] In 1882, Furtwängler recalled reactions to the first finds: 'One expected to find sculptures in the style of the Parthenon pediments and was astonished to see something quite different before one. Some were so disappointed that they lost interest in the subject as a whole; the others were so busy creating hypotheses on the origin of the style, which they sought in almost all the areas inhabited by Greeks, that they generally disdained the clear inferences offered by traditional sources.'[56] This combination of aesthetic disillusionment and search for origins forms part of the context in which the rhetoric of archaeology as a whole now moved gradually away from aestheticism and towards historicism.[57]

Brunn, predictably, was one who did not lose interest but rather threw himself into the search for origins. Although he described the Olympia pediments as 'malerisch,' in contrast to the perfections of Phidias's 'plastisch' sculptures,[58] he was able to see them as the product of a different sort of style, and indeed to ratify a theory he had developed even *before* the excavations had commenced. In a paper presented to the Bavarian academy of sciences in early 1876, Brunn reacted to photos and sketches of the new finds he had seen in Berlin, arguing 'that the sculptures were made in another style than everyone had expected and would have to have expected, as long as Paionios was treated as a student of Phidias.' Paionios was, rather, a *predecessor* of Phidias, and the Olympia sculptures *pre-dated* the Athenian masterpieces. The sketches, Brunn insisted, had confused rather than clarified matters. 'In the study of the originals in and for themselves,' he continued, 'it is to be hoped that we will soon succeed in grasping and defining the stylistic peculiarities of these [works]. But this is possible also in art historical studies that embrace the larger connections, and I have them to thank that I was not surprised by the new discoveries.' Indeed, he insisted, he had said something of the same a year before in print, and two years previously in lectures.[59] So Brunn, it seems, had already arrived at his conclusions about Paionios on the basis of looking at the Paris metopes and carefully rereading Pausanias and the work (on other pediments) of Brunn's contemporary Ludwig Urlichs. He did not need to go to Olympia to draw his conclusions; he had come to them *before* sustained fieldwork had begun, and done so, in essence, by 'antiquarian' means.

It seems, however, that antiquarian means were not enough to convince his contemporaries, and not quite enough to convince Brunn himself, to leave Pausanias completely behind. In 1877, Brunn reiterated his claims and berated his colleagues for offering all sorts of hypotheses without actually *looking* at the monuments themselves (by which he presumably meant the casts, which were now available).[60] He fleshed out his claim that the borrowing had occurred in the opposite direction, that is, that the developmental sequence began not with Attic art, the glorious traits of which were then borrowed by the other Greek city states, but with an ionic style that was perfected, but not invented, by Phidias in Athens.[61] A year later, a frustrated Brunn thundered, 'I hope the time will not be too far off when each archaeologist will be just as convinced of this as the philologist is that Herodotus did not write after Thucydides and was not his student.'[62] But he did not go to Olympia to seek proof for his claim, though he had another two decades yet to live.[63] Indeed, Brunn, despite his ardent graecophilia, never got closer to Greece than Winckelmann's tomb in Trieste, to which he made a pilgrimage as a young man.[64] Nor did he, in the letters that remain, ask his devoted student Furtwängler to go, even though the latter was in Rome by 1876 and in Athens in early 1878. When, in 1877, Brunn pleaded with his colleagues to study 'the monuments themselves,' he meant, quite clearly, the casts.[65]

The time has come now to describe Furtwängler's sojourn at Olympia, which, it should be noted, lasted only eight months in total, during which time Furtwängler also visited Germany and England.[66] He did not go of his own volition, nor on Brunn's recommendation; while studying in Rome on a Deutsches Archäologisches Institut stipend, he was drafted by the Olympia excavators to deal with an unanticipated problem: the uncovering of a plethora of *Kleinkunst* that the foreign 'scientific' team, unlike earlier private excavators, could not simply throw away. Furtwängler was promised that he could return to Rome afterwards to complete his studies, and asked to work alongside Georg Treu, who was assigned to the important temple pediments; his job was to organize and if possible catalogue the increasingly vast number of bronze objects. Furtwängler decided that this paid position was as good as any for a young scholar without the means to remain an unpaid *Privatdozent* for a long period of apprenticeship. Brunn agreed, arguing that it was good for young scholars to engage in a little 'forced labour' (*Zwangsarbeit*).[67] By now, thanks to the Mycenaean project, Furtwängler had some hands-on experience of archaeological cataloguing, but he would still be bowled over by the scale of the Olympia project. Every day, he noted in November 1878, the team of 250 excavators found 40–50 bronze objects, and the same number of terra cottas, plus coins and inscriptions. All these needed to be inventoried and their locations noted, and at the end of each week an extensive report had to be sent to Berlin. To give some idea of the overall scale of the finds, by 1879, Georg Treu could report the location of 1,328 stone sculptures, 7,464 bronzes, 2,094 terra cottas, 696 inscriptions, and 3,035 coins.[68] Furtwängler was overwhelmed, but also, at this point, content with his job, and certain that he was profiting from it. He wrote to Brunn: 'In Rome you wished "forced labour" on me; here I have it on a whole different scale. But I have to say that I feel quite satisfied. If the cataloguing of many small bronze objects, coins, and the like is truly onerous, I am learning so much that one otherwise would have no opportunity [to learn].'[69]

He was still happy in February of that year; Dörpfeld was now on site, and Furtwängler felt he learned much from his architectural insights.[70] The architect introduced the practice of keeping detailed archaeological diaries, from which he could draw material for his weekly reports to the overseers of the excavation (who remained in Berlin). Furtwängler surely profited from this careful attention to detail, as well as from what Klaus Herrmann has called the 'collegial working climate' created by Dörpfeld and probably enhanced by the presence of Richard Borrmann, another architect who would do path-breaking work in the ordering of terra cotta roof decorations.[71] At Easter, Furtwängler explored the surrounding regions with a colleague, an expedition that gave rise to a highly romantic popular essay praising the *Gastfreundschaft* of the Greek peasants and chuckling at their lack of appreciation for ancient monuments.[72] But by the summer of 1879, cataloguing had become oppressive – and, what is more important, Furtwängler felt he had no more to learn. 'This work is very tiring and quite thankless, as we lack books and the inspiration of others almost completely, and thus we don't get very far.'[73] He was beginning to suspect that cataloguing would not further his career very much, and that he ought to habilitate rather than continue with the apparently mechanical labour of classifying objects. Moreover, the conflict between the Institute in Berlin and the Olympia excavators, especially Friedrich Adler, made the situation uncomfortable.[74] Luckily for Furtwängler, he caught malaria in Bologna in July 1879 and was forced by health considerations to return to Freiburg, rather than having to explain to the Institut his other reasons for not returning to the dig.[75] By late 1879 he was working in Bonn and had completed an extensive essay on the bronzes, which, the excavator's protests aside, boasted an impressive quantity of footnotes. Here he used stratigraphic observations, together with recent work by Wolfgang Helbig and Alexander Conze on Geometric pottery, to organize some 7,500 bronzes into chronological groups; later, he would expand his insights to develop a stylistic sequence for Geometric bronzes that has remained central to Greek art history for more than a century.[76] Significantly, like Conze before him, in attempting to create developmental sequences in the absence of texts, Furtwängler in his work on the bronzes drew on the work of antiquarians, collectors, and prehistorians rather than philologists; like Brunn, he started from the monuments themselves, but unlike his mentor he worked with artefacts he had not chosen and did not particularly admire; moreover, unlike free-standing sculptures, these objects could not be attributed to individual makers or elucidated with help from the literary tradition. In the years to follow, he would continue to develop his typologizing eye and depend less and less on texts for dating and interpreting ancient material culture.

Furtwängler's departures from the neohumanist tradition were apparent, too, in his work on the Olympia pediments. The young man saw the sculptures for the first time in June 1878; fresh from the experience, he wrote to Brunn: 'In Olympia the greatest surprise was saved for me; I came to it like a newborn child, without having seen casts or anything. I was amazed by the Alkamenes [West pediment] – what did I find standing there? No trace, no scratch that could have been made by an Attic artist, not to mention by a student of Phidias. On the contrary, the work corresponded to the last detail with the East pediment.'[77] We may take

Furtwängler's 'shock' with a grain of salt; if he had seen no casts, he had certainly read Brunn's essays and was thus intellectually prepared not to see Phidian forms. But we can well imagine that even for this student of Brunn, up to his eyeballs in Mycenaean sherds, the unfamiliar, archaic harshness of the sculptures was difficult to assimilate. Seeing the material evidence, however, made rethinking Pausanias essential. Now it was necessary, as Furtwängler put it in an essay for the widely popular *Preussische Jahrbücher* in 1882, to 'unlearn' (*umlernen*) what scholars had thought they knew, and to put the Olympia sculptures in a new frame entirely. Once this was done, the developmental sequence became clear, and the dissonance between Olympian and Attic art he had felt on his first visit to the excavations disappeared.[78] In subsequent years, Furtwängler would complete the break with Pausanias that Brunn had begun, giving up Paionios and Alkamenes completely. The Olympia sculptures, he wrote in 1893, 'are certainly not works that show the impress of a powerful and intelligent personality. They are average achievements of their age, they are the works of a school and workshop, not works of an artist of the first rank.'[79] Historicized realities now took the place of aesthetic expectations, on-site viewing that of textual interpolation. If Brunn had reversed the chronology while preserving Pausanias's authority, Furtwängler trusted his eye rather than the text – and defended his task as one of ascertaining the historical importance, not the aesthetic interest, of the monuments concerned.

It might be said of Furtwängler that the antiquarian tradition gave him the tools; the later nineteenth century's collecting and publishing mania gave him the material; and positivism gave him the confidence to alter archaeology's balance between words and things. It must also be said, however, that state patronage, both for excavations and for grand-scale museums, was a necessary prerequisite for Furtwängler's achievements. Not only did it make possible his trip to Olympia; after his habilitation, while waiting to be called to a paid teaching post, he continued for fourteen years to work, quite happily, in the Berlin Museums. His work there was of a rather different sort than that of Brunn in the Munich museums; whereas the older scholar worked with and taught from the monuments, he did not catalogue or seek to authenticate masses of *Kleinkunst*, as did his student. In the Berlin Museums, Furtwängler perfected his 'eye' in a way that would have been impossible for a neo-humanistically inclined scholar to imitate; turning from bronzes to the cataloguing of vases, and then to overviews of cut stone and gem collections, he worked intensively with objects (and reproductions of objects) and very little with ancient texts. He travelled to other museums often and, as a result of being sent to auctions to enhance Berlin's collections, came to know well the world of the art dealers.[80] His 1885 two-volume inventory of the Royal Museum's vase collection covered 4,221 artefacts, and his cut stone catalogue, published in 1896, required him to examine approximately 15,000 pieces; his final overview of ancient gems (*Die antiken Gemmen* [Leipzig, 1900]), according to his friend Paul Arndt, entailed the observation of 50,000 to 60,000 objects[81] (fig. 8). Contemporaries insisted that he had made this field, once inhabited exclusively by dilettantes and forgers, respectable.[82] They failed to add that this new respectability of the study of *Kleinkunst* also represented a departure for neoclassical institutions like the Royal Museum and the Gymnasien; but, as we shall see, new respectability did not mean that those institutions would (or could) adopt a fully historicist stance towards the classical past.

Furtwängler, not surprisingly, believed his methods to be wholly scientific and objective, but it is perhaps worth reiterating that the archaeological positivism he represented in fact was shaped by the cultural ecosystem in which it evolved. We have already seen how important the acceleration of state patronage and the new scale of collecting were for the development of the field. But the increasingly conservative tendencies in what Steven Moyano once described as the 'mercantilist' attitude towards art are also clearly visible in Furtwängler's writings;[83] following in the tracks of Winckelmann, Humboldt, and Gottfried Semper, the positivist archaeologist hoped explicitly to improve German art and public taste by means of his endeavours. If Winckelmann, Humboldt, and Semper were envisioning the development of a truly revitalized German classicism, Furtwängler, it seems – like Caylus a century earlier? – was primarily raising up classical models *against* the 'modern' art of his day.[84] He lavished attention on gemstones and vases not simply because they could tell him about Greek cultural history; he also believed the objects themselves beautiful or interesting. Finally, if classicists like Furtwängler found themselves importing ideas from the natural sciences to assist them in the rigorous interpretation of their material, that was, on the one hand, to defend themselves as interpreters of objects against the dismissive attitude of most philologists and historians towards the study of material culture, and, on the other, to give a powerful new impetus to the non-utilitarian study of the ancient world, something proponents of school reform saw as elitist and anti-modern. 'Objectivity' here meant renunciation of modern art and the defensive appropriation of natural science, the adoption of state patronage, and the resistance to mass culture. That does not mean, however, that under these conditions archaeologists did not make lasting contributions to scholarship; it simply underlines the ways in which this new form of antiquarian scholarship was in fact heavily structured by deeply held political and cultural commitments.

Indeed, in pursuing this sort of archaeological *Wissenschaft*, according to Alois Riegl, the great Austrian pioneer in the realm of nonaestheticizing style criticism, Furtwängler by the 1890s had gained 'a comprehensive insight into the apparently so incidental area of the ornamental in Greek art more profound than any other.'[85] He was by this time widely renowned not only for the breadth of his knowledge but also for the accuracy of his eye, and he was frequently called in as an expert when forgery was suspected. His expertise did not, however, win him a university chair, nor the directorship of the Antiquarium in Berlin, nor a seat on the Deutsches Archäologisches Institut's central direction, a set of circumstances that made the scholar suspect an anti-Catholic conspiracy. Anti-Catholicism there certainly was among Prussian classicists, and Furtwängler was famously unclubbable, but more probably he was victim, here, to the persistence of neohumanism's denigration of the 'real.' It took the publication of a large book on Greek sculpture, *Meisterwerke der griechischen Skulptur* (1893), to win him Brunn's chair and real academic recognition. But the fact that a man so clearly oriented to the stuff, rather than to texts, could ultimately attain such a position was a sign of his contemporaries' rising appreciation of visual knowledge.

Unlike his more specialized publications, Furtwängler's *Meisterwerke* created immediate controversies. In a highly positive review of the book, the French archaeologist Salomon Reinach applauded its greatly enlarged corpus of monuments, commenting, 'It is high time that the history of ancient sculpture stop trampling around on the 160 engravings [published by Johannes] Overbeck and that it aspire at least to the direct, complete knowledge of the *thousand monuments* of which [Eduard] Gerhard's renowned formula speaks.'[86] German reviewers, however, particularly classicists of the previous generation, remained doubtful not only about Furtwängler's methods but also about his departures from the heavily philological conventions of German *Altertumswissenschaft*. Adolf Trendelenburg, reviewing the work for the *Kölnische Zeitung*, wrote of the *Meisterwerke*'s author, 'He trusts his trained eye, his feeling for style and his judgment of monuments so unconditionally that he simply throws over his shoulder the literary tradition of the ancients where it doesn't want to agree with the results he has drawn from his critique of monuments.'[87] Another reader complained about Furtwängler's 'natural scientific' orientation and tendency to substitute observation for reading.[88] Even in the interpretation of 'masterpieces,' the legacy of the Olympia experience seemed to live on.

But Furtwängler's *Meisterwerke* was in many ways not nearly as 'modern' a book as his catalogues of gems and analyses of bronzes, and in conclusion I want to compare it, briefly, to two contemporary but quite different products of what may be called the antiquarian tradition: Brunn's final book, a collection of his essays entitled *Griechische Götterideale in ihren Formen erläurtert* (published the same year as the *Meisterwerke*, 1893), and Alois Riegl's 1901 masterpiece, *Spätrömische Kunstindustrie*. The comparison should underline the ways in which, by reconfiguring antiquarian practices, Furtwängler had transformed his field but not transcended it. This is not to fault an enormously learned scholar for not living up to our expectations, but rather to illustrate, as suggested in the introduction, the ways in which classical archaeology, at the fin de siècle, continued to resist integration into modern *Kulturgeschichte*. In this resistance Furtwängler was, of course, not alone.

Heinrich Brunn's *Griechische Götterideale in ihren Formen erläurtert* was, quite clearly, the work of an outdated iconographer; the Munich archaeologist's final book was in fact a collection of essays on individual sculptures, dating back as early as the 1850s. He had considered reworking them all to provide a full pantheon, he noted in the introduction, but had been discouraged by the vastness of new material a now elderly art historian could not incorporate. His methods, he admitted, were highly subjective, and his studies driven by love for particular objects (which were, as Helmut Sichtermann has pointed out, with one exception Roman copies of Greek sculptures).[89] Here is how Brunn, in his introduction, described his art historical practice: 'The first thing that must be done is to engage visually the object of study and to establish some kind of a personal relationship to it. When, then, after long commerce, a certain familiarity with its general character has been reached, external sources can be used to collect one's impressions and thus to work out and formulate scientifically the theme of the essay.'[90] Clearly Brunn's 'science' here was closer to connoisseurship than to fieldwork. If he had made the transition to 'Anschauung,' he had not made the transition to grand-scale, historicist archaeology, which others were making in the twenty years before his death. Brunn was, as Ludwig Curtius put it, 'a teacher whose greatness lay more in the ability to delve deeply into individual, great works of art than in the surveying of great historical eras'; as one elegist wrote in 1898, 'His method is not the purely historical one of today.'[91]

Though much richer in illustrations, Furtwängler's *Meisterwerke* was in many ways a Brunnian book; it focused on well-known masterpieces and reflected a quite conventional neo-Romantic aesthetics. As Curtius claimed, 'Furtwängler's wholly naïve relationship to art was shaped by the waning, neo-Romantic [*romantisch gefärbt*] classicism of the second half of the nineteenth century. The *Meisterwerke* belonged to [that world].'[92] He did not eschew the use of texts, now that he had them; indeed, his central insight was that Roman copies of Greek sculptures could be matched up with the texts that describe ancient sculptures. As copies were probably made precisely of the sculptures textual authors had described, text and image could be reunited, and unidentified pieces illuminated. Indeed, the book attempted many new identifications of masterpieces, the most famous of which was the cobbling together of a body from Dresden and a head from Bologna to create the lost Lemnian Athena known to have been sculpted by Phideas (fig. 9). Some of these reconstructions are now thought brilliant, others – like his Venus de Milo – absurd.[93]

The striking thing for our purposes is that here Furtwängler reverses the usual direction of his analysis, focusing now on the individual piece and seeking to name its maker; no longer is he working from masses of anonymous material in the direction of a new sort of *Kulturgeschichte*; he seems, rather, to be trying to revive the Winckelmannian and iconographic traditions by giving them a new series of masterpieces to add to the canon. And, indeed, maintaining and transmitting this canon became a major activity in the years after the *Meisterwerke*, as Furtwängler took over from Brunn the publication of the *Denkmäler griechischer und römischer Skulptur*, a handbook of masterworks (all sculptural) of Greek art for the edification of German Gymnasium students.[94] Although he continued to travel extensively, he did so primarily in order to visit museum collections, dealers, and auction houses in northern Europe, not to view excavation sites in Greece (he seems not to have travelled to Asia Minor). He returned to the field only in 1901, this time to Aegina, to accumulate information on how to reassemble a major monument – the Aegina pediments – in the Munich collection. And, as for K.O. Müller before him, the experience proved a lethal one; in 1907 he died in Athens, of dysentery contracted in the field.

A brief contrast with Riegl's work should help to underline the point here. Born only five years after Furtwängler, Alois Riegl differed from his south-German contemporary in numerous ways; it is perhaps significant that his father had been a student of the natural sciences and then director of a state-owned tobacco factory. The young Alois grew up chiefly in Galicia, where the medieval Slavic world would have been a more relevant reference point than that of classical antiquity, which was so powerfully present for Furtwängler in Munich's neoclassical city centre. It is certainly significant that his doctoral work was concerned chiefly with medieval architectural history and that the museum job he landed in 1884 was at the Vienna Museum für Kunst und Gewerbe, not an antiquities museum.[95] Like Furtwängler, however, he spent a long time at the museum (thirteen years) before receiving an Ordinarius at the University; during this time he published his hard-to-read rebuttal of Semper's treatment of design dynamics, *Stilfragen* (1893), and continued to develop his taste for unconventional, non-classical periods, especially the Baroque era and the early Middle Ages – a historicist, and Austro-German, set of passions he shared with several important fellow Viennese art historians, Max Dvořák, Franz Wickhoff, and Josef Strzygowski.[96] Through his artefact-oriented publications, his work in the museum, and his active role in the growing movement known as *Denkmalpflege* – the equivalent for a medievalist, I would argue, of fieldwork – Riegl, like Furtwängler, gradually earned a reputation for his erudite eye. But, especially with the publication of *Spätrömische Kunstindustrie*, it was also clear that he wanted to move beyond the sequencing of monuments to the explication of the laws that governed production and the minds (or better, the national-collective mind, or spirit) that made them.

Moreover, apparently untouched by German philhellenic humanism, Riegl neither suffered shock in encountering non-classical *Kleinkunst* nor needed (or wanted) to compose his own version of the *Meisterwerke*; on the contrary, it was his goal to fully historicize the study of ancient art, and to fill 'a somewhat major lacuna, the last in our knowledge of the general history of art of mankind.'[97] In his introduction, Riegl explains why he has chosen to include such a broad range of monuments but not to give them much individual attention: 'I directed my attention not so much toward the publication of individual monuments as to the presentation of the laws governing the development of late Roman art industry; these universal laws ... never have received a more precise definition even for the architecture, sculpture, and painting of the late Roman period, because rooted prejudices held that it was completely useless to look for positive laws of development in late antiquity.'[98] This remark leads him to make a more general critique of the enduring aesthetic prejudices of the scholarly world:

> Indeed, this latest phase of ancient art is the dark continent on the map of art historical research. Not even its name and its boundaries are determined in a manner which can claim general validity. The reason for this phenomenon does not lie in an external inaccessibility of the field. On the contrary it is open toward all sides and offers a great abundance of material for observation, which to a great extent is published. Missing has been the desire to get involved with it. Such an adventure did not seem to offer sufficient personal satisfaction nor easy appreciation among the public. This reveals a fact which cannot be overlooked: in spite of its seemingly independent objectivity, scholarship takes its direction in the last analysis from the contemporary intellectual atmosphere and the art historian cannot significantly exceed the character of the artistic passions [*Kunstbegehren*] of his contemporaries.[99]

The antiquarians, he then explains, have been the ones chiefly responsible in the last thirty years for studying and publishing the monuments of the period of antiquity's 'death throes,' whereas the classical archaeologists have been obsessed with things Greek (Mycenae and Pergamon) and with iconographical studies; the only scholar who has devoted attention to the period is none other than an art historian who hails from an era pre-dating specialization (and professional archaeology), namely, Jacob Burckhardt. It is high time that modern scholars recognize that 'the aim of the fine arts is not completely exhausted with what we call beauty nor with what we call animation,' and that 'modern art, with all its advantages, would never have been possible if late Roman art with its unclassical tendency had not prepared the way.'[100]

In Riegl's work, then, the aim of the explication of the arts of antiquity is to understand the evolution of modern art, not to provide additional examples of ancient effloresence, as it still is, to a large extent, in Furtwängler's. This is an exact parallel, it seems to me, to the post-1860 reversal Momigliano describes in the writing of history; whereas, before this time, ancient models are still very much alive, by the nineteenth century's end, inquiry has begun to be heavily shaped by 'modern' questions.[101] But this chronology does not really hold for our two protagonists, who were almost exact contemporaries (in fact, Riegl died in

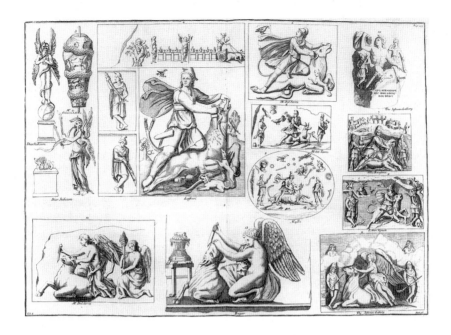

1. This page from the English version of Montfaucon's *Antiquité expliquée* (1721–2) typifies the early modern antiquary's interest in iconography – here, images of Mithras – rather than in the evolution of design, the location of the artefact, or the specific culture-historical meaning of images.

2. Overbeck's 160 illustrations zeroed in on particular – and exclusively Greek
– works of art, but his engravings did not offer much more in the way of technical details or data about the context of the images than did Montfaucon.

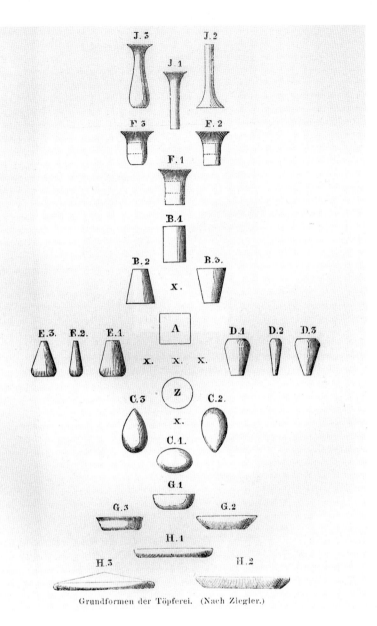

Grundformen der Töpferei. (Nach Ziegler.)

3. This page – 'Basic Forms of Pottery Design' – from Semper's *Der Stil*
(1830–3) nicely illustrates the architect's interest in the structure and use of
artefacts.

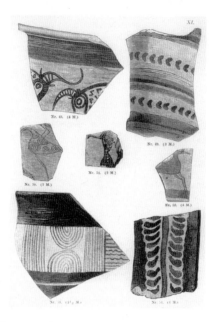

4. Schliemann's 1878 *Mykenae* haphazardly reproduced some of his pottery finds; the author described the content of this illustration simply as 'broken pieces of painted vases from Mycenae.'

5. In their 1886 *Mykenische Vasen*, Furtwängler and Loeschcke tried to sort Schliemann's Mycenaean materials chronologically, arguing that organic designs like those illustrated here preceded the development of more abstract ornamentation.

6. The 'field' at Olympia after Furtwängler's work there. The building in the rear, on the right, is the on-site museum paid for by the German excavators. Copyright DAI, Athens Archive.

7. Two slightly different reconstructions of the West pediment of the Temple of Zeus, Olympia, as presented in the official excavation report, Georg Treu et al., *Olympia* (1890–7).

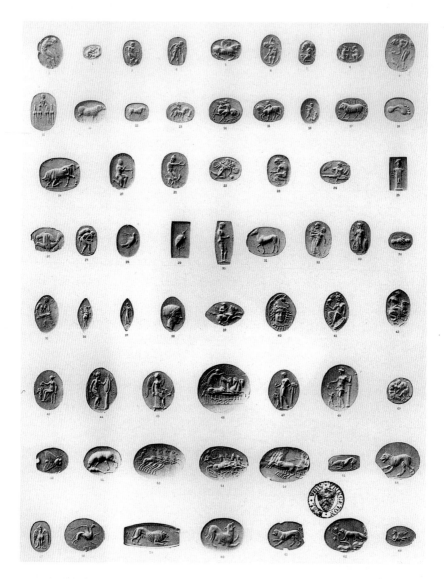

8. A photographic plate from Furtwängler's *Die antiken Gemmen* (1900). The author has placed only Greek artefacts and organized them chronologically, the top rows belonging to the preclassical 'strong style,' and the lower ones to the 'free style' of the fifth to fourth century BCE. Unlike Montfaucon's illustrations, Furtwängler's do not separate objects according to the scenes depicted, but according to date and national provenance.

9. Furtwängler's reconstruction of Phideas's Lemnian Athena, as reproduced in his *Meisterwerke* (1893). The archaeologist used casts to assemble an almost complete sculpture by the renowned Greek artist.

Münchener
Glyptothek

RÖMISCHER SAAL, GESAMTANSICHT

Phot. F. Kaufmann, Mohn.
Amtl. Ausgabe Nr. 215

10. The Roman Room of the Glyptothek as it looked in Furtwängler's day. An anthropological view of culture was hardly compatible with a workplace such as this one. Copyright Glyptothek, Munich.

1905, two years *before* Furtwängler). It is certainly true that for Furtwängler, being an 'Archäolog' in the era of grand-scale fieldwork required that he devote more time and energy to classification than interpretation, relating masses of objects to one another rather than working out from the individual pieces. Brunn, despite wide knowledge of textual sources, coins, vases, inscriptions, and especially, sculpture, could pick and choose his material; he faced the problem of the indentification of objects *after* they had been deemed worthy of acquisition, transport, and discussion by others. For Furtwängler, on the other hand, his Mycenaean and Olympian experiences were those of the cataloguer, on the receiving end of what had become a vast flood of unsorted, mundane artefacts. The change in scale did matter, for with it came changes in the presumptive tasks of the 'Archäolog' and the institutions that framed his work. The balance had shifted in favour of the visual and the historical, making a new sort of antiquarianism respectable, and an older, iconographical art history seem superficial and perhaps even unscientific. But Furtwängler was able to adapt to the new challenges without accepting 'the identity of humankind in culture': he simply focused on the (classical) artefacts and left the task of 'normalizing' the Greeks to non-classicists like Riegl.

We arrive at a paradox: on the one hand, 'going there' functioned to legitimize and even institutionalize a historicist, fieldworkers' science; on the other, this 'science' ultimately did little to disturb classicists' neohumanist proclivities (in so far as they did take place, the changes were, as I argued in *Down from Olympus*, mostly imposed by intellectual and political forces pressuring classics from the outside). Ian Morris argues, most insightfully, that late-nineteenth- and early-twentieth-century archaeologists settled for categorization (which appeared scientific, and thus made them acceptable in university circles) rather than taking on larger historical issues, thereby blinding themselves to the implications of their finds.[102] That is precisely what happened to Furtwängler, who had perhaps the best 'eye' of any scholar of his era. He had excavated in Greece; he knew trajectories of gems, pottery, and bronzes from the Mycenaean era through the Hellenistic period (and was also knowledgeable about Germanic and Scandinavian prehistorical archaeology); his catalogues brought together vast quantities of *Kleinkunst* and are still admired by specialists today.[103] Thanks to new publications, museums, decipherments, institutionalized forms of collecting, and contemporary excavations going on in Greece, Rome, Mesopotamia, the coast of Asia Minor, the Levant, Egypt, and Crete, he was, historically, in a position to appreciate the arts of the Greeks in the context of a greatly expanded – and in many cases, newly accessible – Mediterranean world. Furtwängler had the materials at his command to write a 'Greek Art Industry' that did away, once and for all, with Winckelmannian *Kunstgeschichte*.

Instead, Furtwängler's focus on 'masterpieces' was, quite self-consciously, a revision of Winckelmann's method, without being a critique of his ideals. Furtwängler was, according to his student Ludwig Curtius, 'a son of the scientific positivism of his era, which he naively imbibed and represented ... He viewed modern art history's turn from the purely descriptive to the constructive with concerned disapproval.'[104] Nor was he able to appreciate the critical perspectives on the classical tradition developed in his day; he read but claimed not to understand Riegl;[105] he came to loathe Jane Harrison, whose 'fancies' about the origins of Greek religion appalled him.[106] He showed no signs of being touched by the Nietzschean questions so resonant for Curtius and his generation, one that included Aby Warburg and Stefan George, Oswald Spengler and Erwin Panofsky, all of whom recognized, in various ways, what Furtwängler could not, namely, that something had happened to German neo-humanism, and that 'science' alone could not bring it back. Instead, his heart belonged to an older form of scholarship, in which an abiding love for the objects and the longing to bring antiquity to life remained fundamental. It was, in the end, impossible for a student of Brunn's, and the director of the Glyptothek, to break free entirely from the neoclassical tradition (fig. 10).

But Furtwängler's scholarship did begin the process of accommodating classical archaeology to modern demands, and his influence has been considerable (though not always commendable), especially among those who tend objects or who focus on the objects in themselves, that is to say, museum curators and art historians rather than cultural historians and anthropologists. Had he been able to write a history of classical art that dispensed entirely with texts and with aesthetic judgments in favour of a kind of cultural anthropology, he might be more famous today – and he might, perhaps, have helped to avert German classicism's drift towards conservative anti-modernism and Aryanist racism.[107] But some who committed themselves to such a project, including Fritz Saxl, Franz Cumont, and even Riegl himself, have not exactly become household names. And even those scholars can be said, like Furtwängler, to be products of the antiquarian tradition, which, in developing the means of dating, cataloguing, and authenticating artefacts, ultimately made, and continues to make, an accurate sort of *Kulturgeschichte* possible.

Furtwängler remains an exemplar of classical scholarship's reluctant transition to modernity, a reluctance fully understandable the in light of the social and cultural history of humanism and of the antiquarian tradition's affection for the objects themselves. Good scholarship does not emerge without effort and, often, a struggle with one's predecessors, and it is perhaps right that the fields that have come into the modern world trailing long and distinguished careers – theology, for example, as well as philosophy and classics – should require extra time to accommodate themselves to new institutions and norms. And it may be, too, that some will never become fully modern, in the rather restrictive sense of adopting a kind of full-on cultural relativism. Classical archaeology, for example, may always retain remnants of its own aestheticizing past and antiquarian practices. But if living in the post-modern world is all about the acceptance of contradictions and differences, maybe we can tolerate that too.

Notes

This paper has undergone considerable revision since its presentation at the Olympia symposium in November 2000. I would like to thank the following people in particular for their comments and critiques of the paper: Greg Curtis, Luca Giuliani, Anthony Grafton, Wolf-Dieter Heilmeyer, Thomas DaCosta Kaufmann, Helmut Kyrieleis, Hugo Meyer, and Peter Miller. I would also like to thank John Blazejewski and the Firestone Library staff for producing the images from published sources that accompany this article, and the Deutsches Archäologisches Institut, Athens, and the Glyptothek, Munich, for permitting me to publish images from their collections.

In researching this paper I consulted a number of archival sources, including the papers of Heinrich Brunn, Wilhelm Dörpfeld, and Adolf Furtwängler in the Deutsches Archäologisches Institut Archiv in Berlin (DAI); and the records of the Kaiser's Civil Cabinet (Zivil Kabinet; record group 2.2.1) and the papers of Friedrich Althoff in the Zentrales Staatsarchiv in Merseberg (MZStA) (now in Geheimes Staatsarchiv, Dahlem).

1 Arnaldo Momigliano, 'The Rise of Antiquarian Research,' in *The Classical Foundations of Modern Historiography* (Berkeley, 1990), 58.

2 For the purposes of this paper, I will not discuss these recent (extensive) critiques of positivistic field archaeology; readers may be referred to the works of Ian Hodder, Ian Morris, and Anthony Snodgrass, all working archaeologists with a critical perspective on the history of the discipline.

3 See, for example, Joseph Levine, *Dr. Woodward's Shield: History, Science, and Satire in the Augustan Age* (Ithaca, 1991); Anthony Grafton, *Forgers and Critics: Creativity and Duplicity in Western Scholarship* (Princeton, 1990) and *The Footnote: A Curious History* (Cambridge, MA, 1997); Paula Findlen, *Possessing Nature: Museums, Collecting, and Scientific Culture in Early Modern Italy* (Berkeley, 1994); Maria Grazia Lolla, '*Ceci n'est pas un monument: Vetusta monumenta* and Antiquarian Aesthetics,' in *Producing the Past: Aspects of Antiquarian Culture and Practice, 1700–1850*, ed. Martin Myrone and Lucy Peltz (Aldershot, 1999), 15–34; and Alain Schnapp, *La conquête du passé: Aux origines de l'archéologie* (Paris, 1993). See also the rich literature on palaeontology and history, for example, Paolo Rossi, *The Dark Abyss of Time: The History of the Earth and the History of Nations from Hooke to Vico* (Chicago, 1984); and Claudine Cohen, 'Leibniz's *Protogaea*: Patronage, Mining, and Evidence for a History of the Earth,' in *Proof and Persuasion: Essays on Authority, Objectivity, and Evidence*, ed. Suzanne Marchand and Elizabeth Lunbeck (Brussels, 1996), 124–43.

4 Tamara Griggs, 'The Changing Face of Erudition: Antiquaries in the Age of the Grand Tour,' Ph.D. dissertation, Princeton University, 2003; Giovanna Ceserani, 'The Study of Magna Graecia: Classical Archaeology and Nationalism since 1750,' Ph.D. dissertation, Cambridge University, 2000.

5 For an interesting discussion of Evans's inventions and discoveries, see Joseph A. MacGillivray, *Minotaur: Sir Arthur Evans and the Archaeology of the Minoan Myth* (New York, 2000).

6 In addition to the extensive literatures on racist *Vorgeschichte* and Greek nationalist archaeology, see *Nationalism, Politics, and the Practice of Archaeology*, ed. Philip L. Kohl and Clare Fawcett (Cambridge, 1995).

7 Alain Schnapp, 'Between Antiquarians and Archaeologists: Continuities and Ruptures,' *Antiquity* 76 (2002): 139.

8 See Jan Bazant, 'The Case of the Talkative Connoisseur,' *Eirene* 29 (1993): 84. Thanks to Greg Curtis for referring me to this fine essay.

9 See Helmut Sichtermann, *Kulturgeschichte der klassischen Archäologie* (Munich, 1996), 237–9.

10 See Luca Giuliani, 'Winckelmanns Laokoon: Von der befristeten Eigenmächtigkeit des Kommentars,' in *Commentaries: Kommentare*, ed. Glenn Most (Göttingen, 1999), 296–322.

11 See Suzanne Marchand, *Down from Olympus: Archaeology and Philhellenism in Germany, 1750–1970* (Princeton, 1996), 12–15.

12 In this era, 'Archäologie' could be used to describe both the study of ancient art (*antiquitates*) and the study of political, legal, and economic structures in the manner of the Roman 'antiquarian' Varro. See Marchand, *Down from Olympus*, 40–2.

13 For an interesting late example of this sort of inquiry, see Konrad Wernicke's edition of K.O. Müller and F. Wieseler's *Antike Denkmäler zur griechischen Götterlehre* (Leipzig, 1899).

14 Walter Rehm, *Griechentum und Goethezeit: Geschichte eines Glaubens* (Leipzig, 1936), 6.

15 On Haller, see Eve Gran-Aymerich, *Dictionnaire biographique d'archéologie, 1798–1945* (Paris, 2001).

16 See Hans-Joachim Schalles, 'Klassische Archäologie und Denkmalpflege,' in *Klassische Archäologie: Eine Einführung*, ed. Adolf H. Borbein, Tonio Hölscher, and Paul Zanker (Berlin, 2000), 59.

17 See Schnapp, *La conquête du passé*, 156–219. Furtwängler would later praise Haller for his attempts at rigorous historical reconstruction of ancient architecture and, by the 1870s, find Semper inspirational.

18 Brent Edwin Maner, 'The Search for a Buried Nation: Prehistoric Archaeology in Central Europe, 1750–1945,' Ph.D. thesis, University of Illinois at Urbana–Champaign, 2001, chap. 1.

19 See also Marchand, *Down from Olympus*, chap. 5.

20 See Anthony Grafton, 'The Renaissance,' in *The Legacy of Rome: A New Appraisal*, ed. Richard Jenkyns (Oxford, 1992), 97–124.

21 On Gerhard, see Marchand, *Down from Olympus*, 58–60; Gran-Aymerich, *Dictionnaire biographique*, 294–6. Gerhard's 'Archaeological Theses' (1850) are now available in English in *Modernism/Modernity* 11:1 (special issue 'Archaeologies of the Modern') (January 2004): 173–8.

22 Gerhard, 'Allgemeiner Jahresbericht,' *Archäologischer Anzeiger zur Archäologische Zeitung* 16 (1858): 148–9.

23 See Ernst Vogt, 'Wilamowitz und die Auseinandersetzung seiner Schüler mit ihm,' in *Wilamowitz nach 50 Jahren*, ed. William M. Calder et al. (Darmstadt, 1985), 613–31.

24 Luca Giuliani, 'Antiken-Museen: Vergangenheit und Perspektiven einer Institution,' in *Klassische Archäologie*, ed. Borbein et al. (n16 above), 82.

25 See, for example, Alexander Conze, 'Zur Geschichte der Anfänge griechischer Kunst,' *Sitzungsberichte der Kaiserlichen Akademie der Wissenschaften in Wien* (Phil.-Hist. Kl.) 64 (1870): 505–34; and 'Zur Geschichte der Anfänge

griechischer Kunst,' *Sitzungsberichte: Wien* (Phil.-Hist. Kl.) 73 (1873): 221–50.

26 Quoted in Walter Riezler, 'Adolf Furtwängler zum Gedächtnis,' in Adolf Furtwängler, *Briefe aus dem Bonner Privatdozentenjahr 1879/80 und der Zeit seiner Tätigkeit an den Berliner Museen 1880–1894* (Stuttgart, 1965), 9.

27 Ludwig Curtius, 'Adolf Furtwängler,' in *Badische Biographien*, vol. 6 (1901–10) (1934), 331; quoted in Walter Schuchhardt, *Adolf Furtwängler* (Freiburg im Breisgau, 1956), 6.

28 'Was wollte ich damals vom leben? Nur genuss, unmittelbaren genuss des schönen, wo es mir gerade entgegentrat; ernste wissenschaftliche arbeit kannte ich nicht. Als ich bereits 2 semestriger philologe war, wollte ich allen ernstes die lederne wissenschaft mit der schauspielkunst vertauschen!' (Furtwängler to Brunn, 9 September 1874, DAI, Nachlass Brunn).

29 Schuchhardt, *Adolf Furtwängler*, 7.

30 Furtwängler calls the field 'unerreichbar' in his letter to Brunn, 9 September 1874, DAI, Nachlass Brunn.

31 See Gottfried von Lücken's entry on Brunn in *Neue Deutsche Biographie*, vol. 2, p. 679.

32 For example, Heinrich Brunn, *Geschichte der griechischen Künstler*, vol. 1 (Braunschweig, 1853), 110; idem, 'Archäologische Miscellen,' *Sitzungsberichte der königlichen Bayerischen Akademie der Wissenschaften* (Phil.-Hist. Kl.) 2 1872).

33 Rosemary Bletter, 'From Post to Pillar,' review of Wolfgang Hermann, *Gottfried Semper*, in *Times Literary Supplement*, 24 January 1986, p. 97.

34 Heinrich Brunn, *Archäologie und Unterricht* (Munich, 1885).

35 Furtwängler to Brunn, 9 September 1874, DAI, Nachlass Brunn.

36 Curtius notes, 'Er war Anhänger der deutschen darwinistischen Forschung und las begeistert ihre Werke' (Curtius, 'Adolf Furtwängler' 355 [n27 above]). When asked, sometime after the 1890s, what he owed his instructors in *Altertumswissenschaft*, the mature Furtwängler – who had by this time become enraged with the Berlin classicists and the older generation of neohumanists in general – responded, 'Nothing at all,' and gave full credit instead to his reading of Semper's *Der Stil* and Darwin's *The Expression of Emotion in Animals and Man* (1872) (quoted in Ludwig Curtius, 'Erinnerungen an Adolf Furtwängler,' *Münchner Neueste Nachrichten*, 4 November 1927, DAI, Nachlass Furtwängler, Biographische Mappe).

37 See, for example, Gottfried Semper, *Keramik, Tektonik, Stereotomie, Metallotechnik für sich betrachtet und in Beziehung zur Baukunst*, vol. 2 of Semper, *Der Stil in den technischen und tektonischen Künsten oder praktische Ästhetik* (Munich, 1863), 21.

38 Furtwängler to Brunn, 25 December 1874, DAI, Nachlass Brunn.

39 Curtius, 'Adolf Furtwängler,' 332–3. Bazant suggests that Furtwängler here is practising a new sort of cultural history; it seems to me, rather, that he is still very much beholden to forerunners like Müller and Brunn, and that what is really new about Furtwängler is not his cultural history but rather the formalist-historicist analysis evident in his later works. See Bazant, 'The Case of the Talkative Connoisseur,' 85–7.

40 He continues, 'Doch die hauptsache bleiben ja diese grundrichtigen gesammtanschauungen, die den mann befähigen auch in fällen wo er weniger zu hause, das richtige instinctiv zu treffen, und die über manche kleinen mängel hinwegsehen lassen' (Furtwängler to Brunn, 9 September 1874, DAI, Nachlass Brunn).

41 Furtwängler to Brunn, 20 November 1874, DAI, Nachlass Brunn.

42 Furtwängler to Brunn, 18 February 1875, DAI, Nachlass Brunn. Ludwig Curtius reports his mentor as saying that he wished himself dead rather than to see Hegel come back into fashion, as this would represent the end of science (Curtius, 'Adolf Furtwängler,' 332).

43 Heinrich Brunn, *Cornelius Nepos und die Kunsturtheile bei Plinius und Die Onyxgefässe in Braunschweig und Neapel* (Munich, 1875).

44 Published in 1877–8 as 'Plinius und seine Quellen über die bildenden Künste,' in Adolf Furtwängler, *Kleine Schriften*, vol. 1 (Munich, 1912), 1–71.

45 Curtius, 'Adolf Furtwängler,' 335.

46 *Mykenische Tongefäße*, basically a collection of images, dates to 1879; *Mykenische Vasen* to 1886.

47 Paul Wolters, *Adolf Furtwängler: Gedächtnisrede* (Munich, 1910), 10.

48 Adolf Furtwängler and Georg Loeschcke, *Mykenische Vasen* (Berlin, 1886), iv. This idea might well have come from Max Müller's naturalistic interpretation of the origin of myths in 'diseased' or misunderstood words.

49 Brunn to Furtwängler, 25 February 1878, DAI, Nachlass Furtwängler, Kasten 1.

50 The treaty specified that no artefacts (other than doubles and casts) would be retained by Germany, though the Germans were later able to obtain nearly nine hundred objects. For the German side of the excavations, see Suzanne Marchand, 'The Excavations at Olympia: An Episode in German-Greek Cultural Relations,' in *Greek Society in the Making, 1863–1913*, ed. Philip Carabott (London, 1997), 73–85. A revealing examination of the Greek side of the negotiations can be found in Thanassis Kalpaxis, 'Die Vorgeschichte und die Nachwirkungen des Olympia-Vertrages aus griechischer Sicht,' in *Olympia 1875–2000: 125 Jahre Deutsche Ausgrabung*, ed. Helmut Kyrieleis (Mainz, 2002), 19–30.

51 Bernd Sösemann, 'Olympia als publizistische National-Denkmal. Ein Beitrag

zur Praxis und Methode der Wissenschaftspopularisierung im Deutschen Kaiserreich,' in *Olympia 1875–2000*, ed. Kyrieleis, 49–84.

52 Curtius, quoted in Sichtermann, *Kulturgeschichte* (n9 above), 273.

53 Adolf Furtwängler, 'Die Bronzefunde aus Olympia und deren kunstge-schichtliche Bedeutung,' in *Kleine Schriften*, vol. 1 (n44 above), 340.

54 Sichtermann, *Kulturgeschichte*, 273.

55 Even Jacob Burckhardt, whose taste in any event ran to the archaic, was disappointed by this view of real Greek art, unmediated by Roman copyists or later restorers; he despaired of 'the stiff "Apollo," the undoubtedly naïve but horribly conceived squatting figure, the tangled mob of the centaurs' battle, and the like. The conception itself is far inferior to that of the Aegina [sculp-tures]' (Burckhardt, quoted in Arnold von Salis, *Jacob Burckhardts Vorlesungen über die Kunst des Altertums* [Basel, 1948], 11). Ironically, the Elgin marbles themselves had provoked enormous controversy on their arrival in England; many viewers thought them too harsh and simple to be truly Greek.

56 Adolf Furtwängler, 'Eine Ausgabe der Funde von Olympia in einem Bande,' in *Kleine Schriften*, vol. 1, p. 247.

57 Naturally, this transition did not occur overnight. It was begun long before Olympia and completed long afterwards (if ever!). Furtwängler himself remained very much a devotee of the fifth century (see below).

58 Heinrich Brunn, 'Die Sculpturen von Olympia,' in *Sitzungsberichte der königlichen Bayerischen Akademie der Wissenschaften* (Philos.-Philol. Kl.) (1877), 26.

59 Heinrich Brunn, 'Paeonois und die nordgriechische Kunst,' in *Sitzungs-berichte der königlichen Bayerischen Akademie der Wissenschaften* (Philos.-Philol. Kl.) (1876), 315–16.

60 For example, Brunn, 'Die Sculpturen von Olympia' (1877), 1–28.

61 For an overview of the argument, see Furtwängler, 'Eine Ausgabe der Funde von Olympia,' 245–58.

62 Heinrich Brunn, 'Die Sculpturen von Olympia,' in *Sitzungsberichte der königlichen Bayerischen Akademie der Wissenschaften* (Philos.-Philol. Kl.) (1878), 442–71, on 459.

63 Indeed, in February 1879, Furtwängler tried to persuade Brunn to visit him in Olympia, and go with him to Athens rather than simply returning to Rome: 'Wenn sie doch einmal reisen, muss es doch etwas rechtes sein, nicht nur ihr alten, ewiges Rom.' (Furtwängler to Brunn, 7 February 1879, DAI, Nachlass Brunn).

64 See Hermann Brunn, 'Julius Langbehn, Karl Haider, Heinrich von Brunn,' *Deutsche Rundschau* 218 (January–March 1929): 20–34.

65 Brunn, 'Die Sculpturen von Olympia' (1877), 2. Long into the twentieth

century, even after it became conventional to visit the site itself, the chronology, authorship, and correct disposition of the figures remained controversial. See Hans-Volkmar Herrmann, 'Einführung' and 'Olympiameister – Olympiawerkstatt – Olympiastil,' in *Die Olympia-Skulpturen*, ed. Hermann (Darmstadt, 1987), 1–18, 309–38.

66 He visited briefly in June, on a trip to see Mycenae, then spent the fall and spring at the Olympia excavations.

67 Furtwängler to Brunn, 29 August 1878, DAI, Nachlass Brunn.

68 Georg Treu, 'Die Ausgrabung zu Olympia,' report no. 37 (1879), MZStA 2.2.1–20772, pp. 58–61.

69 Furtwängler to Brunn, 22 November 1878, DAI, Nachlass Brunn.

70 Furtwängler to Brunn, 7 February 1879, DAI, Nachlass Brunn.

71 Klaus Herrmann, 'Bauforcher und Bauforschung in Olympia,' in *Olympia 1875–2000*, ed. Kyrieleis, 112, 115.

72 'Aus der Umgebung Olympias,' in *Kleine Schriften*, vol. 2 (Munich, 1913), 227–44, originally published in *Literarische Beilage der Karlruher Zeitung*, 8 and 15 February 1880. Here Furtwängler describes how he saved a donkey from having to lug a piece of sandstone, carved by water into 'a rather remarkable form,' to the local museum in Dimitzana. He concludes, in a rather orientalist vein, 'Die Autorität der Fremden pflegt überhaupt bei den Griechen eine sehr grosse zu sein; man ist fast allenthalben im Volke überzeugt, dass wir mit Hilfe unserer Bücher ganz genau wüssten, wo jeweils die Tempel und Schätze vergraben liegen' (243). But he also admits, elsewhere, that art dealers and forgers are common, thereby suggesting that the Greeks were not, after all, so ignorant about ancient art and its marketability (237).

73 Furtwängler to Brunn, 1 July 1879, DAI, Nachlass Brunn.

74 Ibid.

75 Furtwängler to Brunn, 21 August 1879, DAI, Nachlass Brunn.

76 See Wolf-Dieter Heilmeyer, 'Einleitung,' in Heilmeyer, *Frühe olympische Bronzefiguren* (Berlin, 1979), 1–6.

77 Furtwängler to Brunn, 6 June 1878, DAI, Nachlass Brunn.

78 Furtwängler, 'Eine Ausgabe der Funde von Olympia,' 252.

79 Adolf Furtwängler, 'Zu den olympischen Skulpturen' (1893), in *Kleine Schriften*, vol. 1, p. 322.

80 Curtius, 'Adolf Furtwängler,' 338.

81 Schuchhardt, *Adolf Furtwängler*, 14–15.

82 Johannes Sieveking, 'Adolf Furtwängler,' in *Biographisches Jahrbuch für die Altertumswissenschaft*, vol. 32, ed. Conrad Bursian (1909), 326.

83 Steven Moyano, 'Quality vs. History: Schinkel's Altes Museum and Prussian Arts Policy,' *Art Bulletin* 72: 4 (December 1990): 585–608.

84 Bazant, 'The Case of the Talkative Connoisseur,' 98.

85 Riegl to Furtwängler, 8 September 1893, DAI, Nachlass Furtwängler, Kasten 7.

86 Reinach's review appeared in *Revue critique d'histoire et de litterature* 28:6 (5 February 1894): 116, DAI, Nachlass Furtwängler, Kasten 11.

87 [Trendelenburg], 'Meisterwerke der griechischen Plastik,' *Kölnische Zeitung* 1029 (24 December 1893), DAI, Nachlass Furtwängler, Kasten 11.

88 See also J. Ilberg, 'Meisterwerke der griechischen Plastik,' *Wissenschaftliche Beilage der Leipziger Zeitung* 152 (21 December 1893): 605.

89 Sichtermann, *Kulturgeschichte* (n9 above), 235.

90 Heinich Brunn, *Griechische Götterideale in ihren Formen erläutert* (Munich, 1893), iv.

91 Curtius, 'Adolf Furtwängler,' 332; H. Bulle, quoted in Sichtermann, *Kulturgeschichte*, 234.

92 Curtius, 'Adolf Furtwängler,' 353.

93 On Furtwängler's Venus reconstruction and the controversies in his day over *Meisterforschung*, see Gregory Curtis, *Disarmed: The Story of Venus de Milo* (New York, 2003), 122–63.

94 See, for example, Adolf Furtwängler and H.L. Ulrichs, *Denkmäler griechischer und römischer Skulptur*, 3rd ed. (Munich, 1911).

95 On Riegl's career, see Rolf Winkes, 'Foreword,' in Alois Riegl, *Late Roman Art Industry*, trans. Winkes (Rome, 1985), xii–xix.

96 For more on the Austrian school of art history, see Suzanne Marchand, 'Professionalizing the Senses: Art and Music History in Vienna, 1890–1920,' *Austrian History Yearbook* 21 (1985): 23–57; idem, 'The Rhetoric of Artifacts and the Decline of Classical Humanism: The Case of Josef Strzygowski,' *History and Theory* Beiheft 33 (December 1994): 106–30.

97 Riegl, *Late Roman Art Industry*, 17.

98 Ibid., 5–6.

99 Ibid., 6.

100 Ibid., 6–8, 11.

101 Arnaldo Momigliano, 'The Place of Ancient History in Modern Historiography,' in *Settimo contributo alla storia degli studi classici e del mondo antico* (Rome, 1984), especially 29–33.

102 Ian Morris, 'Archaeologies of Greece,' in *Classical Greece: Ancient Histories and Modern Archaeologies*, ed. Morris (Cambridge, 1994), 28.

103 There are, however, dangers in accepting as raw data the chronologies that Furtwängler developed; for a discussion of these, see Wolf-Dieter Heilmeyer, 'Olympia und die Entdeckung der geometrischen Plastik,' in *Olympia 1875–2000*, ed. Kyrieleis, 85–9.

104 Curtius, 'Adolf Furtwängler,' 355.
105 Ibid.
106 Mary Beard, *The Invention of Jane Harrison* (Cambridge, MA, 2000), 79.
107 On this trajectory, see Esther Sophia Sünderhauf, *Griechensehnsucht und Kulturkritik: Die deutsche Rezeption von Winckelmanns Antikenideal, 1840–1945* (Berlin, 2004).

chapter ten

Arnaldo Momigliano and the History of Religions

GUY G. STROUMSA

I

It took Arnaldo Momigliano a lifetime of passionate and constant effort to fully explore and express what he had discovered as a young man. At the core of history one finds the contacts between civilizations, and at the core of these contacts, one finds religion. Hence, the study of religions and of their transformations is the ultimate goal of the historian. As a young man, Momigliano had realized that this truth had been more often than not belittled, ignored, or occulted by most historians since antiquity. He also knew, however, that it had already been discovered and explored, during the seventeenth and early eighteenth centuries, by a remarkable group of scholars, whom we call the antiquarians, and who offered more than a new intellectual taste: a real revolution in method.[1] Throughout his life, Momigliano sought to follow their inspiration. The antiquarians came from the various nations and religions of Western Europe, but really belonged to the international and interconfessional *République des Lettres*. If they had been able to discover the true core of history, at the dawn of modern times, it is because they stood at a historical junction, thoroughly committed to the rational investigation of all phenomena, when the various civilizations of humankind, past and present, were being discovered, and also because they usually remained very close, intellectually and socially, to their own religious community. Although Spinoza was not one of them, his *Tractatus theologico-politicus* remains one of the major works pertaining to the history of religions written in the seventeenth century. It comes as no surprise that Momigliano, who had read Spinoza's *Tractatus* as a boy, asked that a passage of the *Ethics* (on the free man's refusal to speak about death) be read at his funeral.[2]

'Ancient History and the Antiquarian' sought to highlight the revolution in historical method that Momigliano had detected in the seventeenth century. This article also in itself represents a revolution in method, in that it introduces a notion of the central importance of religion in the proper understanding of history. The critical study of the Holy Scriptures, the birth of Orientalism, the comparison of dogmas and rituals, the interest in etymologies, all those intense interests of the antiquarians came to play a major role for the eighteenth-century philosophic historian, who was interested in questions about the present. The critique of religion, from Spinoza and Simon to Blount, Bayle, and Le Clerc, was recognized by Momigliano as belonging to the early modern transformation of historical method and sensitivity.

In the constant and acute attention he devoted to the antiquarians and their deep interest in religious phenomena, studied from a non-theological ('unpartheilich,' would say Gottfried Arnold) and comparative viewpoint, Momigliano called attention to a phenomenon that has remained almost unnoticed to this day: that the modern study of religion began two centuries earlier than has usually been thought. Its heroes, who followed the great Spanish *frailes*-turned-anthropologists in sixteenth-century Mexico and Peru such as Bartolomé de Las Casas, Bernardino de Sahagun, and José de Acosta, were figures from the Western Europe of the seventeenth and early eighteenth centuries, such as John Selden, Gerard van Voss, Samuel Bochart, Pierre-Daniel Huet, John Spencer, Edward Pococke, Thomas Hyde, Joseph-François Lafitau, and Isaac de Beausobre. The main thrust of their efforts was to approach all religious phenomena, past and present, from near and far, with the same methods and the same presupposition: that the religions of all societies reflected, in their vastly different ways, a single humanity. At the same time, they sought to retain their basic loyalty to their own religious faiths and communities, and usually succeeded: they were anything, as Momigliano says, but frivolous.[3] Accordingly, he could note that Selden, Bochart, and Huet, for instance, were good representatives of the seventeenth-century effort to reduce differences between ancient Jews and pagans – an effort to which Vico, for all the modern echoes in his writings, remained alien.[4] It is a sad testimony to the chasm between disciplines, at a time when interdisciplinarity works well as a mantra, that so important an insight seems to have been ignored to this day by most historians of religion. Although various excellent monographs on aspects of the birth of the modern comparative study of religion are in existence, we still lack a synthetic work.

In the Italian intellectual and cultural traditions within which Momigliano was educated, the constant dialogue of humanists across generations was natural. It happened as a matter of course, and not as the consequence of any ideology. Latin was still a recognized medium. In a way, a similar situation obtained in other milieux, such as Habsburg Austria, where the Jesuit educational tradition had emphasized the continuity of the Latin tradition (in contradistinction to the turn to Greek in the Humboldtian reform of German higher education). Yet an essential trait of the Italian intellectual commerce with the past, which distinguished it from what was happening elsewhere, was a deeply engrained sense of normalcy. In Italy as nowhere else, the continuity of the great humanist chain was a local tradition. There one had an immediate sense of inserting oneself in this respectable tradition, to a degree that the caesura of modernity, so clearly felt elsewhere, was not easily recognizable. Indeed, for models of intellectual modernity, Italians often looked across the Alps. In the study of the ancient world, modernity usually meant German influences. Hence, as a young scholar, Momigliano could converse with the great early modern humanist scholars, but he *also* read them through the lenses of what happened later, when this tradition was transformed into modern scholarship in nineteenth-century German universities.

It is this dual relationship to the two slopes of modern scholarship and cultural history that explains Momigliano's unique status among twentieth-century scholars. To say simply that he bridges tradition and modernity, by reading the ancients in the light of the moderns and the moderns in the light of the ancients, is presenting only a rather flat picture of what appears to the close reader as a constant intellectual feast. More than other traditional Italian scholars, he was naturally able to raise subversive questions with full power. And, more than German scholars trained with the new critical tools and methods of philology and history, he knew that these tools and methods were best understood when seen in the context of the antiquarian tradition. With people such as Heyne, F.A. Wolf, Creuzer, Mommsen, Usener, and K.O. Müller, modern scholarship of the ancient world had undergone a revolution. The nineteenth century had brought a dramatic caesura in the tradition, imposing new questions and new methods. On the other hand, Momigliano knew that the real cultural significance of modern scholarship was best preserved in the humanist and antiquarian tradition that was now fast falling into oblivion. Momigliano, systematically, refused to choose one of these slopes at the price of ignoring the other. His refusal, which was to become his trademark, was certainly much strengthened with emigration: in England, he realized how unique his fluency in the history of the modern scholarly tradition was, and wisely decided to cultivate it.

But it had been made possible, it seems to me, through a much deeper, much earlier sense of belonging at once to different worlds, and being called upon to bridge them. In his youth, as a Piedmontese Jew, Momigliano realized that he could not claim any single tradition as his own, or rather that he would not let himself become enclosed in any single tradition to the exclusion of others. The antiquarian tradition had remained, very clearly, a Christian one. Its practitioners were enlightened Christians to be sure, and the Hebraists among them had also reclaimed the Jewish tradition, but his point of view could never identify totally with theirs. Hence his immediate willingness and ability to distance himself from the Italian intellectual tradition. At the same time, an early loss of his faith imposed upon him a similar distance from the Jewish tradition. In a sense, he perceived himself, like the early modern Christian antiquarians, as an enlightened Jew, having as his *Beruf* the duty to read the Jewish cultural and religious tradition critically and to integrate it into the cultural history of the Western world. In this task, as he soon discovered to his dismay, he could find precious little help from the modern (mainly German) scholarly tradition, since that tradition quite systematically during the nineteenth century had sought to erase any traces of significant Jewish or other oriental influence on Western cultural history. In many ways, then, he had to invent his own complex standing.

The religious dimension had indeed been an essential one in Momigliano's identity from the time of his youth. Without taking it into account, we cannot begin to understand the complexity of his relationship to both traditional and modern forms of scholarship, and his invention of a sui generis, dialectical symbiosis between them. Since the following pages will focus on his scholarship from the point of view of the study of religious phenomena, an analysis of his attitude to Jewish religious culture is imperative.

The Greeks have left us two means, Momigliano liked to remind us, for understanding religion and its development: philosophy and historiography.[5] Of the two, Momigliano opted for the second, but with a twist. He never declared, but also never hid, an ambition to be a 'philosophic historian,' the kind of historian who never ceases wondering about the ways of the world and about how things would have been different if Cleopatra's nose had been longer.[6] His early interest in philosophy and in abstract thought, as well as his relationship with Benedetto Croce, reflect this ambition.[7] For Momigliano, the main goal of the philosophic historian was to understand the civilizations of the past in their contacts and transformations. Following Montesquieu, the philosophic historian learns to think about civilizations as a whole, searching for deep structure rather than events. In a sense, he seeks to avoid usual patterns of historical work, which emphasize some trends at the expense of others. In that sense, religious history is just as limited as is, say, social, economic, or military history. But with a difference: from his early years, Momigliano felt strongly that historians of antiquity had more often than not failed to notice the major importance of religious phenomena for the understanding of past civilizations. He was interested in religion, and this interest grew as time went on. More precisely, it seems that gradually he discovered the great heuristic power of reflection centred upon the religions of the ancient world; and to it he devoted much of his work during the last twenty years of his life, mainly in a series of brilliant articles stemming from his classes at both Chicago and Pisa.[8] Yet one can easily discern that for him it was a highly existential problem.

Harbouring 'strong anti-theological beliefs,' and wary of any attempt at overarching theories, Momigliano could not follow the methods, or the questions, of most professional students of religion. Indeed, he expressed more than once his suspicion of the (explicit) methods and (implicit) goals of both theologians and phenomenologists, who sought to understand religion outside historical context. We should remember that in both the Italy and the England of his youth and his prime the comparative study of religion for various reasons was not held in high esteem, particularly by his generation. When, in 1924, Raffaele Petazzoni, a scholar for whom Momigliano had great respect, was offered the first Italian chair of the history of religions, Croce objected violently, arguing that the discipline was not needed in Italy.[9] The young Momigliano published in the journal established by Pettazzoni, *Studi e materiali di storia delle religioni.* Things changed later on, of course, but Momigliano retained his strong interest in the Italian history of religions.[10]

Momigliano was never quite in sympathy, however, with the approach of his Chicago colleague Mircea Eliade.[11] Eliade, like Momigliano, was a European, and of the same generation. But he belonged to the other side, as it were, having had to leave Europe in the early 1950s, when his direct association with the Romanian fascist – and anti-Semitic – movement prevented him from getting a job in France (the Americans, of course, could not have cared less). It was precisely during the Chicago years, however, that Momigliano developed most fully his ideas about the religious dimensions of ancient history. One wonders whether his doing so was not also, in a way, an attempt to offer a different, more serious kind of reflection on religion than the one offered by Eliade's unbridled comparativism and ahistorical phenomenology. In various articles and reviews over the years, Momigliano expressed both his interest in the comparative study of religions and his methodological scepticism regarding the discipline, stressing that it was the differences between phenomena from different civilizations, rather than the similarities, that most called for explanation. Yet some of this scepticism, at least, can be understood as a reaction to Eliade's lack of historical method – notwithstanding the name of the journal he founded, *History of Religions*. Despite his suspicion, Momigliano contributed a few entries (on Roman religion and the historiography of religion) to the *Encyclopedia of Religions*, launched by Eliade. In a sense, he was showing his Chicago colleagues (and all of us) what true history of religions can be. At the same time, as we shall see, he expended a great deal of effort in analysing the achievements of some of the most important historians of religions since the nineteenth century.[12]

The philosophic historian, when reflecting on religion, is willing to entertain questions, or follow patterns of thought, that more 'down-to-earth' colleagues would ignore or reject as vain or even illegitimate. For much of his career, Momigliano felt that ancient historians were missing a significant or essential dimension of their field if they did not study religion directly. A Rostovtzeff, for instance, for all his achievements, did not fully recognize the importance of the religious dimensions of Roman history.[13]

Momigliano made that point in particular with regard to the meeting of cultures in the ancient world. For him, this meeting of cultures was not only the obvious one between Greece and Rome, but also, especially, the meeting between Greece and Rome and the various cultures of the Near East: Iran, Egypt, Syria, and particularly Israel, and thereafter Christianity. This multiform meeting, as is quite obvious, carried essentially religious dimensions. Understanding these dimensions would increasingly become one of Momigliano's principal intellectual goals over the years.

Time and again Momigliano spoke about the treble tradition of which he was the proud heir: Jewish, Christian, and classical, well captured in the expression *tria corda,* coined by Ennius and used as the title of a volume honouring Momigliano.[14] He often insisted upon the fact that from his youth he had been brought up to recognize the multiple religious dimensions of history. He was the scion of a well-off and orthodox Jewish family that succeeded in harmoniously combining Torah and *derekh eretz,* Jewish and Italian culture, in a small Piedmontese village. Throughout his life, Judaism would retain an existential importance for him.[15] It seems that he early lost personal interest in religion, and that, like Max Weber, he was 'religiously unmusical.'[16] Yet he felt it his duty as a historian to call the attention of ancient historians to the importance of the Jewish phenomenon, which too often they chose to ignore or underplay.

Momigliano did not partake of any of the ideologies favoured by historians of his generation. He never felt the attraction of Marxism, of religion, of nationalism, or of any of the various intellectual fashions, such as structuralism and post-modernism, that have succeeded one another since the end of the Second World War. One can argue that antiquarianism was his own very personal way of protecting himself, as an exile, from both the threatening outside world and its ideologies. In the Oxford of the 1940s, antiquarianism provided him with an anchor in his own culture and tradition and also with a very special epistemological perspective. The history of historical method became Momigliano's very own method. And it is during that search that he discovered the utmost importance of religion in the history of ancient nations.

II

In Momigliano's library at the Scuola Normale Superiore in Pisa, one can see various books that he inscribed, in Hebrew characters, with his Hebrew name: Aharon Momigliano. From the time of his youth, he was conscious of possessing the tool most essential for understanding foreign cultures: the knowledge of languages, something that, as he noted time and again, the Greeks never managed to acquire.[17] 'As a man trained from early days to read the Bible in Hebrew, Livy in Latin, and Herodotus in Greek, I never found the task of interpreting the Bible any more or any less complex than that of interpreting Livy or Herodotus.'[18] Elsewhere he states, 'I was born in a house full of books ... of *sefarim* and *libri.*'[19]

Momigliano knew that his Hebrew was not at the level of his Greek and his Latin. Yet he read at least the Bible in Hebrew, and retained a

deep interest in Jewish history and culture. Although the Jewish education he received as a child was orthodox in principle, he tells us that he
was introduced to Spinoza's *Tractatus theologico-politicus* before his bar
mitzvah, adding that this introduction prevented any serious conflict
between reason and faith – at the price, one might add, of a strong
atrophy of faith.[20]

Momigliano refers in the following terms to the great nineteenth-
century philologist Jacob Bernays, a particularly dear hero of his, who
remained throughout his life a strictly practising Jew: 'Having received a
faith, he did not have to look to history for one.'[21] One wonders whether
Momigliano did not intend to suggest here that his own all-absorbing
interest in history was meant to replace, in some way, the faith, or at least
the interest in religious practice, that he had lost. In Sylvia Berti's
pregnant coinage, Hermann Cohen's 'Religion der Vernunft' became
for Momigliano a 'Religion der Geschichte.'[22] Peter Green similarly has
spoken of his 'religion of scholarship.'[23]

The Jewish scholar as an avatar of the rabbi: Momigliano called the
philologist Eduard Fraenkel 'a *Yeshivah bocher* if there ever was one,' one
who simply transferred to Aeschylus and Plautus the perseverance and
intelligence with which his forefathers had studied the Talmud.[24] As for
the historian Moses Finley, a Marxist *né* Finkelstein, as Momigliano liked
to recall, he was, like Momigliano himself, an *apikoros* (heretic, literally
'Epicurean'), whose role model was Elisha ben Avuyah, the Talmudic
rabbi turned rebel.[25]

Momigliano clearly enjoyed the status of the *apikoros*, the intellectual
heretic playing with fire on the borders of the Jewish community. It
comes as no surprise that he considered Gershom Scholem, who did
more than anyone else to establish the scholarly study of Jewish mysticism, 'the greatest Jewish historian' of the twentieth century.[26] Scholem
was indeed a great historian of religion, who liked to flirt with heresy
pour épater les bourgeois. Scholem's approach to history was strikingly
different from Momigliano's. Although both recognized in religion the
core of history, Scholem became a straightforward historian of Judaism,
of the faith of his fathers, which he could not share, rather than of the
Jews, being ever in search of the metaphysical, ahistorical element.
Rather than simply studying history, he decided to jump into it, when, as
a young man, he immigrated to Palestine.

Another heretical Jew admired by Momigliano was Leo Strauss, a
historian of medieval philosophy, like Scholem a convinced Zionist, and
also an atheist and inveterate reader of the scriptures, whom he met in

Chicago when he went there to teach in the 1970s.[27] In the lines he devoted to Strauss's memory, he wrote, 'Few men have loved the faith of the fathers with so much austere love as Leo Strauss, who understood it but did not share it.'[28] One may detect here some secret admiration, perhaps even jealousy.

Finally, Elias Bickerman, the great ancient historian who had crossed Europe and its languages before landing in New York. Bickerman remained 'Momigliano's guide since his youth,' in Peter Brown's words.[29] Bickerman claimed that the Jews had learned from the Greeks the value of *paideia*, the highest Hellenic ideal, which they made theirs, and transformed into what eventually became the typically Jewish virtue of Torah learning.[30] Momigliano was so impressed that he made this argument his own, when he noted, for instance, that the Jews were the only people in the ancient world for whom knowing more meant becoming more, not less, pious.[31]

Momigliano probably perceived himself, too, as a *yeshiva bocher* of sorts, of the heretic persuasion. For the late Momigliano, at least, developed a strong conviction of and a serious interest in the specificity of Israel throughout the ages, and not only in the ancient world. Moreover, his interest in the history of scholarship, which had always been there, became more and more a trademark of his. This major importance attributed to the great chain of intellectual tradition strikes me, at least metaphorically, or perhaps atavistically, as reflecting the old Jewish respect for the great chain of tradition.

Glen Bowersock has noted that Momigliano remained 'obsessed' by his Jewish identity ('Ma era ossessionato del fato di essere ebreo'), adding that this obsession, which originated in the religious cult practised in his family, grew especially after the war, during which his parents were murdered in a concentration camp.[32] It is true that from the time of his first works, published while he was still in Italy, he persisted in cultivating a strong interest in themes from Jewish history or of Jewish concern. Such behaviour was – certainly at that time, and in England – fairly atypical for Jewish classicists. Rather than speaking of an obsession, it might be more accurate to speak of Momigliano's simultaneously existential and intellectual deep interest in Jewish topics.

As a Jew, Momigliano remained proud of his identity and of the religion of his fathers, even though he did not practise it, in a world (and in a generation) that had murdered the Jews after having insulted their religion for so long. As he said, at least privately, it was, after all, a matter of dignity.[33] Did he remain free from any apologetic undertone or intention when dealing with the place of Judaism in the ancient world? That is a hard question, which I do not feel qualified to answer.

Momigliano made a conscious effort, especially after the war, to reclaim for the Jews the important place that ought to be theirs in the study of the ancient world. It was precisely his Jewish identity that opened for Momigliano the way to a broader conception of the ancient world, as a place where cultures and religions met. He kept insisting upon the lack of recognition, on the part of most ancient historians, of the significance of Israel, together with that of the other cultures of the Near East, and fought for a full understanding of the ancient world, too often limited to Greece and Rome.[34] Such an insistence may have struck some of his colleagues as a kind of 'overreaction.' But it is now better known, thanks in part to the loud discussions launched by the publication of Martin Bernal's *Black Athena*, that much of nineteenth-century scholarship, particularly in German-speaking lands, sought to reject, ignore, or at least play down 'Semitic' cultures of the Mediterranean.[35] Here too Momigliano was a precursor, though his caveats do not seem to have had the impact they deserved. If that is the case, it might be precisely because he avoided the polemical tone that would have called attention to the problem.

When speaking about modern Judaism and the place of Jews in the modern world, however, he repeated, sometimes 'solemnly,' that the Jews had a right to their religion, the first monotheistic and ethical religion, and that they should be given total religious freedom everywhere.[36] There is a paradox in Momigliano's Jewish identity, and in his perception of modern Judaism. For him, religion was culturally conditioned, and Judaism accordingly was the religion of the Jewish people. But how could Jewish identity express itself for one who believed neither in the God of his fathers nor in national rebirth? The young Momigliano had lost the faith of his fathers, and since he rejected any national Jewish component, he could see no reason to retain his 'official' links to the Jewish community.[37] On the other hand, as a young man he had expressed strong reservations about Zionism, in the hope that Italy would eventually accept Jews as full-fledged citizens and participants in the national culture. I call attention to the paradox of Momigliano's Jewish identity as it is directly related to his perception of the place of religion in general, and of Judaism in particular, in history. Momigliano's basic perception of this place, which is fundamentally correct when he deals with the ancient world, strikes me as paradoxical when he refers to the modern world. His own personal solution, of course, was to live in history rather than in faith: cultural memory had taken for him the place of religion. The great Orientalist Moritz Steinschneider, whom Momigliano never, I think, referred to, once said that all his work on medieval Jewish literature was meant as a decent tombstone for a dead civilization. Obviously, Momigliano had other intentions in his work on Jewish topics. But one wishes they had been made more explicit.

III

More than most other classical historians, Momigliano sought to compare to various cultures of the ancient world, bringing into the general frame Celts, Jews, Egyptians, and Persians, as he did in particular in his *Alien Wisdom*. He reminded us that differences remain more important than similarities in the fields of political, social, and religious history.[38] Differences entail comparison. In the ancient world, religion clearly played an important part in the definition of identity. So the recognition of the complex interplay between peoples and cultures reflects also the interaction of religious worldviews.

For Momigliano, it was obvious that the same principles of study should be applied to the Bible and the classics. The classical scholar can help the biblical scholar, and vice versa. Too often classicists remain ignorant of the Jewish component of christianized Graeco-Roman culture. Their usual channel to some minimal knowledge of Judaism is too often that of the theologians. Better than they do, Momigliano knew that in the ancient world the Jews were very much a people, and not the stiff-necked carriers of a rather desiccated religion that was only waiting to blossom a last time and give birth to its most fragrant fruit, the new faith, which would conquer the world. More than most historians of Greece and Rome, then, and more than the theologians, whom he instinctively distrusted, Momigliano was able to present a complex and lively picture of the place of the Jews and of their faith in the ancient world.

As a classicist, Momigliano approached Judaism, first of all, through the prism of Hellenistic Judaism: Josephus, of course, but also Philo and the Books of the Maccabees. From his intimate knowledge of the history of the field since Scaliger, he was aware how difficult it is to define Alexandrine ('Hellenistic') Judaism. Among the Greek-speaking Jews, only a very few can be called hellenizing Jews (namely, Jason of Cyrene, the source of 2 Maccabees, and Josephus).[39]

The disappearance of 2 Maccabees from Jewish literature was for him indicative of 'the overall rejection of history and historiography by Jews after the destruction of the Second Temple ... The *Encania* became the commemoration for a miracle rather than the celebration of a religious and political struggle, as *2 Maccabees* had described it.'[40] Was this transformation of Jewish memory, to his mind, a sign of the transformation of the Jews into believers in a religion, rather than members of a people? Momigliano does not ask the question, and therefore does not begin to answer it.

Momigliano was never tempted by the interpretations of Goodenough: 'Thus, we should consider, as a reasonable working hypothesis, that the symbols Goodenough studies should be interpreted in the context of a superficial process of Hellenization against which both Philo and the rabbis reacted rather than in terms of a mysteriosophic religion not otherwise documented.'[41] Here too Momigliano presents in clear and strong terms a view of things based on a common sense rarely partaken of by most students of Hellenistic (or for that matter rabbinic) Judaism.

Quite naturally, throughout his life Momigliano devoted much effort to Josephus. The highly complex figure of this Palestinian Jew, a priest and a fighter turned writer who ended his career in Rome, deeply interested him. Momigliano described the French historian Pierre Vidal-Naquet, the author of a remarkable essay on Josephus, as 'a Jew of the modern Diaspora, studying Josephus, a Jew of the ancient Diaspora.' The same description, of course, holds for Momigliano himself. What is more interesting is his strongly critical perception of Josephus, in which he differs widely from Vidal-Naquet. Momigliano notes that Josephus 'does not appear to comprehend the synagogue,' that 'he appears to comprehend even less that the apocalyptic enthusiasm he opposed involved not only Palestinian revolutionary groups but also Jews from the Diaspora.'[42] Momigliano recognized that Josephus, as he sought to bring Judaism within the schemes of the Greek mentality, had remained unable to understand the most powerful religious trends – and the most important institution, the synagogue – in the Judaism of his day. In comparing him to both Yohanan ben Zakkai and Paul, he underlines Josephus's marginality.[43]

Time and again Momigliano insisted upon the radical way in which Jews stopped writing historiography after the first Christian century. It would take at least a thousand years before a successor would be found to Josephus. Momigliano never stopped wondering over this puzzling fact, for which he had no ready solution. (He was highly suspicious of scholars who, because they were intelligent enough to formulate a good question, thought they had to offer an answer.) Of all the peoples of antiquity, the Jews were the only one to have elevated memory of the collective past into a religious duty.[44] In what Momigliano called the 'creative survival' of Judaism, or 'the fundamental reconstruction of religious life,' after the destruction of the Temple and the end of Jewish political life in Palestine, no provision had been made for historiography. (To be sure, nor did Jews write secular literature for many centuries, although Momigliano seems not to have been preoccupied by that fact.) The usual explanation of the Jewish abandonment of historiography, perhaps best expressed by Bickerman, connects it to the loss of political independence.[45] Momigliano remained unconvinced by that explanation. I am inclined to think that he saw in the Jewish retreat from history (or at least from history-writing) a reaction to the Christian appropriation of Israel's past – although he never put such a suggestion in writing. In contradistinction to Greek law, Jewish law (the Bible) was not conducive to history-writing, as it was itself history, or rather the broadest and most universal kind of history-writing possible.[46]

Momigliano once told me (though I did not see this idea in print) that he had no doubt that if the Jews abandoned Greek, at least as a written language (as well as giving up all interest in the Septuagint), it was precisely because of the Christian 'threat.' By their 'creative survival,' in their willingness to give up so much of Greek culture, the Jews actually became the only people of antiquity who withstood the charms of Greek civilization.

Yet the Jews did not give up all elements of Greek culture. Following Bickerman, whom Peter Brown has described as 'Momigliano's guide since his youth,'[47] Momigliano pointed out that the Jews adopted the most important idea in Hellenism, *paideia*, and transformed it into the religious virtue par excellence. This originally Hellenic idea would become the keystone of the transformation of Judaism after the destruction of the Temple.[48] Although he never worked seriously with rabbinic texts or on questions of rabbinic Judaism, Momigliano liked to refer to the Talmud. Indeed, he never made the mistake of forgetting that, as he wrote more than once, 'Jerusalem, not Alexandria, was the city where the future of Judaism was at stake.'[49]

IV

It stands to reason that Momigliano's perception of Christianity was doubly conditioned, by his interest in both Judaism and Roman religion.

His interest started here with historiography. First, he noted that the essential point of contact between Jews and Christians was their common faith in the imminent end of the world, as reflected in both Daniel and Revelation.[50] Only the progressive erosion of early Christian apocalyptic permitted the birth and development of Christian historiography in the Roman Empire. The Christians learned to do, in a strikingly new way, what the Jews had stopped doing, and Momigliano underlined the dynamism and the efficacy of Christian historiography, which encapsulated much of Christianity's superiority over paganism.[51] He noted that Christian historiography was responsible for introducing the pagans to Jewish history. To become a Christian (or a Jewish) proselyte meant having to learn a new history.[52] Christian historiography, however, remained strikingly different from Roman historiography: Eusebius is no Ammianus Marcellinus. The way in which Christian intellectuals wrote about the past was so unique, represented such a departure from Greek and Roman models, that a leading historian of Roman religion, Hubert Cancik, has recently questioned the legitimacy of speaking about Christian historiography.[53]

Momigliano was strongly dissatisfied with the approach of most Roman historians to the decline of the Roman Empire. They talked about social change without really taking into account the most important of all social changes, Christianity. This strange occultation, he pointed out, stemmed from the fact that even the greatest scholars of early Christianity, Harnack and Troeltsch, as theologians had been more interested in Christianity than in Christians, thus strongly limiting their influence upon ancient historians.[54]

Momigliano saw more clearly, and perhaps with more sympathy, than most ancient historians some of the dramatic transformations brought about in the Roman world by Christianity. He insisted, for instance, upon the erosion of the chasm between elite culture and popular culture in late antique Christianity. In a seminal article 'Popular Religious Beliefs and the Late Ancient Historians,' he showed that Christianity succeeded in erasing the traditional opposition between high- and low-class religion, and between religion and superstition.[55] From the second half of the fourth century, there would be no sensible difference between religion and superstition. 'Christian intellectuals succeeded where pagan intellectuals had failed for centuries, both in transmitting their theories to the masses and in sharing the beliefs of the masses.' Here, it seems that he was successful, and that his argumentation had a direct and profound impact on scholarship.[56]

One of the most striking departures from the traditional leadership was the new role played by women and saints. Momigliano was particularly sensitive to the decisive role played by women in the propagation of Christianity in the Roman Empire.[57] In the wake of his studies on Greek biography, he was able to add some significant insights; in particular, he noted the transformation of both biography and historiography with the rise of the holy man in late antiquity.[58] In his study of Marcel Mauss and the history of the concept of person, he pointed out that the development of hagiography had as a consequence the exclusion of the divine from historiography.[59]

Erik Peterson's seminal book *Monotheismus als politisches Problem* was written in 1935 as a reaction to Nazism (more specifically, to Carl Schmitt's theory on *politische Theologie*). Peterson argued that Christianity eventually rejected the direct connection (through the concept of God's *monarcheia*) between monotheism and Empire. In a brillant article, Momigliano was able to modify Peterson's conclusions by calling attention to some fundamental ambivalences of Christianity towards the political realm, as well as to the transformation of the main parameters of identity, from cultural to religious, in the christianized Empire.[60]

Momigliano's coquetry brought him to belittle his own theological competence. Yet, on Christianity as on other topics, a constant flow of book reviews on early Christianity reflects the depth of his knowledge and the permanence of his intellectual openness and curiosity. Reviewing T.D. Barnes's book on Tertullian, for instance, he showed how finely tuned he was to theological issues, and when writing about Wayne Meeks's *The First Urban Christians*, he pointed out the great value of combining form criticism with sociological analysis.[61]

V

In writing about Fustel de Coulanges's *La cité antique*, which had much to say on the subject of archaic Greek religion, Momigliano noted that for Fustel, a good representative of the leading intellectual trend in the late nineteenth century, only Indians figured together with Greeks and Romans. There were no Hebrews, no Phoenicians. Like most ancient historians of the late nineteenth century, Fustel sought to eradicate all traces of the Semitic peoples from the Mediterranean world.[62] On the other hand, the creative philology of Hermann Usener, a scholar who slowly became aware 'of certain possibilities of philology which he and others had not grasped before,' deeply impressed Momigliano, who was able to offer a detailed analysis of Usener's significant contribution to the understanding of Greek religion.[63]

Momigliano did not write very extensively on classical Greek religion. What interested him most in ancient religion was directly linked to transformations and contacts among the classical tradition, Judaism, and Christianity. The most dramatic of these transformations and contacts had taken place in the Roman Empire, which was 'religiously an agglomeration of competitive groups,' a fact that prompted Momigliano to devote much energy to Roman Imperial religion.[64] Asking whether the cult of the emperor was an element of a state religion, he concluded that it was primarily a sign of indifference, or doubt, or anxiety about the gods.[65]

The interpretation of Roman religion had an important epistemological value: 'it provides questions for the whole discipline of the science of religion.'[66] If it had not been studied well enough, that was due to a lack of concrete case studies of individual religious experience, and also of a comparative approach that would not isolate pagans from Jews and Christians.[67] Momigliano was acutely aware of the specific problems posed by Roman religion, and insisted on the epistemological dangers of asking the same questions about different societies. He called attention, for instance, to the fact that religion was a culturally defined notion: whereas Roman religion and Christianity shared the clearly defined realm of 'the religious,' differentiated from other activities of daily life, the same was not true of Greek religion and of Judaism, where the borders between the different domains of life remained blurred, and the realm of religion was ill defined.[68] His work on ancient biography taught him to focus on the religious experience of the Romans, to ask himself how people in the ancient world lived their religion. He spoke about men and women in Roman religion, ever seeking concrete instances.[69]

His interest in daily religion, in the religion of simple people, and in the role of women in a highly official and ritualized religion did not mean his forgetting the faith and practice of the intellectuals. In his essay on the theological efforts of the Roman upper class of the first century BCE, Momigliano told how some intellectuals, such as Varro and Cicero, had learned to think in earnest about religion.[70] But he liked to repeat that the equation true of Rome, as well as of Greece, concerning education and religion – that the more educated one was, the less religious one would be – has never been true of Israel, where only the learned man can be truly religious ('ein am ha-aretz hassid' as the Mishna has it).[71] In the first century CE, indeed, Judaism was an intellectual faith, more clearly so than any other religion. In that sense, it was 'a religion of philosophers,' and the rabbis, later followed by the Fathers, to some extent acted as the philosophers in Rome. In dealing with Seneca, Momigliano pointed out that 'the type of priest who is also a spiritual director and a confessor remained almost unknown in Greece and Rome until oriental religions came to replace the old cults. No man is likely to be an effective spiritual guide if he is a priest only in his spare time.'[72]

This interesting insight, which seeks to highlight the transformation of the very concept of religion in the christianized Empire, does not carry full conviction.[73] When thinking about spiritual direction, Momigliano probably had in mind principally the Desert Fathers of late antiquity. But the monks (or the rabbis) were probably more closely related to the prophetic schools of ancient Israel than to the Temple priests, who were not particularly known for the quality of their spiritual direction. It seems that here Momigliano's insight might have been sharpened by a systematic and comparative study of spiritual direction in antiquity.

Momigliano had scant sympathy for some French patterns of thought and scholarship, which seemed to him to suffer from too much theory and too little common sense. He did not trust the structuralist effort of Georges Dumézil to reconstruct archaic Roman religion on the basis of his overall conception of Indo-European 'tri-functionalism.' To his refutation Momigliano added, in the 1980s, a violent polemic against Dumézil's alleged 'sympathy for Nazi culture' in the 1930s and early 1940s. The polemics, which soon spread to two communities of scholars across the Alps, added little to the clarification of basic problems of Roman – or Indo-European – religion.[74]

VI

As is by now pretty clear, Momigliano's contribution to our understanding of ancient religions amounts to much more than a series, even an impressive one, of studies on aspects of Judaism, Christianity, and Greek and Roman religion. Throughout his lifetime, the main thrust of his effort was to insist upon the need to think about ancient civilizations together. He often called attention, for instance, to the importance of Iran as the context of both the Greek and the Jewish intellectual and religious transformations. Yet his principal interest remained in 'thinking together' the three sides of the 'triangle' of Mediterranean culture and religion: the Graeco-Roman heritage, Israel, and Christianity, which sought to offer a synthesis of the other two. The comparative study of ancient religions was not intended as descriptive only: he insisted on the need to theorize it.[75]

Momigliano's attitude to theory, however, remained ambiguous: he felt on slippery ground in the presence of sociological and anthropological notions applied too forcefully to ancient religion. Yet despite his demand for concrete examples, he did not shy away from comparative overviews and the search for major transformations in ancient religion. A case in point is his daring 'Empietà ed eresia nel mondo antico.'[76] Marshalling evidence from Babylonia and Egypt through Greece and to early Christianity, Momigliano was able to sketch the birth and early development of the complex idea of heresy and the passage from tolerance to intolerance in late antiquity. It is noteworthy in our present context that he began this study with an invocation of Pettazzoni ('la cui memoria mi è cara'), who taught in Rome when Momigliano was studying there with Gaetano De Sanctis, a Roman historian who was a Catholic with strong religious interests, for instance in prayer and in early Christianity.[77]

In his reflection on Karl Jaspers's theory of an 'Axial Age' (*Achsenzeit*), 'The Fault of the Greeks,' Momigliano stated that the foundation of the *collegium trilingue* was primarily a Roman and Jewish affair, and called attention to the fact that 'it was precisely in the atmosphere of the Augustan peace that the Jews produced a sect that soon turned to Greek proselytes and to Greek language as its main sphere of action.'[78] Even in the study of early Christianity, the most obvious place to look for the Jewish influence on religion in the Roman world, Momigliano noted that classical scholars had too often sought to ignore the Jewish dimension. That was true, in particular, for Droysen, the great nineteenth-century student of Hellenism.[79]

Comparison, hence, meant first of all a confrontation between the sacred history of the Hebrews and the profane history of the Greeks and Romans. Momigliano used to repeat that his childhood education had permitted him to move freely between these borders: 'I never found the task of interpreting the Bible any more or any less complex than that of interpreting Livy or Herodotus.'[80]

In his seminal essay 'Religion in Athens, Rome, and Jerusalem in the First Century BC,' Momigliano studied the semantic fields of 'hope' and 'faith' in Greek, Latin, and Hebrew.[81] Calling attention to the different places and roles of education in the three religions, he analysed the cultural differences and their consequences for the perception of religion.[82]

One of the most fruitful loci for the passage of religious ideas Momigliano found, in one of his very last essays, in the prophecies conserved in the Sibylline Oracles, with their Greek origin, their Roman development, and the Jewish and Christian *engouement* with them, which led to their transformation and offered Jews and Christians a common ground in the face of the pagan perception of history.[83]

VII

The 'philosophic historian' sought to understand profound mutations in religious and intellectual sensitivities. It is, then, precisely because he was a 'philosophic historian' that Momigliano also came to write as a comparative historian of religion *sans le vouloir*, or rather *sans l'avoir voulu* (unlike Molière's M. Jourdain, who spoke prose *sans le savoir*).

The important posthumous essay 'From Bachofen to Cumont,' one of a series of lectures given at Chicago in 1986 under the general heading 'Questions on the Historiography of Religion,' offers many insights into Momigliano's perception of the modern study of religions, its tasks and achievements.[84] The philosophic historian will seek to write about religion as a cultural historian, interested in history as a whole. Hence stems Momigliano's suspicion of professional historians of religion. To paraphrase Clemenceau's famous *mot* on war and generals, he considered religion too serious a topic to be left to its own specialists. What Momigliano offered, then, was an enterprise of creative transformation, the *Aufhebung* of the history of religions, as it were. As he put it, 'in order to understand Greek and Roman religion, you had to understand what in ordinary parlance is *not* religion.'[85]

A religious agnostic, Momigliano could probably have said, like Salomon Reinach in the late nineteenth century, that it was not necessary to be a believer in order to study religion in scholarly fashion, but it did not hurt to have been one. He was not averse to work done by religious historians, provided it was good work. What worried him were wrong methods, not strong beliefs. Total honesty in observing and analysing the evidence was what counted most: a building was not a place of cult just because its historian was religious.[86] He could be sarcastic, even ferocious, however, when dealing with the work of theologians, especially of the German persuasion, since their primary, 'Vichian' epistemological principle – the great divide between the history of Israel and that of the nations – ran against Momigliano's most deeply ingrained methodological attitude.[87]

He did not ignore or despise problems connected to the (productive) tension between scholarship, or, more broadly, reason, and religion. In the last lines of *Alien Wisdom*, he quoted (in reference to the Hellenistic world) A.D. Nock's remark (about Protestantism) that there could be no stopping in the compromise between revelation (or tradition) and reason once the process had been started.

His intensive and constant involvement with the antiquarians could not have left Momigliano indifferent to these problems. The antiquarians, the first modern comparative students of religion, lived in an age when both religious identities and the new belief in the powers of science were particularly strong. Indeed, much of their work reflected a conscious effort on their part to master their cultural and religious heritage. In a sense, then, it was not only Momigliano's effort to avoid more fashionable ideologies that kept him attentive, for more than half a century, to the early modern historiographers of religion. Their fight became his fight, their struggle to find, define, present, and defend their complex religious and cultural identity, he made his own.

In that sense, Momigliano was perhaps the last denizen of the *République des Lettres.*

He was, then, fundamentally a humanist, and he approached history, or rather lived in it, as Richard Rorty would later propose we live with philosophy, in a permanent dialogue of sorts with the great minds of the past.

For him, antiquarianism was a humanism; it expressed the continuity of culture in times of upheaval, when the barbarians were at the gates, or even when they had invaded the city. Momigliano, who had a strong sense of the tragedy of history, spoke of his excitement when he read, for the first time, the suggestion made in 1895 by Otto Seeck concerning the decline and fall of the Roman Empire. Seeck had claimed that the process was due mainly to a negative selection of elites, to an inverse Darwinism, as it were, a survival not of the fittest but of the worst: 'Die Ausrottung der Besten.'[88] In Momigliano's bleak century, there was no doubt much suggestive power in Seeck's words (the new century does not seem to have begun much better; the guns speak, literally within earshot, as I write this essay in Jerusalem in August 2001).

In his piece 'What Flavius Josephus Did Not See,' Momigliano had claimed that for all his intellectual powers, Josephus was unable to perceive the crucial importance of apocalyptic trends in contemporary Judaism.[89] He had sought to read Judaism with Greek lenses, remaining blind to the revolution in Palestinian Judaism, a revolution that would highlight the religious experience of the individual. Momigliano was of course aware that in order to understand ancient religion, one had to understand the religion of the individual. But his lack of religious 'musicality' did not encourage him to invest too many effort in that direction. That task he left to others. The transformation of the religious history of late antiquity in the last generation, thanks in great part to his student Peter Brown, owes much to Momigliano's pioneering efforts. Despite the general recognition of Momigliano's impressive stature and achievement, however, one is left with a sense that the thrust of his impact is not usually acknowledged enough.

I have compared Momigliano's lack of religious 'musciality' to Weber's. As in Weber's case, Momigliano's superior intellectual powers permitted him to open new trails in research precisely because of his boundless intellectual *curiositas,* which, throughout his life, constantly revealed to him new problems and new cultures. For a manifesto of antiquarianism as 'la science pour la science,' one can do worse than quote Momigliano once more: 'The only justification for the history of scholarship is the promotion of scholarship itself. We must go into the past of the discipline we profess in order to learn something new or to be reminded of something which we had forgotten.'[90]

Notes

I should like to express my thanks to Riccardo Di Donato for his comment on a draft of this paper.

Most of Momigliano's articles were reprinted in a series of nine *Contributi alla storia degli studi classici e del mondo antico,* published by Edizioni di Storia e Letteratura in Rome from 1955 (the first *Contributo*) to 1990 (the ninth and last *Contributo,* published posthumously, edited by Riccardo Di Donato). These volumes are referred to by the title *Contributo* and a Roman numeral in the notes below. Full details about the first publication of the different texts are given in the *Contributi.*

1 See, for instance, Momigliano's 'Historiography of Religion: Western Views,' in *Contributo VIII,* 27–44, as well as his 'Ancient History and the Antiquarian,' *Contributo I,* 67–106.
2 The same passage of the *Ethics* (IV, prop. LXVII) is inscribed on the tombstone of my own mentor, Shlomo Pines, in Jerusalem.

3 'The antiquarians were not frivolous. They were aware that their attempt to combine Christian devotion with pagan tradition could succeed only if it was supported by the strength of Greek thought and by the continuity of imperial tradition' (*Contributo III*, 198–9).

4 'Roman "Bestioni" and Roman "Eroi" in Vico's *Scienza Nuova*,' *Contributo III*, 161.

5 See, for instance, 'Prophecy and Historiography,' in Momigliano, *Essays on Ancient and Modern Judaism*, ed. S. Berti (Chicago and London, 1994 [Italian ed., Turin, 1987]) [hereafter *EAMJ*], 102. See also 'Historiography of Religion: Western Views' (n1 above)

6 See Momigliano, *Alien Wisdom: The Limits of Hellenization* (Cambridge, 1975), 1.

7 On his relations with Croce, see C. Dionisotti, *Ricordo di Arnaldo Momigliano* (Bologna, 1989). Dionisotti records Croce's invitation to Momigliano, in 1946, to become director of the institute he had established in Naples.

8 See, for instance, G.W. Bowersock, 'Arnaldo Momigliano e la storiografia dell'antichità in USA,' in *Omaggio ad Arnaldo Momigliano: Storia e storiografia sul mondo antico*, ed. L. Cracco Ruggini (Como, 1989), 43–51, especially 49; G.W. Bowersock and T.J. Cornell, 'Introduction,' in A.D. Momigliano, *Studies on Modern Scholarship*, ed. Bowersock and Cornell (Berkeley, Los Angeles, London, 1994) [hereafter *SMS*], xviii; P. Brown, 'Arnaldo Dante Momigliano, 1908–1987,' *Proceedings of the British Academy* 74 (1988): 404–42, especially 438–9; G.W. Bowersock, 'Momigliano's Quest for the Person,' in *The Presence of the Historian: Essays in Memory of Arnaldo Momigliano*, ed. P. Steinberg (*History and Theory* Beiheft 30 [1991]), 27–36, especially 27–8.

9 D. Sabbatucci, 'Raffaele Pettazzoni,' *Numen* 10 (1963): 1–41, especially 2. A similar argument was made a few years later at the Hebrew University of Jerusalem, when Gershom Scholem proposed to appoint Martin Buber to a chair of comparative religion. See G.G. Stroumsa, 'Martin Buber as a Historian of Religions: Presence, not Gnosis,' *Archives de sciences sociales des religions* 101 (1998): 1–17.

10 See, for instance, 'Per la storia delle religioni nell'Italia contemporanea: Antonio Banfi ed Ernesto de Martino tra persona ed apocalissi,' *Contributo IX*, 701–21.

11 See, for instance, his review of Eliade, *Cosmos and History: The Myth of Eternal Return* and *Birth and Rebirth: The Religious Meaning of Initiation in Human Culture*, in *Contributo III*, 755–8.

12 Most of these studies are reprinted in *SMS*.

13 See, for instance, 'Christianity and the Decline of the Roman Empire,' in *Contributo III*, 74; *SMS*, 43.

14 See, in particular, J. Weinberg, 'Where Three Civilizations Meet,' in *The Presence of the Historian*, ed. Steinberg (n8 above), 13–26.

15 See, for instance, 'After-Dinner Speech on the Occasion of the Award of the Degree of D.H.L., L.C. at Brandeis University, 22 May 1977,' in *Contributo VIII*, 430–432, especially 431.

16 See R. Di Donato, 'Materiali per una biografia intellettuale di Arnaldo Momigliano,' *Athenaeum* 83 (1995): 213–44, especially 225–7. On Max Weber, see 'A Note on Max Weber's Definition of Judaism as a Pariah Religion,' in *EAMJ*, 171–7.

17 See, for instance, *EAMJ*, 15, and *Alien Wisdom*, passim.

18 *EAMJ*, 3.

19 'Prologue in Germany,' in *Contributo IX*, 543–62, on 543.

20 'After-Dinner Speech' (n15 above), 431.

21 *Contributo IV*, 152.

22 *EAMJ*, xxiv.

23 Peter Green, 'Ancient History and Modern Historians,' *Times Literary Supplement*, 22 July 1955.

24 'In Memoriam – Eduard Fraenkel,' *EAMJ*, 213–16.

25 'The Use of the Greeks,' in *Contributo VI*, 322.

26 *EAMJ*, 190.

27 Momigliano had already held a visiting professorship at Chicago in 1958.

28 'In Memoriam – Leo Strauss (February 1977),' *EAMJ*, 189.

29 'Arnaldo Dante Momigliano,' 434.

30 For his last statement, see E. Bickerman, *The Jews in the Greek World* (Cambridge, MA, 1998). Cf. *Contributo I*, 364.

31 'Religion in Athens, Rome, and Jerusalem in the First Century B.C.,' *Contributo VIII*, 91.

32 Bowersock, 'Arnaldo Momigliano e la storiografia dell'antichità in USA' (n8 above), 48.

33 This sentence was reported to me by Ada Rappoport-Albert. When she asked him why he was so interested in Judaism and Jewish identity, he answered, 'It is so undignified not to be, when you are one.' See also Bowersock and Cornell, 'Introduction' (n8 above), xvii.

34 See, for instance, 'Fattori orientali della storiografia ebraica post-esilica e della storiografia greca,' in *Contributo I*; 'J.G. Droysen between Greeks and Jews,' in *Contributo V-1*, 109–26; 'Time in Ancient Historiography,' in *Contributo IV*, 13–41; 'The Fault of the Greeks,' in *Contributo VI-2*, 509–23; 'Biblical Studies and Classical Studies: Simple Reflections upon Historical Method,' *EAMJ* 3–9.

35 M. Bernal, *Black Athena: The Afroasiatic Roots of Classical Civilization*, vol. 1, *The Fabrication of Ancient Greece, 1785–1985* (New Brunswick, NJ, 1987).
36 See, for instance, the last sentences of his preface to *EAMJ*, xxvvi–xxviii.
37 See Di Donato, 'Materiali' (n16 above).
38 'Biblical Studies and Classical Studies (n34 above), 7.
39 'Jews and Greeks,' in *EAMJ*, 26–7. See also most articles reprinted in part 1 of *EAMJ*.
40 'The Second Book of Maccabees,' in *EAMJ*, 46–7.
41 'Problems of Method in the Interpretation of Judeo-Hellenistic Symbols,' in *EAMJ*, 57. See also his review of Goodenough's introduction to Philo Judaeus, in *Contributo IV*, 625–7.
42 'What Flavius Josephus Did Not See,' in *EAMJ*, 70.
43 'An Apology of Judaism: The *Against Apion* by Flavius Josephus,' in *EAMJ*, 58–66, especially 66.
44 'Time in Ancient Historiography' (n34 above), 36.
45 See, for instance, 'Remarks on Eastern History Writing,' in *Contributo III*, 237, and the reference there to Bickerman, *Revue biblique* 59 (1952): 44–5. See, further, 'Persian Historiogaphy, Greek Historiogaphy, and Jewish Historiography,' in Momigliano, *The Classical Foundations of Modern Historiography*, with a foreword by R. Di Donato (Berkeley, Los Angeles, Oxford, 1990), 5–28, especially 22.
46 'Persian historiography' (n45 above).
47 'Arnaldo Dante Momigliano,' (n8 above), 434.
48 'Problems of Method' (n41 above), 57.
49 'Biblical Studies and Classical Studies' (n34 above), 19, for instance.
50 'Prophecy and Historiography' (n5 above), 105.
51 'Christianity and the Decline of the Roman Empire' (n13 above), 85.
52 'Pagan and Christian Historiography in the Fourth Century A.D.,' in *Contributo III*, 91.
53 See his 'Geschichtsschreibung,' in *Religion in Geschichte und Gegenwart* 4, vol. 3, pp. 803–14; in oral communication, Cancik expresses his view in stronger terms.
54 'Christianity and the Decline of the Roman Empire,' 74–5.
55 The article, originally published in 1971, is reprinted in *Contributo V-1*, 73–92.
56 See, for instance, A. Murray's words: 'Of the model of an elite religion contrasting with a popular religion ... Arnaldo Momigliano's devastating critique had once and for all delivered us' ('Peter Brown and the Shadow of Constantine,' *Journal of Roman Studies* 73 [1983]: 191–203); and R. Lane Fox's reference to 'Momigliano's insight that the old pagan barrier between

upper-class propriety and "popular superstition" was dissolved for Christian historians' ('The Life of Daniel,' in *Portraits: Biographical Representation in the Greek and Roman Literature of the Roman Empire*, ed. M.M. Edwards and J. Swain (Oxford, 1997), 179.

57 See 'The Life of Saint Macrina by Gregory of Nyssa,' in Momigliano, *On Pagans, Jews, and Christians* (Middletown, CT, 1987) [hereafter *PJC*], 206–21, especially 208.

58 See in particular 'Ancient Biography and the Study of Religion in the Roman Empire,' in *PJC*, 159–77.

59 'Marcel Mauss e il problema della persona nella biografia greca,' in *Contributo VIII*, 179–90, especially 189–90.

60 'The Disadvantages of Monotheism for a Universal State,' in *PJC*, 142–58. See also 'Some Preliminary Remarks on the "Religious Opposition" to the Roman Empire,' ibid., 120.

61 Respectively, in *Contributo V*, 710, and *VIII*, 399.

62 'The *Ancient City* of Fustel de Coulanges,' in *SMS*, 162–78.

63 'New Paths of Classicism in the Nineteenth Century,' in *SMS*, 251–66.

64 See 'Ancient Biography and the Study of Religion in the Roman Empire' (n58 above), 163. For a thorough analysis of Momigliano's studies of Greek and Roman religions, see M. Mazza, 'Arnaldo Momigliano e la storia delle religioni classiche,' in *Omaggio*, ed. Cracco Ruggini (n8 above), 141–58.

65 'How Roman Emperors Became Gods,' in *PJC*, 92–107.

66 'From Bachofen to Cumont,' in *Contributo IX*, 597.

67 'Ancient Biography and the Study of Religion in the Roman Empire,' 160, 165.

68 'From Bachofen to Cumont' (n66 above), 593–607.

69 'Men and Women in Roman Religion,' in *Contributo IX*, 577–91.

70 'The Theological Efforts of the Roman Upper Classes in the First Century B.C.,' in *PJC*, 58–73.

71 'Religion in Athens, Rome, and Jerusalem in the First Century B.C.,' in *PJC*, 81ff.

72 'Seneca between Political and Contemplative Life,' in *Contributo IV*, 239–56, on 239.

73 See G.G. Stroumsa, 'Du maître de sagesse au maître spirituel,' in Stroumsa, *La fin du sacrifice: les mutations religieuses de l'Antiquité tardive* (Paris, 2005), 189–214.

74 See G.G. Stroumsa, 'Georges Dumézil, Ancient German Gods, and Modern Demons,' *Zeitschrift für Religionswissenschaft* 6 (1998): 125–36. In that article, I expressed some criticism of Momigliano's decision to avoid mentioning his own membership in the Fascist party when accusing Dumézil of Nazi sympa-

thies. The document recently published by G. Fabre, 'Arnaldo Momigliano: Materiali biografici/2,' *Quaderni di storia* 27 (2001): 309–20, certainly reinforces one's sense that Momigliano's behaviour in this regard was less than heroic. One should not forget, however, the very difficult conditions of life in Fascist Italy. See how Momigliano himself, in October 1940, justified his own party membership, in R. Di Donato, 'Nuovi materiali per una biografia intellettuale di Arnaldo Momigliano,' *Atti della Accademia Nazionale dei Lincei, Rendiconti*, ser. 9, IX, vol. 11, fasc. 3 (Rome, 2000), 391.

75 In his review of a *Festschrift* for Jacob Neusner, in *Contributo VI*, 775.

76 *Contributo VI-2*, 437–58. The study was published in 1971, but Momigliano's work on the topic dates from the forties and fifties. See R. Di Donato's introduction to A. Momigliano, *Pace e libertà nel mondo antico* (Florence, 1996), xxviii–xxix.

77 'In Memory of Gaetano de Sanctis (1870–1957),' in *SMS*, 54–71, especially 55.

78 *Contributo VI*, 509–23; see especially 518.

79 'Droysen between Greeks and Jews' (n34 above), 109–26. See also 'Hellenismus und Gnosis: Randbemerkungen zu Droysens Geschichte des Hellenismus,' *Saeculum* 21 (1970): 185–8.

80 'Biblical Studies and Classical Studies' (n34 above), 3.

81 *PJC*, 74–91. Cf. Joanna Weinberg's thorough discussion in 'Where Three Civilizations Meet' (n14 above).

82 Cf. Brown, 'Arnaldo Dante Momigliano' (n8 above), 439.

83 'From the Pagan to the Christian Sibyl: Prophecy as History of Religion,' in *Contributo VIII*, 725–44.

84 *Contributo IX*, 593–607.

85 'From Bachofen to Cumont,' (n66 above), 595 (emphasis mine).

86 'Le regole del giuoco nello studio della storia antica,' in *Contributo VI*, 19.

87 On this, see, for instance, his review of the Norwegian theologian Thorleif Boman's *Das hebräische Denken im Vergleich mit dem griechischen*, in *Contributo II*, 759–64.

88 'After Gibbon's Decline and Fall,' in *Contributo VI*, 265–84, especially 271–2.

89 *EMAJ*, 67–78.

90 'New Paths of Classicism' (n63 above), 223–85.

chapter eleven

Arnaldo Momigliano and Gershom Scholem on Jewish History and Tradition

MOSHE IDEL

1. Amadio Momigliano: A 'Betrayed' 'Grandfather'?

No one is capable of choosing his progenitors; all of us are, however, able – if we wish – to decide whom to select and adopt as our predecessors. The search for illustrious predecessors is, to be sure, not only the patrimony of some epigones; giants of Jewish thought did so, too. Franz Rosenzweig believed he was the transmigration of the famous twelfth-century medieval poet and thinker Rabbi Yehudah ben Shmuel ha-Levi, whose Hebrew poems he translated into German,[1] just as Gershom Scholem chose the sixteenth-century German humanist and Kabbalist Johann Reuchlin[2] as his imaginary forebear. I assume that the two Jewish thinkers spoke metaphorically; I guess that neither really believed in any form of metempsychosis.

However metaphorical these statements of ancestry, and of course however unable they are to exhaust the rich and variegated achievements of these modern thinkers, they nevertheless contain a grain of truth, perhaps even a clue to something of the way in which those figures imagined themselves. The parallelism between the strategy used by one of the arch-anti-historicists, as Rosenzweig was, and that of a thinker like Scholem, who was commonly described as a quintessential historicist figure – in my opinion true, though it constitutes something of an exaggeration[3] – is indeed astonishing. It even constitutes something of a historical irony: there were few Jewish philosophers who – unlike Rosenzweig – attributed such a great importance to historical events as ha-Levi did; and Reuchlin, the idol of Scholem, was basically a perennialist, certainly not a historian.

Unlike Rosenzweig and Scholem, who were, to a great extent, also theologians, Arnaldo Momigliano was a professional historian. Whereas the two German Jews adopted theologians as their predecessors, Momigliano looked for a predecessor who, naturally, was a historian, a Jewish one, and an author who, quite understandably, lived in Italy.

In the following essay, I shall attempt to compare some some strands in the view of Jewish history and tradition in the writings of Scholem and Momigliano, though I shall also invoke Franz Rosenzweig's approach from time to time. The relationship between history and tradition preoccupied Momigliano. His essay 'Tradition and the Classical Historian' ends with this statement, related to the writings of Joseph Levenson, a historian of Chinese society and traditions: 'He typifies the difficulty of reasserting tradition within a historiography of change, such as we have inherited from the Greeks.'

Nor are comparisons between Momigliano and Scholem fortuitous: Momigliano not only wrote about Scholem, offering some interesting insights into his cultural background, but expressed himself in a manner that may help us understand better some implicit positions of the distinguished historian concerning Judaism. Moreover, as I shall attempt to point out, not only was Kabbalah a matter of Scholem's research in the field, it also has something to do with the manner in which Momigliano understood Judaism, prior to and independently of his acquaintance with Scholem's scholarship. Momigliano addressed both Kabbalah and its main researcher explicitly, and I shall try to use his succinct, illuminating formulations to make a modest contribution towards understanding him. No claim is made here for a comprehensive picture of Momigliano's thought, and much of what is discussed has to do with statements he made in the last part of his life. I do not know to what extent the formulations suggested below belong to the earlier Momigliano, or even whether these problems were of interest to him.

A perusal of Momigliano's writings concerning Judaism shows the dominant role played by the brother of his grandfather, Amadio, who became something of a 'grandfather.' He was an adopted – and adored – progenitor, who was responsible for much of his grand-nephew's early Jewish education. Arnaldo's admiration for him is without restraint, though he does not conceive of himself as his follower. In fact, between Amadio and the medieval early Jewish chronicler from Oria, the famous Rabbi Ahimaatz, Arnaldo chooses the latter as his intellectual predecessor.[4] It is an interesting choice, about which I shall have more to say later on. Here let me simply note that, for whatever reasons, Momigliano did not adopt the much more eminent sixteenth-century historian Azariah de Rossi as his predecessor, despite the remarkable similarities between them – they knew the same three ancient languages, and both took a more critical stance towards their own tradition – but opted instead for a much more traditional and obscure medieval figure. Raised by a late-age Kabbalist,[5] Arnaldo chose history as his academic field. As I shall attempt to show, however, his allegiance to history is not a total one, and we shall explore his resistance to a complete submission to a certain sort of history, namely, historicism. This complexity seems to me characteristic of his background more generally, and also of his decision not to divorce himself from some aspects of his religious background. I would say that my assumption will be that in Momigliano's case, as in that of any great figure, a deeper understanding does not consist in finding out the one basic assumption, but in detecting the different and divergent vectors and voices that interact in the life and the thought.

There is a distinct tone of sadness in the manner in which the discontinuity between his 'grandfather' and the future historian is formulated. Amadio never spoke with anyone about the content of the Zohar. Neither had his experiences been a topic of discussion even with his beloved 'grandson.'[6] Momigliano had the distinct feeling that a certain rupture took place between the form of Judaism his grandfather cultivated and the orthodoxy of his own family after his grandfather's death. The historian quite explicitly states that there was a failure to transmit the Jewish tradition among Italian Jews, *and that he was part of this process.*[7] The grandfather, as he describes him, using a phrase of André Schwarz-Bart's, was 'the last of the Tzaddiqim' of Italy.[8]

It should be mentioned, however, that despite the explicit choice between history and traditional experience, Momigliano does not work with the opposition between the historical and the mythical that is characteristic of Mircea Eliade, whose views Momigliano opposed.[9] Momigliano does not see himself as fallen in history, but as enacting a spiritual and intellectual mode already in existence not only in the academy but also in Jewish tradition, though it seems that some form of nostalgia for the mystical past of Judaism in Italy is also evident.

2. A Transcending Experience in Judaism

Let me start with what seems to me to be a major statement about Judaism, which may help make sense of some of Momigliano's other, less explicit formulations. When he describes his grandfather, we may discern that he attributes a kind of sublime status to Amadio: 'The whole development of Judaism led to something ahistorical, eternal, the Law, the Torah ... History had nothing to explain and little to reveal to the man who meditated the Law day and night.'[10]

This is a seminal statement. I read it as assuming the possibility of a combination in Momigliano's thought of both anti-historicism and historicism. Though dealing with the manner in which his grandfather experienced his study of the book of the Zohar, Momigliano generalizes and claims that it is just a particular example of a larger development that shaped Judaism in a certain manner: 'the whole development of Judaism.' Thus, we may assume that for Momigliano Judaism developed from a more historically oriented religiosity, perhaps the biblical Judaism, to an ahistorical one, probably commencing with rabbinic Judaism. What this passage says is that history does not explain, religiously speaking, something valuable to those Jews who were immersed in the study process or in the ritual, because it was not conceived of as a message delivered in a direct manner, like the canonical scriptures. The master key was felt to be already found in the fathoming of their content. This does not necessarily mean that Jews, whether or not great scholars, did not, for the sake of their religious, economic, or political survival, learn, understand, and accommodate their religious and secular practices – or often misread the meaning of the historical circumstances of their lives. The question, as formulated by Momigliano, is to what extent the traditional forms of post-biblical Judaism conceived the book of history to be a meaningful text. His answer seems clear and in the negative. Judaism in the manner contemplated by Momigliano is conceived of as frozen in its gravitation around the contemplation of the text. It does not take into consideration the centrality of ritual, customs, and communal life, so cardinal for the manner in which Jews traditionally lived.

Again, Momigliano's Judaism stands at the opposite pole from Eliade's description of Judaism as the historical religion par excellence. In fact, Momigliano's approach is echoed in the praise of his friend Joseph Levenson, a historian of China's traditional culture. Levenson, had he not died in an accident, would, according to Momigliano, 'have reinterpreted Judaism – the faith of his fathers, and his own faith – in terms of a recurrent affirmation of life according to traditional patterns.'[11] Momigliano conjures up Levenson, as he will do later the dead Rosenzweig, in order to depict a certain form of Judaism, consonant with his own understanding of the trans-historical experience of the traditional student of the Law. I shall have more to say below about patterns, models, and tradition. I am not acquainted with the plans Levenson might have had to turn his expertise in traditional Chinese studies in the direction of Judaism. Though Momigliano may correctly diagnose some hidden intention of his friend, the statement may just as well point to his own hidden agenda. How the categories used by Levenson to elucidate Chinese traditional culture could be applied to traditional Judaism is a matter that transcends both my expertise and the framework of this modest study. But it seems that what he expected from Levenson he had once expected from another figure he admired, Rosenzweig.

3. Gershom Scholem versus Franz Rosenzweig

Momigliano seems to extrapolate from his acquaintance with the manner in which his 'grandfather' allegedly experienced his study of the book of the Zohar, to what he conceived to be a major development in Judaism. But this extrapolation does not hold water. Momigliano himself, as has been pointed out, reported that his grandfather never revealed anything about his Kabbalistic studies. Neither do I assume that the young Arnaldo, no more than sixteen years old at the time his grandfather died, was capable of drawing the aforementioned conclusion from observing Amadio. So the question is, how did he know about the transcending experience related to the study of the Law? I would suggest that his description of his grandfather, and of the 'whole development of Judaism,' comes, at least in part, from a much later source: Rosenzweig's vision of Judaism as an ahistorical religion (compared to Christianity as the historical religion).

In her introduction to Momigliano's essays on Judaism, Silvia Berti has pointed out the affinity between the anti-historicist casts of mind of two other Jewish thinkers of Momigliano's generation, with whom he was well acquainted: Leo Strauss and Scholem.[12] I am confident that with Strauss anti-historicism was a basic approach. With Scholem, however, the situation is much more complex. In my opinion, if as a phenomenologist Scholem was much closer to the anti-historicists, as a historian and a Zionist he was, on some main points, much closer to the historicists.

In our context, the question is how Momigliano saw Scholem's scholarly project in the light of his own view that some forms of Judaism, like Kabbalah, both transcended and sublated history. Let me quote a fascinating remark of Momigliano's that only a thinker who had himself transcended historicism could produce. He claims that Rosenzweig, 'if he had lived longer, would have been the only scholar capable of challenging Scholem's interpretation of Judaism.'[13] This conjuration of a thinker dead for more than forty years is indeed formulated in the context of Scholem's vision of Judaism, but we may only guess what might have been the direction of Rosenzweig's alternative interpretation from the philosopher's relatively articulated anti-historicist legacy. Such a reading would be consonant with the manner in which Momigliano conjured up the hypothetical reinterpretation of Judaism by Levenson, as quoted above: dealing with permanence rather than with changes. All this despite *his* understanding of history as having nothing to do with permanence: 'I cannot forsee history ever becoming a science of the permanent.'[14] For him history 'is always a choice of facts fitting into a static or dynamic situation which appears worth studying.'[15] Momigliano then adduces a passage in which Scholem himself pointed out the profound political differences between himself and Rosenzweig.[16] As important as this passage is, however, I believe that Momigliano's remark hints at a divergence that is more systemic.

My assumption is that between Scholem, the scholar of Kabbalah with a strong historical orientation, and Rosenzweig, who was rather allergic to mysticism but had been interested to a certain extent in Kabbalah, Momigliano conceived of Rosenzweig's thought as more consonant with what he understood to be the 'whole development of Judaism.' Or, to put it in other terms, between Scholem, whom he conceived of as a sort of anarchist,[17] and Rosenzweig, the conservative figure, Momigliano definitely preferred the latter. As great a historian as he was, when he thought about Judaism, he was much more inclined to envisage it as a phenomenon that transcended history, at least in the moments of intensely experienced Torah study. Again, there may be a difference between a more historical Momigliano's apparent embracing of an evolutionary vision of religion, and Rosenzweig's essentializing approach to the structure of Judaism as ahistorical. I do not claim Rosenzweig as the specific source of Momigliano's vision of Judaism, but his statement about Rosenzweig's ability to offer a different interpretation than Scholem's demonstrates that Momigliano wished that such an interpretation would be offered.

4. Tradition, Mysticism, and Messianism
in Momigliano and Scholem

It seems that Momigliano's adherence to an anti-historicist orientation à la Rosenzweig, as opposed to the more change-oriented approach espoused by Scholem the historian, is nowhere more pronounced than in the case of messianism. In his description of the culture of Italian Jews, Momigliano emphasizes the fact that Kabbalism survived better – held on longer – than Talmudism. But with his grandfather an end comes to it, too. In this context, Momigliano wrote rather elegiacally, 'Jewish culture has seldom been transmitted in the sense we Jews intended it to be transmitted.'[18] This is no doubt a general statement about the decay of traditional study of Judaism in Italy. However, its context is much more personal: it has to do with the discontinuity between the study of the Zohar by Amadio and its non-transmission to the next generation. It is in fact Arnaldo himself who did not continue this tradition. He, who studied Hebrew under Amadio, was a natural candidate to continue the tradition. Here we have a tension between his awareness of the need for transmission, and of tradition in general – 'we Jews' – and the fact that he nevertheless did not perpetuate his grandfather's tradition. Still, the adolescent Arnaldo could hardly blame himself for not continuing the tradition, since the grandfather refused to discuss it with anyone. Interestingly enough, Momigliano was not content with surveying the Kabbalistic tradition in Italy: as he confessed, he attempted to find out whether his grandfather was part of a broader Kabbalistic tradition in the family but in the end did not find any evidence of such a possibility.[19]

Elsewhere, Momigliano identifies the orthodox Kabbalists with Tradition itself: 'When the Kabbalists turned into apostates or illuminists or, finally, Zionists – and then gather in the streets to march into a promised land – no model and no tradition can serve Scholem.'[20] Momigliano also describes Scholem as unclassifiable at the point where 'his Zionism and his kabbalistic pursuits intersect.'[21] 'Tradition' and 'model' are thus rather similar categories, and I would like to learn something from the term model: it implies a relatively fixed pattern that is recognizable beyond variants and thus may be classified. Thus, it is reminiscent of the concept of permanence attributed to Chinese and Jewish traditions, as envisioned, at least in principle, by Joseph Levenson. I assume that this permanence is embodied by spiritual preoccupations rather than by other forms of religious activity.

Interestingly enough, the tradition, or the Kabbalah, is described by Momigliano as connected also to Scholem's statement that if he believed in transmigration he would conceive of himself as the incarnation of Johann Reuchlin – again an instance of some form of permanence.[22] It seems that Momigliano suspected that Scholem had some affinities with the great religious anarchists he described in his academic studies.[23]

It is here that the orthodoxy of the historian becomes quite evident. He draws a sharp line between the Kabbalistic phenomena, which are understood to constitute tradition, and their antinomian transformations, which presumably include also Zionism. As long as study is the focus of a certain approach, it remains in the domain of tradition. Any attempt to put it into practice turns it into anarchy. This stark distinction may constitute the background of Momigliano's insistence that 'the world that was closest to him was not one of practice but of theory.'[24] So what Scholem conceived of as a major development in Judaism, namely, the intersection between theory and praxis, or the entrance of Jews into history by creating a messianic movement and then Zionism – the culmination of a tradition – Momigliano conceived of as its moment of break. In his essay 'The Apocalypse and Exodus,' he wrote about messianic time not as apocalypse but as an aeon in which the strengthening of the 'joy of a contemplative life under the Law' took place.[25] I suspect that the resort to the concept of contemplation is reminiscent much more of the meditative manner in which Philo described the evasive sect of Therapaeutes in his *De vita contemplativa* than of the actual practices of any ordinary rabbinic yeshiva. It is in this essay, in which the attitude towards messianism and apocalypticism becomes quite reticent, that he reveals his reserve also towards Scholem's academic project. 'The anomic impulse is repressed by normative Judaism practically until the nineteenth century: anomie was brought back into fashion by G. Scholem in the twentieth century.'[26] I assume that 'anomie' is a word paralleling 'antinomianism.' This statement is, in my opinion, true: Scholem identified his vision of messianism as apocalyptic above all, and as disruptive of the rabbinic order. So, for example, Scholem states: 'The very historical research of the topic of messianism is new. Today, we are all wise, we all understand [this topic], we all read *Zion*, we all read books on messianic movements.'[27] Elsewhere he states that to the extent that messianism entered 'as a vital force in the messianism of the mystics, it is permeated by apocalypse and it also reaches ... utopian conclusions which undermine the rule of the Halakhah ... in the days of redemption.'[28] He also writes, 'When the Messianic idea appears as a living force in the world of Judaism ... it always occurs in the closest connection with apocalypticism.'[29] At least in an implicit manner the 'historical consciousness' mentioned by Scholem in this context has to do with his own studies of messianism. His acknowledgment of the affinities between the national renascence and his own deep concern with history is quite explicit.[30] Thus the combination of mysticism and messianism is conceived by Scholem as having been the very motor of history since the seventeenth century, to the extent that an active attitude has been adopted by Jews.

Momigliano, however, divorced nationalism and religion, allowing the expression of national feelings and activities to Jews in Italy.[31] But, by contrast, a Jewish religious movement, especially a messianic one, would constitute a sort of aberration, at least in so far as Italian Jews were concerned. It would mean, according to Momigliano's logic, a betrayal of their national commitment to the surrounding society and politics by adopting independent forms of activity, and a betrayal of the spiritual or the metahistorical structure of Judaism by submitting it to the vicissitudes of history. Therefore, there is no deep structural difference between Scholem and Momigliano: both regard nationalism as part of historicity, but whereas the former integrates nationalism and religion into an inseparable unity, the latter starkly distinguishes between the two. It takes, however, only a superficial reading of Scholem's monumental *Sabbatai Sevi*, to discern how deeply immersed Italian Jews and their spiritual leaders were in the course of the Sabbatean movement.

In fact, according to Scholem, it is not only the 'intersection' between messianism and mysticism that created public effervescence but even mysticism itself, in many of its manifestations. According to his analysis, the mystical experience of some form of contact with a nebulous, ineffable realm of existence is inherently in tension with a more structured tradition as accepted by society.[32] It is therefore not only the messianic fervour but also the mystical act of transcending the normal mode of experience and existence that creates a tension between the ways in which the mystic understands reality and religion. This tension is also registered in the way they are understood by the common communal apperceptions. Scholem is interested less in the manner in which tradition colours the experience itself than in the contribution of the nebulous experience to tradition at the moment when it is formulated in terms of that tradition. To borrow spatial imagery, Scholem's mystic has access to an ontological realm higher than and, axiologically speaking, superior to tradition. By ascending to it, the mystic feels capable of offering, or compelled to offer, another interpretation of what ordinary people accept. In a quite anti-historicist manner Scholem writes:

> What exactly is this 'secret' or 'hidden' dimension of language, about whose existence all mystics for all time feel unanimous agreement, from India and the mystics of Islam, right up to the Kabbalists and Jacob Boehme? The

answer is, with virtually no trace of hesitation, the following: it is the symbolic nature of language, which defines this dimension. The linguistic theories of mystics frequently diverge when it comes to determining this symbolic nature. But all mystics in quest of the secret of language come to share a common basis, namely the fact that language is used to communicate something which goes way beyond the sphere which allows for expression and formation: the fact also that a certain inexpressible something, which only manifests itself in symbols, resonated in every manner of expression.[33]

Here Scholem adopts an approach that unifies all mystics throughout history in some form of linguistic universalism. Kabbalah, as a generic term, is perceived as intending to reach a transcendental realm, in so far as that is possible: 'In Kabbalah, one is speaking of a reality which cannot be revealed or expressed at all save through the symbolic allusion. A hidden authentic reality, which cannot be expressed in itself and according to its own laws, finds expression in its symbol.'[34]

I am unable to understand the meaning of 'an authentic reality' in a frame of thought other than the anti-historicist. Mysticism and Kabbalah are therefore united by a symbolic mode, and thus transcend the differences created by the particular traditions that hosted them, at least by a certain linguistic strategy, which articulates in words what is not articulated or articulable in experience. For Scholem, there is a universalistic moment in the transcendence of the tradition and experiencing of the ineffable, which only subsequently becomes a particularistic tradition after it has been articulated in words and concepts.

For Momigliano, however, the traditional Jew contemplates tradition or the Law as a structured and already articulated order, and thus his contemplation reinforces that tradition as it already is, rather than reinterpreting it. The contemplative Jew does not live under the aegis of God, but under Law, as Momigliano put it in the two cases adduced above. According to Momigliano, it is the structured Law, not an amorphous divine realm or its intuited experience, that governs the sublime religious experience. Given this articulated experience, the religious man does not have to struggle for his own formulation or look for specific meaning in history. He already has a spiritual anchor. Like Amadio, he can be silent as he constantly re-experiences this transcendental dimension. Instead of the 'ineffable,' understood as a basic category in Scholem's phenomenology of mysticism, and attributed by him to the experience of the mystic elite, Momigliano was interested in the more traditional forms of spirituality, and in the post-revelatory forms of contemplation that are strongly related to a reconfirmation of tradition. Their discussions touch different social layers and different moments in the development of the Jewish tradition. Scholem dealt more with the exceptional, Momigliano with the ordinary.

5. Did Amadio Indeed Study the Book of the Zohar?

Let me return for a moment to speculate about why Amadio did not speak with his family about the content of his studies. One way to account for it is to assume that an experience of the ineffable cannot, by definition, be conveyed in words. Scholars sometimes make such an assumption about the nature of mystical experience. This is also the case of Kabbalah, as understood by Scholem and his followers.[35] So, for example, Scholem might assume that profound truth demands silence.[36] Yet I wonder if a more down-to-earth explanation might not be more appropriate in our case. If the reading of the book of the Zohar was conceived of as study in the normal manner, namely, the digesting of the content of a book by its perusal, it is hard to understand why nothing of its content lived in Amadio's family. After all, Kabbalah was conceived of by the older and more authoritative friend of Amadio, the famous Rabbi Elijah ben Amozegh of Leghorn, as a lore that had already become an exoteric sort of knowledge. However, if we assume that the text of the Zohar had been read loudly without an effort made to fathom its meaning, but just as sacramental recitation, the absence of discussion of its content by Amadio becomes more understandable. Indeed, this was the manner in which the book of the Zohar had been studied for generations in North African popular circles.[37] Like the custom of the North African Kabbalists, Amadio is reported to have sung the famous song *Bar Yohai* during the feast of Lag Ba-'Omer.[38] Since this custom could have been known also in Northern Italy, especially given the great concentration of North African Jews in Leghorn, I see no problem with assuming an acquaintance with it by Amadio.[39] After all, how could one begin at an advanced age to understand a rather complex book without studying with a more accomplished master, or possessing a pertinent library of Kabbalistic books? In general, studies of Kabbalah by traditional Kabbalists are not so much concerned with this book as with Lurianic texts.

6. A 'Spiritual Orientation,' or: How to Write Jewish History

In a review of Cecil Roth's *History of the Jews in Venice* written early in his academic career, Momigliano made the following remark:

In order to prevent our history of the Jews of Venice from being treated as a series of superficial representations, or from limiting the story to the usual generic episodes that characterize every Jewish community and differ only in minor details depending on the individual cases, we must pay attention above all to the spiritual orientation of the Venetian community and focus the narration of events on this spiritual orientation. This means that we should narrate the history of the penetration and exchange with the surrounding culture that took place within the ghetto, the conflicts and compromises to which it had to adjust ... It goes without saying that the writer of this note considers this solution as absolutely definite, and not only for the Jews of Venice.[40]

For Momigliano, it is a principal requirement for writing Jewish history to pay special attention to a 'spiritual orientation' in lieu of an anecdotal report of external events. This spiritual orientation is understood as involving exchanges with the surrounding culture. Momigliano's calls for another form of history, which focuses on spiritual activities rather than on other aspects of life, like the economy, society, or politics for example, is interesting in itself. Unlike Cecil Roth's approach, which saw the Italian Jews during the Renaissance as intellectually dependent upon Christians' possessing higher culture, Momigliano seems to imply a more interactive approach. There is, after all, an inner spiritual orientation, which can come into contact with an outer intellectual world.

I see this spiritual orientation as reminiscent of the concept of tradition and as connected to the concept of permanence in matters of spirit. This orientation can enter into a variety of exchanges with other spiritual orientations. In his essay 'Historicism Revisited,' Momigliano distinguishes quite sharply between the preliminary moral or religious judgments that precede historical research and the practice of the historian, and he assumes that not only writing history but 'even the notion of transforming history by studying history implies a metahistorical faith.'[41] I wonder whether this 'metahistorical faith' has something to do with the concept of spiritual orientation he mentioned in the passage quoted at the beginning of this section. In any case, whether the equation is accepted or not, this last formulation is reminiscent of the combination of historicist and anti-historicist factors.

7. Some Conclusions

The confrontation between the two forms of tradition expounded by these two giants of scholarship reflects their initial biographical starting points: the orthodox piety of the Piedmontese Jewry, and a version of the early twentieth-century flirtation with anarchism that still reverberated in Scholem's later vision of apocalypticism. Momigliano, as a Jew who internalized a rabbinic stance – even if he did not practise it – was fascinated by continuity, or permanence, in good rabbinic fashion. Scholem, who broke with the cultural orientation of his family towards some acculturation of German culture, was much more fascinated with antinomianism and ruptures. While Scholem celebrated his departure from his family geographically, ideologically, and culturally, Momigliano first underwent a much slower development, which brought him, after the Holocaust, far away from some of the religious aspects cultivated in his family, and from the places in which he had previously preferred to live and work. Interestingly enough, Momigliano the historian envisioned Judaism as primarily a spiritual orientation, which had little to do with other forms of history. Momigliano was suspicious of acts triggered by messianic aspirations. Scholem, on the other hand, the scholar of mysticism, was obsessed by the need to enter history and envisioned the peak of Jewish mysticism as the convergence between it and messianism, creating a popular movement.

The divergences between Momigliano and Scholem go even deeper. For Scholem, there was a very strong connection between spiritual orientations and the communal body of persons that was supposed to support them. That is why he did not believe in a double identity, or in a Jewish-German dialogue and coexistence. In a way, this is the expression of Scholem's ardent Zionism. Nevertheless, he never stopped writing and lecturing in German and in Germany.

Momigliano, on the other hand, was very proud of his – to use a modern term – hyphenated identity, as his essay on Italian Jewry amply demonstrates. He assumes that one may be a good religious Jew, confessing one's ancestral religion, and, at the same time, a good Italian citizen, participating in Italian national projects. Nevertheless, he himself was a rather cosmopolitan scholar, who mastered Greek, Latin, and Hebrew and who embraced in his scholarship a variety of ancient cultures. He constantly circulated between Pisa, London, and Chicago and sometimes visited Jerusalem. He followed the pattern that he described with reference to the major Greek historians: 'To acquire and convey his knowledge and wisdom, the historian had to detach himself from the surrounding society. In Greece the "great" historians were almost invariably exiles or at least expatriates.'[42] It would be interesting to compare this positive vision of expatriation as a condition for creativity with

George Steiner's vision of the cosmopolitan, cultured Jewish intellectuals who are creative precisely because of their detachment from a specific commitment to place or nationalism.[43] The two European scholars not only lived far from the places where they were born, using languages different from those they were born into, but also chose double academic addresses and, perhaps, also multiple passports. Like Momigliano, Steiner also sees in the text some form of motherland. Scarcely surviving the Holocaust, they both attempted to diversify their life and status by not subscribing to a single allegiance. Last but not least, both were fascinated by Scholem's scholarship – as becomes obvious from Steiner's recent *Errata* – because, in my opinion, he constituted the most important example of someone who made a historical choice very different from theirs and nevertheless succeeded tremendously from an intellectual point of view.

Scholem spent most of his life, from the time of his *'aliyah* in 1923, in the same city, Jerusalem, where he died in 1982. He concentrated his scholarship on a vast, complex, and rather neglected mystical literature pertaining to one form of religion. If, at the end of his essay on Italian Jewry, Momigliano is quoting R. Ahimaatz, a medieval Jewish author who describes the welling of the Torah from Oria and Bari, Scholem, I assume, would subscribe to the biblical verse that Torah will emerge out of Zion. We have here just another interesting variant of the well-known tensions between Jerusalem and Babylonia.

For Momigliano, the question was how to preserve Jewish religion (not Jewish history) by detaching it from the temporary, conceiving of it as governed by devotion, contemplation, or meditation on an immutable Law. Scholem was much more concerned with dramatic processes, changes, and ruptures in the development of Judaism: in the past, in the present, and, we may assume, also in the future.[44] Those changes are, for the Italian historian, more at the level of society, but do not, so to speak, concern piety. I would say that the phrase Momigliano uses in order to describe the nineteenth-century classicist Eduard Fraenkel, 'He dismissed with a characteristic ancestral gesture what was not orthodox,'[45] also fits his own approach. Immersed in historicism as a historian,[46] he still believed that there was another level of reality in which, for some Jews at least, history could be imagined as irrelevant or as a 'metahistorical faith.' I return again to a statement Momigliano made in his essay on Jacob Bernays: 'Having received a faith, he did not have to look in history for one.'[47] If his characterization of Bernays's approach is applicable to his own, then a 'metahistorical faith' is not just a certain general

worldview but also a rather religious one. What is the relationship between the practice of history and the metaphysical faith? According to
the context of his reference to metaphysical faith, the practice of history
is impossible without such an underlying faith. This faith may be explicit
or not, but it seems always to be active. Such an assumption follows from
the manner in which Momigliano described Emile Durkheim's understanding of Australian tribes: 'It is interesting that Australian totemic
society should have been Judaized by Durkheim and should have come
to resemble one of those small communities, no longer agitated by waves
of mysticism or Messianism,[48] that Durkheim, born in 1858, must have
known in the Alsace-Lorraine of his precocious and earnest childhood.'[49]

The possible impact of the rabbinic background of Emile David
Durkheim on the manner in which he described the importance of the
communal life of archaic tribes, alluded to by Momigliano, has not been
accepted, for the time being at least, in scholarship,[50] and it is not my
concern here to discuss its correctness or plausibility. It is fascinating,
however, to see the emphasis on the dissipation of the messianic fervour
as something that causes the return of the small communities to their
'rabbinic' mode, part of Momigliano's aforementioned anti-apocalyptic
propensity. It suffices to note that Momigliano formulated so explicitly
the nexus between Durkheim's religious background and the specific
claims he made as a sociologist. Might this strong, historicist affinity,
suggested by Momigliano, hold true, albeit in a looser manner, for
Momigliano's own way of understanding history? Has he, too, judaized
Hellenistic history, as he claimed Durkheim did to the totemic Australian aboriginals? My ignorance of the intricacies of the main fields to
which Momigliano contributed so much prevents me from offering a
meaningful answer, and I turn to more learned colleagues to supply one.
I would, however, say that this is not a more absurd question than
assuming that David Durkheim, alias Emile, unconsciously adopted rabbinic communal patterns for analysing distant tribes who knew even less
about rabbinism than did the Greeks.

Or was Momigliano a more detached, dispassionate scholar in the
manner in which he envisioned the dissociation between 'faith' and
scholarship in Jacob Bernays? I suspect that no simple answer is available. Faith, in the way Momigliano apparently understood it, does not
need historical action, or historical confirmation. To learn from Amadio,
even speaking might be superfluous. Faith transcended and perhaps
sometimes informed the historical approach but was in any case *not* to
be attracted into history. On the basis of a statement of Momigliano's

concerning Greek historians – 'At least the "best" historians would provide men of action with models of explanation and behaviour for what was felt to be transient in society'[51] – one would expect the metahistorical to inspire the practice of historians, if not politicians. History, therefore, is understood as addressing the meaning of mundane, contingent affairs, unlike the metahistorical, which dealt with more permanent and continuous factors. I see here a parallel to the manner in which Momigliano described the development of Judaism as reaching a moment in which history was not relevant by studying the Law. His resort to the term 'model' is reminiscent of his use of it in the context of the impossibility of relating the historical acts of the Kabbalists as described by Scholem, to prior models. However, at least in so far as modern Judaism is concerned, Momigliano did not make any effort to supply models for understanding its history. Perusing the content of Silvia Berti's wonderful collection of essays, one may ask whether a more pertinent title would not be *Essays in Ancient Judaism and Some Modern Jewish Scholars*. For modern Judaism is hardly the business of his discussions: neither the Holocaust nor the establishment of the State of Israel elicited special or elaborated treatments. Of course, he did not have to discuss them, as his main academic fields were so remote. By choosing not to do so, however, he adopts a certain attitude to modern history. His parents' death during the Holocaust and his visits to Israel were not, presumably, topics that invited his analysis, since they did not represent exchanges between Jewish thought and external cultural approaches. Those historical events are, however, dramatic upheavals that do problematize Momigliano's vision of Jewish history as mainly a cultural interplay. Nor could a 'metaphysical faith' make simple sense of them. Or, did he, perhaps, fear that by treating these events he ran the risk of becoming another 'minor' historian, dealing with local topics or tribal events, a traditionalist, as he described some Greek historians in his essay 'Tradition and the Classical Greek Historians'?

Scholem's view, however, was much more dialectical. On the one hand, historical events, or at least major traumas, were conceived of as having shaped religion, and, on the other, religious systems could shape history, as he showed in the various forms of connections he suggested between the expulsion of the Jews from Spain, the Safedian Kabbalah, Sabbateanism, and the repercussions of the latest messianic movement in quite diverse phenomena such as Hasidism, Reform, Enlightenment, and perhaps also Zionism. Unlike Momigliano, Scholem dealt at length with the crises and dramatic developments, even political ones, of his generation, and was in close contact with persons who were involved in political processes in Israel. Moreover, according to one of Scholem's statements, the experience of the trauma of the Holocaust could possibly help the scholar to understand Kabbalah better, which was itself, sometimes, a response to crisis. 'In a generation that has witnessed a terrible crisis in Jewish history,' Scholem writes, 'the ideas of these medieval Jewish esoterics no longer seem so strange. We see with other eyes, and the obscure symbols strike us as worth clarifying.'[52] It is not easy to explain how exactly a scholar might learn from the Shoah about events in medieval Spain. I suspect it was, according to Scholem, the relevance of the Kabbalistic theories about the power of evil, and the centrality of the myth of exile and redemption. But that means some form of permanence in history, or at least Jewish history – a certain type of recurrence that transcended the major changes in particular circumstances over centuries. I would say that Scholem started to believe in the pertinence of history immediately after it gave the strongest blow to the Jews. His shift from Enlightenment and Romanticism to historical modernism is – to follow a view of Reinhold Niebuhr – 'not so much confidence in reason, as faith in history. The conception of a redemptive history informs most diverse forms of modern culture.'[53] Scholem and his school of research were, indubitably, great believers in the power of history to shape Kabbalah, and in the power of Kabbalah, especially in its messianic forms, to shape the course of Jewish history. He himself assumed, as we have seen, that history might, sometimes, even teach the scholar of Kabbalah how better to understand this lore, itself a history-saturated sort of literature.

Scholem's strong emphasis on the historicity of Kabbalah notwithstanding, a description of his opus as belonging in its totality to historicism does not do justice to his more complex intellectual position. Earlier in his career Scholem embraced an anti-historicist stand, looking, as he confessed, for the essence of reality by resorting to historical tools. In a 1937 letter addressed to Zalman Schocken, a friend of Scholem's and a patron of the nascent Jewish studies in the land of Israel, Scholem described his expectations from the study of Kabbalah: 'I arrived at the intention of writing not the history but the metaphysics of the Kabbalah.'[54] He intended to 'penetrate through the symbolic plane and through the wall of history. For the mountain, the corpus of facts, needs no key at all; only the misty wall of history, which hangs around it, must be penetrated. To penetrate it was the task I set for myself.'[55]

At this relatively early stage in Scholem's career, history is no more than a misty cover that disguises the core of reality and, as such, had to be overcome. The message he was looking for was not found within history but beyond it. Scholarship is conceived of not as a construction of history but as its necessary deconstruction en route to something more valuable. This core may be understood as more articulated and much less ineffable, unlike the views about the Absolute that Scholem adopted later in his career. I assume that the trauma of the Holocaust contributed much to this change of mind. Beginning in the 1940s, Scholem searched Kabbalistic metaphysics, especially in the special structure of Lurianic theosophy, for a transfigured reverberation of Jewish history rather than one representing an ontological core of reality.[56]

To summarize some of the points made above: my assumption is that there is a stark divergence between Momigliano's and Scholem's visions of Judaism: whereas Momigliano saw the Sacred Scriptures as the ultimate object of study, elevating Jews beyond history, for Scholem it is the Gnostic antinomianism that represented what David Biale called a 'counter-history,' helping bring Jews 'back into history' through the detonation of the messianic impulses – found already in earlier Jewish mysticism – in the Sabbatean movement. Scholem emphasized developments within Judaism, and hoped for some type of convergence between Judaism and Jewish nationalism in a certain form of cultural Zionism.

With Momigliano, however, religion and history coexist, for Jews at least, on two different and unrelated spheres. That is why he insists that Scholem, notwithstanding his recurring assertion concerning the meaninglessness of the Jewish-German dialogue in his writings, nevertheless was imbued with the German culture of the beginning of the twentieth century; he even designates Scholem as belonging to German 'Catholic romanticism.'[57] I assume that by projecting upon Scholem's intellectual *Bildung* the phrase 'Catholic romanticism,' he was trying to place Scholem's mindset in a cultural framework to which he himself belonged. It is possible that he was indeed right. Scholars are rarely able to detach themselves fully from the intellectual soil that nourished them in the formative part of their academic life. As ardent a Zionist as Scholem was, and as successful a scholar as he was in Israel and abroad, it is difficult to deny the existence of a certain sense of alienation on his part from some aspects of life in the State of Israel.[58] Nevertheless, unlike Momigliano (and for our purpose also unlike George Steiner), Scholem was able not only to open a new field of research but also to establish a whole school of research, given the critical mass and the unexpected relevance of his chosen field for a broader audience, first in Israel and more recently abroad.

Last but not least: the most important divergence between the two scholars is a phenomenological one. Momigliano embraced a traditional vision of Judaism with the study of Law at its centre, in a vein not so different from that of Rabbi Ahimaatz, the first Jewish Italian historian. Scholem was much more concerned with the drastic historical developments and subversive triggers, like Gnosticism and apocalypticism,[59] that changed traditional Judaism into the much greater variety of religious outlooks that is evident in the modern period. If Scholem the historian was in search of changes in faith and history as they run together, for Momigliano the changes are reduced to history, and the faith remains part of a trans-historical sphere. Scholem, a scholar of mysticism, tuned his ears after the Holocaust to the lessons of history. Momigliano, the historian immersed in the Book of the Maccabees, preferred to listen to the voice of the rabbinic tradition he had observed in his childhood, long after the experience of the Holocaust and the establishment of the State of Israel, as if these historical events had never taken place. Maybe the true historian knows too well that there is not much to be learned from them or from other historical events. However, in order to really understand such a stance one would first have to become such a historian.

Notes

Many thanks are due to Professor Carlo Ginzburg and David N. Myers of the Department of History at the University of California, Los Angeles, for their helpful remarks, and to the editor, Professor Peter N. Miller, for his many improvements.

1 See the 1929 letter to his mother, in *Franz Rosenzweig, His Life and Thought*, ed. Nachum Glatzer (New York, 1953), 167. It seems that the importance of someone's name for inspiring his life is important in Rosenzweig's thought, and this statement should be read in that context.

2 *Die Erforschung der Kabbala von Reuchlin bis zur Gegenwart* [Pforzheim, 1969], 7.

3 My assumption is that Baruch Kurzweil's sharp polemic against Scholem's studies of Sabbateanism polarized the much more complex thought of Scholem, who came to be understood as a historicist historian, a fact that does not fit many of Scholem's own statements On this controversy, see

David N. Myers, 'The Scholem–Kurzweil Debate and Modern Jewish Histori-ography,' *Modern Judaism* 6 (1986): 261–86.

4 See Momigliano, 'The Jews of Italy,' in his *Essays on Ancient and Modern Judaism*, trans. Maura Masella-Gayley, ed. Silvia Berti (Chicago, 1994), pp. 133–4.

5 See the introduction in Momigliano, *Essays on Ancient and Modern Judaism*, ed. Berti, ix.

6 Ibid., xxv–xxvi.

7 Ibid., 133.

8 Ibid.

9 See Moshe Idel, 'Some Concepts of Time and History in Kabbalah,' in *Jewish History and Jewish Memory: Essays in Honor of Yosef Hayim Yerushalmi*, ed. E. Carle-bach, J.M. Efron, and D.N. Myers (Hanover and London, 1998), 153–88.

10 Momigliano, 'Persian Historiography, Greek Historiography, and Jewish Historiography,' in his *The Classical Foundations of Modern Historiography* (Berkeley, 1990), 23; and the remark of Robert Chazan, 'The Timebound and the Timeless: Medieval Jewish Narration of Events,' *History and Memory* 6: 1 (1994): 31–2.

11 Momigliano, *Essays in Ancient and Modern Historiography* (Middletown, CT, 1977), 175.

12 Momigliano, *Essays on Ancient and Modern Judaism*, ed. Berti, xxi.

13 Ibid., 192.

14 Momigliano, *Essays in Ancient and Modern Historiography*, 369.

15 Ibid., 367.

16 Momigliano, *Essays on Ancient and Modern Judaism*, ed. Berti, 192–3.

17 Ibid., 141.

18 Ibid., 133.

19 Momigliano, *Essays on Ancient and Modern Judiasm*, ed. Berti, xxvi.

20 Ibid., 198.

21 Ibid., 196.

22 Ibid., 197–8.

23 Ibid., 197.

24 Ibid., xxvi.

25 Ibid., 93. See also a similar remark, pp. 193–4, where he expressly describes anomia as lawlessness. As to contemplation, compare his resort to the concept of meditation above.

26 Ibid., 93.

27 G. Scholem, '*Od Davar, Explications and Implications* (Tel Aviv, 1989), 240 (Hebrew). See also his *Kabbalah* (Jerusalem, 1974), 68, 71–2; and *The Messi-anic Idea in Judaism and Other Essays* (New York, 1971), viii.

28 Scholem, '*Od Davar*, 234–35.

29 Scholem, *The Messianic Idea*, 4.

30 Ibid., viii.

31 See Momigliano, *Essays on Ancient and Modern Judaism*, ed. Berti, 226–9.

32 G. Scholem, *On Kabbalah and Its Symbolism*, trans. R. Manheim (New York, 1969), 5, 33.

33 G. Scholem, 'The Name of God and the Linguistic of the Kabbalah,' *Diogenes* 79 (1972): 60, also 62, 165, 193; idem, *On the Kabbalah and Its Symbolism*, 36; idem, *Major Trends in Jewish Mysticism* (New York, 1967), 27. Compare Scholem's earlier view that a mist covers the core of reality, and that this mist can be penetrated by historical research (n54 below).

34 G. Scholem, *On the Possibility of Jewish Mysticism in Our Time and Other Essays*, trans. Jonathan Chipman, ed. A. Shapira (Philadelphia, 1997), 140.

35 See nn 32–3 above.

36 Scholem, *On the Possibility of Jewish Mysticism*, 140.

37 See Harvey Goldberg, 'The Zohar in Southern Morocco: A Study in Ethnography of Texts,' *History of Religion* 29 (1990): 249–51; and Boaz Huss, '*Sefer ha-Zohar* as a Canonical, Sacred, and Holy Text: Changing Perspectives of the Book of Splendor between the Thirteenth and Eighteenth Centuries,' *Journal of Jewish Thought and Philosophy* 7 (1998): 295–6.

38 See Momigliano, *Essays on Ancient and Modern Judaism*, ed. Berti, 133.

39 See Riccardo di Segni, 'Commento al Bar Yochai,' *Rassegna mensile d'Israel*, 67: 1–2, i–xx (Hebrew part).

40 Momigliano, *Essays on Ancient and Modern Judaism*, ed. Berti, 226, also 227.

41 Ibid., 370.

42 Ibid., 174.

43 See Moshe Idel, 'George Steiner: prophète de l'abstraction,' in *Steiner*, ed. Pierre-Emmanuel Dauzat (Paris, 2003), 122–43.

44 See Harold Bloom's introduction to Gershom Scholem, *From Berlin to Jerusalem* (New York, 1988), xx. For the importance of ruptures in modern scholarship on Judaica, see Ivan Marcus, 'Beyond the Sefardi Mystique,' *Orim* 1 (1985): 35.

45 Momigliano, *Essays on Ancient and Modern Judaism*, ed. Berti, 213.

46 See his 'Historicism Revisited,' in *Essays in Ancient and Modern Historiography*, 365–73.

47 Momigliano, *Essays on Ancient and Modern Judaism*, ed. Berti, 169.

48 I assume that Momigliano refers to the decline of the Sabbatean movement.

49 Momigliano, *Essays on Ancient and Modern Historiography* (n11 above), 340.

50 See Ivan Strenski, *Durkheim and the Jews of France* (Chicago, 1997).

51 Momigliano, *Essays on Ancient and Modern Historiography*, 175.

52 See Scholem, *On the Kabbalah and Its Symbolism*, 3. See also his *On the Possibility of Jewish Mysticism*, ed. Shapira, 70–1. Compare also the very same idea expressed by Isaiah Tishby, *Paths of Faith and Heresy* (Ramat Gan, 1964), 22 (Hebrew). Compare also with Bloom's description of Scholem as being in 'an obsession with the imagery of catastrophe' (Harold Bloom, 'Scholem: Unhistorical or Jewish Gnosticism,' in *Gershom Scholem*, ed. Harold Bloom [New York, 1987], 217).

53 See Niebuhr's *Faith and History: A Comparison of Christian and Modern Views of History* (New York, 1949), 6, also 203. Compare Scholem's interesting remark that in his classes at the Hebrew University he does not teach reason but history, in his *On Jews and Judaism in Crisis*, ed. Werner J. Dannhauser (New York, 1976), 46.

54 Translated in David Biale, *Gershom Scholem, Kabbalah and Counter-History* (Cambridge, MA, 1979), 31.

55 Ibid. Compare, however, the different view of Scholem adduced above, according to which the supernal divine realm is not an articulated structure but a nebulous one.

56 For this shift, see more in Moshe Idel, 'Zur Funktion von Symbolen bei G.G. Scholem,' in *Gershom Scholem, Literatur und Rhetorik*, ed. S. Moses and S. Weigel (Cologne, Vienna, Weimar, 2000), 51–92.

57 Momigliano, *Essays on Ancient and Modern Judaism*, ed. Berti, 193–6.

58 See Irving Wohlfarth, '"Haarscharf an der Grenze zwischen Religion und Nihilismus." Zum Motiv des Zimzum bei Gershom Scholem,' in *Gershom Scholem zwischen den Disziplinen*, ed. Peter Schaefer and Gary Smith (Frankfurt am Main, 1995), 176–256.

59 See Moshe Idel, 'Subversive Catalysts: Gnosticism and Messianism in Gershom Scholem's View of Jewish Mysticism,' in *The Jewish Past Revisited: Reflections on Modern Jewish Historians*, ed. David N. Myers and David B. Ruderman (New Haven and London, 1998), 39–76.

chapter twelve

Momigliano, Benjamin, and Antiquarianism after the Crisis of Historicism

PETER N. MILLER

Momigliano's short essay on Walter Benjamin, published in 1980, is not a contribution to his history of classical studies. It belongs, instead, to the late Momigliano's autobiographical commentary on the German-dominated intellectual world of his youth, and to his grapplings with Scholem in particular. Less an essay in the 'problem of understanding Benjamin' – whom he seems neither to have much liked, nor understood – than a commentary on the way in which the friendship between Scholem and Benjamin informs the latter's work, Momigliano actually reverses the balance of influence between the two, seeing Scholem as the greater thinker, an opinion that became widely diffused only a decade or so later.[1]

But there is more to this encounter, seen from the perspective of our volume, than the biographical. Indeed, even if Momigliano had consigned no words to the work of Walter Benjamin, the two would make a pair, however unlikely. For while we know that Momigliano, the precocious home-schooled boy from Piedmont who had to leave his parents behind to their fate in 1939, is the most important twentieth-century historian of the antiquarian tradition, it is forgotten that Walter Benjamin, the mandarin from Berlin who killed himself on the Spanish border in 1940 when he feared that same fate for himself, is one of the most important, if overlooked, twentieth-century scholars to turn back to that same tradition. Their approaches to antiquarianism, from the different vantage points of the historian of antiquarianism who was also a bit of a practitioner, and the practising antiquary who was also alert to its history, and which converged on key figures like Bachofen, were explicitly developed *against* 'Historicism.' And however different they are, and however different the worlds they belonged to – indeed, perhaps because of these differences – placing them alongside one another makes us realize how bound up history and antiquarianism still were in the middle of the twentieth century.

By the 1920s, confidence in the German way of doing history and thinking about history – *Historismus* – was beset, and a wave of publications proclaimed its crisis.[2] Academic study of this discussion has tended to be written as a narrative of antinomies that were generated from within a disciplinary practice whose uniformity is otherwise assumed.[3] As a result, no one has perceived that, nor understood how, a focus on the practice and study of antiquarianism under these conditions could constitute a constructive response to a sense of crisis in the everyday workings of historians. This blind spot is in large measure to be explained by the disappearance of any familiarity with the history and reality of antiquarian scholarship by 1900, even among historians of scholarship, let alone historians of philosophy. Placed against this backdrop, Benjamin's interest in the varieties of antiquarian experience in the two decades before the war, and Momigliano's in the four that followed, appear for what they are: a way out of a dead end.

I

Historismus, or 'Historicism,' is a word that meant – and means – many things. It meant that every generation was equal in the eyes of God, that everything and everyone was shaped by its context, and that all judgments must be made within that horizon. It also refers, specifically, to the particular historical sensibility developed in late eighteenth- and early nineteenth-century Germany that made it possible to imagine thinking oneself back into each and every one of these epochs. A corollary of the first meaning was that no judgment of others could be reached, owing to incommensurable conditions; of the second, that judgment across horizons was in fact possible because empathetic understanding was possible – but only by Germans.[4]

The thoroughgoing contextualist side of *Historismus* could be viewed as the culmination of a process that began with the Renaissance discovery of anachronism. But the prospect of a completely historicized reality, however desirable for the historian, entailed a relativism that terrified the moralist and the moral absolutist alike. Max Weber thought he had found a way to accommodate both the diversity of facts and the historicized position of the inquirer (while showing no inclination to see in the

German soul any especial advantage). Coherence could be preserved if the inquirer could be made a sufficiently self-disciplined methodologist. Otto Hintze followed Weber in emphasizing the science of inquiry. Meinecke, in his famous *Entstehung des Historismus* (1936), looked back to Dilthey rather than Weber. He identified *Historismus* with an epoch in the intellectual history of Germany in which sensitivity to the principle of individuality, whether referring to a community or a person, emerged as the central value.

Meinecke's book is the best known of the contributions to the pre-war debate on the future of *Historismus*. Momigliano had immediately (1937) digested the argument and reached some limited conclusions about it.[5] But it is in the years afterwards that we can watch him immersing himself in the theoretical literature on 'Historicism,' of which Meinecke's was only the most recent work. These were also, however, the years of Momigliano's exile, of his flight from Italy to freedom. The conjunction of personal and intellectual itineraries is not coincidence.

In a notebook dated 'Oxford 1939–42' (but containing references to works published through 1944), Momigliano listed nearly all the major sources on 'Historicism.' Divided up into specific rubrics related to the question of historical method and social science, the notebook suggests some of the scope of Momigliano's reading during the initial period of his exile in England. Topics included 'Storia, Storicismo, Historismus, Sociologia, Sociologia II–Max Weber, Marxismo, Burckhardt, Burckhardt-Nietzsche, Crisi-Nietzsche, Humboldt-Razza, Filosofia Religione, Freud, Gibbon, XVII-XVIII secoli, XVIII secolo.'[6] This is the tip of an iceberg of reading that only occasionally obtrudes into his contemporary studies of ancient history, as in the footnotes to his 1936 study of the modern historiography on the Roman Empire and 1946 essay on Friedrich Creuzer.[7]

The first few pages of this notebook contain a series of self-conscious reflections that link events in Germany with his own condition and with the state of historical scholarship. In a text dated 30 May 1939 explaining that history is about change not immutability, and is a record of a past that is sought out, or of facts that are the explanation for other facts (including what is in the minds of those who perform the deeds that are those facts), the example that Momigliano chose to illustrate this point was the persection of Jews. 'To seek the reason for the persecution of the Jews consists in seeking the facts, or presumed ones (that is, the fact that some facts were presumed), that some people think necessary or suffi-cient in order to persecute the Jews.'[8]

A bit less than a year later, at the end of his first Cambridge lecture in the course 'Peace and Liberty in the Ancient World' (January 1940), Momigliano emphasized the importance of the history of historiography at that precise moment in time. 'For you also, I believe, the importance of the history of historiography is beyond question. No real understanding of history is possible where it is no longer possible to discover the meaning that past generations gave to the facts we are studying ... We must know the meaning of the problems, from which our problems derive.'[9]

By 1945, or as late as 1947, as Grafton has shown, Momigliano came to the conclusion that Meinecke had not really grasped the *Entstehung des Historismus*, thinking it an achievement of Voltaire and Gibbon, without realizing that they stood on the shoulders if not of giants, then of giants of erudition.[10]

Sometime between 1948 and 1951, while he was teaching at Bristol, Momigliano jotted down some 'Rules for Ancient Historians,' a title he later changed to 'Suggestions to Future Ancient Historians' and finally to 'Thoughts for the cupida antiquae historiae iuventus.' The context is obviously instructional, but the title carries us forward a quarter of a century to the 'Regole del giuoco nello studio della storia antica.' In jocular tone, Momigliano advanced some important points about the tools needed for handling evidence: knowing how to read texts and knowing how to read things. For instance, that (no. 2) 'knowledge of German does not replace the knowledge of Greek; yet knowledge of German philology is less dangerous than renounce [*sic*] of it .... (no. 4) Inscriptions and papyri give you facts only: literary texts also ideas. That is why historians ought to read especially poetry. (no. 6) Monuments do speak; but whether you believe or not to understand their language, it is better you call in an archaeologist as an interpreter. Monuments do speak, but like the Italians they talk all at the same time. The real nicety is to carry individual conversation under these conditions.'[11]

Most important, however, because of their extended focus on the importance of evidence, are three lectures in a notebook from the year 1950.[12] The first is about Benedetto Croce. What Meinecke was to German discussions of *Historismus*, Croce was to the Italian literature on *Storicismo*. Carlo Dionisotti and others have described the debt and distance the younger man felt for the older scholar.[13]

Momigliano explained that by 1914, at the latest, Croce's optimistic Hegelian belief in progress was gone. The main theme of history might be liberty, but that did not mean every story had a happy ending. For

Croce, historical knowledge was linked to moral action, not outcome. 'When a man is faced by a situation, he must know how it came about in order to act properly.'[14]

Later, Croce amended this definition, but we cannot be sure whether what Momigliano presented was his paraphrase of Croce or his interpretation of Croce. 'A sober, truthful analysis of concrete situations is what is called for from the historian, if history is to be the necessary presupposition of moral action.'[15] Momigliano's emphasis, as he drew the article to a conclusion, came back to the matter of concreteness. In that vein, he opined that Croce's greatest contribution lay not in his systematic thought but in his erudition. 'He has produced original solutions for thousands of problems of European history, literature and philosophy.' In other words, it was as a philologist, if not as an antiquary, that Croce was most successful. Finally, in summing up, Momigliano described Croce's achievement as 'a philosophy of history accompanied by and leading to solid historical research.'[16]

This, surely, is not how most people in 1950 would have characterized Croce's achievement. In this definition, as well as elsewhere in the article, one suspects that Momigliano was re-packaging Croce in the light of his own ideas about the importance of basic philological research. The conjunction certainly suggests that Momigliano's interest in antiquarianism needs to be viewed alongside his reflections on 'Historicism.'

The second essay is the text of a lecture delivered that summer, in Italy, that is Momigliano's own 'supercommentary' on the article that was to appear in December in the *Journal of the Warburg and Courtauld Institutes*. Here, as in the published piece, Pyrrhonism features, for the first time, as a causal agent. How – and why – it replaces the focus on 'Historicism' is a crucial question.

After summarizing the forthcoming article's main points, Momigliano ended by asking two questions. First, how did antiquarianism manage to survive *after* the creation of this new history for the nineteenth century? Momigliano's description of the nineteenth-century answers stressed the parallel between these and those given in the twentieth century to differentiate sociology from history – study of essences or statics over and against becoming. 'The relations between the dying antiquarianism and the rising sociology are worthy of study,' he opined. Second, 'What can the methodological experience of the antiquaries teach us *today*?' Here his answer was more complex. First of all, by denying the existence of what passed for sociology, he denied any distinction between sociology and history.

As for the methods of the antiquaries, they were now more necessary than ever.

> The method of the antiquaries – as a collection of critical experiences that helped vanquish the crisis of Pyrrhonism – is more relevant than ever. Today, as everyone knows, we are in a phase of scholarship in which too many historians, at least of antiquity, interpret the facts before being certain that the facts exist. Already we see, as if in reaction, a new Pyrrhonism, of those weary of seeing scientific journals and books full of ill-founded conjectures. Extreme conjecturalism is inevitably accompanied by Pyrrhonism. Against conjecturalism and Pyrrhonism there is only the old remedy: the cautious and methodical examination of documents with all the skills that were developed in the collaboration of antiquaries and textual critics in the seventeenth and eighteenth centuries.[17]

In 1936, in his essay on the historiography of the concept 'Hellenism,' Momigliano had argued for the need to return to studying the founders of classical philology in order to attain 'a more exact understanding of their intuitions and the speculative demands that animated them.'[18] In 1950 the discovery of 'intuitions' and 'speculative demands' no longer described the purpose of the history of scholarship. Now, against one tendency to generalize based on limited, or even inadequate, evidence, and another to dismiss all evidence out of despair that anything could be true, Momigliano counterposed, as if therapeutically, the antiquaries' painstaking attention to detail. The historical reference is telling, too: 'Pyrrhonism,' in the seventeenth century, was a corrosive scepticism associated with the Hellenistic philosopher Pyrrho of Elis that denied the possibility of knowing anything, let alone deciding between two things, and which as a guide to living therefore collapsed into an extreme conventionalism. 'Pyrrhonism' was Momigliano's way of describing Germany's collapse – or, more precisely, its intellectuals' collapse – after 1933.[19]

Methodological discussions in the inter-war years were, in Momigliano's words, heavily influenced by Schleiermacher's idea of hermeneutics. Wilhelm Dilthey's adaptation of Schleiermacher's 'hermeneutical circle' amounted to an attempt to provide a philosophical foundation – borrowed from theology, as Momigliano noted – for Prussian School history in which the individual, unique, and plural was coordinated with the communal, general, and environmental. Dilthey's failure to find a scientific foundation for history as a 'human science' precipitated the 'Crisis of Historicism.' If this was in some way responsible for the outbreak of sloppy historical thinking, then the alternative was a root-and-branch replacement of one hermeneutic by another. 'There exists,' Momigliano wrote, 'a hermeneutic of the antiquaries, much more complex and more productive than that of the theologians, which merits attention in any future theory of the historical document.'[20]

What Momigliano may have had in mind by 'antiquarian hermeneutic' is the focus of a third lecture, given by Di Donato the working title 'Philology and History.' In the beginning, there was the historical problem, by which Momigliano meant 'a situation which can be explained only with the help of some evidence which at the moment is not available, or if it is available, is not fully clear.' The historian, when he finds any evidence, has to determine what it says and if it is reliable before he can decide if it is useful for him. Interpretation, then, includes both understanding the meaning of the document and understanding its relevance. Understanding the meaning of the document 'implies the capacity of putting oneself into the position of the man who wrote a note or built a palace (or perhaps destroyed it), in order to attribute to it exactly that meaning that it had in the mind of its author ... If so, historical interpretation always means the understanding of what some people thought or did.' Interpetation of a document, or piece of evidence, is also therefore an interpretation 'of the purpose of the speaker or writer,' which is another way of saying that we want to grasp 'what was in the mind of the author of the document.'[21] (Recall that in 1939 Momigliano had used the persecution of Jews as an example of just how this worked.)

The next step, after ascertaining that the author wished to tell the truth, was to find out whether what he thought true was, in fact, true. If so, then the historian comes to the second question: Is this piece of evidence useful, or relevant, to the solution of the problem? If it is, then the foregoing 'philological process of interpretation becomes part of the historical process when we recognize that a document is relevant to research.' If it is not, however, then the philological process of dis-authentication is terminal, without being part of a historical interpretation.

'If that is true,' Momigliano concluded, 'some consequences follow: Croce argued that the basic distinction is between history and chronicles. History interprets the facts, the chronicle remembers the facts.' Philology, for Croce, was to all intents and purposes identical with chronicles – a tool for remembering; but what mattered was the interpretation, so Croce's history of historiography was really a history of interpretation.

Momigliano, in 1950, was much more sceptical than Croce ever had been. 'All that is not so certain,' Momigliano countered. 'Men indeed put aside recollections of facts in various ways: monuments, inscriptions, chronicles, documents. The historian needs chronicles as [he needs] any other document. But he must interpret them just as much as any other document to make sure that they are relevant to his problem.'[22] Philology was part of history, even – in so far as history is about evidence and philology offers tools for evaluating evidence – 'the most basic part of history.'[23] In other words, facts were not 'givens,' nor the tools of evidence 'auxiliary' or preparatory. Croce, Momigliano wrote in that other essay of 1950, 'knew the difference between search for truth and propaganda and despised those who mistook the latter for the former ... which explains his later hostility towards the Fascist regime.'[24] But it was Momigliano, not Croce, who drew the consequences for the practice of history. If the fascists had taken the search for truth too lightly, the only response was to take it even more seriously. 'Exactness,' he continued in 'Philology and History,' 'is not irrelevant to the historical inspiration, it is indeed [an] essential part of it ... Any historical research starts by understanding and checking evidence and concludes by making the evidence so checked a part of our living experience by telling how things happened and solving the probem. Historical experience is so given a widened maturity.' Mistakes, of course, were always possible. But mistakes made at the philological stage were the most 'dangerous' because they were the 'most difficult to contest.'

The intensity with which Momigliano turned to focus on the proper handling of evidence as the core of historical practice and, therefore, the most important narrative thread in the history of historiography, marks the line of demarcation from Croce and also from the last attachment to *Historismus*. It fully justifies Di Donato's assertion, elsewhere in this volume, that for Momigliano antiquarianism is not an object of study in itself but part of a much vaster investigation of the forms of historical knowledge. There is an overtly moral fervour to Momigliano's discussions of historical method after 1950. The essays of 1954–5, 'A Hundred Years after Ranke' and 'Il linguaggio e la tecnica dello storico' are decisive in this regard. In the first, he worried about the 'little respect' and 'actual contempt' for the rules of doing history. Others denied the power of ideas, rejected progress, and submerged the individual in some collective body or consciousness. 'You can explain the French Revolution as you like,' Momigliano wrote, 'but there is always a moment in which you have to take account of the fact that a certain individual was either angry or in love or ill or drunk or stupid or cowardly.' How was this to be accommodated to a perspective that left no place for individuals?[25]

The proliferation of facts and of narratives, Momigliano concluded with characteristic understatement, made the historian's work difficult. His answer was no more and no less than a return to rigour. 'It is more than ever essential to be strict in the examination of evidence. We must not allow people to get away with doubtful pieces of evidence.'

He also urged the need for self-knowledge. 'The clearer we are about the theme of our own research, the clearer we become about our own bias.'[26] (This statement surely, is unobjectionable, though probably unsatisfying to those whose arguments emphasized unconscious drives or class commitments.) In this essay, Marxists, psychoanalysts, racialists, Catholics, and sociologists fill the role of modern Pyrrhonists, calling the very enterprise of historical scholarship into doubt. And Momigliano, like Sebastian Le Nain de Tillemont or Jean Mabillon, insisted on the curative powers of a discriminating method. Perhaps these various disquisitions on method are the public acknowledgment of his own 'bias.' So too his acid observation on the subject of racialist theories of history that it was too soon to 'pronounce the funeral oration or to offer up a balanced judgment of a theory that was elevated to the philosophy of a sadistic assassin.'[27]

In his open letter to N. Abbagno of 1955, 'Il linguaggio e la tecnica dello storico,' Momigliano continued along these same lines. He offered that 'the true difficulty in the profession of the historian seems to me to lie in the relation that there is between stabilizing the facts and interpreting.' Stabilizing facts can be so difficult at a distance of decades or centuries or millenia that fulfilment of these two tasks could be separated by generations. The final synthesis might be 'the ideal to which the historian tends' with the purpose of orienting himself in the world.[28] But that was a distant goal and always subsequent to the historian's daily skirmish with the evidence.[29] In this essay, the epistemological problem of the historian judging his sources is expanded into the moral problem of judging historical figures – impossible from a historicist perspective.

'We judge and are judged.'[30] If one aspect of both German *Historismus* and Crocean *Storicismo* was a retreat from judgment out of either a hypersensitive fear of anachronism or a pure relativism, then Momigliano, whose parents had been killed by the Nazis, could not be a 'Historicist.' In 1958, as Peter Brown has noted, he chose for his own tombstone the epitaph 'His faith was that of a freethinker, without dogma and without hatred. But he loved with a son's devotion the Jewish tradition of the Fathers.' In a review published in 1959, he exposed Helmut Berve's Nazi past – as in most such cases, an open secret – and in 1967 he wrote more generally about the close connections between German scholars of ancient Greece and National Socialism.[31] His response to their scholarship was to urge better scholarship. His response to the general desire not to be reminded of such uncomfortable facts was to insist upon the cathartic power of the history of historiography.[32]

'Historicism' à la Meinecke, with its deep roots in early Romantic German thought, sought to find in the detail of history itself a transcendent moral identity for the inquiring individual. Momigliano rejected this basic claim in his significantly titled article 'Historicism Revisited.' 'Either we possess a religious or moral belief independent of history, which allows us to pronounce judgment on historical events, or we must give up moral judging. Just because history teaches us how many moral codes mankind has had, we cannot derive moral judgment from history.'[33] Hence his appreciation for Jacob Bernays, of whom he wrote so revealingly that 'having received a faith, he did not have to look to history for one.'[34] But hence also his sensitivity to Leo Strauss, whose anti-'Historicism' is the subject of a searching but sympathetic article whose key point is that Strauss's critics had overlooked the extent to which the flip-side of his anti-'Historicism' was a theism. Momigliano would also have appreciated, and understood, the link between Strauss's anti-'Historicism' and his training as a philologist.[35]

Momigliano was not blind to the fact that the plurality of historical reality threatened a free-fall into relativism, but neither was he intimidated by it.[36] The historian had other recourse. He could, for example, turn to genres like biography, which had discrete, undeniable subjects. The concrete – and Momigliano frequently remarked on the parallels between biographical and antiquarian research – was his answer of choice to the perils of 'Historicism.' But even the history of historiography, seemingly 'the inevitable corollary of historicism,' could serve as an anti-'Historicist' tool. For standing between any historian and any given past was a body of evidence. This meant that however immured in the present, the inquirer – the honest inquirer – was by necessity confronted by voices expressing the reality of other periods. 'Consequently the historian will worry less about his own inevitable situation in history than about the historical situation of his evidence, previous historians in-

cluded.'[37] The history of historiography, therefore, 'like any other historical research, has the purpose of discriminating between truth and
falsehood.'[38]

The historian pursued truth. About this Momigliano had no doubt.
'There is an inescapable question of truth,' he wrote in 1972, 'if the
historian is to be a responsible actor in his own society and not a
manipulator of opinions.'[39] Facts mattered. Hence his scorn for those
modern students who found nothing objectionable in the assertion that
the Athenians ate potatoes and tomatoes at their symposia and finished
the meal with sugared coffee. 'Theory' – his phrase is 'le parole astratte' –
was become in large part responsible for legitimizing ignorance after the
war, as 'Historicism' had before.[40] Momigliano, indeed, was formed as a
historian 'in an age of ideologies,' and he repeatedly counterposes
antiquarian scholarship to the politicized scholarship characteristic of
the Nazi era.[41]

In his later essays the connection was tightly drawn. The challenge
facing universal history in the modern age was relativism: once an
evolutionary hierarchy of civilizations was rejected, then what remained
was a series of parallels that could not easily be ordered. E.A. Freeman
and Max Weber faced this, but also 'such different cultural historians as
Dilthey, Lamprecht and Huizinga were involved in this search.'[42] In later
decades the situation had been radicalized still further, as there existed
historians who 'relativize all the historians – whether belonging to the
classical world or to other ages – and consider them the mere exponents
of ideologies or even more narrowly of centres of power. Historiography
is therefore deprived of any value in the search for truth.'[43]

Confronted by this continuing threat, Momigliano argued for nothing
less than a return to antiquarianism, 'to the traditional public, private,
military and religious antiquities; we return, it is understood, with the
precaution of calling it sociology ... Because sociologists, as I have often
noted, are nothing but armed antiquaries.'[44]

Momigliano's positive identification of sociology as the twentieth-
century form taken by early modern antiquarian inquiry can make still
more precise our understanding of his reaction to 'Historicism.' For as
late as 1950 he had explicitly denied sociology's existence.[45] In 1954 he
linked it to the relativizing enemies of truth. But by 1961 he was presenting the French historiographical style institutionalized in Braudel's VIe
section of the Ecole Pratique des Hautes Etudes as the successor to the
German tradition of 'Historicism.'[46] And in 1962 he explicitly identified
a continuity between early modern antiquarianism and modern sociol-

ogy.[47] In writing about Leo Strauss in 1967, he showed that he no longer shared Strauss's unequivocal rejection of 'Historicism' and sociology; Strauss had remained where Momigliano was in 1950.[48]

'Armed,' then, but with what? With facts. This kind of continuity between antiquarianism and sociology may explain Momigliano's great, late respect for Max Weber.[49] Weber's argument that the rigour of the inquirer enabled him to transcend his context while remaining attuned to that of his subject must have appealed to Momigliano. His own emphasis on philology and history is an answer of the same sort to the same problem. It was in the context of thinking about Weber's contribution that Momigliano, in 1986, offered his last and most inclusive definition of the nature of antiquarianism in the modern world. The richness of the passage warrants its citation in full.

> In what precise relation Max Weber himself was putting history and sociology becomes a secondary problem once it is realised that there have always been two types of history, the history which pursues the fleeting event and the history which analyses permanent or long-lasting structures. Whether you call the second type of history antiquarianism or 'histoire de la longue durée' or anthropology or sociology or structural history is less important than the relation which at any given moment exists between these two types of history. As far as Max Weber is concerned, he found in the elaboration of the notion of ideal types an original method for keeping structural research separate from, but connected with, the study of the individual facts. This went together with a rigorous refusal to avail himself of certain notions which were fashionable in his time when one talked about history.[50]

The best modern historians, he wrote, with Marc Bloch in mind, actually obviated the need for sociology by doing it even better.[51] They got the facts right, but went further, by bringing them to life. Momigliano devotes some of his most beautiful writing to this theme in his classic 'Le regole del giuoco nello studio della storia antica' (1974), a document whose origins lie in those methodological remarks, published and largely unpublished, of the early 1950s. 'The historian finds in a letter the man who wrote it, in the legal decree, the legislative body that promulgated it in precise circumstances; he finds in a house the one who inhabited it, in a tomb the faith of the group to whom the deceased belonged ... The historian interprets documents like signs of the men who have disappeared.'

The real historian did not study documents, he studied – and resuscitated – the lives implied by the documents. 'It is this capacity to interpret the document as if it were not a document but a real episode of a past life that, in the end, makes the historian.'[52] With this formulation from 1974, Momigliano moved beyond the ancient distinction between *historia* and *antiquitates*, beyond his own division between ancient historians and antiquarians, and even beyond that between historians of fast and of slow moving change. Now the difference is between those who, whatever their methods, are able to bring the past to life, and those who cannot.

This very creativity, Momigliano came to believe, reflected the historian's awareness of his own position. What enabled him to breathe life into some old document or artefact was the recognition that it belonged to a 'situation' that continued to work in the present. 'The historian transfers what survives to the world that does not.'[53] This same self-consciousness was also a second firebreak – after methodological rigour – between the historian and the perils of 'Historicism.' 'We must get used to the fact that the purpose of our research has an influence on the methods of the research itself,' he began. 'A candid admission of the purpose of one's own study, a clear analysis of the implications of one's own bias helps to define the limits of one's own historical research and explanation.' He argued that being aware of one's own interests actually made for better work. Syme's *Roman Revolution*, he suggested, would have been an even greater book if its author had asked whether Augustus's revolution was a fascist revolution. Because people 'still inevitably turn to history in order to clarify their own mind about ideas such as freedom, honor, justice, or even marriage, war, trade ... The clearer we are about the theme of our own research, the clearer we become about our own bias. And the clearer we are about our own bias, the more honest and efficient we are likely to be in our own research.' 'Self-examaination,' he concluded, 'is a necessary step not only to personal redemption, but also to objective historical research.'[54]

Nor, in fact, was 'personal redemption' far from Momigliano's thoughts, even if he got there by ways alien to Meinecke and the German tradition. Momigliano observed that stabilizing the distinctions between history, philology, and antiquarianism 'was not without a connection to *otium* and *negotium*, the *vita contemplativa* and *vita attiva*.'[55] Towards the end of his life, he put this another way, with the emphasis not on the differences between forms of inquiry into the past, but on their cumulative effect on the inquirer. 'The historical thought that takes seriously these things,' he once said, 'is a form of religious life' ('Il pensiero storico che guarda seriamente a queste cose, è una forma di vita religiosa').[56]

Being a good historian was a good in and of itself, independent of its being necessary for the discovery of truth, in the same way that a religious life was good in itself independent of its 'outcome.' Perhaps this notion lies behind Momigliano's comment, reported by Edward Shils, that Weber's greatness 'lay in his understanding that religion is the foundation of society.'[57]

This same 'greatness' was something Momigliano also associated with Johann Jakob Bachofen. He returned to the Basel-born and bred scholar repeatedly in the last years of his life.[58] In 1986, Momigliano argued that he was best understood in the context of history of religion, and that Bachofen had understood himself to be working in that area. 'It was his deepest belief that religion determined history in those ages which really counted for the history of mankind.'[59] This reflected Bachofen's own view of religion as the best guarantor of tradition; that is to say, a 'religious attitude towards the past and the present' was the sine qua non of the historian.[60]

Bachofen began to develop these ideas in the 1850s, and they informed the *Gräbersymbolik* (1859) and *Mutterrecht* (1861).[61] The core of his teaching was the idea that religion encoded the history of deep antiquity, which, if deciphered, could reveal a stage of human thought beyond the reach of surviving documents and more intimate than anything that would ever be recorded in a document.

Bachofen realized that to understand the antiquity of Europe it had to be compared with other ancient societies. This would have been a great discovery before 1600. Bachofen's corollary, that to understand Graeco-Roman religion you had to understand things that were not typically viewed as religion at all, such as deviant aspects of society, types of family organization, and patterns of cosmology, was a huge discovery in 1870.[62] But it was his practical efforts between 1870 and 1890 to draw on existing non-European primitive societies to reconstruct that deep layer of prehistory that made an epoch in scholarship.

It was this step, from antiquarianism to anthropology, that most interested the late Momigliano.[63] And yet, as Bachofen's eccentric, brilliant insight became a commonplace, his achievement fed the very 'Historicism' that the return to antiquarianism was supposed to counter. The anthropological turn, far from making the past clearer, seemed only to open on to a vast hall of mirroring cultures. 'Whether the world civilization emerging from the Second World War can help us in the same task,' Momigliano wondered aloud in one of his last works, 'remains to be ascertained.'[64]

II

At the end of 'Ancient History and the Antiquarian,' Momigliano observed that 'the survival of the antiquarian approach to history' was not a wholly German affair. 'France,' he continued, 'remained traditionally the best home for the antiquaries until not so many years ago.' Although he believed that 'the idea of *antiquitates* is now dead because the corresponding idea of political history founded upon literary history is dead,' he did not deny the possibility of future antiquarian projects. 'Occasional relapses into the antiquarian state of mind must be expected even in the future.'[65]

Walter Benjamin lived in Paris while he was composing *The Arcades Project*, and more or less continuously from 1933 until 1940. With all the oceans of ink that have been spilt over him since his death, only a trickle has dealt with him as a historian – as opposed to a *theorist* of history – yet his sole completed book, *The Origins of German Tragic Drama*, and his unfinished masterwork, *The Arcades Project*, were both, fundamentally, studies of the past. While no one, to my knowledge, has examined his practice as an antiquarian in Momigliano's sense of the term, Roland Kany has, indeed, placed him in the trajectory of antiquarian study of the history of religion, from Vossius through Usener and Warburg.[66] And whereas Benjamin's critique of *Historismus* in the name of a 'historical materialism' in his later works has been noted, the 'survival' of the antiquarian tradition that drives this very idiosyncratic 'historical materialism' has not. Benjamin's intellectual interests were many, and philosophy and criticism probably loom largest, but there is a kind of antiquarian disposition, or 'state of mind', to use Momigliano's term, that runs throughout his work. For that very reason, 'Benjamin the antiquary' also points us towards the as yet unexplored realm of the forms of antiquarianism in the twentieth century.

Scholem described Benjamin as someone who 'united the insight of the Metaphysician, the interpretative power of the Critic, and *the erudition of the Scholar*' (my emphasis). Although Benjamin admitted to a distaste for the kind of wide reading that characterized the 'real' historian,[67] and although there was a strong philosophical and present-centred cast to his writing, he always identified strongly with philology understood as pure research. In 1921, while still a student, he shared with Scholem his view of the relationship between philology and history.[68] And in December 1938, near the end of his life, Benjamin responded sharply to Adorno's rejection of his article on Baudelaire, with a defence of the importance of philology for his method. 'When you speak of a "wide-eyed presentation of the bare facts,"' he wrote, 'you are characterizing the genuinely philological stance.'[69] Two months later, in February 1939, responding to a second hectoring letter from Adorno, Benjamin began simply but pointedly, 'On est philologue ou on ne l'est pas.'[70] The implication was clear.

In the fragment 'Methodical Arts of History,' probably dating to sometime between 1918 and 1921, Benjamin described three kinds of historical writing: the 'pragmatic,' which was chronological in scope and useful for controversy; the 'phaenomenal,' which studied non-chronological material (for example, history of science or art history); and 'philological' history, which concerned itself with neither the purely temporal nor the purely structural. He described it as a 'developmental history' (*Verwandlungsgeschichte*) because it offered the 'highest continuity' between things and words. Whereas 'pragmatic' and 'phaenomenal' history could have no fruitful offspring, Benjamin thought, either could happily mate with philology, the former coupling producing source criticism (*Quellenkunde*) and the latter interpretation. However, he added, in terms that recall Momigliano's identification of philology with the history of historiography, 'the link is all the closer the older the Pragmata or Phänomena ... With the same justice – or, better, injustice – with which literary history or history of philosophy are called auxiliary sciences for *Geistesgeschichte*, source criticism is given the designation of auxiliary science for history. Methodologically ancillary, it has, nevertheless, a fully autonomous worth.'[71]

Over and against this stood the 'sterility' of the still dominant 'Philosophy of History of the Late Romantics and the Historical School.' In the fragment with this title, from 1921, Benjamin blamed the mistaken model of a disengaged historian observing a distant and inanimate past for the falsification of a teleological history that followed from it; Benjamin's word was 'growth.' Historians of the Prussian School had come 'openly to abandon true historical – that is to say, religious and pragmatic – observation,' so their work was without 'the power to disentangle the various strata of the real world.'[72]

Benjamin's discomfort with history as an overarching narrative was given a more focused impression in a letter to a friend, Florens Christian Rang, of December 1923, as he began work on *The Origins of German Tragic Drama*. Benjamin explained that he was preoccupied with 'the question of the relationship of works of art to historical life.' His conclusion was that there was 'no such thing as art history' – only individual works of art. The construction of a narrative tended to be based on some pre-existing schema, whether of subject matter or form. Benjamin noted that the same approach was often taken by historians of philosophy, who reduced their subject to a series of problems whose story could be narrated. His own goal in the *Trauerspiel* book, he explained, was to be true to the object itself without ignoring its context.[73]

Benjamin's study of seventeenth-century German tragic drama does indeed demonstrate a serious familiarity with its intellectual context – reason of state, the role of women in baroque drama, emblemata, hieroglyphics, astrology, polymathy, and neo-stoicism – some of which was decades ahead of widespread scholarly interest.[74] He likened the moral ostentation of the stoic kings on stage to the ostentatious learning of their playwrights.[75] He noted that the constant metaphorical and allegorical displacement of ideas into things and things into ideas 'made the same rigorous demands on the learning of the authors as did the precise handling of historical sources. Thus the writers share the cultural ideal of the polymath which Lohenstein saw realized in Gryphius.'[76] The 'significance of baroque polymathy for the *Trauerspiel*,' Benjamin argued later, was that the genre could not have existed in any other climate.[77]

But as he had explained to Scholem in March 1924, 'History as the Content of the Trauerspiel' was only the first of the book's three parts (it was later divided into two); the others were 'On the Occult Concept of Melancholy in the Sixteenth and Seventeenth Centuries' and 'On the Nature of Allegory and Allegorical Art Forms.'[78] Things and their study in the seventeenth century thus lie at the core of the final two-thirds of the work. The antiquarian attention to material culture turned history into collecting and landscape into text. The more erudite the society, the more historically attuned it necessarily was, and the more easily it could identify places and things with events, turning even nature into a museum – or a *Wunderkammer*. The conception of history in the seventeenth century 'is determined by such a collection of everything memorable.'[79]

Benjamin's famous 'theory' of the ruin grows out of this description of the seventeenth century's conception of history, in which ruins, quite literally, were observed, described, compared, and collected by contemporary antiquaries.[80] It is true, of course, that not all stoics were antiquaries. Yet very many antiquaries *were* stoics. The pursuit of the 'philosophical foundation of baroque philology' was crucial to Benjamin in a way that has typically not been shared by the historians of scholarship or art who have dominated study of the antiquarian tradition.[81]

The importance of things separated ancient tragedy from the modern mourning play, but it also reflected the role of the antiquary. 'The function of the mass of scholarly annotations is to point to the night-mare burden of *realia* on the stage action.'[82] If the melancholic's vision restores some feeling, albeit of mourning, to a world drained of it by that combination of Lutheranism and stoicism that Benjamin saw at work in the German *Trauerspiel*, it has the effect of infusing those deadened remains with a new vitality: allegory.[83] Accordingly, the objects found in the landscape, the things strewn about the feet of Dürer's *Melancolia*, the stage props of the *Trauerspiel*, all these are ruins, emptied of their origi-nal contents and ready to be infused with a new meaning through allegory. 'Allegories are in the realm of thoughts,' Benjamin tersely proclaimed, 'what ruins are in the realm of things.'[84] The 'cult of the ruin' in the seventeenth century, which from the perspective of the history of scholarship is manifested in the beginnings of modern archae-ology, represents for Benjamin an epistemological leap forward, a new way of assigning meaning to the world. 'Nature was not seen by them in bud and bloom, but in the over-ripeness and decay of her creations. In nature they saw eternal transience, and here alone did the saturnine vision of this generation recognize history.'[85]

Benjamin was not writing a history of antiquarianism. And yet, he produced a cultural history founded on the presumed centrality of antiquarian vision in seventeenth-century Europe. This project brought him into contact with the world of sources and genealogies studied by Momigliano, figures like Winckelmann, Creuzer, and Usener – all of whom figure decisively in the argument[86] – and, most important of all, Aby Warburg. The 'survival of the pagan gods' in allegory, and the survival of both their Olympian and their demonic aspects, marks the point of closest convergence and closest intellectual dependence on Warburg.[87] Here is the most important clue to Benjamin's historical thought in the 1920s and into the 1930s.

Benjamin's sympathy for Warburg, who once called himself a 'contem-plative antiquary,' reflects a shared affinity for the antiquarian, but also for a new kind of cultural history.[88] In his essay 'Pagan-Antique Prophecy in Words and Images in the Age of Luther' (1920), which Benjamin had read carefully, Warburg proclaimed the need to study 'image-making in all its forms' regardless of aesthetic appeal, and noted that 'the idea of examining a mere "curiosity" for its relevance to the history of human thought is one that comes more naturally to historians of religion than to historians of art.' This kind of careful examination would enable him to show the persistent polarizations of the rational and demonic in

European history. With such examination, Warburg concluded, 'the historian of civilization furnishes new grounds for a more profoundly positive critique of a historiography that rests on a purely chronological theory of development.'[89] In his 1926 lecture on Rembrandt, Warburg identified this kind of chronological vision with *Historismus*. He acknowledged that the oft-invoked 'spirit of an age' was usually the spirit of the historian's time retrojected onto the past ('Certainly anyone who has made an effort in this direction has experienced the crushing truth of this verdict in all its weight'). Yet as long as the interconnections between contemporary cultural forms have not been studied, as long as 'not all the methodological resources have been used to make the spirit of the age speak with the voice of the age itself,' Warburg was willing to allow 'the accused *Historismus*' to continue trying to illuminate the age with its own evidence.[90]

Benjamin was a careful reader of Warburg. He was years ahead of other scholars in recognizing that Warburg's argument – that in the Renaissance 'heavenly manifestations were conceived in human terms, so that their demonic power might be at least visually contained' – was conceived 'out of deep spiritual kinship.'[91] Warburg's 'demonic' was contained by distance, and distance was precisely what allegory offered. Benjamin even mused about taking over this core of Warburg's thought and using it in a study of fairy tales.[92]

Warburg's thinking about the heavens gives shape to the fragment 'To the Plantetarium,' which concludes *One-Way Street*, a collection that Benjamin worked on concurrently with the *Trauerspiel* book and saw published in 1928. The teachings of antiquity could be summed up, he wrote, in the phrase 'They alone shall possess the earth who live from the powers of the cosmos.' Nothing more distinguished modern from ancient man than the gulf between their respective experiences of the heavens. The ancients' 'intercourse' with the cosmos was 'ecstatic' and thus, necessarily, 'communal'; the moderns' (Kepler, Copernicus, and Tycho are named) has been through telescopic observation. It was 'the dangerous error of modern men,' Benjamin wrote, to relegate that ancient experience to the realm of the 'unimportant and avoidable' while replacing it with the rhapsody of the poetic individual. The experience of the last war, Benjamin concluded, in an uncanny recapitulation of Warburg's vision of the unending polarization and re-polarization of the basic human response to nature, and of the related conclusion to his 1923 lecture on the 'Snake Dance,' showed that it was impossible for either nations or generations to escape the grip of heavenly powers.

'Human multitudes, gases, electrical forces were hurled into the open country, high-frequency currents coursed through the landscape, new constellations rose in the sky, aerial space and ocean depths thundered with propellers, and everywhere sacrificial shafts were dug in Mother Earth.'[93]

Benjamin sought an institutional relationship to the intellectual circle that had gathered around Warburg.[94] The K.B.W., for its part, owned Benjamin's book, and it was Warburg himself who had brought it to Fritz Saxl's attention.[95] But neither this nor various third-party efforts succeeded in establishing any connection between Benjamin and Warburg.[96] For Benjamin, the key challenge inherited from nineteenth-century criticism was to be both concrete and philosophical. Looking back to the seventeenth century, Benjamin reflected on how its scholars had tried to coordinate these two registers of evidence. Divergent facts were accommodated at a higher level by the contemporary category of *historia sacra* – the belief that the organization of the world was providential and that meaning inhered, needing only to be excavated.[97] In the move from the seventeenth century to the nineteenth, across the frontier of Spinoza and Simon, the matter of joining the detailed to the general demanded a new answer. Having rejected Hegel and 'Historicism,' Benjamin had to find his own way. In the very same letter of 1928 in which he asked Scholem to approach Saxl on his behalf, he explained that he was hoping to finish his work on the 'Arcades' of Paris and, he wrote, 'Then I will have put to the test the extent to which it is possible to be "concrete" in the context of the philosophy of history.'[98]

Indeed, in an early draft entitled 'The Arcades of Paris,' presented to Horkheimer and Adorno in 1929, Benjamin returned to the 'Planetarium,' but now in order to apply the notion of a 'Copernican revolution' to the vast field of 'historical perception.' To the 'what has been' of the 'Historicists' was juxtaposed the meaning that the past had *in the historian's own present.* That was what was intended in the affirmation that 'politics attains primacy over history.' And the means to the desired concreteness is located in collecting.[99]

But even with the articulation of this 'political' goal, which intensified during the decade of the 1930s – and which cannot be identified exclusively with Marxism since it reached its culmination in the anti-Marxist 'On the Concept of History' – Benjamin remained 'under the spell of the living Warburg tradition.'[100] As he groped towards an alternative kind of history in several short pieces from the beginning of the decade, the specific problem of writing a new kind of cultural history was central.

In 'Literary History and the Study of Literature' (1931), Benjamin's defence of breadth of vision in the *Trauerspiel* is turned into a polemic against disciplinization and its discontents. But was there an actual discipline of literary history? Rather than looking back to the *historia literaria* of the seventeenth and eighteenth centuries as an intellectual historian might today – but which no one would have done at the time – Benjamin identified its growth in the nineteenth century with the Prussian, or National, school of history-writing. This, echoing the fragment of ten years' earlier, he described as a 'narrative comforter,' removed from real historical engagement and successful only at reifying the preconceived notions of the day. He called this 'the false universalism of the methods of cultural history.' And, for Benjamin, 'universalism' meant 'Historicism' – trying to empathize with the past in order to recover it. The pre-eminence of this approach meant that 'research was demoted to the status of an auxiliary in a cult in which the "eternal values" were celebrated.'[101]

'Research' (*Forschung*) is the key word in charting Benjamin's response to *Historismus* during these years. If research was one of its first victims, it would also be the agent of its undoing. Benjamin's hopes for a new kind of cultural history lay in a synthesis of the material and the marginal. He proposed paying attention to new kinds of writing, not just poetry and belles-lettres, but anonymous forms like 'calendar stories and colportage – as well as ... the sociology of the reading public, writers' associations, and the history of the publishing industry.'[102]

The emphasis on 'research' is given its sharpest presentation in a review of the first volume of the Viennese *Kunstwissenschaftliche Forschungen*. There Benjamin shifted his specific target from literary history–as–cultural history to art history–as–cultural history. In the review, written at the end of 1932 and published pseudonymously in July 1933, Benjamin used the occasion of a collective product of the Vienna school to attack the received form of cultural history as it pertained to art. 'Only from the perspective of the current situation does it become evident to what extent the understanding of art history as universal history – under whose aegis eclecticism had free play – fettered authentic research.'[103] Hence Benjamin's approval of Sedlmayr's '*investigation of individual works*' (Benjamin's emphasis).[104] This extended to a general attention to 'the insignificant,' but always with the understanding that sometimes the insignificant only seemed so. 'But what animates this esteem, if not the willingness to push research forward to the point where even the "insignificant" – no, *precisely* the insignificant – becomes significant? The bedrock that these researchers come up against is the concrete bedrock of past historical existence [*geschichtlichen Gewesensein*].' The inconspicuous can survive and be the key point of interpretation, 'which constitutes the point where the content reaches the breaking point for an authentic researcher.'[105] Because of this focus on materiality, the real forefather of the Vienna school was not Wölfflin but Riegl. His *Spätromische Kunstindustrie* showed that 'sober and simultaneously undaunted research never misses the vital concerns of its time.' In the 'new type of research' represented by this volume, 'the more crucial the works are, the more inconspicuously and intimately their meaning-content is bound up with their material content.' In the final sentence of the published review, Benjamin again returned to the contrast between *Historismus* and 'research.' The 'hallmark of the new type of researcher,' he wrote, 'is not the eye for the "all-encompassing whole" or the eye for the "comprehensive context" (which mediocrity has claimed for itself), but rather the capacity to be at home in marginal domains.' In the second, unpublished version, this assertation was amended slightly, and crucially, to credit as exemplary in this regard the Germanistik studies of Burdach and the religious-historical works associated with the 'Bibliothek Warburg.'[106]

Warburg was, then, an intellectual interlocutor, on into the 1930s, when Benjamin was supposedly already deep into his 'Marxist' phase. In the fragment 'On Astrology' (1932), Benjamin identifies the 'attempt to procure a view of astrology from which the doctrine of magical "influences," of "radiant energies," and so on has been excluded' with inquiries 'into the historical origins of the concepts of a scientific humanism.' This was of course the domain of Warburg and the K.B.W. Benjamin adds that he had already 'shown the intensity it conferred on the concept of melancholy. Something along these lines could be adduced for many other concepts.' What would it look like?

Benjamin presents a condensed version of his 'doctrine of the similar' to explain the general process whereby natural resemblances stimulated the 'mimetic faculty' in human beings that in turn perceived and generated additional resemblances. He then turns back to the specific example of astrology, at which point the complementarity of his notion of the mimetic faculty and the generation of Warburg's *Pathosformeln* becomes clear.[107]

Benjamin even identifies their projects and, at the same time suggests how his own could contribute to the broadening of Warburg's already capacious category of 'transmission': 'As students of ancient traditions, we have to reckon with the possibility that manifest configurations, mimetic resemblances, may once have existed where today we are no longer in a position even to guess at them.' The arrangement of the heavenly bodies was just one such configuration. Hence the concluding sentence of the fragment: 'This, then, is the complete prolegomenon of every rational astrology.'[108]

Benjamin developed his notion of the 'similar' or 'mimetic' in two unpublished essays of 1933. In addition to spelling out in much greater detail exactly how this faculty worked, and alluding in passing to the macrocosm and microcosm, he posed the question of whether the clearly decreased number of such resemblances in modern times relative 'to that of the ancients or even that of primitive peoples' was a matter of decay or of transformation. Astrology again provided a model, and – once again using the first person plural – he wrote, 'As researchers into old traditions, we must take account of the possibility that sensuous shape-giving took place' where today one no longer even suspected it.[109] Dance, Benjamin suggests, could have been one such way primitive peoples embodied resemblance – though when he wrote these words so closely paralleling Warburg's own thought, it is extremely unlikely that he could have known of Warburg's 1923 lecture on the Pueblo Indian Snake Dance, which remained locked away until published in truncated form in 1938, in English translation.[110]

But where Warburg looked to images as an archive of non-sensuous similarity, Benjamin turned to language. 'From time immemorial,' he acknowledged, 'the mimetic faculty has been conceded some influence on language.' But up until now it had always been 'without foundation' and without a history. Moving beyond the obvious onomatopoeia, Benjamin argued for the power of words – spoken and written – as a container of mimesis. But if written language was, somehow, an 'archive,' then reading became a key to its decipherment.

If, at the dawn of humanity, this reading from stars, entrails, and coincidences was reading per se, and if it provided mediating links to a newer kind of reading, as represented by runes, then one might well assume that this mimetic gift, which was earlier the basis for clairvoyance, very gradually found its way into language and writing in the course of a development over thousands of years, thus creating for itself in language and writing the most perfect archive of nonsensuous similarity. In this way, language is the highest application of the mimetic faculty – a medium in which the earlier perceptual capacity for recognizing the similar had, without residue, entered to such an extent that language now represents the medium in which objects encounter and come into relation with one another. No longer directly, as they once did in the mind of the augur or priest, but in their essences, in their most transient and delicate substances, even in their aromas. In other words: it is to script and language that clairvoyance has, over the course of history, yielded its old powers.[111]

In the second 'version' of the argument, Benjamin concluded with a more pointed – and much more Warburgian – ending: 'In this way, language may be seen as the highest level of mimetic behavior and the most complete archive of nonsensuous similarity: a medium into which the earlier powers of mimetic production and comprehension have passed without residue, the point where they have liquidated those of magic.'[112] Additional echoes of Warburg remain audible even in the depths of *The Arcades Project*, and perhaps it was these echoes, along with Benjamin's dedication to 'philology' or 'research', that made Adorno bristle so inelegantly at the late works.[113]

But when Benjamin turned directly to confront the challenge of cultural history, it was another student of the marginal, and of visual culture, whom he chose for his case study: Eduard Fuchs. Benjamin was commissioned to write 'Eduard Fuchs, Collector and Historian' in 1933 or 1934, began it in 1935, and saw it published in 1937.[114] In a way, his essay on Fuchs occupies the place in his historical thinking that 'Ancient History and the Antiquarian' occupies in Momigliano's: it is a history of practice that is also a model of the practice of history.

Fuchs was an autodidact – in this perhaps not so unlike Benjamin himself, but the polar opposite of Momigliano – who moved from printing to journalism to scholarship. He wrote about neglected subjects while drawing heavily on neglected, or overlooked, types evidence. He began with caricature, a universal as well as non-elitist form of art and social comment. He mined it for his books on the history of European peoples from antiquity, on the World War, on Jews, and on women and marriage. Even more daring was a series of publications drawing on objects in his own collection – German ceramics, T'ang funerary sculpture, and Chinese acroteria – which he entitled 'Kultur- und Kunstdokumente.' The extraordinary program for the series, and the effort to ground material artefacts in their cultural context that outlined the shared structure of the three volumes has never been properly examined or appreciated.[115]

In Benjamin's interpretation, when Fuchs first began writing, cultural history was little more than a diversion for the working poor ('History was loosened up and yielded *cultural history*').[116] It was from Engels by way of Mehring that Fuchs was able to develop, for the first time, 'the cultural historical researches of historical materialism.'[117] Benjamin refers to a long letter sent by Engels to Mehring in 1893 and adds, 'The more one considers Engels's sentences, the more one appreciates his insight that every dialectical presentation of history is paid for by a renunciation of the contemplativeness which characterizes historicism ... Historicism presents the eternal image of the past, whereas historical materialism presents a given experience with the past – an experience which is unique.' With this experience, 'the immense forces bound up in historicism's "Once-upon-a-time" are liberated.'[118]

Fuchs's work on manners and style 'partakes of the problematic that is inseparable from cultural history' – and, in a way, this was what interested Benjamin in Fuchs.[119] Once the power of disciplinary divisions was negated – and with this we are back to the 1923 letter to Rang, and the later essays on literary and art history – what remained was cultural history 'as the inventory which humanity has preserved to the present day.' On the other hand, this move dispensed with 'the varied and problematic unities which intellectual history embraces (as history of literature and art, of law and religion) merely by a new and more problematic unity.' What was needed was, once again, to go beyond cultural history as conventionally understood.

Acknowledging these internal contradictions of a 'materialist cultural history,' and acknowledging also Fuchs's only limited success in escaping from the unthinking notion of history as 'development,' Benjamin insisted that Fuchs's collecting practice did provide the crucial 'destructive element.'[120] Objects brought Fuchs into 'marginal areas' that hitherto had been ignored, like caricature and pornography, and helped shatter the still dominant 'classicist conception of art.'[121] But things also offered new ways back to the past, 'and threads may have been lost for centuries that the present course of history erratically, inconspicuously picks up again.'[122]

Benjamin described Fuchs's 'family tree': on the French side was the collector, on the German the historian.[123] What he meant by the former is relatively clear, and was echoed by Momigliano in the famous 1950 essay – the collector was much more central to France. By the latter, however, he intended the smug moralizing that attended the German tradition. Looking back beyond Balzac's fictional Cousin Pons, Benjamin remarked that 'as a rule collectors have been guided by the object itself. A great example on the threshold of the modern age is the humanists, whose Greek acquisitions and travels testify to the single-mindedness with which they collected.' Other examples were drawn from the seventeenth and eighteenth centuries: the Marolles transformed by La Bruyère into a type, and the Comte de Caylus, whose publication of his own collection 'is the first great achievement of archaeology.' 'Fuchs,' Benjamin concluded, 'belongs in this line of great and systematic collectors who were resolutely intent on a single subject matter.'[124]

This critique of *Historismus* in the name of a new kind of material cultural history is further articulated in 'Konvolut N' of *The Arcades Project*, entitled 'On the Theory of Knowledge, Theory of Progress.'[125] Ranke, the father of history and founder of the Prussian Historical School, was the first to be arraigned. Benjamin writes that his approach, 'the history that showed things "as they really were" – Ranke's "wie es eigentlich gewesen" – was the strongest narcotic of the century.'[126] Fustel de Coulanges and Johan Huizinga were other targets. Fustel was a follower of Savigny, and the establisher of the historical school of French law. He was the teacher of Durkheim. As an author he is remembered for *La cité antique*. Benjamin quotes Julien Benda's citation from Fustel: 'If you want to relive an epoch, forget that you know what has come after it.' 'That is the secret Magna Charta,' Benjamin adds, 'for the presentation of history by the Historical School.'[127] Benjamin thought this precondition humanly impossible, and those who accepted it self-deluded. For example, Huizinga's account of the continuity of 'ragpicker' imagery from the Middle Ages to Rembrandt was denounced as an 'example of a "cultural historical" perspective in the worst sense.'[128]

Cultural history as practised was the elevation of 'the collective intellectual development of society' to the entire contents of history.[129] What Benjamin wished to do was fix the 'demarcation from cultural history' by establishing his own 'cultural historical dialectic.'[130] He rejected the idea that the past existed, 'out there,' beyond the passions of the present-day historian, just waiting to be reconstructed as it was. 'Forming the basis of the confrontation with conventional historiography and "enshrinement" is the polemic against empathy (Grillparzer, Fustel de Coulanges).'[131] 'Historicism' had implied the 'enshrinement as heritage' of the past.[132]

It is against this view that Benjamin's theory, and practice, is devoted. The 'object of history is to be blasted out of the continuum of historical succession.'[133] He writes about the 'destructive momentum in materialist historiography' – that concrete things offered a way both to break the smooth narrative of political history and to reconstruct it on another basis.[134] Collecting was the model for this new kind of history, since the 'true collector detaches the object from its functional relations' in the very process of acquiring and reordering.[135] The collection of citations – literally, fragments of books – marked another way of doing just this. Things that were marginal and insignificant often held the key to the whole. 'To assemble large-scale constructions out of the smallest and most precisely cut components. Indeed, to discover in the analysis of the small individual moment the crystal of the total event ... To grasp the construction of history as such.'[136]

'The constructions of history' – referring to the grand narratives of the great historians of the nineteenth and early twentieth centuries – were comparable to military orders that disciplined the true life and confined it to barracks. On the other hand: 'the street insurgence of the anecdote. The anecdote brings things near to us spatially, lets them enter our life. It represents the strict antithesis to the sort of history which demands "empathy," which makes everything abstract.' Benjamin terms this pitfall, with an obvious nod to Nietzsche, the 'pathos of nearness.'[137]

The moral and epistemological deadening achieved by 'Historicism' represented everything Benjamin opposed. This combination of ideas was spelled out fully in the seventh section of 'On the Concept of History,' written in the first half of 1940:

> VII. To the historian who wishes to relive an era, Fustel de Coulanges recommends that he blot out everything he knows about the later course of history. There is no better way of characterizing the method with which historical materialism has broken. It is a process of empathy. Its origin is the indolence of the heart, *acedia*, which despairs of grasping and holding the genuine historical image as it briefly flashes up. Among medieval theologians it was regarded as the root cause of sadness. Flaubert, who was familiar with it, wrote: '*Peu de gens devineront combien il a fallu être triste pour ressuciter Carthage*' [Few can imagine how sad one had to be to bring Carthage back to life]. The nature of this sadness stands out more clearly if we ask: With whom does historicism actually sympathize? The answer is inevitable: with the victor.[138]

In this last essay on history, Benjamin names historical materialism as the champion appointed to slay 'Historicism,' though what he means by a practice he identifies as much with theology as scholarship is not easy to determine.[139] Yet he remains clear about the target: 'historicism offers the "eternal" image of the past; historical materialism supplies a unique experience with the past (section XVI).' 'Historicism,' Benjamin continues (section XVII), 'rightly culminates in universal history. It may be that materialistic historiography differs in method more clearly from universal history than from any other kind.' 'Universal history,' by contrast, 'has no theoretical armature. Its method is additive; it musters a mass of data to fill the homogeneous, empty time.' Materialist history, by contrast, 'is based on a constructive principle.' In conclusion, Benjamin claimed that 'historicism contents itself with establishing a causal connection between various moments in history,' but that, in fact, not all connections were causal. They became 'causal,' or 'historical,' only afterwards, sometimes 'through events that may be separated from [a particular moment] by thousands of years.' The historian who recognizes that history is made long after the event, in the eyes of later beholders, 'ceases to tell the sequence of events like the beads of a rosary.' Narrative gives way like a false facade. Instead, the historian 'grasps the constellation into which his own era has formed with a very specific earlier one.'[140] The 'weak messianic power' of the historian, referred to in section II, stands behind the contrast Benjamin draws between universal history as properly understood and as practised in the world. 'The authentic concept of universal history is a messianic concept. Universal history, as it is understood today, is an affair of obscurantists.'[141]

Another isolated historical thinker who attracted Benjamin's attention in the mid 1930s, just as he began shifting his focus from Warburg to Fuchs, was Johann Jakob Bachofen. Benjamin seems to have made Bachofen's acquaintance around 1916.[142] But he first appears in Benjamin's oeuvre later, in the essay on Goethe's *Elective Affinities*.[143] Benjamin reviewed Bernoulli's *Johann Jakob Bachofen und das Natursymbol: Ein Wurdigungsversuch* in *Die literarische Welt* in 1926.[144] Already then he had hit upon the justification for interest in Bachofen: the paradoxical fact of his non-existence in the eyes of professional classicists at the same time as his enormous and increasing presence 'where sociology, anthropology and philosophy attempt to venture from the beaten track.'[145]

In 1934, Benjamin returned to Bachofen. He wrote an essay entitled simply 'Johann Jakob Bachofen,' in French, for the journal *Nouvelle revue française*. It was not published until 1954. It has the form of an introduction to Bachofen for a general audience. But upon receiving a copy of it for the first time, in 1961, Gershom Scholem wrote, 'It is as if the author were conducting a sort of general inventory of all of his oldest themes, without identifying them as such.'[146]

Unravelling the riddle of Bachofen's strange popularity was the ostensible task of the essay. Engels and later communists had been attracted by the idea of a matriarchy with shared property; anthropologists and Freudians by Bachofen's focus on archaic symbols, death cults, and fertility rites; and the 'Müncher Kosmiker' and George circle by the pre-logical prehistory he seemed to have excavated. Bachofen's attention to the irrational in society had more recently found a new audience for him among Europe's fascists.[147]

Like Fuchs's, Bachofen's work seemed stretched across a tension. He was interested in tombs and death, but for philosophical rather than the usual erudite reasons.[148] On the one hand, Bachofen's researches were 'so vast and yet so precise,' and on the other 'there was nothing in them that recalled the positivists' method.' His concoction of passion and philology transcended philology, and that, as well as his focus on symbols, made him the legitimate heir of Winckelmann.[149]

This was only the first of the explicit links Benjamin traced back from Bachofen to the earlier antiquarian tradition. A second located him in a line of seigneurial savants. The type was, he thought, inaugurated by Leibniz and continued down to the present day in 'certain noble and remarkable spirits like Aby Warburg, founder of the library that bears his name and that has just quit Germany for England.' Always viewed as somewhat 'dilettantish,' this sort of scholar tended to gravitate to the frontier zone where disciplines uneasily met. Benjamin saw this gravitation as chiefly a function of a financial independence that freed such scholars from the demands and jealousies of patrons on the one hand and of colleagues on the other.[150] 'On all these points,' Benjamin concluded, 'Bachofen presents striking analogies.'[151]

III

Meinecke's 'Historicism' was opposed to what might seem to us today a caricature of eighteenth-century French thought: mechanism, encyclopaedism, and natural law. If *Historismus* was supposed to be the philosophical expression of German modernity, the crudeness of its dialectic seemed to both Momigliano and Benjamin to sanction a flight from the concrete facts of history into fields of fancy where truth could no longer be distinguished from propaganda. And in these fields the dragon's teeth sprouted. Indeed, by the time Meinecke returned to consider the 'Crisis of Historicism' in 1942, he was ready to proclaim it a thing of the past, its relativism defeated by the 'Renewal of our whole national life' since 1933. The historical sciences were also affected by this change, which 'sought to raise up certain new interpretations of the past as guiding principles of historical thought, that until that point were discussed but unmoored, concerning the importance of *Volk* and Race for history.' The outbreak of war offered the hopeful horizon of 'a new European Order' (*'einer neuen europäischen Ordnung'*).[152]

Long after war's end, the publication of a book about 'Historicism' in contemporary thought provided Momigliano with an opportunity to reflect on the fate of German *Historismus*. Unlike the book's author, he thought it dead: without followers in Germany, France or Italy – each for different reasons – and, in the two countries possessed of a sizeable number of German-born and trained scholars, the United States and Great Britain, tamed and transformed by local approaches to social science and philosophy. Most illuminating, however, was the brief history of 'Historicism' that preceded the nation-by-nation analysis. For Germany, Momigliano began with Dilthey, and then turned to the revision of his work undertaken in the following generation by Troeltsch, Weber, Simmel, and Meinecke, and by the leaders of the next cohort, Karl Mannheim, Karl Löwith, and Fritz Saxl. But, Momigliano wrote, 'the oppression of all free voices, and the exile (as opposed to legal assassination) imposed on many historians (Jews, or born to Jewish parents, or simply anti-Nazi), amounted to a suspension of all that work of revision of historicism.' Momigliano then, in an extraordinary intellectual tour de force, deftly enumerated the different strands in that suspended project of revision: Meinecke's and Troeltsch's insistence on the anti-relativism of the Individual, Lukács's and Mannheim's determinism, Spengler's fatalism, Alfred Weber and Scheler's Weberian rejection of ideology. Even Heidegger belonged to the story, inserting the theory of history into existentialism. Among practicising historians 'the suspension was no less dramatic.' Jaeger's neo-humanism had to relocate to America; Stefan George's 'great man' history, which had enlisted also Kantorowicz and Gundolf, was shut down; and 'the revision of the inheritance of the classical world undertaken by A. Warburg and embodied in his Institute at Hamburg, could no longer express itself in German.'[153]

A generation's task had been interrupted by war. Is it too much to see Momigliano's turn to the historical recovery of antiquarian practice as his, also belated and also dispersed, contribution to that generation's work? And what of Scholem's achievement? Could Momigliano's late fascination with him reflect the sense that he, too, belongs to this story? (To be fair, in his *tour d'horizon* of the German-Jewish historical diaspora Momigliano had explicitly put Israel to the side.) And surely Benjamin, too, belongs to the generation that struggled with 'Historicism,' killed off before he could bring his project to any completion.[154]

'Historicism' as a problem had, in fact, led Benjamin to explore a new kind of material history which was embodied by Eduard Fuchs and was to be demonstrated in his own *Arcades Project.* 'Historicism' as a solution – Meinecke concluded his essay with the Dilthey-like vision of an individual buoyed by the 'life forces' of Religion and Fatherland – propelled Momigliano in the opposite direction, to a post-war immersion in the study of Europe's antiquaries and their hermeneutic.[155]

In the Italian lecture Momigliano delivered at Malcesine in the summer of 1950, he described the intellectual breakdown in pre-war Germany in terms of debilitating scepticism and misology – a 'new Pyrrhonism' (*nuovo pirronismo*). But the long arc of Momigliano's post-war writings bridges the Pyrrhonism of *Historismus* and the Pyrrhonism of post-modernism. 'Historicism Revisited' was not only the title of an article, but a war correspondent's dispatch from the front lines. And yet, there was something about the 'novissimus Pyrronismus' that Momigliano didn't get – as his unsuccessful struggle to decipher Foucault shows. For the Heideggerian critique of historicity, upon which Foucault rests, and with him post-modernism generally, was much more far-ranging, challenging the very foundation in subjectivity that was presupposed by the entire Western historical tradition.[156] If Meinecke's caricature of eighteenth-century thought does not seem so ludicrous today, it is because it resonantes with the anti-Enlightenment commonplaces of so much post-modernism.[157] Momigliano's answer was loud and clear, even if those he was criticizing could not hear it. 'But when we come to our own society we need to know what we can believe rather than what is believed. There is an inescapable question of truth, if the historian is to be a responsible actor in his own society and not a manipulator of opinions. This need, incidentally, seems to be taken too lightly by the various sociologies of knowledge, including the novel one of Foucault.'[158]

Both Momigliano and Benjamin turned back to the antiquarian as a response to the intellectual culture of fascism, of societies unhinged by unreasonable doubt. Among historians of scholarship, Momigliano is best known for his study of those who studied ruins in early modern Europe. Among historians of literature, Benjamin's is the best-known attempt to explain the wider cultural import of ruins in early modern Europe.

There will be need for antiquaries as long as ruins exert their pull. But as grasping the great destruction wrought by the Second World War has become a cultural priority, people have been drawn to different aspects of Europe's antiquarian heritage. At different extremes, the novels of W.G. Sebald and the *yizker-bikher*, or memorial books, of the destroyed Jewish communities of Eastern Europe bring together antiquarianism and remembering. These works – and one could name others, too – remind us of the life-giving power of the study of ruined fragments, but also of a passion for the past that has been largely suppressed among professional historians, and yet 'lingers on, but with a dimmed and manic glow, in antiquarians, researchers, and bibliomaniacs.'[159]

Notes

1 Momigliano, 'Walter Benjamin,' in *Settimo Contributo*, 509–13. The nine volumes of Momigliano's *Contributi alla storia degli studi classici e del mondo antico*, published in Rome from 1955 to 1990, are referred to in short-title form here and in the notes below.

2 The key texts are Ernst Troeltsch, *Der Historismus und seine Probleme* (Tübingen, 1922); Karl Heussi, *Die Krisis des Historismus* (Tübingen, 1932); Friedrich Meinecke, *Die Entstehung des Historismus* (Berlin and Munich, 1936); idem, 'Von der Krisis des Historismus,' in his *Aphorismen und Skizzen* (Leipzig, 1942 [1939]). For a recent review of the 'Crisis of Historicism,' see Donald R. Kelley, *The Fortunes of History: Historical Inquiry from Herder to Huizinga* (New Haven and London, 2003), 327–33.

3 The revival of interest may be dated to Thomas Nipperdey, 'Historismus und Historismuskritik heute,' in his *Gesellschaft, Kultur, Theorie: Gesammelte Aufsätze zur neueren Geschichte* (Göttingen, 1976), 59–73, but has accelerated in the last decade: Horst Walter Blanke, *Historiographiegeschichte als Historik* (Stuttgart, 1991); Annette Wittkau, *Historismus: Zur Geschichte des Begriffs und des Problems* (Göttingen, 1992); Friedrich Jaeger and Jörn Rüsen, *Geschichte des Historismus: Eine Einführung* (Munich, 1992); Georg G. Iggers, 'Historicism: The History and Meaning of the Term,' *Journal of the History of Ideas* 56 (1995): 129–52; Charles R. Bambach, *Heidegger, Dilthey, and the Crisis of Historicism* (Bloomington, IN, 1995); *Historismus in den Kulturwissenschaften: Geschichtskonzepte, historische Einschätzungen, Grundlagenprobleme*, ed. Otto Gerhard Oexle and Jörn Rüsen (Cologne, Weimar, Vienna, 1996); Otto Gerhard Oexle, *Geschichtswissenschaft im Zeichen des Historismus: Studien zu Problemgeschichten der Moderne* (Göttingen, 1996); *Historismus am Ende des 20. Jahrhunderts: Eine internationale Diskussion*, ed. Gunter Scholtz (Berlin, 1997); Johannes Heinssen, *Historismus und Kulturkritik: Studien zur deutschen*

Geschichtskultur im späten 19. Jahrhundert (Göttingen, 2003); and Reinhard Laube, *Karl Mannheim und die Krise des Historismus: Historismus als wissens-soziologischer Perspektivismus* (Göttingen, 2004).

4 The following paragraphs draw mainly on the work of Peter H. Reill, *The German Enlightenment and the Rise of Historicism* (Los Angeles and Berkeley, 1975); Georg G. Iggers, *The German Conception of History: The National Tradition of Historical Thought from Herder to the Present,* rev. ed. (Middletown, CT, 1983); Otto Gerhard Oexle, *L'historisme en débat: De Nietzsche à Kantorowicz* (Paris, 2001), with full bibliography; and the very perceptive comments of Glenn W. Most, in his preface to *Historicization = Historisierung,* ed. Most (Göttingen, 2001), vii–viii.

5 Momigliano, 'Note marginali di storia della filologia classica. Il contributo dell'autobiografia alla valutazione del Gibbon,' in *Contributo,* 380. Earlier evidence – perhaps going back as far as 1933 – shows Momigliano exploring the roots of historicism in Wilhelm von Humboldt's thinking about classical antiquity ('Genesi storica e funzione attuale del concetto di ellenismo,' in *Contributo,* 175–6).

6 Pisa, Archivio Arnaldo Momigliano, N-b 1, *Archivio Arnaldo Momigliano,* ed. Giovanna Granata (Pisa, 1998 [privately printed]), 127. Like all others who have used the Momigliano Archive in Pisa, I am deeply grateful to Riccardo Di Donato for making access possible and for guiding me through its organization. For the general context, see *Die Historismusdebatte in der Weimarer Republik,* ed. Wolfgang Bialas and Gérard Raulet (Frankfurt and New York, 1996).

7 'La formazione della moderna storiografia sull'impero Romano,' in *Contributo,* 123 n62; 'Friedrich Creuzer and Greek Historiography,' in *Contributo,* 245 n32.

8 'Cercare la ragione della persecuzione degli Ebrei consiste nel cercare i fatti o presunti tali (cioè il fatto che determinati fatti fossero presunti) che talune persone considerarono necessari o sufficienti per perseguitare gli Ebrei' (Riccardo Di Donato, 'Materiali per una biografia intellettuale di Arnaldo Momigliano. I. Libertà e pace nel mondo antico,' *Athenaeum* 83 [1995]: 228–30).

9 Riccardo Di Donato, ed., *Pace e libertà nel mondo antico. Lezioni a Cambridge: gennaio–marzo 1940* (Florence, 1996), xxii; Di Donato, 'Materiali I' (n8 above), 234.

10 Momigliano, *Contributo,* 245 n32

11 Riccardo Di Donato, 'Materiali per una biografia intellettuale di Arnaldo Momigliano. II. Tra Napoli e Bristol,' *Athenaeum* 86 (1998): 245.

12 In fact, the same notebook preserves the two essays on antiquarianism, the

one in English and the other in Italian, and the lecture on Croce (Pisa, Archivio Arnaldo Momigliano, N-f 62).

13 Carlo Dionisotti, 'Arnaldo Momigliano e Croce,' *Belfagor* 43 (1988): 617–42, repr. in Dionisotti, *Ricordo di Arnaldo Momigliano* (Bologna, 1989).

14 'Benedetto Croce [1950],' in *Nono contributo*, 539.

15 Ibid., 540.

16 Ibid., 541.

17 'Ma appunto perciò il metodo degli antiquari – come raccolta di esperienze critiche le quali contribuirono a vincere la crisi del pirronismo – è piu che mai attuale. Oggi come a tutti è noto, noi siamo in una fase degli studi in cui tropi storici, almeno dell'antichità interpretano i fatti prima di essere sicuri che i fatti esistano. Già si profila per reazione un nuovo pirronismo di chi è stanco di vedere le reviste scientifiche e i libri pieni di congetture mal fondate. Il congetturalismo a oltranza è inevitabilmente accompagnato dal pirronismo. Contro al congetturalismo e al pirronismo non c'è che il vecchio rimedio: l'esame cauto e metodoico dei documenti con tutti gli avvedimenti che furono elaborati dalla collaborazione di antiquari e critici testuali nei secc. XVII e XVIII' ('Antiquari e storici dell'antichità,' Pisa, Archivio Arnaldo Momigliano, N-f 56, quoted in chapter 2 in this volume, Riccardo Di Donato, 'Arnaldo Momigliano from Antiquarianism to Cultural History: Some Reasons for a Quest').

18 'Genesi storica e funzione attuale del concetto di ellenismo' (n5 above), 166.

19 For a more subtle presentation, see Markus Völkel, *'Pyrrhonismus historicus' und 'fides historica': die Entwicklung der deutschen historischen Methodologie unter dem Gesichtspunkt der historischen Skepsis* (Frankfurt am Main and New York, 1987); and Lorenzo Bianchi, *Tradizione libertina e critica storica: Da Naudé a Bayle* (Milan, 1988).

20 'Antiquari e storici dell'antichità' (n17 above): 'Esiste una ermeneutica degli antiquari ben più complessa e più produttiva di quella dei teologi, che merita attenzione in ogni futura teoria del documento storico.'

21 Di Donato, 'Materiali II' (n11 above), 243.

22 'Philology and History,' Pisa, Archivio Arnaldo Momigliano, N-f 56, quoted in chapter 2 in this volume, Di Donato, 'Arnaldo Momigliano from Antiquarianism to Cultural History.'

23 Ibid.

24 'Bendetto Croce' (n14 above), 541.

25 'A Hundred Years after Ranke,' in *Contributo*, 371.

26 Ibid., 372.

27 'Gli studi di storia antica,' in *Secondo contributo*, 330.

28 'Il linguaggio e la tecnica dello storico,' in *Secondo contributo*, 371: 'Ci voglia-
    mo orientare nel mondo.'
29 Ibid., 372.
30 Ibid., 371.
31 'Prospettiva 1967 della storia graeca,' in *Quarto contributo*, 45, 51. Emphasiz-
    ing the importance of these biographical facts should not be considered
    anachronistic; during the war itself, Momigliano contributed texts to the
    BBC Italian service, and eight of the twenty-eight are on the subject of
    National Socialism and German racism.
32 Review of H. Berve, *Storia greca*,' in *Terzo contributo*, 708. Grafton hints at
    this connection in his 'Einleitung' to volume 2 of Arnaldo Momigliano,
    Ausgewählte Schriften zur Geschichte und Geschichtsschreibung, ed. Anthony T.
    Grafton (Stuttgart, 2000), xv.
33 'Historicism Revisited,' in *Sesto contributo*, 28.
34 'Jacob Bernays,' in *Quinto contributo*, 152.
35 'Ermeneutica e pensiero politico classico in Leo Strauss,' in *Quarto con-
    tributo*, 124, 126.
36 'Historicism Revisited' (n33 above), p.25.
37 Ibid., 30.
38 Ibid., 31–2.
39 'A Piedmontese View of the History of Ideas,' in *Sesto contributo*, 335.
40 'Prospettiva 1967 della storia graeca' (n31 above), 51.
41 As in 'Dopo Max Weber,' in *Sesto contributo*, 310.
42 'Two Types of Universal History: The Cases of E.A. Freeman and Max
    Weber,' in *Ottavo contributo*, 122.
43 'The Place of Ancient Historiography in the Modern World,' in *Settimo
    contributo*, 32.
44 'Prospettiva 1967 della storia graeca,' 51. Momigliano further noted, how-
    ever, that the concreteness of sociology also attracted many former Nazi
    classicists who were seeking a 'sphere of objective and (like Weberian) non-
    valuative analysis, after the unhappy experience of politics' ('Dopo Max
    Weber' [n41 above], 310). Recent scholarship on the history of social
    history in Germany after the war has confirmed this intuition. See Peter N.
    Miller, 'Nazis and Neostoics: Otto Brunner and Gerhard Oestreich before
    and after the Second World War,' *Past and Present* 176 (2002): 142–86.
45 'Chi, come il sottoscritto, si rifiuta di ammettere l'esistenza della sociologia
    sebbene sia informato che qualcosa chiamato sociologia si muove a passi
    rapidi nel mondo' ('Antiquari e storici dell'antichità' [n17 above]).
46 'Lo storicismo nel pensiero contemporaneo,' in *Terzo contributo*, 279.

47 'Conclusion,' in *The Classical Foundations of Modern Historiography* (Berkeley and Los Angeles, 1990), 155.

48 'Ermeneutica e pensiero politico classico in Leo Strauss' (n35 above), 177.

49 Edward Shils pointed out that all six essays about Weber were written in the last years of Momigliano's life ('Arnaldo Momigliano and Max Weber,' *Storia della storiografia* 16 [1989]: 58).

50 'Two Types of Universal History' (n42 above), 128. The essay was originally written in 1979.

51 Review of Paul Veyne, *Comment on écrit l'histoire*, in *Sesto contributo*, 759.

52 'Lo storico trova nella lettera l'uomo che l'ha scritta, nel decreto il corpo legislativo che l'ha emanato in precise circostanze; trova nella casa che l'ha abitata, nella tomba la fede del gruppo a cui il defunto apparteneva. Lo storico interpreta documenti come segni degli uomini che sono spariti. È questa capacità di interpretare il documento come se non fosse documento, ma episodio reale di vita passata, che da ultimo fa lo storico' ('Le regole del giuoco nello studio della storia antica,' in *Sesto contributo*, 20–1). This one learned from reading great historians, not great manuals; the names he offered were Herodotus, Guicciardini, Burckhardt, and Marc Bloch.

53 'Le regole del giuoco nello studio della storia antica' (n52 above), 20.

54 'A Hundred Years after Ranke' (n25 above), 372–3. See also Giuseppe Giarizzo, 'Storia sacra, storia profana: la tradizione come unita vissuta,' *Rivista storica italiana* 100 (1988): 391.

55 'L'eredità della filologia antica e il metodo storico,' in *Secondo contributo*, 465.

56 In conversation with Silvia Berti, quoted in Berti, 'Autobiografia, storicismo e verità storica in Arnaldo Momigliano,' *Rivista storica italiana* 100 (1988): 306.

57 Shils, 'Momigliano and Weber' (n49 above), 62. This also explains something of the appeal of Bachofen at the end of Momigliano's life.

58 No fewer than three discrete articles on Bachofen emerge from the last year of Momigliano's life. Bachofen was also the subject of what turned out to be the last of the Pisa seminars on the history of scholarship. The earliest mentions are less than flattering: 'Tre figure mitiche: Tanaquilla, Gaia Cecilia, Acca Larenzia [1938],' in *Quarto contributo*, 463, 456; and 'Friedrich Creuzer and Greek Historiography [1946]' (n7 above), 233; more respectful is that in 'C.G. Lewis, Niebuhr e la critica delle fonti. I. Il metodo del Niebuhr [1952],' in *Contributo*, 250; and 'A Hundred Years after Ranke [1954],' 369.

59 'Johann Jakob Bachofen: From Roman History to Matriarchy,' in *Ottavo contributo*, 91.

60 Ibid.

61 'Bachofen tra misticismo e antropologia,' in *Nono contributo*, 776; 'Johann Jakob Bachofen: From Roman History to Matriarchy' (n59 above).

62 'From Bachofen to Cumont,' in *Nono contributo*, 595.

63 'My interest in Bachofen is focused on this later development, which turned him from a Romantic thinker into a pioneer of modern anthropology' ('Johann Jakob Bachofen: From Roman History to Matriarchy,' 94).

64 'From Bachofen to Cumont' (n62 above), 607.

65 'Ancient History and the Antiquarian,' in *Contributo*, 102.

66 Michael P. Steinberg, 'The Collector as Allegorist: Goods, Gods, and the Objects of History,' in *Walter Benjamin and the Demands of History*, ed. Steinberg (Ithaca, 1996), 88–118; and, most recently, Vanessa R. Schwartz, 'Walter Benjamin for Historians,' *American Historical Review* 106 (2001): 1721–43. By contrast, see Roland Kany, *Mnemosyne als Programm: Geschichte, Erinnerung und die Andacht zum Unbedeutenden im Werk von Usener, Warburg und Benjamin* (Tübingen, 1987); and idem, *Die religionsgeschichtliche Forschung an der Kulturwissenschaftlichen Bibliothek Warburg* (Bamberg, 1989).

67 'My foundation is remarkably – indeed, awfully – narrow: a knowledge of some few dramas, by no means all the relevant ones. An encyclopedic reading of these works in the tiny amount of time available would have inevitably evoked an insurmountable *dégoût* in me' (Benjamin to Florens Christian Rang, 10 January 1924, in *The Correspondence of Walter Benjamin*, 227). Or: 'Some instrinsic defects are clear to me. Calderón is essentially the subject of the study; in some passages, my ignorance of the Latin Middle Ages has required me to be profound when precise knowledge of the sources would have made this unnecessary. And yet if a work such as this were to be based exclusively on original sources, it might never come into being' (Benjamin to Scholem, 22 December 1924, in *The Correspondence of Walter Benjamin, 1910–1940*, trans. Manfred R. Jacobson and Evelyn M. Jacobson, ed. Gershom Scholem and Theodor W. Adorno [Chicago, 1994], 256).

68 Benjamin to Scholem, 14 February 1921, in *The Correspondence of Walter Benjamin* (n67 above), 176.

69 Benjamin to Adorno, 9 December 1938, in *The Correspondence of Walter Benjamin*, 589.

70 Benjamin to Adorno, 23 February 1939, in *The Correspondence of Walter Benjamin*, 596.

71 Benjamin, 'Methodische Arten der Geschichte,' in his *Gesammelte Schriften*, 7 vols in 14, ed. Rolf Tiedemann and Hermann Schweppenhäuser (Frankfurt am Main, 1991), vol. 6, p. 94. Compare Momigliano: 'The process of

discovering, interpreting and checking the subjective bona fides of the documents is an essential part of historical work, even if it leads to the conclusion that the document is irrelevant. If philology is this activity, philology is the most basic part of historiography. Indeed, when the document is recognized to be relevant to the research, philology becomes ipso facto historiography' ('Philology and History' [n22 above]).

72 Walter Benjamin, 'The Philosophy of History of the Late Romantics and the Historical School,' in Benjamin, *Selected Writings*, ed. Howard Eiland and Michael W. Jennings, 4 vols (Cambridge, MA, 2003), vol. 1, pp. 284–5.

73 Benjamin to Florens Christian Rang, 9 December 1923, in *The Correspondence of Walter Benjamin*, 223–4.

74 For the book's place in the history of German baroque studies, see Herbert Jaumann, *Die deutsche Barockliteratur Wertung-Umwertung. Eine Wertungs-geschichtliche Studie in systematischer Absicht* (Bonn, 1975), 571–89.

75 Walter Benjamin, *The Origins of German Tragic Drama*, trans. John Osborne (London, 1977) [orig. 1926], 89.

76 Ibid., 91.

77 Ibid., 229.

78 Benjamin to Scholem, 5 March 1924, in *The Correspondence of Walter Benjamin*, 238.

79 Benjamin, *The Origins of German Tragic Drama*, 92.

80 See, for example, Nicole Dacos, *Roma quanta fuit: Tre pittori fiamminghi nella Domus Aurea* (Rome, 1995); Sabine Forero-Mendoza, *Le temps des ruines: Le goût des ruines et les formes de la conscience historique à la Renaissance* (Seyssel, 2002); and *Ruinenbilder*, ed. Aleda Assmann, Monika Gomille, and Gabriele Rippl (Munich, 2002).

81 This blind spot was most emphatically not that of Don Cameron Allen, among a few others. See his *The Star-Crossed Renaissance: The Quarrel about Astrology and Its Influence in England* (Durham, NC, 1941); *The Legend of Noah: Renaissance Rationalism in Art, Science, and Letters* (Urbana, 1949); *Doubt's Boundless Sea: Scepticism and Faith in the Renaissance* (Baltimore, 1964); and *Mysteriously Meant: The Rediscovery of Pagan Symbolism and Allegorical Interpretation in the Renaissance* (Baltimore, 1970).

82 Benjamin, *The Origins of German Tragic Drama*, 133, also 124.

83 Ibid., 183–4.

84 Ibid., 177.

85 Ibid., 179. We cannot discuss here the other aspect of Benjamin's theory of the ruin, namely, its usefulness for the extraction of meaning from individual works of art or entire genres – the *Trauerspiel* and baroque opera are examples he gives here (ibid., 182, 84, 235, 212, 189; Benjamin, *The Arcades*

Project, trans. Howard Eiland and Kevin McLaughin [Cambridge, MA, 1999], [N2,3], p. 460; 'Goethe's *Elective Affinities*,' in Benjamin, *Selected Writings* [n72 above], vol. 1, p. 296).

86 Benjamin, *The Origins of German Tragic Drama*, 164, 223–4, 226.

87 Ibid., 220–1.

88 In the huge and growing literature on Warburg and on Warburg and Benjamin, there is almost no discussion of this point. See Wolfgang Kemp, 'Walter Benjamin und die Kunstwissenschaft. Teil 2: Walter Benjamin und Aby Warburg,' *Kritische Berichte* 3 (1975): 5–25; Kany, *Mnemosyne als Programm* (n66 above); Momme Broderson, '"Wenn Ihnen die Arbeit des Interesses wert erscheint ..." Walter Benjamin und das Warburg-Institut: Einige Dokumente,' in *Aby Warburg. Akten des internationalen Symposions Hamburg 1990*, ed. Horst Bredekamp, Michael Diers, and Charlotte Schoell-Glass (Weinheim, 1991), 87–94; and Matthew Rampley, *The Remembrance of Things Past: On Aby M. Warburg and Walter Benjamin* (Wiesbaden, 2000). However, Momigliano did mark – by dog-earing the page in his copy of Giulio Schiavoni's *Walter Benjamin: Sopravvivere alla cultura* (Palermo, 1980) – a page-length footnote that begins 'Forse l'unica "scuola" cui l'idea benjaminiana di filologia si avvicina è quella warburghiana' (131).

89 Aby Warburg, 'Pagan-Antique Prophecy in Words and Images in the Age of Luther,' in Warburg, *The Renewal of Pagan Antiquity*, trans. David Britt, introduction Kurt W. Forster (Los Angeles, 1999), 598–9.

90 Though Gombrich notes that in this very lecture Warburg used contemporary evidence – Rembrandt's work – to show resistance to and fragmentation of that supposed 'spirit of the age.' Quoted in E.H. Gombrich, *Aby Warburg* (Chicago, 1970), 313–14.

91 Benjamin, *The Origins of German Tragic Drama*, 221. Elsewhere, he explained that 'for the Baroque, even for the Renaissance, the marble and the bronzes of antiquity still preserved something of the horror with which Augustine had recognized in them ... Or, as Warburg puts it, with reference to the Renaissance "a double herma, which had one dark, demonic countenance, that called for a superstitious cult, and another, serene Olympian one, which demanded aesthetic veneration."' The extent of Benjamin's sympathy for a point of view associated so immediately with Warburg is extraordinary. See, for example, 'Goethe's *Elective Affinities*' (n85 above), 303, 316–19.

92 'Having attempted to lay bare the philosophical, moral, and theological content of allegory, I would now like to perform the same task for the fairy tale as an equally fundamental and originary repository of certain traditional themes – at the disenchantment of the sinister powers embodied in the saga' (Benjamin, 'Curriculum Vitae (III),' in *Selected Writings* [n85 above], vol. 2, p. 78).

93 Benjamin, 'To the Planetarium' in *One-Way Street*, in *Selected Writings*, vol. 1, p. 486. In 1927, that is, after the text was finished but before it was published, Warburg staged an exhibition of his history of astrological thinking at the Hamburg Planetarium. Presenting the same material a year earlier, he had explained that 'European civilization is the result of conflicting tendencies, a process in which – as far as these astrological strivings for orientation are concerned – we should look for neither friends nor enemies, but rather for the symptoms of psychological oscillations swinging uniformly between the distant poles of magico-religious practice and mathematical contemplation – and back again' (quoted in Gombrich, *Aby Warburg* [n90 above], 262–3). There is no way of knowing whether Benjamin knew of the exhibition or of these words, or whether he could have known that Kepler was a hero to Warburg for creating 'Denkraum' through his astronomical calculation (Fritz Saxl, 'Warburg's Besuch in Neu-Mexico,' in *Aby. M. Warburg: Ausgewählte Schriften und Würdigungen*, ed. D. Wuttke [Baden-Baden, 1979], 314). But the convergence is striking.

94 In October 1926 he wrote to Hoffmannsthal, 'I may also be able to hope for the interest of the Hamburg circle around Warburg ... In any case, I would first expect to find academically qualified and, at the same time, sympathetic reviewers among the members of that circle (with whom I myself have no contact)' (Benjamin to Hoffmansthal, 30 October 1926, in *The Correspondence of Walter Benjamin* [n67 above], 310). By the beginning of 1928 it was clear that this attempt at gaining an entrée had failed, apparently on the shoals of Panofsky, though his 'cool, resentment-laden response' apparently has not survived (Benjamin to Scholem, 30 January 1928, ibid., 324). In April of that same year, Benjamin urged Scholem to contact Saxl on his behalf (Benjamin to Scholem, 23 April 1928, ibid., 333). We know that Benjamin held Panofsky and Saxl in the highest esteem for their work on *Melancolia*, which he owned, used, and recommended to Scholem in the warmest terms (Benjamin to Scholem, 22 December 1924, ibid., 256). On 21 July 1928, writing to Krakauer, Benjamin not only identified 'our approach to things' with the K.B.W., but implied that the opening to Saxl had succeeded (Benjamin to Krakauer, 21 July 1928, in *Walter Benjamin. Gesammelte Schriften* [n71 above], vol. 1, p. 910).

95 Broderson, 'Wenn Ihnen die Arbeit des Interesses wert erscheint' (n88 above), 90, illus. 1.

96 Scholem's later explanation was that Panofsky discerned Benjamin's distance from Cassirer at a time when the latter's influence in the K.B.W. was at its peak (Scholem to Kemp, quoted in Kemp, 'Walter Benjamin und die Kunstwissenschaft' [n88 above], 7).

97 Benjamin, *The Origins of German Tragic Drama*, 216.

98 Benjamin to Scholem, 23 April 1928, in *The Correspondence of Walter Benjamin*, 333.

99 Benjamin, 'The Arcades of Paris,' in *The Arcades Project* (n85 above), 883.

100 H.D. Kittsteiner, 'Walter Benjamins Historismus,' in *Passagen: Walter Benjamins Urgeschichte des neunzehnten Jahrhunderts*, ed. Norbert Bolz and Bernd Witte (Munich, 1984), 163–97; trans. as 'Walter Benjamin's Historicism,' *New German Critique* 39 (1986): 179–215, offers the standard interpretation of Benjamin's idiosyncratic historical materialism as his alternative to *Historismus*. See also Harro Müller, 'Einige Anmerkungen zu Benjamins Historismuskritik,' in *Global Benjamin: Internationaler Walter-Benjamin-Kongress*, ed. Klaus Garber and Ludger Rehm, 3 vols (Munich, 1999), vol. 1, pp. 153–60.

101 Benjamin, 'Literary History and the Study of Literature,' in *Selected Writings*, vol. 2, p. 460.

102 Ibid., 462. The success of the literary history emerging from the George circle, by contrast, was of a different sort: 'antiphilological' and 'designed to exorcize the historical' (463).

103 Benjamin, 'The Rigorous Study of Art,' in *Selected Writings*, vol. 2, p. 666.

104 Ibid., 667.

105 Ibid., 668–9.

106 Benjamin, *Gesammelte Schriften* (n71 above), vol. 3, p. 374.

107 Benjamin's thinking so closely approaches Warburg's here that one would think that he must have had access to Warburg's *Gesammelte Schriften* (Leipzig, 1932). Not only is there no positive evidence for this, however, but his unsettled life at the time – Benjamin left Berlin in April 1932 and did not return until November before leaving for good on 18 March 1933, whereas these essays were composed in 1932 and the first part of 1933 – seems to suggest that parallel development is more likely. This dimension of the parallel between Benjamin and Warburg is not examined in Matthew Rampley, 'Mimesis and Allegory: On Aby Warburg and Walter Benjamin,' in *Art History as Cultural History: Warburg's Projects*, ed. Richard Woodfield (n.p., 2000), 121–50.

108 Benjamin, 'On Astrology,' in *Selected Writings*, vol. 2, p. 685.

109 Benjamin, 'The Doctrine of the Similar,' in *Selected Writings*, vol. 2, 695; for the micro/macrocosm, 'On the Mimetic Faculty,' vol. 2, p. 720.

110 Benjamin, 'On the Mimetic Faculty,' 721.

111 Benjamin, 'The Doctrine of the Similar' (n109 above), 697–8. Cf. 'On the Mimetic Faculty,' 722.

112 Benjamin, 'On the Mimetic Faculty,' 722.

113 For example, the survival of the ancient gods in Baudelaire took him back

to the work of Warburg's colleague Friedrich von Bezold and *Das fortleben der antiken Götter im mittelalterlichen humanismus* (Leipzig and Bonn, 1922) (Benjamin, *The Arcades Project* [n85 above] [J79,1], p. 367); this is only one of many echoes in the *Konvolut* on Baudelaire); the farewell on a station platform evokes the *Pathosformel* (*The Arcades Project*, [L1,4], p. 406); 'only a thoughtless observer' was said to be capable of denying 'that correspondences come into play between the world of modern technology and the archaic symbol-world of mythology' [N2a,1]; the 'immediate proximity' of the idea of antiquity 'to the extremely modern image of America' [M15a,4]; and, whereas in his lecture on Manet, Warburg talked about the gods being 'archaeologically sterilized,' Benjamin, later, wrote of the effort 'to sterilize them ornamentally' (quoted in Gombrich, *Aby Warburg* [n90 above], 277; Benjamin, *The Arcades Project*, [S8a,1], p. 557).

114 On this, see Steinberg, 'The Collector as Allegorist' (n66 above), 89.

115 Scholarship on Fuchs has been limited and poor. The following is a fairly complete survey of the literature: Thomas Huonker, *Revolution, Moral und Kunst. Eduard Fuchs: Leben und Werk* (Zürich, 1985); Ulrich Weitz, *Salonkultur und Proletariat. Eduard Fuchs: Sammler, Sittengeschichtler, Sozialist* (Stuttgart, 1991); and Luciana Zingarelli, 'Eduard Fuchs, vom militanten Journalismus zur Kulturgeschichte,' *Asthetik und Kommunikation* 25 (1976): 32–53. I hope to address this soon.

116 Benjamin, 'Eduard Fuchs, Collector and Historian,' in *Selected Writings*, vol. 3, p. 265.

117 Ibid., 260.

118 Ibid., 262.

119 This was noted by contemporaries. See Horkheimer to Benjamin, 13 April 1937: 'Es ist ja der große Vorzug Ihrer Fuchs-Arbeit, daß sie sich nicht so sehr aus dem Interesse an Fuchs als aus der Polemik gegen den Begriff der Kulturgeschichte herleitet' (Benjamin, *Gesammelte Schriften* [n71 above], vol. 2, bd. 3, p. 1342).

120 In his notes, under the heading *Kulturgeschichte*, Benjamin wrote: 'Die Unmöglichkeit einer Geschichte des Rechts, der Literatur etc./ Ist materialistische Kulturgeschichte möglich?' (Benjamin, *Gesammelte Schriften*, vol. 2, bd. 3, p. 1358).

121 Benjamin, 'Eduard Fuchs' (n116 above), 268. See also the preparatory note on Fuchs and Winckelmann, in *Gesammelte Schriften*, vol. 2, bd. 3, p. 1357.

122 Benjamin, 'Eduard Fuchs,' 269.

123 Ibid., 276.

124 Ibid., 283.

125 For whatever it might be worth, Momigliano folded down the page in his

copy of Schiavoni's book that initiated a discussion of '"Salvazione del Passato" e *Historismus*' (Schiavoni, *Walter Benjamin* [n88 above], 328–30). Kelley devotes a paragraph to Benjamin and 'Historicism' in *The Fortunes of History* (n2 above), 335.

126 Benjamin, *The Arcades Project* (n85 above), [N3,4], p. 463.

127 Ibid., [N8a,3], p. 472.

128 Ibid., [N15,4], p. 481.

129 Ibid., [N14,1], p. 479.

130 Benjamin, 'Materials for the Exposé of 1935,' in *The Arcades Project*, [N1a,3], p. 912.

131 Benjamin, *The Arcades Project*, [N10,4], p. 475.

132 Ibid., [N9,4], p. 473. Jonathan B. Knudsen has remarked on the different approaches of Meinecke and Benjamin but seems not to have noticed how pointedly Benjamin's practice was directed *against* everything that Meinecke represented ('Friedrich Meinecke [1862–1954],' in *Paths of Continuity: Central European Historiography from the 1930s to the 1950s*, ed. Hartmut Lehmann and James van Horn Melton [Cambridge, 1994], 57–8).

133 Benjamin, *The Arcades Project*, [N10,3], p. 475.

134 Ibid., [N10a,2], p. 475.

135 Ibid., [H2,7], p. 207.

136 Ibid., [N2,6], p. 461. Such *maxima in minimis* is emphasized strongly in Kany, *Mnemosyne* (n66 above), 242.

137 Benjamin, *The Arcades Project*, [S1a,3], p. 545.

138 Benjamin, 'On the Concept of History,' in *Selected Writings* (n72 above), vol. 3, p. 391. I have modified the translation slightly. A narrower emphasis on the relationship between study and melancholy is found in *The Arcades Project* [m5,3], with further references to Mallarmé, Baudelaire, and Goethe.

139 In more or less contemporary remarks on historical method, Benjamin defined commentary on reality as theology and commentary on a text as philology (*The Arcades Project*, [N2,1], p. 460).

140 Benjamin, 'On the Concept of History' (n138 above), 397. In a related fragment composed for this essay but not included, Benjamin specified three lines of attack on historicism: 1) the notion that there was enough of a universal human experience for universal history to be written; 2) the idea that history could be narrated at all; 3) and the idea that history, especially the history of culture, was 'the inventory of spoils displayed by the victors before the vanquished' (Benjamin, 'Paralipomena to "On the Concept of History,"' in *Selected Writings*, vol. 3, p. 406).

141 Benjamin, *The Arcades Project*, [N18,3], p. 485.

142 Gershom Scholem, *Walter Benjamin: The Story of a Friendship* (London, 1982), 31.

143 Bernoulli's *Johann Jacob Bachofen und das Natursymbol* (1924) is cited in Benjamin, 'Goethe's *Elective Affinities*' (n85 above), 349.

144 We know that Momigliano borrowed the book, probably from the Warburg Library, on 10 January 1949 (Pisa, Archivio Arnaldo Momigliano, N-f 57).

145 Benjamin, 'Review of Bernoulli's *Bachofen*,' in *Selected Writings*, vol. 1, pp. 426–7.

146 Scholem to Peter Szondi, in *Gershom Scholem: A Life in Letters, 1914–1982*, ed. Anthony David Skinner (Cambridge, MA, 2002), 365–6. For recent discussion, see Giulio Schiavoni, 'Benjamin – Bachofen: Cur Hic?' in *Global Benjamin*, ed. Garber and Rehm (n100 above), vol. 2, pp. 1045–56.

147 Benjamin, 'Johann Jakob Bachofen,' in *Gesammelte Schriften*, vol. 2, bd. 1, pp. 220, 228–9, 230.

148 Ibid., 221.

149 Ibid., 222.

150 Ibid., 224.

151 Ibid. Benjamin's *Nachlass* preserves an outline for a nine-part essay (the final version has ten) that reveals a parallel to Momigliano's later interpretation: Vico, Burckhardt, and Winckelmann are the key precursors ('Johann Jakob Bachofen' [n147 above], vol. 2, bd. 3, pp. 967–9).

152 'Neuaufbau unseres ganzen nationalen Leben,' which 'auch auf die geschlichtlichen Wissenschaften übergegriffen und bestimmte neue, bis dahin noch als flüssig und diskutabel geltende Auffassungen der Vergangenheit über die Bedeutung von Volkstum und Rasse für die Geschichte zur festen Richtschnur historischen Denkens und Verstehens zu erheben versucht' (Meinecke, 'Von der Krisis des Historismus' [n2 above], 114, 122). For a discussion of these lines in the context of Meinecke's own development, see Otto Gerhard Oexle, 'Meineckes Historismus. Über Kontext und Folgen einer Definition,' in *Historismus in den Kulturwissenschaften*, ed. Oexle and Rüsen (n3 above), 167–8. For the National Socialist critique of 'Historicism' that Meinecke was parroting, see Gadi Algazi, 'Otto Brunner – *Konkrete Ordnung* und Sprache der Zeit,' *Geschichtsschreibung als Legitimationswissenschaft*, ed. Peter Schöttler (Frankfurt am Main, 1997), 166–203.

153 'Lo storicismo nel pensiero contemporaneo' (n46 above), 268–9.

154 For a rich, but different, look at this same question, see Innocenzo Cervelli,

'L'ultimo Momigliano: costanti e variabili di una ricerca,' *Studi storici*, 30 (1989): 59–104, especially 74–5. I thank Professor Di Donato for bringing this reference to my attention.

155 Historicism, Meinecke conceded, worked to weaken the life force in so far as it led to an 'Anarchy of Thought': 'Er steigert das Leben, wenn er das Lebensrecht sowohl der eigenen Innerlichkeit wie der ihn umgebenden und nährenden Lebensmächte, – Religion und Vaterland vor allem – bewußt und tief empfindet und aus ihm heraus auch handelt' ('Von der Krisis des Historismus' [n2 above], 126). In this light, the disappearance of *Historismus* from post-war German historiography is not surprising (Oexle, 'Meinecke's Historismus' [n152 above], 191). That Momigliano was especially concerned about 'Historicism' can be ascertained by comparison with Ernst Cassirer's interpretation. In *The Problem of Knowledge: Philosophy, Science, and History since Hegel* (New Haven and London, 1950), Cassirer surveyed the same terrain worked over by Momigliano, from Herder to Usener, with a similar interest in historical method. But his conclusion was much less fearful: 'We do an injustice to 'historicism' when we stress only its negative and destructive side and regard it merely as the forerunner of skepticism and relativism' (324).

156 Iggers, 'Historicism: The History and Meaning of the Term' (n3 above), 142; more generally, Allan Megill, 'Why Was There a Crisis of Historicism?' *History and Theory* 36 (1997): 416–29.

157 This was noted by Pietro Rossi, 'The Ideological Valences of Twentieth-Century Historicism,' *History and Theory* Beiheft 14 (Essays on Historicism) (1975): 18; but not by the contributors to *Historismus am Ende des 20. Jahrhunderts*, ed. Scholtz (n3 above).

158 'A Piedmontese View of the History of Ideas' (n158 above), 335.

159 Benjamin, 'One-Way Street' (n93 above), 465.

Index